RVing

(Caravanning)

into

Canada's Arctic

by
John & Liz Plaxton

Copyright © 1998 by John Plaxton

Canadian Cataloguing In Publication (CCIP) Data
Plaxton, John, 1941-
RVing into Canada's Arctic

 Includes index.

1. Plaxton, John, 1941- --Journeys--Canada, Northern. 2. Plaxton, John, 1941- --Journeys--British Columbia, Northern. 3. Plaxton, Elizabeth, 1942---Journeys--Canada, Northern. 4. Plaxton, Elizabeth, 1942- --Journeys--British Columbia, Northern. 5. Canada, Northern--Description and travel. 6. British Columbia, Northern--Description and travel. 7. Recreational vehicle living. I. Plaxton, Elizabeth, 1942- II. Title.

FC3956.P54 1999 917.1904'3 C99-910285-0F1090.5.P54 1999

ISBN 0-9680314-2-0

Edited by Elizabeth Plaxton and Geraldine Himmelsbach

Photographs by authors of the various articles and diaries. Cartoons by Doug Urquhart, sketch by Bob Heinrich.

PRINTED IN CANADA

Travel 'N Write
1998

To our many friends
who are becoming separated from us
by distance and time

and

especially to my loving wife
who was and is a great navigator.
(If we haven't been here before, we can't be lost.)

Foreword

We travelled by ourselves for five and a half months in a 7.2 m Class C motorhome, living our mottos "Take a risk carefully, it's more fun" and "We'll go where few RVs have gone before." Today in northwestern Canada, risks are very few and RVs are many. In this book Recreational Vehicles (RVs) are considered to be campervans, caravans, truck campers, trailers, motorhomes and trucks with fifthwheels.

Although out of contact with our family and friends more than we would have preferred, use of free Internet services in Canadian public libraries and a few long distance phone calls helped ease the isolation we sometimes felt.

This illustrated book consists of a series of articles by the author followed by his wife's daily journal and two appendices that summarize food and gasoline costs.

Two additional appendices include five supplemental diaries or letters that also describe travelling in Yukon, Alaska and Northwest Territories from 1992 to 1998.

All these provide a balanced view of driving in Canada north of 60⁰N because they cover different time periods and different areas visited (and the same areas revisited at different times) by people with different interests and different numbers of vacation days than we had. All include personal incidents – joys, frustrations, feelings of what was seen and what was done – and a few suggestions and hints for those who follow in or by our tire tracks.

The last appendix briefly mentions some other useful sources of information, and concludes with miscellaneous notes.

We, John and Liz, travelled on a limited (retirement) monthly budget. At least for us, once again we confirmed that having lots of time was much more important than having lots of money, as long as we had some money.

Unless otherwise noted, our photographs were taken with a simple "point and shoot" 35 mm camera or an old manual camera without a flash. Because I can't buy flash bulbs any more it has no need for batteries, and it can be used any time. Liz and I wanted to show travellers that reasonable pictures can be taken by novices using inexpensive equipment. Certainly there were occasions when we wanted telescopic and wide angle lenses, but the cost of postcards was a lot less than the expense of those accessories.

Liz and I enjoyed ourselves most of the time. Fortunately we never encountered long periods of rain or swarms of insects that could have kept us inside our motorhome.

Conditions change almost daily in Canada's sub-arctic. Where we experienced sun, others experienced cold and wind. When we canoed in a lake, others flew above the overcast in airplanes. While we enjoyed a sunset, others went to a night club, lounge or a movie to escape rain. When we cooked supper inside or barbequed outside our RV, others went to restaurants, and vice versa.

We've enjoyed writing this book, and we believe that you and your travelling friends will enjoy reading it while you learn how others travelled in Canada's north.

You can write to us at the address below. We try to reply to everyone, although our answers might take several weeks or months to get back to you. We'll be somewhere else in this wonderful country called Canada, and at irregular times our mail will be forwarded to wherever we happen to be or expect to be.

John or Elizabeth Plaxton
1362 Maple Road
Kelowna, BC Canada
V1X 4Y4
E-mail: RVing@ogopogo.com

Please send us corrections for any typographical and grammatical errors you find. Also, we will be pleased to consider your suggestions and comments to make this a better book.

We want to provide an accurate and balanced view of getting to and travelling in northern British Columbia, Yukon and Northwest Territories in a recreational vehicle (RV); that is,
RVing* into Canada's Arctic.
(*"Caravanning" is the European equivalent of "RVing")

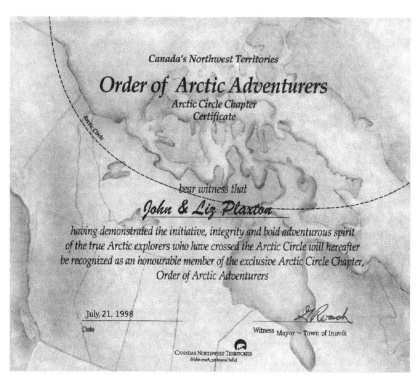

Remember to get your certificate!

The authors in the Beaufort Sea.
(Arctic Ocean)

This indexed, illustrated appendix is an enjoyable "Must Read" because it complements the previous articles, and is almost as long. Because it is a chronological record of events, it was difficult to assign sub-titles, so none were.

Index

Summary of Areas Visited

British Columbia

We drove from Kelowna, British Columbia along Highway 97 to Prince George, BC then on to Yukon Territory, usually referred to as Yukon. Many travellers from the neighbouring province of Alberta also pass through Prince George en route to Yukon.

There are two major routes to get into Yukon (YT) from within British Columbia (BC). One way is via Highway 97 which includes part of Canada's Alaska Highway that starts at Dawson Creek, BC. The other is westward via a continuation of the Yellowhead Route, or Highway 16, and northward on the Stewart-Cassiar Highway, or Highway 37. Interestingly, the distance of either route to Whitehorse, Yukon from Prince George, BC is almost the same.

Each route has wonderful scenery and places to visit. If sufficient vacation time is available, both should be travelled.

We chose to travel the Stewart-Cassiar into Yukon, then weeks later drove on part of Canada's Alaska Highway out of Yukon into British Columbia (and into YT into BC into YT into BC) and then on to the Northwest Territories via the Liard Trail.

While in Yukon we diverted south to Atlin, BC and also south through British Columbia and then into Alaska to use the Skagway-Haines marine ferry. Atlin can only be reached by road from Yukon, using Highway 7 southeast of Whitehorse. This quiet, magical community was definitely worth the trip.

Because of our selected routes, we did not travel all of the Alaska Highway. We missed two Canadian sections – Haines Junction, YT to Whitehorse, YT and from Dawson Creek, BC to Fort Nelson, BC – and everything west of Tok, Alaska.

Yukon

The Yukon encompasses a huge area and many hundreds of kilometres of uninterrupted highway. Such distances would probably astound most Asians or Europeans. Liz and I spent almost two months of 18+ hours of sunny days in the Yukon, some of it driving hundreds of kilometres from place to distant place. The time and effort were usually worth it.

The highlights of our visit were being in Dawson to celebrate the 100th Anniversary of the Klondike gold rush, travelling the constantly changing Dempster Highway and enjoying the awe-inspiring Top of the World Highway.

Contrary to all those horror stories we heard, the Alaska Highway was probably the least exciting portion of our travels. Statements like "I survived the Alaska Highway" were true once. But now a driver almost can select Cruise Control for his/her large motorhome then go back to the kitchen for a drink of juice and a sandwich. (Don't!) Always pretty, occasionally scenic, the Alaska Hwy is certainly no challenge.

Did we have a great time? Yes. Would we go back? Certainly, maybe in a couple of years. But there is still much more of Canada we want to see.

Alaska

We travelled briefly into Alaska, primarily to circumvent having to retrace Canadian highways.

The highlight of this portion of our travels was the scenery along the Carcross-Skagway and Haines-Haines Junction highways, especially Tormented Valley and Rock Glacier which are both in British Columbia. Even allowing for those cold, overcast days while we were there, the low point was picturesque Skagway, which seemed to us to be nothing but a summer town selling trinkets to tourists.

Northwest Territories

The Northwest Territories has the best territorial/provincial parks in western Canada, excellent gravel and asphalt roads, several interesting historical and naturally scenic locations, great lakes and rivers, but too many kilometres of monotonous, return-trip highways.

1998 was the 50th Anniversary of the MacKenzie Highway, which now extends from Grimshaw and High Level, Alberta to Fort Simpson and on to Wrigley, NWT. Liz and I decided that we would celebrate this anniversary by driving every kilometre of the eight major highways in the NWT. And we did, with several digressions along secondary and tertiary roads. We took almost two months to travel 3960 km.

The highlight of this adventure was volunteering and helping during the tenth Great Northern Arts Festival (GNAF) in Inuvik, inside the Arctic Circle. The low point was washing the sandy silt off our motorhome for the umpteenth time after yet another overcast day of rain as we travelled muddy roads and trails.

Did we have a great time? We had a good time camping and canoeing. Would we go back? Yes, but not soon. Although the Dempster Highway and Great Northern Arts Festival beckon, there is still lots more of Canada for us to visit. But if you haven't been there, then go!

Let the Journey Begin....

A Slow Start

Wednesday we were in Savona, BC. Today, Friday, we are camped in Juniper Park, just east of Cache Creek. Why have we travelled only 24 km?

Nothing is as simple as it appears. In reality we've travelled 640 km.

We left Kelowna on Sunday, April 19th at 6:30 pm (1830 hrs) and did it ever feel good to finally be on our way! We were no longer house-bound, family-bound, friendship-bound and activity-bound. We were on the road, carefree again, beholden only to ourselves and our meagre bank account.

We camped in the O'Keefe Ranch parking lot immediately after our lights failed intermittently. We hadn't gone far — 45 km — but we were on the road. I could work on the lights at our next campground. Meanwhile we would make sure we didn't travel at night. What is there to see at night anyway?

By early afternoon next day we were in Steel Head Provincial Park and settled in for our first night beside a lake.

We'll have to re-learn to open cupboard and refrigerator doors slowly. A few items ended up on the floor. I doubt that we could survive in a fifth wheel. We wouldn't hear those door-swinging, door-slamming, fallen-object-thud sounds that indicate potential problems.

I plugged my trusty old SLT286 portable computer into a 12V DC outlet, turned it on and, for the first time in eleven years, the screen displayed ERROR. I tried out a couple of fault-finding ideas, but nothing worked. Oh well, tomorrow I'll fix it. Right now it is time for the first fire of our trip. (Gosh but I'm good at procrastinating.)

The fire — started with one match placed on a couple of handfuls of dead, dry leaves buried beneath several layers of small, bleached-white driftwood and a couple of bigger pieces— burned beautifully. No doubt about it, life can be great.

Especially when one's loved one is close by and both of us are sitting near a smokeless, warm fire under a black sky filled only with twinkling stars while orange and grey wavering ribbons of Savona's street lights are reflected on Lake Kamloops.

Computer Problem and Solution

Next day I spent a fruitless three hours trying out various ideas, without my computer technical manuals which had been lost in a minor flood while they were stored in my son's basement. Eventually I decided I might as well take the machine apart. I had nothing to lose.

Bit by bit I found the secretly hidden screws. Finally I got through layers of plastic and sheet metal, a floppy drive, a hard drive, a power supply and several ribbon cables to the motherboard at the very bottom of the computer case. That is where I expected to find a worn out CMOS battery. I didn't find it, but if it were there it was soldered in very well. Everything was! There was nothing left to do but put the bits and pieces back together. All in all, it was instructive and entertaining, and I had only one screw and a bit of broken plastic left over. But when I turned on the power the error message was still there.

Now, what to do? I need a computer to write our stories and articles as we travel to Inuvik and back. Could I write them by hand? No, doctors come to me for lessons in how to write illegible prescriptions. Could I use a typewriter? Sure, but I'd have to go to an antique dealer to get one that didn't require 110V AC. Besides I'd waste too much paper correcting bad grammar and retyping my many mistakes and relocating changed ideas.

Liz and I decided that we should drive back to Kelowna, shop around the computer stores I knew, buy an old portable (called a laptop nowadays), then re-install what I could from my supply of software diskettes and CDs. The money spent on gasoline would be considerably less than buying new programs. And that is what we did. Almost.

This is being written on a new, state-of-the-art laptop computer, with a colour display (just try to get one in black and white), lots of RAM, CD drive and a humongous hard drive. Of course, within six months it will be outdated even if it does everything I need. But if this computer also lasts eleven years I'll have got my money's worth.

I put most of my software on the hard drive. It didn't use half the space. Good. I can write and save hundreds of articles.

Being a laptop, it will run for a couple of hours (maybe) on its internal battery, but then what? Liz and I don't want to be constrained to living in electrified, 'citified', crowded campgrounds because of the need to constantly recharge computer batteries. We like to drycamp where there are no facilities available, usually in out-of-the-way places. (RVers from Canada and USA call this boondocking.)

A dealer suggested that I buy an inverter that would convert 12V DC to 110V AC. That reminded me that I already had one built into my uninterruptible power supply, or UPS. It was in my oldest son's basement feeding secure power to my big and not-so-old desktop model which he was storing for me.

So I took my UPS back, drilled a couple of holes in its side, added a couple of wires, a fuse and a heavy-duty diode, and hooked it up to the over-sized deep cycle battery that powers the lights, water pump and furnace fan in our Class C motorhome. Now this laptop can operate on its own tiny battery or for many, many hours from the huge RV battery, or from protected 110V AC in whatever campsite we might be in. Thanks to an uninterruptible power supply , we are free to camp and park wherever we want.

Having said our Kelowna goodbyes again, we were on our way. We stopped by RV and Truck Wash just outside of the city on Highway 97 North to use their sanidump, then kept on going.

Lac La Hache

En route, we saw a black bear poking its head through a barbed-wire fence on a hillside, observing vehicles speeding by on the highway below. I wonder if it considered going back to quiet hibernation to escape the noise.

We also saw two interesting signs indicating place names. One was "Todd's, My Hall" and the other was a carving of a spoon followed by large letters "ers."

La hache is french for 'the axe', which explains why a small axe is called la hatchette or, in English, a hatchet.

Tiny Lac La Hache has a post office and a couple of motels and restaurants. Six kilometres north, on the left of the blacktop, is the "Fir Crest Resort." A few kilometres farther north is the Kokanee RV Campground. The latter is beside the highway - where trucks seem to pass in both directions 24 hours a day - next to a gas and propane station. The former is about a half kilometre from the road and very quiet. (The new owners hope to have some winterized cabins and RV sites in by winter 1998. I wonder how quiet it will be then?)

Liz and I enjoyed full hookups and unlimited water and electricity for seven days. Although I can run my computer safely from my UPS and RV battery, I'm glad I didn't have to. My little portable was on for at least 30 hours.

But it wasn't all paper and digital slavery. We did get our canoe down off the roof, once I managed to untie some interesting knots – a graduate Boy Scout I am not – and spent many a pleasant hour on the quiet water, or sitting beside a warm camp fire, or walking around the area.

Our canoe sits on a second spare tire and a "bug-free" kitchen tent.

Every year the first trip in our canoe is always exciting. A canoe is so tippy. By the time we were 100 m (yds) from shore we were nervous wrecks, and our water trail showed we had changed directions several times. But five minutes later we were still dry and starting to relax.

Springtime is a marvellous time to be canoeing through a marsh. There are so many birds and sounds. Mallard and merganser ducks, Canada Geese, blackbirds with waxy-red on their wings, big birds, tiny birds, brown birds with colourful heads, squawks, chirps, honks, musical arias, all are wonderfully relaxing when silently floating amidst an avian opera. Whenever we paddled by a goose's nesting areas, a female would fly out in front of us, seemingly injured, and flop around trying to get us to follow her away from her nest.

A near-sighted muskrat almost ran into our canoe before submerging and reappearing on the other side.

We'd better move on. We've been here so long, a spider has spun its web in the RV's steering wheel. Hopefully the rest of our trip will be as enjoyable.

Quiet waters, peaceful scenery.

Williams Lake

Liz and I are parked on the south side of Williams Lake in a small pullout overlooking the lake and the Scout Island Nature Centre, with its sandy beach, picnic area and boat launch. Although it is unseasonably hot, we are cooled by breezes wafting up from the lake and the very occasional truck driving past on this dead-end road.

The Nature Centre offers a relaxing break - and a dusty gravel parking lot - for those travellers that have time to drive a couple hundred metres off Highway 97 for a picnic lunch or a break from driving. If you go there look for water fowl, the fish tree with a desiccated corpse hanging over a branch, a tree with a huge goiter or bole, and a beaver house. Don't be surprised to see many trees with wire wrapped around their lower trunks. There is more than one beaver on Scout Island.

The tourist information kiosk on the right side of the highway (heading north) is open from September to May from 9 am - 4 pm, Monday to Friday, and open 8 am - 6 pm everyday in June, July and August. Our sources indicated it was open all year round and we assumed that meant everyday. Because we arrived on Saturday in early May, we drove around a city of 20,000 people without any idea where we were or where we were going. Ah well, being lost and exploring are part of our adventure.

For those RVers who are real snowbirds and not the kind who migrate south for the winter, you might want to travel to Williams Lake for their January 2 festivities. It seems they have some kind of a civic holiday, an extra day off, called "Wrestling Day." Local opinion believes it is only fitting for New Year's to have its own version of "Boxing Day."

Drivers, be alert in this city.

The duration of the orange caution light in the stop lights seems very short. I watched one set of lights change from green to orange, and by the time I hit the brakes they went from orange to red and I was slowing down in an intersection. Because I couldn't stop safely, I kept on going. I don't know why I didn't get a ticket from the only car waiting at the intersection, you know, the one with red and blue lights on top. Maybe the RCMP saw the "Student Driver" sign in my RV's window and took mercy on me. Or maybe the orange light really is too quick to be lawful.

Last night, we parked in the paved parking lot of the Kiwanis complex. When leaving I inadvertently drove by a fire hall just as some men were dusting off a hotdog stand. I love hotdogs. I just had to stop and find out what was going on. The end result was that we and about seventy locals participated in a Boot Drive that raised several hundred dollars for the Multiple Sclerosis Foundation.

Thank heavens the roof didn't leak.

A photographer from the Tribune newspaper, Angie M., took pictures of our RV being scrubbed with biodegradable soap, water and brushes and then being doused and rinsed by a water-fall roaring down from the top of a ladder of a pumper truck. My recently patched and painted RV roof worked well and no water got inside, even though it had to wait inside the deluge for several minutes until my dear wife had also taken a picture or two.

As full-time RVers, it sure is nice to have the time to stop and smell the roses, paddle our canoe up a creek, or search some archives. Unlike most other travellers, Liz and I have many

Mass manufacturing of log homes, and not a log apartment block as I initially thought, near Williams Lake.

weeks to get to Inuvik and back. Once again, we are reminded that for some full-timers it is better to have much time and a little money than only a little time and much money. Of course, the best would probably be lots of time and lots of money. But for us right now we'd rather travel cheaply than not travel at all.

Marguerite Ferry

Driving to Quesnel from Williams Lake on Highway 97, we drove past Marguerite Ferry. I stopped, turned around, and drove back. I thought I hadn't been on a cable ferry (sometimes called a reaction ferry) since I left Saskatchewan decades ago. Here was an opportunity to do so again. But Liz reminded me we've ridden the Needles Ferry, also a cable ferry but bigger, across the Arrow Lakes in BC. I wanted to ride on this ferry anyway.

And I did. Just because. And I'm really pleased because it was the ferry's inaugural day for this year, and only the third trip that day.

Apparently hundreds of visitors to Canada take this same fifteen minute trip over the Fraser River and back, mostly as

foot passengers. This tiny ferry is not accessible to many RV's because a steep incline results in a sharp bend just before the level approach. Even our 7.2 m (23 ft) Class C scraped its rear bumper getting on and off the ferry.

Marguerite ferry and ramp

A cable ferry has no power of its own. It uses the power of moving water to push it aside, to tack from river bank to river bank, and back.

A cable is strung across the river and fastened to strong towers on each side. One roller of a double pulley is placed on this large cable, and a different cable is fed through the other

11

roller. Ends of the smaller cable are attached to the front of the ferry's two pontoons via some ingenious, magical windlass arrangement. If the ferry operator spins the windlass, the cable loop is pulled along, and so too is the bow of the ferry. By turning the pontoons of the ferry at an angle to the current flow, the ferry is pushed aside by the rushing water. Depending upon the direction of its axis, the ferry will move from left-to-right or right-to-left. Do you remember watching your arm move up and down after putting your open hand out of the window of a fast moving car or truck while turning your wrist in the air flow? A cable ferry works in the same way.

During our conversation as we travelled across the river, Captain Martin said "You should have been here last year. High water peaked in only three days, the water level was at least five feet higher than this year, the rushing and roiling current was extremely fast, and it was my first time in charge of a ferry. So many huge logs and thousands of pieces of debris shot by that there are probably none left for this year. One log must have been 110 feet (35 m) long with a root system that must have been as big as a car. As it rushed towards me and the ferry, I noticed someone had nailed a STOP sign to the trunk. I stopped and let it go by."

Cable ferries do not work in the winter when rivers are covered in ice. People can cross here using a small cable car that is suspended above the river from two towers a few metres farther upstream. Almost no one does though. It is slow travelling because the car is moved 'handraulically'; that is, the people have to manually winch the car along its cable.

Water resource personnel do use this cable car to take bi-weekly measurements of water depth and speed in springtime.

Quesnel

As you drive into Quesnel, stop in at the tourist bureau. Then carry on for another few hundred metres and drive into the area beside Front Street across from Ceal Tingley Park. It has a sani-dump, recycling bins, and some of the very best drinking water in the area. The water tastes so good that we had to wait in line to top off our tank. By the time we were finished four other people – locals, not tourists – were waiting. There is no camping overnight but this is a convenient place to park your RV while you walk about the area.

For those RVers who feel the need for exercise after sitting in a cab for hours, a 5 km asphalt walking, jogging, roller-blading and bicycling loop is within a 100 m. It is a pleasant walk that takes you by two rivers, through a park and around some industrial sites. Or, you can pass over the Fraser River on a nearby pedestrian bridge and enjoy a 4.3 km walk on the residential west side of this town.

Barkerville

Too bad this snow won't be here during a sweltering August day!

On May 4th, we filled up with gas and propane and emptied our holding tanks (black water or toilet water first, then grey or sink water last) at the Chevron Station in Maple Park Mall about five kilometres before Quesnel. Then we stopped at the tourist bureau – on the right shortly after crossing the bridge – and headed up BC Highway 26 for Barkerville.

I've discovered that it isn't too difficult to talk gas station cashiers out of a free cup of coffee after spending more than $50 on fuel.

Driving along I remarked to Liz that this was a really enjoyable drive because we could poke along at 60-70 km/hr and not hold anybody up because there was no traffic. I should've known better. No sooner had the words passed from mouth to ear than I noticed an antique-gold-coloured school bus behind us, completely filling the rear bathroom window. At the first opportunity I pulled off onto a side road to let it pass.

First stop en route was at the Cottonwood House Historic Site which, naturally, had 'closed' pasted over its entrance sign. We expected that, but stopped in anyway because we could probably stroll around the buildings. Laura met us with a smile and a paintbrush in her hand.

Knock knock. Anyone home?

After explaining that we were writing a book, and because the site wasn't open except to maintenance vehicles and photo opportunities, she allowed us to actually drive on one of the few stretches of the original Caribou Waggon Road (read the sign carefully) from Quesnel to Barkerville.

She even let us park under the last remaining portion of the original telegraph line in front of the last original — not restored — roadhouses along that trail.

Laura also mentioned nearby calcium deposits where animals often go for a lick or two. Although it was late afternoon when we got there we did see a black bear, who watched us for a while then snorted disgustedly at us because we wouldn't go away. Eventually it turned about and lumbered off into the woods.

At the top of Mexican Hill I pulled off onto the tiny Lovers' Leap pull out and, repeating history, threatened to drive over the steep bluff as we edged up to it unless I got a kiss from my feminine passenger. Changing history, she agreed and happily I was able to drive away with a smiling wife.

When we arrived at Barkerville a Class A, a Class C, and a Fifth Wheel were parked in the asphalt parking lot to the right. We chose to park down in the dirt overflow area to the left, next to famous gold-producing Williams Creek and the soothing sound of cascading water. Knowing that the provincial parks (campgrounds) were not yet open, Liz correctly foretold that we would be by ourselves before dusk.

I hope those other tourists had seen everything they wanted to see. I'd hate to think they left just because a sign declared "No camping and parking overnight." Mind you, in the tourist season when 1100 people and hundreds of vehicles visit this historic site each day, one would be wise to heed the warning. It might even be wise to make reservations when planning on staying overnight nearby.

Alone, we stayed the night. We awoke a couple of times thinking the furnace fan was producing a lot of noise. Finally we realized the burbling hiss was from the rushing snow-melt flowing down Williams Creek. Come daybreak we dressed, ate a leisurely breakfast, and strolled up to the park, being the second and third visitors that day. I don't know how long that man had been sitting in his car waiting for the gate to open at 8 am.

Barkerville seemed so empty (there were no shop keepers, no miners, no visitors), so dull and grey (very few of the weathered buildings are painted, and trees hadn't filled out with green leaves), so cold (piles of snow were still on the grounds although the main walkways had been cleared), and so much like an unpopulated ghost town. We could only wander around the buildings and look through windows, or walk among the old equipment and under the working flume feeding a braked water wheel.

Both Liz and I were disappointed. It was nothing like the time that I was there with our four children almost two decades ago. The place was lively, bustling, busy, exciting. And of course, it will again be so in the summer when 'living history' walks the land mingling with guests and aromas from the restaurants and bakery and root-beer salon.

Because the bakery didn't open until 11 am, we took a small break for a mid-morning coffee back inside our RV. Heading back we passed a couple from Holland who were spending four weeks touring British Columbia and Alberta. We asked them to join us. Martin and Tonie spoke excellent English and we had a very enjoyable conversation. Once again Liz and I were reminded that our being uni-lingual can be very limiting.

After they drove away to visit acquaintances in Prince George, we returned to Barkerville. The sun and temperature had risen to a comfortable level. The staff had finished their meeting and opened many of the buildings' doors. Now we could walk inside most of the buildings and scrutinize many antiques and artifacts close up. And main street was host to several newly arrived visitors. When we finished our much more interesting second look-around, we walked out of town and uphill to see Richfield and the oldest Court House in BC.

Although only just 1.3 km, this trip seemed to take forever. This trail hadn't been plowed. The snow, which had been packed by snowmobiles and cross-country skiers, hadn't melted very much. It was half a metre (a foot and a half) thick in many places. Fortunately the crust was quite thick and hard and, although we slipped fairly often, we seldom broke through it.

Our legs felt as if they were weighted down with lead, and we seemed to have no energy. Eventually we realized that we were 780 m (2500 ft) higher than we were yesterday and we were probably affected by the increased altitude.

Part way to the Richfield Courthouse Liz wondered aloud if there were any bears about, grouchy from hibernation. That added a new thrill to our hike because I had seen two or three week-old paw prints that were from a cougar or mountain lion. It was hard to tell exactly because the snow had melted somewhat and the edges of the prints were rounded. So I whistled a few songs as we trudged along, warning any beast of our presence.

When we arrived safely at Richfield the door to the restored building was locked. Naturally. The windows were so far above ground we couldn't see in. It didn't matter. To prevent birds from trying to fly through the invisible panes of glass, they were completely covered with matte black panels on the inside, which blocked any possibility of our viewing the inside. Ah well.

The downhill trip back was much more pleasant. In fact it was so warm that, although our running shoes were soaked from melted snow and miniature waterfalls, we took off our jackets and sweaters and bared our backs to the tanning sun.

Leaving Barkerville we passed through the main building and interpretive centre, where we watched an interesting but brief audio-visual presentation of the history of the area.

Back at our RV I packed up our portable table, put away our folding chairs, and checked the outside compartments and tires. Liz secured the inside cupboards doing whatever she does to keep dishes from breaking and cans and bags from falling onto the floor as we travel.

On the way back to Quesnel, we found and took the 3 km side trip along Stanley Road which we had missed before, and stopped at Robbers' Roost and Blessing's grave. Sadly, we saw little that appealed to us, and no bears or moose.

Barkerville should be visited for a minimum of four hours when it is officially open to tourists. But because we'll be north of 60^0N at that time, we had to settle for an enjoyable visit instead of an exciting one.

Hush Lake Rest Area

A few kilometres north of Quesnel on Highway 97, on your left you'll see a small lake full of lily pads and a sign that says

Why does the top log of log fences always rot away before the ones below do? The local people we talked to don't know either.

Rest Area. Picnic tables and pit toilets are there. So too is a boat launching site which is level and can accommodate several vehicles.

Although there is the usual "No camping or overnight parking" sign in the rest area, there is none in the lower launching area next to the water. So we spent the evening and night there. Eventually we were joined by five other vehicles. Two arrived after midnight — the scrunch of tires on gravel woke us up — but everybody had left by the time we finished breakfast.

I parked as close as I could to the lily pads because I hoped to be able to see a moose come out of the woods and chew on a few of them. But to do so meant being right next to some trees and bushes which blocked our view. So, while Liz was preparing supper, I got out our green indoor-outdoor carpet and our two lawn chairs and set them up on the roof, beside our canoe and between the tie-down ropes. Our binoculars and camera were next, soon followed by warm plates and utensils, and finally, Liz.

There we were, eating our supper, perched precariously but comfortably on our roof, looking through binoculars at a pair of mallard ducks and a solitary silent loon when the first visitors arrived. The startled woman on the passengers' side was busy pointing and talking to the driver. They parked as far away from us as they could.

The water was so still that I could watch a water bug leave ripples as it crossed the lake a hundred metres (yards) away. It was like a mirror, marred occasionally by circular rings moving away from where a fingerling had surfaced to swallow an insect. Among the lily pads, more fish jumped. And red-wing blackbirds hopped from pad to pad — sending out more circular rings — looking for nourishment, and finding it.

But no moose appeared.

Burns Lake

This is one hilly town, great for walking if you want some exercise after several hours of sitting and driving.

It also has a free municipal campground with eight small spaces for campers and RV's, most with their own fire pit and some free wood. There are no pull-throughs but a nearby level gravel parking lot can accommodate vehicles of any size. Visitors can pull in for a picnic, for a night, or camp for up to 72 hours. Beach and playground access is readily available, with a boat launch only a block away.

This campsite is only a few hundred metres along the road to François Lake, which is accessed at the east entrance to the town.

We selected our site. While Liz organized supper I rounded up some wood, chopped it with my axe, and laid a fire. I didn't light it though because we decided we needed a walk. An hour later we returned to find all our wood gone. Five campsites over, six older teens were enjoying a roaring fire.

I wandered over and we had a conversation. Amazing! They had no idea that the wood next to a motorhome was mine, nor did they wonder why it was all in small pieces and lying neatly inside a circle of rocks. I guess beer and cigarettes really do damage and destroy brain cells.

I wonder if they saw any moose shapes in their sweet-smelling smoke?

As we drove along west of Burns Lake, rolling hills suddenly transformed into a picture of towering glaciated mountains. We were going to have to drive through that wall of stone and ice!

We stopped in at yet another Canadian tourist bureau that has more information about Alaska than about British Columbia or Yukon. What is wrong with these people?

A little farther west is Hagwilget Bridge, near New Hazelton

Hazelton

As we continued to drive west (actually it must have been southerly because the setting sun was not in our eyes) the towering walls of white snow, ice and rock were wonderful whenever they appeared on the clear blue horizon. To me, they were more impressive than the Rockies we've seen on the TransCanada Highway.

Old Hazelton

Internet is everywhere, even here in a tiny library and museum next to the 'Old Salts Fish & Chips' boat in the hamlet of Old Hazelton. Although the historic town was a disappointment, the 'Ksan Historic Village, accessed by a suspension bridge over a gorge, was a pleasure. Totem poles and long houses are in excellent condition and are there to be enjoyed.

Totems and Long Houses at 'Ksan Historic Village

Having lost all government support, this educational site now charges $2.00 per person just to walk among the totem poles, or $7.00 for a guided tour in English, French or German. The tour takes one into the long houses to see artifacts and hear about these Indians' culture. The large adjacent RV park was well maintained.

Kitwanga

The dozen totems in Kitwanga village and the twenty or so in Kitwancool were impressive, even though some were badly weathered. I wish I had had a brochure or a modern Rosetta Stone so I could have interpreted the stories told by each totem. Were they celebrating a marriage, or a great battle, or detailing a family's history (truly a family tree)? Why does only one totem, and it was in Kitwancool, have a man carved upside down? I'll never know.

Battle Hill at Kitwanga National Historic Site is accessed by 165 steps down and up from a pullout on the side of the highway. It has no artifacts or buildings. However, the seven interpretive panels along the way tell an intriguing story of an Indian warrior chief called Nekt. It seems to me he almost rivals Alexander the Great in his strategic and tactical abilities.

21

Driving back from Kitwancool, 21 km north on the Cassiar Hwy, we saw a golden fox on the side of the road. Even travelling only 80 km/hr we were far past it before we got stopped. No other vehicles were visible, so I backed up slowly and parked on the shoulder of the highway. At first I thought it had gone into the nearby bushes. But then Liz spotted it a little farther away and I snapped a quick shot. We were about to get a better second picture when a tow truck, brakes squealing as if a giant were scraping its fingernails on a blackboard, pulled up beside us to see if we needed help. We didn't. He left without making money. The fox was gone.

Seven Sisters Lookout

These awesome peaks can be seen from several locations.

If stopped on Hwy 16 and looking at the impressive Seven Sisters mountains, look to your left and check if you can see what appears to be a large dark cone sitting on the bare-rock top of the highest mountain. Even with binoculars, we couldn't be sure what it was. And the few people we talked to didn't know what it was either.

Cedarvale Café

This restaurant, seemingly out in the middle of nowhere, served Liz an excellent prime rib of roast beef. It was so tender Toothless Tony could and would have enjoyed it. Much to the delight of my dear wife, who occasionally exhibits signs of being a throwback to the days of cave women, they served her the bone as well. She quickly stripped it clean of any and all meat. When she was finished, the image of white, desert-parched bones flashed across my imagination.

I was not hungry when we ordered, and requested only a cup of coffee. However when Liz was served that plate of inch-thick beef, a mountain of mashed potatoes covered with gravy-from-a-can, a ladle full of mixed vegetables, and a Yorkshire pudding so light that it was anchored to the plate, my stomach juices started making noises. She ate all she wanted, which was considerable, and I sampled everything, especially the meat. When it was all gone, we didn't need dessert. Liz was shocked that I didn't order half a pie or several pieces of cake. But we were both full.

So. If you get a chance to stop by the Cedarvale Grill/Café near meal-time, I suggest you do so. I think you too will appreciate what they serve.

Kleanza Provincial Park

This is a very clean, very orderly and quiet provincial park, with some sites adjacent to a creek that lulled us to sleep with the soothing hiss of water flowing over rocks and boulders. This park does not accept reservations, and I suspect you had best plan on pulling in early in the afternoon or morning if you want to get a site during July and August. (Almost all sites in all parks have been available to us in May, which is an excellent reason for travelling early in the year.)

Dry and aged firewood was provided freely; unfortunately this amenity might not be available in future years . We toasted cheese buns and roasted our first wieners of the year over glowing coals of spruce and birch. It is difficult to surpass that first mouth-watering bite into a warm hotdog in a toasted bun filled with butter-fried onions. But, I'd forgotten the 'wiener sticks' and had to use metal shish-ka-bob lances which were much too short. The wieners were polish sausages, I was smoked.

Contrary to the description in our two-year-old magazine, "The Milepost", which read "Short trail to remains from Cassiar Hydraulic Mining Co. gold-sluicing operations here.", those remains have been nonexistent for over a decade. Still, the walk up the trail overlooking that area was mild exercise and a pleasant walk through the woods.

Next to the tall cedar in our campsite, we discovered a tiny grave. The tombstone, which was a mousetrap made in China, bore this hand-printed inscription in pencil. "RIP; Mouse; 15. Sept '97; by this trap; on this trip; by Kleanza Creek; T. AC from Germany; We're

Better a mouse than you or I.

sorry."

I wonder how long it will stay there? If I had known of its existence before getting ready to leave, I would have made a little picket fence as an enclosure.

Humphrey Falls

Humphrey Falls is worth seeing, even if it means you have to walk 2 km from the highway into the bush, and 2 km back. Sneakers or hiking boots are recommended for climbing the short, mist-dampened path to the top of the roaring falls.

Humphrey Falls, on the road between Terrace and Kitimat, is about 200 m (0.1 mi) north of Humphrey Creek. Great instructions when heading south, right? We drove over the bridge, turned around on the highway when no cars were visible, and drove back to the unmarked road.

The nondescript gravel road, immediately opposite a gravel pullout, is great for hiking. But it's not so good for driving on with a new or rented vehicle that is eight feet wide, or in a motorhome with a long overhang, or in one that is underpowered. This discontinued logging road is rough in places.

A sign at the beginning says one should have a 4x4 truck to drive on it. That is a gross overstatement. Any truck could make it without difficulty. But a driver has to exercise a little skill in a couple of places, and about three-quarters of the way in there are four chewed-up hummocks which would stop most cars. There is no place for turning around.

One tree, bent over and partially uprooted by last winter's snow, straddled the road at windshield height. I got out, then Liz drove while I pushed its leafy branches up and over our canoe on the roof of our RV. A second victim of heavy snow also hung over the road but it looked high enough that we thought we could drive under it. But no. Once again Liz slid into the driver's seat as I climbed up onto the roof. There a branch had snagged one of three ropes holding our canoe in place. As I pulled it free, another branch caught me behind my left knee and almost brought me to twisted ankles on the ground below. Fortunately, it was a small branch and I regained my balance. Hah! Once again, a careless city slicker triumphed over nature.

Nature rewarded our efforts. A high volume, fast flowing creek roared into a small crevice then dropped almost 10 m (30 ft) in a solid, roiling torrent of off-white, tannin-stained water which crashed into the other side of the crevice, sending tendrils of mist skyward while creating two pools of swirling, bubbling water cascading over huge boulders.

Seeing Humphrey Falls in spring is worth the effort it takes to get there.

Terrace

The Terrace Tourist Info centre was well stocked with local information and lots, lots more on many parts of BC, Yukon, and Alaska. Sani-dumps are available behind the building, and across the street at a propane distributor. Check out the gas coupons and prices in the nearby 'wholesale' store. We were pleasantly surprised, and topped up our tanks here for the drive north to the lava beds and Highway 37 North. If you want to change your engine oil, and have containers for it, the Mohawk station in Terrace accepts used oil for recycling.

The Heritage Park features several types of log cabin construction, and each is representative of a different aspect of pioneer life. We arrived on a Monday, only to discover this park is closed on Sundays and Mondays. We were unable to enjoy a guided tour.

Nevertheless, I could see all the exteriors of all the buildings. I was surprised to see that none of these original buildings used dovetailed corners such as were used in Fort St. James and other settlements to the east.

On the same street as Heritage Park, but several blocks away, is a private residence with an amazing Japanese-style garden. Northern Lights Gardens used to be open to the public, and might be again, but not now. This is a shame because it is a remarkably relaxing place. In fact, I'm not sure whether its calm, peaceful atmosphere or the jade sidewalk next to a goldfish pond is the more enjoyable.

Our heartfelt thanks for this special visit.

Nisga'a Highway

I've finished changing the engine's oil and filter, and now we're parked in Terrace's Canadian Tire parking lot. Like the Mohawk Gasoline station in the city, Canadian Tire on the western edge of the city also accepts oil for recycling.

Earlier we had agreed to stay here for the night, but I just didn't want to park on asphalt when we could be parked beside a turquoise lake 31 km farther along our chosen path northward. Until now, the Yellowhead Route from Prince George to Prince Rupert has seemed as if we were marking time, even though the latter half has been spectacularly beautiful. (People who don't live in BC would probably think the first half was beautiful too. Remember, Liz and I are used to big mountains.) We had to travel those kilometres from east to west, but both of us felt that our trip would really begin when we start heading north. And so we packed up and drove away.

By taking the Nisga'a Highway, we would save several dozen kilometres compared to driving back to the Stewart-Cassiar (37 North) Highway. This route also would take us to the Nisga'a Memorial Lava Beds, site of the most recent volcanic eruption in Canada, which happened about 300 years ago. Unfortunately it will take us over 95 km of gravel and clay road after 63 km of asphalt.

Surprise. When we arrived at the Kitsumkalum Lake pullout there was no sign saying that we couldn't park there overnight. So we did.

As we scanned the lake for whatever we could see, I heard a noise almost directly below us, near the shore about 40 m below. Although it hadn't made the noise, there was an animal swimming. I asked Liz to keep an eye on it while I got our binoculars. Just as I returned and focused on the correct spot, it dived down and out of sight. Drat.

Liz and I both searched but could see nothing. Suddenly, Liz shouted and there it was, walking up on some rocks. It turned around a couple of times, nose to the stone, then waddled back into the lake, barely making a ripple. That was the biggest beaver I had ever seen. That was one, huge, fat rodent. We were able to watch it for about two more minutes before it swam around a rock and disappeared.

(Earlier, at the 65 km marker from Prince Rupert, I had seen a sea otter, or a seal, in the Skeena River. It seemed to me to be very unlikely, but I know it wasn't a log or an almost-submerged rock. Could it have been a beaver? I think not, its body was too long. Note. When I was in Stewart, I talked to an ex-resident of Prince Rupert and he confirmed that such a sighting was probable, but a bit sooner than usual. It seems seals and sea otters often swim up the river in pursuit of small fish.)

Although we watched for a few more minutes, the beaver was gone from sight. We sat on the edge of the parking lot for almost an hour, watching the sky and the land slowly darken and enjoying the quiet. It was interrupted only occasionally by a bird's chirp or by the presence of civilization as a car or truck whizzed by, tires humming on the blacktop.

A few cars pulled in for a smoke break, or perhaps to watch submarine races, but they didn't stay long. Maybe we scared them away. It was a remarkably quiet spot during the night.

Next morning we arose to glaring white, snow-capped mountains on the other side of the lake. My senses were almost overwhelmed by the contrast of white snow above the saw-tooth pattern of dark evergreens, rusty-brown of clear-cut areas, pea-green deciduous trees near a grey strip of sandy shore and the green-white-blue of the pebbled surface of Kitsumkalum Lake.

Having time as we travel, we stop at all the locations mentioned in our two major sources of tourist information, BC tourist information guides and the Milestone.

The water tree is interesting, and water is available all year. A visitor has to look very carefully to find the secret. It has quite a history.

We didn't get it all but this is what we were told by two locals who stopped by for some drinking water. This water is certified safe to drink by government inspectors. There was a previous water tree located nearby, with a plaque, that was created by a local group of French Canadians in 1943. I didn't find out what happened to the original — I suspect highway construction was involved — but it was replaced by the current water tree due to the efforts of Mr. Don Parmeter. Of course, it has become much larger and is much older than it was thirty years ago. Occasionally dead branches will fall during high winds.

The flower box is a memorial to a young woman who was getting water when her vehicle rolled into the creek, killing her. This creek is fed from a spring and it never changes, regardless of the seasons. Springs are so plentiful in this area, that Mr. Parmeter built himself a water-powered generator to supply most of his household electrical needs.

As we were making notes, we observed a fox coming toward us, walking on the left side of the road. He was cautious but sauntered by with hardly a look in our direction. It crossed over about 100 m (yds) ahead of us and kept trotting down the road and past a house on its left.

Nisga'a Highway and Lava Fields

The Nisga'a Memorial lava fields are interesting, but only a very small portion can be seen while taking the path to the lookout. Visitors are not allowed to travel any farther into the lava beds because they might damage the fragile environment.

Liz relaxing before leaving the "valley" which is now filled with solid lava.

However, small groups of visitors can hike along a controlled pathway to the source accompanied by a guide, provided that reservations are made in advance. Good hiking boots would be an asset but running shoes would probably be OK.

I understand that hikers who make it to the faraway beginning of the lava field would see where the Vetter Creek disappears into the lava but continues to flow beneath the lava to nearby Lava Lake. There is also a large rock that shows the turbulent nature of liquid lava. It displays several intermingled flow patterns.

The really amazing thing about these lava beds is not how wide and how long they are, but how deep they are. After leaving the lookout area and heading north, Liz and I drove past lava rocks for at least ten kilometres. It is difficult to imagine that most of the floor of the valley is buried beneath lava which is hundreds of metres thick. All we saw was the top 0.1% and most of that was covered in grey lichen.

It seems to me that the Nisga'a people could start a profitable business utilizing this natural resource. Many of our gardens produce healthy fruit and vegetables, but  some have used the same land for the same crops for so long that most of the trace elements have been used up. By digging, crushing, sifting, packaging and marketing powdered lava as a mineral supplement for home and commercial gardens, they could help to restore soil to its original condition. Perhaps adding crushed lava would even improve the soil. Untreated powdered lava should be acceptable for use in organic farming.

Tiny Beaupré Falls was a pleasant walk — notice the change in growth when nearing the falls — but Vetter Falls wasn't worth our time.

Stewart-Hyder Highway

If you travel the Stewart-Cassiar Highway, then you should also travel the Stewart-Hyder Highway. It has some of the most spectacular scenery we've seen so far, and you'll get to see it twice. The Lions' Rainey Creek Municipal Campground in Stewart was very clean and well maintained, and cost less than $20 for full hookups.

This is the only southern highway that crosses the border between British Columbia, Canada and Alaska, USA.

The scenery started immediately after turning at Meziadin Junction. Kilometre-long beds of brassy-yellow dandelions — they make a great salad green if picked early — grew in the highway's gravel shoulders, making a natural border of spring-time gold. And towering above them were the pristine-white, snow covered mountain peaks. I suspect that much of this snow will disappear during the summer, but certainly not all of it.

By the time that Liz and I got to Stewart, we both had stiff necks from straining to look up, and up, and up. Those driving cars, trucks and Class A's with big windshields probably won't have a problem with an overhanging bedroom.

At kilometres 13-14 from the junction, there is a small gravel pit on the right side. Stop, get out your binoculars, and look at the tops of the mountains. Observe the many 'hanging' glaciers, ice-fields that reminded me of a cobra's hood or a nun's white head-piece. Notice too, that some of the glaciers seem to have coniferous trees growing amid the ice and snow covering the mountains.

A couple of kilometres more, there will be a pullout on the left. Pull in and study some other glaciers from there. Amazing. But you won't see any of those hanging glaciers.

Driving on, when your first see Bear Glacier stop on the side of the road if it is safe to do so, remembering to turn on your warning or hazard lights. Then study the glacier through your binoculars. Up to now, all the glaciers we've seen had been reasonably smooth. But not Bear Glacier. It makes the badlands of Drumheller look like a stroll through a tidal wetland. In addition the foot, or toe, of this glacier looks like sun-bleached and sun-cracked blue Styrofoam.

Once done, drive the short distance to the pull-outs in front of Bear Glacier. Take even more time to safely enjoy this snow-turned-to-river-of-ice phenomenon, which extends from a few metres in front of you to thousands of metres above you. When

you get out of your vehicle you will probably enjoy it more wearing a sweater or wind-breaker. No photograph shows the cool mass of air that constantly flows down the glacier's frozen surface.

We could not drive to the summit overlooking Salmon Glacier past Hyder because the road was still blocked by remnants of winter snow. Everyone we talked to said the view was more impressive than that of Bear Glacier.

Ah well, we can't have everything. We got to see fresh vibrant colours that will have darkened or disappeared by summertime, and we safely travelled at 70 km/hr and even stopped with our vehicle on the side of the road without holding up the hundreds of summer visitors. We pulled over to observe bears — singles or in pairs — eagles, and a badger.

But we have yet to see any elusive moose or skittish mountain sheep.

Hyder, the 'friendliest ghost town' is very small with perhaps a hundred residents. Stewart's population has declined steadily in the last six years, to about 450 persons. Nevertheless, once again a Canadian Customs building is situated at the end of blacktop at the Canada-USA border, and duty must be paid on liquor, cigarettes, etc. if the time spent in Hyder is less than 48 hours. One exception being no duty on seafood, which

is fortunate because Alaska Premier Seafood does package excellent smoked fish and delicious Candy Salmon.

Significantly cheaper than at Meziadin Junction, gasoline was available in both communities. Their prices were the same because the Canadian dollar is accepted at par in Hyder. In fact, except for the Post Office, all business in Hyder is conducted in Canadian currency; there is no local bank. Both automobile and bottled propane were available in Stewart. There was a cardlock system for diesel, but we did not find out if it were available to transient tourists.

We stopped in at the Rainey campground to use their payphones, and noticed that this campground was painted in Canada's colours — red and white — and thought "How nice". Talking with managers Al and Sheri, we learned they found five barrels of red paint when they took over last year and used them to beautify the place.

Besides, Al's truck is red. Wrong reasons, correct result.

Last summer, Al saw a grizzly bear wandering by one of the picnic tables so he rushed home and got his weapon then, like a cagey hunter, hid himself behind a tree waiting for the grizzly to get closer. At five metres he fired, scoring four hits on the left rear flank. The grizzly escaped into the nearby bushes, with Al following at a safe distance. When the bear headed back into the campground, Al shot again, scoring a direct hit in the head. The grizzly had enough, and left with five bruises and a rainbow of paint on its fur. Al's Paint Ball Rifle had saved the day.

I think the well stocked and tastefully organized Museum is worth the $3.00 I paid, even though I rushed through it. Unfortunately, we had used all our change elsewhere and we had no bills smaller than fifties [stupid]. With only a few tourists in the area, the museum's cash box resembled Mother Hubbard's Cupboard, so Liz couldn't get in.

As compensation, I agreed to let her spend all the time she wanted at the Stewart cemetery. For one as lively and interested in life as is my dear wife, I do not understand her interest in graveyards. But then, there are still many things I don't understand about my beautiful bride of thirty-two years.

Speaking of the cemetery, we were intrigued with the several upside-down Yield signs that we noticed in there as we drove into Stewart. These upside-down signs only make sense to me if the dead are diving towards the centre of the Earth. Could it be ...?

As in most situations, the answer is simple. People die, some during winter. Because several metres of snow fall upon Stewart each year, these signs were set up to mark the already-occupied locations. When it is necessary to dig a new grave, the snowplows and tractors know where to go without disturbing the residents.

We left Stewart several hours after we arrived in order to have supper at the base of Bear Glacier. En route, about 28 - 31 km from Stewart — sorry, even though I topped up with gasoline, we drove around town afterwards and I don't have an accurate record of distances travelled, and I was too busy gawking at everything to pay attention to my odometer — at a pullout on the left with two litter barrels under powerlines on hydropoles, we noticed a humongous black billboard on the top of a mountain in front of us. Using binoculars we noticed two nearby structures, but we could not determine if the billboard was a billboard, a channel marker for ships on the Portland Channel, an array of solar panels, an array of solar-heating panels, or whatever. Perhaps you will be able to ask the locals to clear up this mystery, then write us with an answer.

A short time later, we rounded a corner where, high and to our left, we saw the original road to Stewart. It is about 130 m (400 ft) above the present highway. It was built way up there because at the time of its construction, Bear Glacier was much thicker and ended at the foot of the mountain where today's road is. Tens of metres later, we drove by the entrance to that old highway. I suggested we should go back and explore the high road but Liz gave me that 'Not!' look she does so well and we stayed on blacktop. Good thing. We saw a couple of washouts where waterfalls have made the old road impassable.

After supper, we stayed the night in the pullout adjacent to the glacier. Two new calves, or pieces of glacier, had fallen into the shallow water. The tiny pieces we had seen previously had been blown to the northern side of the glacial lake.

We wanted to confirm that this glacier really glowed in the dark. We set our alarm for 1 am, after the moon had set, and hoped for cloudy overcast to hide the stars. Wakened by an annoying squeal, we looked outside. Stars were plentiful and the glacier was easily seen. So too was the snow on the sides of the mountains. The 'glowing' glacier was nothing but celestial light reflecting off a white surface.

We went back to our comfortable bed, only to arise seven hours later to solid overcast about 300 m above us. As we prepared and ate breakfast, the sun broke through and lit up several mountain peaks and the head of the glacier. Quite a contrast in colours.

The low overcast (fog?) lasted almost all the way back to Meziadin Junction and Hwy 37.

Cottonwood River Rest Area

I see a wolf on a side road. Brakes on. Back up. Liz watching for traffic. My trying to stay near the middle of the road. There. Do you see it, trotting down the middle of the old asphalt highway?

Uh oh. It's only a dog. What would a dog be doing out here?

Oh well, since we're here, let's check out this rest area. Yes Sweet, I know it's only four thirty, but I could use a leg stretch. After all, we've been driving nonstop for at least a half hour.

Hey, this isn't bad. Listen to the Cottonwood River. I wonder how much higher it will get in the next two or three weeks? OK. We'll stay for supper. What the heck, we'll spend the night here. It should be quiet, I doubt anybody else will drive in. Maybe we'll see a moose.

Liz starts making supper. I walk around picking up dried grass, dry spruce needles, small twigs, and several dry dead branches. Some of the branches I make smaller with my El Salvador machete, then lay out a small fire, with no paper. I don't need to build a ring of rocks because an old campfire had spread out and now a large non-flammable area surrounds my small pile of wood.

Sheesh. Pop cans, beer cans and plastic bags — there must be a half dozen abandoned here. Oh well. As I pick them up, I find a 2 L container which I fill with water and put it beside my fire-to-be. It'll be ready when I put my fire out. I get out our indelible black marker and write "Please use this to douse your campfire before leaving." I wonder if anyone will use it.

There. Done.

Scrunching of tires on gravel. Who's coming? Well for heaven's sake, it's that overloaded suburban that passed us, then passed us again, then met us as it was going back to somewhere. Hi.

Paul Smith, from Australia? There are six of you in there? Where? This is a great place for a walk-about. Your wife, three boys, and your mother will probably enjoy the leg stretch. You saw a moose yesterday?!

Oh, you pulled in because you thought you had another flat tire. Where's the nearest garage? You don't have a guide book? Just a minute, I'll get one of ours. There you are. Take a few minutes to read about what is ahead on this stretch of highway.

Boys, being boys, have to throw stones in the river. Mother is upset because they might get wet. So the youngest finds a snow drift and makes granular ice balls, throws them and one hits his brother on the head. Cries, tears, and a frustrated mother.

With Dad's permission, I call the boys over to the fire area, give the oldest a pack of paper matches and ask him to light the fire. Only three tries later, he succeeds. Dad took a couple of pictures of his boys. The children are excited, as if it were the first campfire they've seen. And perhaps it is.

Next day I heard another Aussie couple say they never light fires in the world's smallest continent because of danger of fires in dry grass.

The boys are tired of games and throwing frisbees and races. They are walking instead of running. Mom and Dad are relaxed after a cup of Liz's tea and some pastries. Grandma is in the car, recovering from a slight asthma attack. Once again, it's time to move on.

Everyone piles into the car, but it doesn't sag any lower. Maybe the 130 kilos of books plus clothing plus food plus who-knows-what-else that is piled on the roof rack have already flattened the springs.

I walk around the car before they leave — just as I always do before I drive away — and notice that their left rear tubeless tire has seemingly broken its bead. Paul gets out, I get my tire gauge, and we find out that the tire pressure registers only 12 psi. He has a spare, but it's only one of those half- size wheels, buried somewhere under all that stuff in the car. When in Kitimat I had bought a battery-operated air pump that was on sale, the kind that will produce up to 250 psi if you have a week to spare. Paul is the first to use it. Happily, in less than ten minutes the tire registers 35 psi.

Paul squeezes back in the car and heads off to Jade City or Goodhope looking for a garage or at least another air pump. We never met again, so he must have got his tire repaired, again, somewhere, somehow.

Around 8 pm a Class A from Florida, USA pulls in beside us. Seems the couple had been here a few years ago and stayed where we are parked. (That time a moose walked past their RV to get a drink from the river, almost rubbing against their motor-home.) Earlier this morning they had seen two moose. Two!

Shortly after setting up they pointed out a white speck way up on the side of a nearby mountain. It was probably a Dall Sheep, possibly a mountain goat, or maybe a walking snow drift. We couldn't be sure, even using our binoculars.

Next morning, Liz and I get out of bed by eight. The Florida couple are gone, probably an hour earlier because I heard a noise about that time. We eat breakfast, then ensure everything is secure. As I 'walk the circle' I discover our tail pipe is hanging lower than usual. A wire clothes hanger and twenty minutes later, I've got it tied up.

We're back on the highway. Maybe we'll see a moose today.

Telegraph Creek

We debated about going to Telegraph Creek, but when we talked to a couple of Dease Lake residents, they were enthusiastic about the awesome scenery. Although leery of 18% and 20% grades, we were assured that we would probably have no problems. After all, cars, half-tons, and logging trucks drive the road regularly.

Nevertheless, I put in just enough gas plus a little extra to get us there and back without too much extra weight. Having two tanks, I put regular (Octane 87) in one tank and supreme (Octane 91) in the other. I thought it might be useful to have high octane fuel to prevent engine pinging when climbing up those steep inclines. I didn't need it.

The gravel road to Telegraph Creek, with a population of around 400 in the area, is narrower but in better shape and less dusty than the under-repair gravel portions of the Stewart-Cassiar Highway.

The first 60 km of reasonably flat road truly reflects the saying, "You can't see the scenery and forests because of the trees". We were both amazed at the amount of deciduous trees; Liz and I expected to see mainly spruce. But we didn't see much else.

The last half of the road is completely different It *is* hilly.

Our 7.5 L engine easily met the challenge of pulling our RV's 4,500 kg (5 tons) up 20 degree slopes, and the brakes had only a little trouble keeping our speed at less than 70 k/h (45 mph) when going downhill at the same 20 degree angle. Traces of the old road were visible and I'm glad we didn't have to travel on them.

Only one part of the road was nerve-wracking to me who has travelled many steep and winding and curvy side roads in

*If you think getting down to this river is bad,
wait until you go back up.*

BC. Someone directly from the Prairie Provinces might have had a heart-stopping experience.

Having to drive up a sandy, snake-like road that is only one and one-half vehicles wide, with vertical stone walls on your right and a near-vertical drop directly into the raging Stikine River, was interesting. Liz said I was almost sitting in her seat. Exaggeration, I'm sure. However, on the way back down that stretch of road she was in my lap.

The highlight of this side-trip was stopping near a gorge — a big parking lot and picnic tables were appreciated — then looking over the river at a vertical wall made up of six thick and distinct layers of lava rock. Beautiful colours and breath-taking scenery.

And paleomagneticists could learn a lot from that readily accessible magnetized rock formation. The truly interesting aspect of the formation was one huge "lava bubble" that existed in three of the layers. How did it get there? At what age (10,000 or 10,000,000 years old?) would each of the layers be dated? I wish I had the tools and lab equipment to explore this potential paleomagnetic anomaly. But you don't have to be a scientist to enjoy the grandeur of that gorge, you merely need a little adventure in your soul.

Once in Telegraph Creek I decided to check the motorhome's brakes. Mid-way down the second steep hill I'd had the impression that those brakes were not working properly. The front disc brakes looked and tested alright. That meant that I had to take off the rear wheels (echoes of our Central America trip). The right brakes were okay. Whew, one down. Off came the left dual wheels, then the axle was pulled out, finally the brake drums removed. Only then did pieces of asbestos-like material fall onto the plastic sheet below. Large pieces. Small pieces. Half of the forward brake pad had been torn from its shoe and had been lying on the drum.

(If it had jammed between the rest of the brake and drum while we were moving, we could have ground to an abrupt halt, maybe turning sideways because only one wheel was stopped, sliding off the road and over a vertical wall of the gorge and down into the rushing Stikine River where, after a quick 200 m plummet straight down into raging water, our battered, broken and bleeding bodies would have gasped for air until body and soul went separate ways. Or, we could have veered in front of an oncoming van, crashed into it and killed a young family on the way to their ill parents, leaving us feeling guilty for years. Much more likely, we would have come to a slow but frightening controlled stop on level ground. But none of that happened.

Isn't it amazing how one's mind, my mind, can imagine the most horrifying incidents, improbable as they are? I feel sorry for people who don't venture off the beaten track because of unfounded fears. Fortunately Liz and I live by the motto "Take a risk, carefully", and it really is a lot of fun. But I digress.)

So here we are in tiny historic Telegraph Creek, 120 km from the nearest garage, with a jack and logs stuffed under the RV frame, with wheels and an oil-covered axle and bits and pieces of a brake system slowly being covered in dust. What am I going to do?

Luck is with us. I talk to Francis who is a retired heavy-duty mechanic. He won't do any work (he really is retired, although probably in better shape than I am) but he will offer advice and let me use any of his equipment I need. That's a relief, I've neither taken a brake system apart or, more important, never put one back together.

Whew ... but where do I get a brake shoe? Where?

Wait a minute. Didn't I see one in my storage compartment? I've got to be kidding myself. No wait, I did see something. Could it be?

It was.

Behind extra belts, fuses, light bulbs, fuel and air filters, fifty feet (15 m) of one-inch (3 cm) nylon tow-rope, a short chain, a cardboard box full of nuts and bolts and screws and nails, a metal box full of tools, and gloves and rags was hidden a small yellow box with words in español written on the side. I opened it and, sure enough, one set of brake shoes appeared. Unbelievable. It's been there for three years. Once again I'm glad I never throw out anything that has to do with this vehicle. Who would ever think that I'd need just one brake shoe?

Two hours later, the brakes are fixed, the axle is back, the wheels are on, and all equipment is cleaned and put away, and our four hands are clean. Francis did help a little; the one essential tool of his I needed to do everything myself had been lent to his son. Now it's time for an ice-cream, then coffee and pie to celebrate. Yes sir!

Liz had finished her walk about the village and joined us. Shortly thereafter, we were on our way back to Highway 37.

What an extraordinary trip. We saw gorgeous scenery, challenged a fearful road, met some great people, and I discovered I can fix complicatcd things, with help. And best of all, we got to drive a side road most travellers won't. Life is good.

Boya Lake Provincial Park

I'm having a hard time writing this article. I'd rather be outside canoeing in the multi-hued waters that are so clear I can see down beyond 6.3 m (20 ft), which is the longest piece of fishing line that I have. Our shadow, wavering sinuously under ripples, often followed us as we paddled between islands and into shallow bays.

Our first surprise was canoeing at the end of the lake closest to the horseshoe pit and boat launching ramp and finding an underwater spring. Several tiny mud pots bubbled and writhed, just like those in El Pozo Vivo (Living Waters) in Nicaragua. Only a little distance away, we canoed over a much larger hole that is, or probably was, another aquifer outlet.

Our second surprise was how frequently this lake changes colour. It depends upon the position of the sun, amount of cloud cover, and from which direction breezes blow. This irregular shaped body of water could easily have been called Jewels Lake, jewels such as pale jade, florescent turquoise, aquamarine, laser grey-blue, and gun-metal blue. When no breeze causes scintillating ripples, the water mirrors the bottle-brush trees, the brown mountains and the polar-bear-white, snow-filled crevices or rose tinted mountain tops as the sun sets.

Contrary to signs indicating that much patience is needed to catch fish here, last night one fisherman cast his line from his site, and within minutes caught a Char. There are only Char in this lake, whereas most of the others nearby have Rainbow Trout.

I wish I had a GPS receiver. After a couple hours of paddling and drifting, we would really like to know where our motorhome is. Even travelling at paddle-speed, Liz and I could easily get lost in all the bays and inlets and among the many small islands and sandbars, all populated with dark-green coniferous and lime-green deciduous trees. Many have beaver lodges, and some have beaver dams built between them. In the really shallow waters between land, we often saw moose-prints heading to or from an island. This is one of the few times that I wish I had a small motor that would quietly zip us along at 5-7 knots for hours on end.

Back in site 3 - those tourists who go where an entrance sign points to campsites will miss this area - we've seen sea gulls, swallows, three varieties of duck (all I recognize is mallards), and a partridge or ruffled grouse who lives here, or at least searches the woods behind us for seeds. The gulls came by as soon as we were set up, looking for handouts and scraps. Who says wild animals and birds are dumb? They must have remembered how to beg from last summer's visitors.

The peaceful quiet is truly invigorating. Even the wind has its own language, from a hushed whisper, to a gentle soughing through newly unfurled leaves, to a harsh Sshhh that bends the tops of spruce, poplars and willows. Even with the sibilant hush, I can hear a gull land on the water. And the occasional lapping of wavelets on rounded rocks. There are no sirens. There is no traffic noise. The constant hum of transformers and electrical lights doesn't exist here. I don't even hear the sound of an RV's generator ... could it be that the drivers of three RV's in the other section are too enthralled with quiet whispers of nature that they will do without their microwave oven or TV?

Nine thirty and I've decided we have to have a fire. I cut the wood last night, but never got a chance to use it. Too bad, because yesterday was considerably warmer than today. But on the positive side, we weren't bothered by any mosquitoes tonight. Even though the sky is hidden behind a solid layer of thin cloud, the flames are almost invisible in the bright dusk. The deep pink blush on the clouds is prettier than the flames.

Ten o'clock, and Liz and I are watching a beaver (it's huge!) gnaw on a branch, then go for a couple of swims. It disappeared into the tall grass, maybe its lodge isn't built yet. We'll drop by tomorrow morning and pay our respects, if we can find the entrance.

The Alaska Canadian Highway

Excerpts [and my additional comments in square brackets] have been taken from The Alaska Highway, *A personal and historical account of the building of the Alaska Highway* written by Brebner, Phyllis Lee, 1915 - ; published in 1985 by The Boston Mills Press, Ontario, Canada; ISBN 0-919783-26-0.

[To ensure minimal comments while maintaining clarity, some of the excerpts are placed in a different order than they appeared in the book.]

'Alaska is a name derived from the Eskimo word "Alaskh-Skhak" which means "great country." ['Eskimo' is now considered an insult to many natives because that word can be translated as "eaters of fat ." 'Inuit' is more correct and preferred.]

'By 1943 the word "Alcan" as the highway had been commonly called in the early days of construction — a derivation of Alaska and Canada — was disliked by everyone who worked on the project. Its unpopularity was mainly due to its derogative twist into "oilcan." Whatever the reason, the word Alcan was not a popular name choice for this important road being carved out of the bush under extreme and harsh conditions, and on July 19, 1943 the Government of Canada concurred with the proposal that the name be changed to the "Alaska Highway."

'The birth of the Alaska Highway was and remains a miracle. Imagine in nine months building a road winding through 1,523 miles [2483 km] of [untouched] mountainous terrain, muskeg, lakes and rivers, over which trucks could haul loads of supplies? Fighting bitterly cold weather, spring break-ups and flooding conditions that could not only break a man's spirit but immobilize his equipment? From the beginning there were men in Washington [,USA] who said "it can be done" and "it must be done." Their voices were heard above all the dissenters, and the Trail of '42, one of the most amazing feats of its time, was begun.

'Before formal agreement was reached with Canada, President Roosevelt, on Feb 11, 1942 authorized work to begin at once on the construction of a pioneer road from Dawson Creek, British Columbia to Big Delta, Alaska. The road was to be constructed by United States Army Engineer troops, who would be followed by contractors furnished by the Public Roads Administration; the contractors would improve the pioneer road to the

44

authorized highway standard. Three days later the War Department directed the Chief of Engineers to proceed.

'... Yet it wasn't until five days after the President authorized the work to commence that informal discussion began between the United States and Canada with a view to securing rights-of-way through Canadian territory. ... On March 6th, 1942 the Canadian government announced approval of the recommendation [that is, construction of the Alaska Highway] and acceptance of the offer by the United States to build the highway. The Canadian section was responsible to the Prime Minister.

'... exchange of notes between the two countries took place on March 17th by the American Minister to Canada and Canadian government. On the 18th, the United States Army Engineer troops were pouring into Canada ... and construction began in earnest.

'1,523 miles [20% in Alaska, 80% in Canada] of the "Road to Tokyo", announced on February 11th ,1942 was officially opened on November 20, 1942, or 279 days later, for an average of five and a half miles [almost nine kilometres] per day of reconnaissance, surveying, and construction of roads and bridges during some of the harshest conditions imaginable.

... 'The average Canadian received $0.86 per hour, compared to $1.57 paid an American worker.

'The next month, the United States decided to use a civilian airline for military transport en route to Alaska, and attempted to do so before receiving authority from Canada for such service. Canadian authorities were unhappy about this, concerned that an American airline was attempting to establish itself in Canada to obtain a postwar advantage, and one of the planes landing at Edmonton [,Alberta] was impounded. ... On March 15, 1944, the War Committee decided to revert to the policy of construction by Canadian contractors and Canadian labour. ... For the nine bases constructed, Canada paid the United States $76,811,511. [A number of these airports were under construction by Canada prior to the war.] The United States ... was not paid for items of nonpermanent value, amounting to $13,872,020.

...

'Canadian officials were also becoming alarmed at the enlarged scope of American activity in the Canadian northwest. They felt that it represented a menace to the system of controls which Canada had imposed on its wartime economy.

'Canadian officials were also becoming aware of a tendency on the part of the Americans to disregard Canadian sovereignty. Concerned only with getting the job done, American officers and officials, with the high priority of their jobs, were none too interested in the niceties of international diplomacy and often went ahead without first obtaining approval, acting as if they were in the United States.

'It is little wonder that at that time [Canada's Prime Minister] Mr. King began to grow apprehensive as to the ultimate designs of the Americans. ...

'In the course of the war, the North-West Staging Route was valuable for the delivery of aircraft to the Soviet Union, and for the logistic support of American forces in Alaska and American projects in Western Canada. More aircraft for the Soviet Union than for the Alaska base were flown over this route,
...

'By the end of 1943 the United States had evacuated the equipment that was not needed for maintenance. ... The end of construction did not signal that work on the highway was over. The highway had to be maintained, and on April 1, 1946 the Royal Canadian Engineers Corps took over the Canadian sector of the road to Alaska ... The last chapter in the Alaska Highway saga come on Wednesday morning, April 1, 1964, when the responsibility of the Northwest Highway system was turned over by the Canadian Army to the federal Department of Works.

'The Alaska Highway ... is significant now as the one overland artery linking Alaska to [Canada and] the rest of the United States. ... The highway has been not only of incalculable value for transportation purposes in exploration and development, but during the Royal Canadian Engineers' tenure of maintenance, techniques were developed in northland construction and soils research that have been priceless in opening up areas of the north.

"The highway was something like a huge practical laboratory — everyone learned something new up there."

'... [It] has opened up the Yukon for exploration, winding through some of the most spectacular scenery in the world ...

'Lying north of 60 degrees latitude is the largest piece of undeveloped real estate in the world. Northern Canada alone has more lakes that the rest of the world combined. ... South Nahanni River, located some 40 miles below Fort Liard, has a sheer drop of 350 ft. — twice the height of Niagara Falls. The Yukon River with its 1,600 miles of navigable water, equal to that of the Great Lakes and the St. Lawrence River combined, has already been harnessed for power in the Peace River district of British Columbia."

Watson Lake

I wrote to the Mayor of Watson Lake, YT concerning the amount of litter in the sides of the western highway leading into his community, and especially the garbage surrounding the town's sign declaring this community to be litter free.

Since that time I have been informed that roadside litter is an annual occurrence, resulting from winter winds blowing across this community's land fill, or garbage dump. Animals and birds scrounge in the land fill, tearing open bags in search of food scraps and releasing paper and plastic to the windy whims of wintery nature. Each spring Watson Lake residents, via a community organization, do a Spring Clean-up. Therefore, only early pre-season travellers to this area should come across a lot of highway litter.

We were surprised at the number of commercial signs along the highway as we drove into Watson Lake.

Once in Watson Lake, conditions did improve.

We were surprised to note that ounces, pounds and miles were still in common usage. Some stores don't even acknowledge the metric system, which might be against Canadian law. I suspect the influence of Alaska and visitors from the southern 48 states are two reasons for maintaining such an archaic system of measurements. On the other hand, maybe Yukoners just want to be different than the rest of Canadians.

The oldest attraction – Signpost Forest – supposedly contains over 34,000 signs from around the world, nailed to hundreds of posts. In fact there are so many, I doubt that most people will spend the time it would take to see them all.

I suggest that you bring a sign with you, perhaps one you had made especially to your specifications, and donate it to the Sign Forest..I wouldn't worry too much about duplications. I doubt that your sign will be placed next to its twin, even if there is one.

Your sign can be an actual highway or street sign or community-name sign, or it can be one that you created, perhaps listing the names of visitors. Other than your own creation, do not expect automatically to be able to hang up or nail up a unique sign.

Do not climb the posts, ask for help in putting up your sign. When we were there, workers were replacing six old posts that were rotted at the base. They were doing so because someone had climbed a post and it fell over. The young man was not seriously injured.

The newest attraction is the Northern Lights Centre. This building is across the road from the visitor information (tourist) centre, and is easily accessible by an entrance on the west side. A parking lot provides ample parking space for any size of vehicle.

The show is forty-five minutes of a laser, pictures and graphics that explain the myths and scientific cause of the Aurora Borealis. Before or after the show, one can easily spend another half hour looking at the space exhibits that surround the huge overhead dome.

Although we both enjoyed the show, we had hoped to see more actual photographs or film clips of the Aurora Borealis than we did. Of course we passed on our comments to staff members. Maybe you will see more of them than we did. Postcards also offer many a majestic sight.

Surprisingly, we saw no real Northern Lights while we were in the Yukon.

Why?

The sun shone too many hours of each day!

We did see several celestial Northern Light displays while in the NorthwestTerritories during late August and early September. Sadly, many other opportunities were hidden by clouds and overcast conditions.

The visitor information centre staff were very pleasant, with lots of information about Yukon events and sights, including its own gallery and slideshow. They even provided a cup of coffee for a nominal donation.

But getting to this info centre might be a bit tricky. Driving east, take the last left turn before the Signpost Forest.

Driving west, take the first right turn after the Signpost Forest. Drive only a few metres along a city street then turn right into a small parking lot. Big motorhomes can be accommodated. Do not take the street before the Sign Forest. This will take you to a gasoline station to your right or to a souvenir shop to your left. Although these places might be worth visiting (we thought so) you cannot drive to the tourist centre parking lot from there, unless you go back on the highway.

When driving west, there is a dirt side road that passes directly in front of the Forest, and eventually goes to the parking lot. But the first time we were on this road we thought we'd done something wrong. I suggest you stay on paved streets.

Watson Lake also provides a free picnic area next to Wye Lake, which is a bird sanctuary. The boardwalk is a pleasant stroll as it meanders through low reeds and bushes. The picnic tables offered us a welcome change from eating at our dinette inside our RV.

To 280 km West of Watson Lake

The 450 km from Watson Lake to Whitehorse aren't very exciting except for brief moments. Although we scheduled ourselves for an average of 100 km per day, we left Watson Lake at 4 PM and stopped 218 kilometres and five hours later. Even near the end of May, the sun shines for many hours.

This highway is in excellent condition, with only a couple of very short stretches of construction. I noticed some areas of the latest upgrading had an extremely wide base of crushed rock. The road resembled a long, thin multi-tiered cake. I understand they use such a wide base because the sharp angular shapes of the rock fragments prevent the rocks from moving and thus distribute the loading stresses over large areas such as a marshy or boggy surface.

It will be interesting to see what the cost of gasoline is as we travel west. We were told that much of it comes from Alaska. Watson Lake prices varied from 70.9 to 65.5 cents per litre, maybe a price war was going on. I should have filled up yesterday when we arrived, today all the cheapest gasoline was sold out.

There was an excellent photo opportunity at kilometre 700, or thereabouts. Canada's Alaska Highway wove sinuously amongst the trees, which were dwarfed by snow-covered mountain peaks. We stopped on the side of the road for pictures. Unfortunately, there was an even more picturesque view a kilometre or so farther on. By the time I convinced myself I should have stopped a second time and taken more pictures, we decided we were too far away.

The scenic Alaska Highway is paved as far as the eye can see.

Rancheria Falls Recreation Area was closed. But how do you close waterfalls, especially in the spring? We drove in, parked in a large empty area, and walked to the falls. This attraction is designed for access for those who are physically handicapped and/or in wheel chairs. Humphrey Falls near Kitimat are still the best we've seen. These were OK, with lots of volume but little height, and the walk there and back was an enjoyable break from constant driving. (Yes, I know some people drive for hours without stopping, but Liz and I often consider an hour, a full sixty minutes, an outrageous 3600 seconds, to be an exhausting experience.)

We stopped in at Walkers for pieces of pie, only to discover the next café had three trucks and a tour bus parked outside. Their rhubarb pie — a house speciality — was very good, although more costly than I expected, and I can't help wondering if the next stop might have been better. Probably not.

Why does living require so many choices? Because it is fun to be alive.

As we were driving along we saw five RV's parked in a level area only a few metres from the highway. It seemed as if they were travelling together. We were tempted to stop for some conversation and company, but agreed that we wanted to get closer to Teslin. Question. Are we starting to suffer from "Goalitis", also known as "Destination Fever"?

Shortly thereafter I noticed a car-carrier catching up to us. Using Channel 19 on the Citizens' Band transceiver (CB) we had a most pleasant conversation with truck-driving Mel and his wife. Because they haul goods from Seattle to Alaska once or twice a month, as well as driving up on holidays every two or three years because they like the ever-changing scenery, we were learning of several places worth visiting.

But about 9 pm we decided we had driven far enough, saw an area that looked promising, and at exactly kilometre 1136 we pulled off the highway onto an unmarked road on our right and into a secluded lakeside field. Having delivery deadlines to meet, Mel and his wife couldn't join us ... that is the only complaint those two had about all their trips on this beautiful highway. Our little campfire of collected twigs and small branches didn't smoke, the pumpkin-orange sunset was marvellous, and mosquitoes and bugs were somewhere else.

Interestingly enough, next evening we met those five RVers at Mukluk Annie's. They had spent the night close to the highway hearing trucks and other noisy vehicles constantly rushing by. They spotted us partially hidden amongst trees as they drove by in the early morning (around 8 am) and were curious how we had found our camping spot.

Me, if I see a side-road that looks like it might go somewhere interesting, I turn onto it. But don't we get lost, or trapped, you ask? Nope.

Our scratched and dented motorhome with two solid steel bumpers and a powerful engine weighs 4,500 kg (5 tons) on six tires while being only 7.2m (23 ft) long. This explains how I can turn around on an awfully narrow path surrounded by bushes and small flexible trees when it turns out to be a path to nowhere.

But the truth is most roads go somewhere and usually it's very easy to turn around.

Teslin

A 'native' Altar

Teslin is a clean, neat village easily accessible from the highway. Based upon my own figures in Appendix B, prices in this community's trading post are some of the lowest I've seen in Yukon. This opinion was confirmed by a survey done by someone else. Unfortunately I cannot give credit to whomever did that study because any reference was missing in the photocopy I was given.

The selection of canned, packaged, frozen and fresh produce in the Trading Post is reasonable, certainly more than we expected in such a tiny community. We discovered the Trading Post in the real part of the village, a short distance from the highway.

We mistakenly chose not to visit the Museum, which can be seen from the highway. Now we understand that it is well worth a visit, if only to study the life-like poses of its taxidermy displays. I wonder how this museum and Adam's Igloo (on Highway 16) compare?

The Catholic church in Teslin is worth a quick visit. It's only a few metres from the Trading Post. The interior design captures the feeling and history of its congregation. Check out what's on the altar.

Take time to drive into Teslin, a community with pride.

Letter to YTMC

By the time Liz and I had travelled BC highways 16 and 37 and part of the Alaska Highway to Whitehorse, we were truly angry with Canadians who refuse to advertise their own country. We did manage to attend a scheduled tourism meeting, but our comments were essentially ignored. We did not receive a promised reply to a letter - which I had written and mailed a couple of weeks before the meeting - and discussions held after the meeting.

This portion of the letter is included as my rebuke to bad manners.

To: Yukon Tourism Marketing Council (YTMC)
Subject: Public Meeting of YTMC on Friday, May 29th

I hope to be able to attend your meeting ...
Yesterday, I was told a story about a resident of the USA who was travelling northward en route to Alaska. He had just crossed the British Columbia-Yukon border. While paying for his gasoline purchase he drawled "I've just left Canada. Where am I?"

That tale reminds me of all the people who responded "Oh, you're going to Alaska" whenever I said I was going North. Most times I managed to control my pique, but occasionally my anger broke through. "No, we're going to the Yukon and Northwest Territories!"

I wonder how many people know that, except for Hyder (which chooses to use Canadian currency in all its stores), one cannot drive a car, truck, motorhome or trailer on a road to Alaska without going through Canada's Yukon?

How many of the Marketing Council members have ever driven the Kitwanga-Yukon Highway (BC 37) and, while hoping to see some mention of Yukon, have counted the numerous Canadian commercial signs that advertise Alaska? If no one has, someone should. Why have a sign that reads "Highway to Alaska" when there could be one that displays "Highway to Yukon and Alaska" or "Highway to Alaska via Yukon", or better yet, one that says "Highway to Yukon?"

Perhaps, a YTMC-sponsored researcher could carry brochures and publications that describe the beauty and businesses of the Yukon. Then, after counting the number of northern Canadian and Alaskan brochures in tourist information centres, he or she could give some brochures to those places that don't have any, or perhaps not enough. (Even I managed to get a couple of BC Info centres to request more Yukon and NWT publications for display and handout.)

Did you know that some British Columbia Tourism publications have more references to a foreign country than they do to the Yukon and Northwest Territories? And I am not referring to paid commercial advertisements. Perhaps the YTMC should hire someone to read all of Alberta's and BC's tourism publications (or the computer files thereof) and search for places where the word 'Alaska' could be replaced with 'Yukon' or at least have the words "Yukon and" added to a phrase or sentence.

Even the federal Department of Highways sometimes chooses to advertise that same foreign destination on its green and white signs rather than direct travellers to northern Canada.

Why do northern residents themselves seem to advertise Alaska more than they extol the magical, marvellous mysteries of the Yukon? Are they happy merely to receive a few dollars from passing tourists heading west, just like beggars and panhandlers on a busy thoroughfare?

As an aside, Canadians providing free advertisements for another country reminds me of the marketing genius who decided to put corporate logos on T-shirts, charge those corporations for advertising, then charge the buyers twice as much as they would otherwise have paid so they can walk about providing advertising in places where radio, TV and newsprint can't.

Reading the article "Tourism's website catches flak from locals" in The Yukon News upset me. I am aware of the need for international marketing. But it seems to me that the website designers forgot or were not told that many Canadians and Americans also check the Web for information on the Yukon.

I am looking forward to being at your meeting. However, if I don't make it there, perhaps this letter will help to generate some fruitful discussion.

Yours truly,
John (& Liz) Plaxton

Even fog can be beautiful.

Atlin

This is a town you must visit, *unless* you are prone to instant decisions and you don't like several things about the place where you now live. Several people have come to Atlin and never left. Truly. Others came, then came back to stay.

Although warned by the gas attendant at Jake's Corner that the gravel road might be slippery during rain, we decided to take our chances. At 50-70 km/hr there was absolutely no danger, and bumps and construction were non-existent. However, washboard occasionally set our stove a-rattling. At the Tagish turnoff to Atlin, severe vibration released the catch on Liz's overhead spice rack, filling our cab with the aroma of Basil and the kitchen floor with bags and bottles that could have come from an ancient alchemist's shelves.

20 km down this muddy road I looked out our back window. Or at least I tried to, but couldn't. All I could see was a brown opaqueness with occasional silver vertical wiggly lines.

Camouflague, who needs it? I'd rather someone see my brake lights.

The rain was intermittent but the overcast was constant. Yet the scenery was spectacular. We saw clouds being formed as moist air was forced up and over mountain peaks. We saw a

56

mountain (or perhaps just a cliff of solid rock, we couldn't see the top) emerge from wisps of fog and low hanging clouds. We watched other clouds change a bright, colourful scene to ghostly grey. Carpets of fog and mist rose and settled over lakes, revealing and hiding islands of black spruce.

This is another reason I stopped. What a beautiful sight.

(Next day the mists and clouds disappeared by noon, and a whole new vista of mountains and glaciers and colours revealed itself to our awestruck eyes and minds. We have had the best of two worlds.)

After 60 km of painting the lower half of our RV in natural colours, and immediately before advancing onto smooth blacktop, I stopped and started backing down a side road to a small creek.(I wish drivers wouldn't tuck their vehicles close in behind our motorhome, out of sight of my mirrors. Fortunately, the driver behind us had quick reactions.) As our vehicle started to slide sideways I decided this might not be such a great place to wash our vehicle, slipped the transmission into Drive and, spewing clumps of mud from the traction treads of snow tires, slowly created a lengthy pair of deep ruts back to the highway.

A few kilometres of asphalt later, we pulled onto another side road and stopped by the banks of the Fourth of July Creek.

Liz made supper while I spent forty minutes washing off the mud, using dozens of pots of water and a soft, long-fibre brush. If only I had brought along a battery operated pump, I could have attached the car-cleaning brush to our drinking-water hose and saved those many toe-soaking trips to the creek. Being so sandy, the mud came off easily. It just required several splashes of water for each small area. Wisely, I wore my rubberized rain jacket and kept my clothes spatter-free.

Wouldn't you know it? This morning I had spent an hour washing the motorhome, using lots of biodegradable car-wash soap and lake water. My bottle of wax turned out to be a second bottle of foaming liquid soap. Nevertheless, until then, I hadn't realized how light and bright the painted aluminum siding was.

I mean, this vehicle almost shone. Then it had to rain.

Surprisingly, after our Atlin road and creek water experience, it still looked great. Except for the highest 35 cm which I couldn't reach. But the diarrhea-brown, antique-brass, and off-white colours went well together. At least, I think so.

'I guess that "No RV's" sign wasn't a bluff after all!'[1]

[1] A cartoon extracted from "R.V.S.P. - Rec Vehicle Survival Pamphlet " (C) 1988 Doug Urquhart, a Guide to Life in the Leisure Lane

An old jail for people, and one for their feathered friends (Jailbirds).

Being unincorporated, Atlin has no bylaws. People can build whatever they like for homes or businesses, but most seem to have opted for restoring and using historical buildings, or building new residences and stores that co-exist with an historical theme. It is an established community, but modern in its outlook of old-fashioned ideals.

There is money here, but ostentatiously hidden away behind trees surrounding subdivisions or set back from Discovery and Warm Springs roads.

Atlin is a clean community where every downtown street is paved. It has a unique ambience, one that is initially and instantly appealing. Buildings are multi-coloured, and many are coloured differently than its neighbours. And weathered pine is slightly different than

Check Liz's diary to see what is beyond this fog-enshrouded island.

weathered spruce. Town people really seem to care about its appearance and other residents. Every person we met was friendly.

This community may make money from visiting tourists — it was open to tourism almost from its inception — but it gives back as much enjoyment as it gets. Atlin — the name comes from the native Tlingit word "ahltah" or "A Tlen" which means "big water" — is cost-effective.

We met Diane Smith, co-author of "Atlin" (which won the Governor General's award for a first book) at the informative and well-organized historical museum. She is a wealth of information, fully recollected and pleasantly told.

In the museum is a hidden treasure, still available to some visitors. I understand that some of the hilarious books of cartoons by Doug Urquhart, who has a wonderfully warped sense of northern humour, are out of print. Get yours while you can.

Outside, sadly subjected to weathering, are several pieces of mining equipment, two of which have sunk into the ground. Whoever thinks that our ancestors were unimaginative in the use of wood and steel — ask Diane about Atlin's corkscrew snowplow — are not too smart themselves. If I had the money to restore just one piece of equipment, it would be the drill.

Permanently dry-docked, the 119 feet boat MV Tarahne offers tours and 1920's weekend pleasantries that we, as early arrivals, could not experience: Friday Night BarBQ's, Saturday Mystery Dinner Theatres and Sunday Brunches. We couldn't even get inside this luxuriously restored vessel because three days previously, volunteers had stripped the wax off the original linoleum and today's stripping chemicals had reacted with the 1916-17 flooring. A team of professional restorers were hard at work, and we were barred from the interior.

Mateus is a congenial Swiss whom we meet several weeks ago in Lac La Hache, south of Prince George. He drove his rented Class C into the RV park on the far side of the village, pulled out his binoculars to scan the area — as 99 and 44/100 percent of the people who visit Atlin will do — and recognized our green canoe on the roof of our ancient but durable Class C. He immediately unhooked from full services, and drove over to our RV, only to discover we weren't there. But he had driven by us at an intersection, recognized us in retrospect, and tracked us down in the Food Basket. We had a long conversation in the aisle between canned soup and green vegetables.

What a pleasant surprise. Later Liz and I walked over to his RV, but it and he were gone. Mateus is not the type of person to stay in one place very long, especially when there is so much to explore and beauty to see.

Atlin has been inaccurately called "Little Switzerland". But as Mateus said, not so. Switzerland has high mountains and deep valleys that sometimes seem very confining, Atlin has high mountains and wide open spaces that beg one's spirit to expand.

Traces of Discovery, a tent town of 10,000 people, no longer exist except for a rusty safe on the side of a gravel road. But a trip to the Spruce Creek Mine is worthwhile, because it shows the reality of modern gold mining techniques. Pine Creek Falls could probably be best enjoyed by scaling down the canyon walls, which we didn't do only because we didn't have a safety rope. We two pre-Baby-Boomers really do believe in our travelling motto "Take a risk, carefully."

We were disappointed in Warm Springs (warm compared to snow melt and glacial water, provider of fresh Water Cress for salads), intrigued by the tiny Grotto, and enthralled by the

Believe it or not, we got within 3 m of the beaver in this picture.

Parker Lake pullout because we could venture out on this shallow lake in our canoe.

In two and half hours in our silent canoe during the first night (by the clock, not by darkness) we observed a solitary eagle high in a tree, several one kilogram (two pound) Pike resting in the tannin-clear shallows, a yearling moose which kept running away, a beaver chewing on a branch then swimming with an occasional slap of its tail and some shallow dives, several ducks, a woodpecker, a grey jay, gulls, possibly an Arctic Tern, and several birds we couldn't identify. We also saw three other people, a motorhome, a camper, a four metre boat with a 5 HP motor, and a successfully-used fishing pole mounted on a kayak. We stayed two more days and nights, peacefully, quietly alone.

Remember to visit Atlin as you travel the Alaska Highway, regardless of the weather.

Skagway vs Haines

Skagway, like "Soapy" Smith's grave site, is not real. Haines is real, a town with real businesses and real people.

Skagway should be considered the end of a destination. The destination is southern Klondike Highway, or the Golden Circle Route, that passes through beautiful parts of Yukon, British Columbia and Alaska.

From Whitehorse, YT this ribbon of asphalt will take you past Emerald Lake, YT which, at least when the wind blows and ripples the lake's surface, we consider to be less colourful than Boya Lake, BC on Highway 37. Then it passes by the Carcross Dunes which is sometimes incorrectly called Carcross Desert and past but preferably through Carcross, YT where you can visit the Carcross Barracks and one of the oldest General Stores in Yukon. And it goes past Log Cabin, BC where you must walk on train tracks to get there even though you are warned not to do so. Then through desolate Tormented Valley with its multi-hued lichen and grotesquely stunted trees. Eventually it passes through Canada Customs, up and over a windy summit, through USA customs, down and down a long and twisting road to within two miles of Skaguay, AK.

Skaguay is the old spelling, Skagway is the modern one.

Once there you can continue on into the village, or you can choose to turn right. We suggest making the right turn and travelling a short distance on blacktop to a viewpoint overlooking the community. This will help orientate yourselves with the two streets of gift and trinket stores, places to park or rest, places to eat, and other establishments. All are meant to ease the worry and burden of having too much money in your wallet or bank accounts.

After resetting your watch to the time displayed on a giant pocket watch painted on the mountain side, you could drive nine miles (15 km) on a narrow gravel road to Dyea, a ghost town that is truly a metaphysical location because there is almost nothing physical left there to clothe its history.

The story behind this graveyard attests to the greed and carelessness of some of mankind.

Or better yet, drive to the Slide Cemetery – also called Avalanche Cemetery – where most of the grave sites contain nothing but restored grave markers. Almost all have the same date, April 3, 1898. After this adventure, you can camp at the inexpensive State Park or continue back to Skagway.

There are *some* things worth seeing in and near Skagway. Foremost is Reid Falls. It was a pretty sight even though it was cold and windy and overcast the day we saw it. It's only a short walk beyond the Gold rush Cemetery and Soapy's grave. On a hot summer day, with light mist from glacial water landing on overheated skin, it should be heavenly.

If you walk along the railroad tracks to get there, you might be lucky enough to see the old White Pass and Yukon Route steam engine being fired up to haul a trainload of passengers over the pass.

The main street — Broadway; Main is a side street — beautifully maintains the historical theme of the Gold Rush days. If the paved streets were dirt and covered with horse droppings and if hundreds of tourists — like prospectors of old rushing somewhere else — were dressed in last century's fashions, they would blend in among faithfully restored buildings, 1800's false fronts, and wooden boardwalks.

The authentic driftwood front of the Arctic Brotherhood {AB} Hall is unique.

The diesel engines of the narrow gauge train of the White Pass and Yukon Route Railway can take you through spectacular scenery, although I suspect you would see similar scenery on the southern portion of the Klondike Highway. I was told that once a month that train is powered by a steam locomotive for an especially nostalgic trip.

The airport — it could be referred to as Airstrip Street — and landing pads were constantly in use when we were there. Small planes and helicopters were taking off and landing after flying sightseers over glaciers and down mountain valleys.

Skagua — meaning 'windy place' or 'home of the north wind' in Tlingit — is a tourist town, a town that insists on being famous because its ancestors were. I think it doesn't deserve the recognition.

We and several other RV's were lucky enough to be allowed to park in the ferry parking lanes overnight, because there was only one ferry running. This is not usual.

For those who are taking the ferry to Haines, drivers of big Class A motorhomes and long fifthwheels could find getting in and out of the side hatch of the ferry MV Malispina interesting. "Organized confusion" is too kind a word for the manner in which vehicles were loaded onto the ferry. The very last fifthwheel was squeezed in between two others, literally with centimetres between them. They were so close the owner couldn't do it and a driver from the ferry staff had to. And yet directly in front of us was room for at least one more motorhome and beside us was room for another car or truck.

Unloading of vehicles took an exceptionally long time. Last on, first off, that's the rule, by necessity. But the first-off was so close to two others that the owner damaged his friend's fifthwheel while trying to inch forward. Almost an hour after docking it finally managed to leave the ferry, but only after being shifted forcibly sideways by chains and winches. The owner should have let the ferry staff take it off. Once that fifthwheel exited, a couple of vehicles could drive off. But all others near the hatch had to backup, turn around in very cramped quarters, then drive off.

A driver of one large Class A was so upset with the delay that once he got pointed towards the exit ramp, he gunned his engine and shot up the ramp. Because of low tide, the ramp formed a fifteen to twenty degree angle with the ferry deck and that motorhome almost left its bumper behind on the ferry. It did scrape, but barely. He was one lucky impatient driver.

Along with a dozen other people, Liz and I spent almost forty-five minutes watching the machinations near the exit hatch, during both loading and unloading. This spectacle alone was worth the cost of the trip.

Haines doesn't pretend to be what it isn't. It is a small town with a small airport, a ferry terminal, a small-boat harbour, and a couple of grocery stores, churches, four gas stations and people who live there year round. One gas station accepts only credit cards, another gives a 5 cents/L discount for Canadian licence plates. All have prices considerably less than in Skagway. Also in Haines are four RV campgrounds, the American Bald Eagle Foundation, and Fort Seward which has been converted to homes, condos and apartments.

Please plan on spending at least forty-five minutes at the Bald Eagle Foundation's expanded but inexpensive interpretive centre. Anyone can learn a lot by talking with David Olerud, either near the continuously-running video or in the unusual transitional sky-land-water diorama. Try to find the seventh bird on the central tree. No. It is not a woodpecker hiding inside the tree trunk.

If you decide to have relatively inexpensive fish and chips try the Grizzly Bear, which is in downtown Haines. Although it had the aroma of a greasy spoon and the appearance of a 1950's fast food parlour, the food was reasonable. There are several other restaurants, but some don't open until supper time. Liz and I were surprised at the cost of seafood, considering that much of it is caught by local fishermen.

Our 7.5 L engine powering a 4500 kg vehicle consumes one litre of gasoline for every 2.9 kilometres of highway driving. That is equivalent to about 6 ½ mpg. As a result, our ferry trip was only slightly more expensive than if we had driven from Skagway to Haines by highway, looping north back to Whitehorse then south to Haines.

But we did miss the drive from Whitehorse to Haines Junction. We heard later that it is a scenic mountain drive. Ah well, next time.

The ferry trip was shorter than we hoped for. Although we saw several waterfalls we saw only one small glacier. However, by driving through Haines and then along Mud Bay Road we saw several large glaciers across the water, as well as juvenile (speckled brown and white) and mature (white heads and tail feathers) American Bald Eagles.

Driving left past the Alaska State Park turnoff we proceeded to the end of the gravel highway, then a hundred yards or metres down a tiny road to the right, where we parked overnight with our dinette window overlooking Lynn Canal. Because this two-rut path eventually leads to a private residence, we had to park on a tiny grass strip next to the rocky shore. We were momentarily awakened by a truck driving past at 5 am. Life is hard.

A Tale of Two Cyclists

"Here's to roughing it ... Seniors' Style" I toasted my smiling wife with red wine in green goblets, as we sat on the soft cushions of our dinette inside a cozy motorhome parked level on a cold and windy beach. We could have been eating oven-baked potatoes and propane-barbequed steaks on warm plates next to a mixed green salad and three dressings.

Outside, a young couple, Andy and Tyra, were dressed in insulated jump suits, toques and mitts after parking their bikes and setting up their nylon tent on uneven and rocky ground. They had opened plastic packages of dehydrated nutrition and were shaking the mixture into a tiny pot of lake water heated by a miniscule stove. "Been there, done that" remained unsaid.

'I guess you could call us "The Counter-Coleman" Culture.'[1]

We first met them at The Cinnamon Bakery – several kilometres before Carcross Dunes, where we spent many minutes strolling barefoot in sun-warmed sand – where we jokingly offered them a ride to their and our destination, Skagway. Their super-light touring bicycles were weighted down with five bags bulging with supplies. Naturally, being athletic and enthusiastic, they refused.

Later we pulled up beside them as they were parking next to the boardwalk in front of the Carcross Tourist Information Centre. Brief smiles and acknowledgments and another offer of a ride refused.

Liz and I set off to visit a 1902 church, Yukon's longest-in-use General Store, a walk across a short foot bridge, and Carcross Barracks. During our walk-about I wished I had worn my Canadian Tilley hat instead of the baseball cap which kept being blown off by the same cold wind that blew sand in our eyes.

At Carcross Barracks beware of red-coated "Sergeant Calamity" who will introduce you to Skookum Jim sitting in his red woollen Stanfield underwear. She'll lock you up with him if you haven't shaved in two days, if you're wearing a plaid shirt or sandals or running shoes, if you are rich or poor, if you are male, and if you are female.

An hour and some minutes later we were back on the highway heading for a picnic area on Tutshi Lake, 42 km closer to Skagway and a recommended overnight camping spot. Several times I wondered about our motorhome's steering mechanism, but I finally realized that a southerly breeze had turned into a high-speed headwind whose fluctuations and whorls were inducing unexpected zigzag motions. That realization and the knowledge that we were continually climbing also explained why our gasoline gauge was dropping much too quickly towards E for empty.

As we pulled into the pullout overlooking an abandoned and weathered wooden mill we saw our cycling acquaintances once more. Bent over into the wind, I struggled over and offered them yet another chance for a ride. Being young, winded, chilled to the bone and exhausted, they agreed. We securely lashed our RV door open while they stripped the bikes of their bags. Hurriedly riders, bicycles and everything else were squeezed through that narrow door and pushed inside our motorhome. Only then were the lashings undone and the door closed and locked against the mini-hurricane outside. Bags were packed properly, pillows and t-shirts were placed between walls and repositioned bike frames, and seats with seatbelts were readied for our guests.

We had several laughs, made a pot of hot chocolate, drove away in our warm home and stopped several times en route for picture taking. Eventually we camped at Tutshi Lake.

Next morning, we offered our riders the opportunity to travel with us again because it was even colder and windier than the day before. After a brief private discussion, they accepted, and we loaded them and all their equipment inside again.

Heading south we stopped several times en route for picture taking, especially of the stark Tormented Forest, eventually turning into a pull-out overlooking ground made of granite partially covered with lichen, moss and patches of snow. Being near the top of a hill and the Canadian-USA border, our guests asked to leave us. They wanted to pedal over the summit then coast down to Skagway. And I'm sure they did. But the true summit was an unexpected several kilometres past the top of that windy hill.

Andy H. and Tyra G. are hoping to cycle all the way to one of the original 13 States, raising pledges and money for a worthwhile cause. We're glad to have helped them on the third day of their trek, the day when overtaxed muscles start to seize up. Hopefully when we get all our mail we'll read about the rest of the trip made by these two hardworking cyclists.

On the left, our two cyclists; on the right, us; and in the centre a German fellow who let his wife take this picture.

While we were unloading and the cyclists were putting on their protective clothing, a couple from Germany drove up in a rented camperized van. They were a pleasant twosome but our lack of any German and their struggling English made for difficult conversation. Liz and I do admire travellers who visit a country without knowing the local language. At times it has to be lonely or frustrating.

But scenery in British Columbia and Yukon is worth it.

Haines to Haines Junction

We're on our way to Yukon's fabulous Top of the World Highway. Of course, we'll have to go back into Alaska to get to Tetlin Junction and the Taylor Highway, but that's ok. Maybe gasoline will be cheaper there. We might even divert to Eagle, just to say we've done it.

Driving north from Haines was a pleasant surprise. Being next to water, the road is flat for tens of kilometres.

Fish are netted, lifted out of water, fall and slide into boxes at the sides.

The sight of our first fish wheel was an unexpected delight, even if it was tied up next to shore and the brake was on. I understand this efficient and effective time-saver was invented after the turn of the century. The original design had two scoops whereas this one had three.

The overhang which houses our bed above the RV's cab is a nuisance now. It is a pain in the neck, literally, because we are constantly looking up trying to spot an eagle or twenty. No luck. We're here at the wrong time to see hundreds or thousands of eagles nesting in the Chilkat Bald Eagle Preserve and fishing salmon in nearby inlets, bays and rivers. November would have been a better time.

Liz, and most other people, think the eagle is a spectacular-looking bird. Me, I think smaller hawks and falcons are just as impressive although, granted, they do not have the wing span of an eagle. Maybe if I saw an eagle swoop out of a tree and grab a fish in its talons, just like an osprey did ten metres from our canoe, then I might change my mind. Truth be known, I'd rather watch a flock of ravens flying, diving, cavorting, arcing, doing barrel rolls, and generally having fun on a summer day than gaze at a solitary eagle perched on a tree like a sleeping owl. I always was different.

At Canadian and USA customs we stopped for a short exploratory visit of the border and interesting conversation with an agent. This particular road was also initially built because of the Alaska Canadian (Alcan) Project in the early-1940's, although several years of improvements were necessary before it became an all-weather, all-season road.

Once more on our way Liz said we had to stop at Rock Glacier, YT. She's *the* navigator and I do what she says.

As an aside, it took me a long time to learn to do that.

For example, when we first got this motorhome and I was backing it into or out of some parking spot, Liz would give me directions by hand waving and yelling above the noise of the engine. Of course, I'd be looking in the mirrors and sometimes would do what I thought was better. This lead to some interesting parking alignments, followed by private discussions inside our RV.

About six months later we bought a walkie-talkie for Liz and I listened on our CB. This greatly improved my hearing, understanding and backing up. I highly recommend most couples do the same.

But the real breakthrough came one day when I said "enough." As I started to back up, I closed my eyes and did exactly what I was told.

After all, which is more important? Is hitting a tree or rock which results in hundreds of dollars of repairs more or less costly than having an argument and a few hours of the "silent" treatment or "I told you so" treatment? I told Liz what I was doing, and kept my eyes closed as WE backed up. And it works, most of the time. Once in awhile Liz uses an expression that I misinterpret – straight back, which means to me to straighten the steering wheel but to her it means straight down the driveway – but we've never had a serious accident and the motorhome remains dent-free.

But back to the present.

Liz said we should stop at Rock Glacier. I'm thinking "Why can't we just look at it from the highway?" but I say "Good idea." When we got there, we pulled into a parking lot, and levelled the vehicle to prepare a snack. ("Why do you always have to be so level. I can't feel any difference in a couples of degrees." "I can.")

Then we spent a fantastic forty-five minutes climbing and exploring one of nature's unique attractions. If we hadn't climbed to the end of the trail, we would never have experienced the amazing result of rocks flowing like ice. We even added to the length of the path and wrote our names with stones.

As we continued driving to Haines Junction we did see other rock glaciers from the highway. Compared to actually climbing on one, the experience was bland.

Manmade "Muffin Mountain" and all its animals.

Watch for Muffin Mountain when in Haines Junction, at the junction. It's an interesting man-made monument and worth a picture or two if the sun is in the right location.

Also you might be able to save a little money. When we were there, gasoline prices were two cents per litre cheaper on the highway two or three kilometres west of the junction.

Rock Glacier

Rock glaciers can only be appreciated by walking on them. You must walk on one.

When travelling to or through Haines Junction, take the time to drive 40 km (25 miles) south on Haines Road to Rock Glacier and spend half an hour climbing on this amazing natural phenomenon. Running shoes and sneakers are adequate footwear, even sandals could be used. Hiking boots are overkill if you stay on the path.

As you climb to the top of this rocky glacier there are four small activities you can perform. Unobstructed by trees, look around and admire the view of Desadeash Lake, the valleys below and those mountain peaks above. Write your name using stones, replacing the name that is already written on a large flat rock. Move a couple dozen stones at the very end of the unofficial path and lengthen it every so slightly. Lastly, carefully study the lichen that covers undisturbed rocks; the variety might surprise you.

Lovely Liz resting near the top, reading a sign.

Please don't do what one couple did as we were preparing breakfast below this extrusion of shattered stone, this grey tongue of a granite giant. They drove their camper into the large parking lot. He waved to us, she looked up above the trees. They drove the few metres back to the highway and disappeared within seconds. If they know where they were they can at least say they were there.

As I'm writing this another couple in a fifth wheel drove in, stopped for a minute, then drove away. I am so glad that we have the time to stop and smell the roses. (Yes, the wild roses are in bloom and their fragrance is wonderful. Also blooming are lupens, fireweed, bitter vetch, buttercups, lily of the valley, bluebells or harebells, something with deep maroon flowers, another plant with hundreds of miniature white flowers creating a snowball of petals, and one with flowers so soft I call it rabbit's paw.) Considering that we spent thousands of dollars and several weeks to get this far, we'd be foolish not to spend a few more minutes to explore this area.

We've walked on ice glaciers (frozen water), lava beds (melted rock) and now on a rock glacier (cold rock). It is difficult to imagine these millions of rock shards, formed by stones cracked by frost, flowing down the side of a mountain. Or flowing anywhere, for that matter. I thought engineers used crushed rock to stabilize road beds because it wouldn't move. But over the centuries, flow it did. What an uncommon natural marvel.

When you get a chance, walk on a rock glacier. Liz and I both agree that this stop was the highlight of our scenic trip from over-commercialized Skagway to Haines Junction.

Sheep Mountain

We stopped in at Yukon's Sheep Mountain Interpretation Centre, only to realize that once again we had been fooled by the sun. Just because it was high above the horizon didn't mean that the Centre still would be open at 8 pm.

Nevertheless we scanned the mountainside with our eyes and binoculars, and the high power telescope outside the building. We saw no sheep. One white rock had us fooled for awhile.

Some deserted cabins can be seen from highways, many more are hidden only a few kilometres away along gravel side roads.

A couple from Florida drove in and parked near us. The driver was exhausted from driving while looking around a base-ball-sized hole in his windshield, which was the result of a large stone falling off of an approaching gravel truck. They and ourselves decided to park overnight in the parking lot. Although windy, it was level. There was no sign saying 'no camping.'

Within an hour four other vehicles joined us. A 40' diesel pusher, a 32' Class A with gasoline engine, a new Class C, our old and dirty Class C, a truck connected to a six-wheeled fifthwheel, and a car towing a pop-up tent trailer made for an interesting mix of vehicles. During the night, a van and another van pulling a trailer had joined our group. Liz and I had the only Canadian licence plates.

Even after several weeks of almost 24 hour daylight, I still find it hard to write 'night' when I have to close curtains in order to read my computer screen. That night, social interactivity and chatting were minimal. I think everybody was tired and/or making supper and/or chilled by the wind and nobody felt like being outside without sheep to see.

Early next morning — that is, when we opened our eyes and saw the sun high overhead — one fellow was standing next to a woman and pointing up the mountain. We quickly dressed, grabbed our binoculars and joined them. Sure enough, there was a herd of seven sheep walking across the mountain side, like a faraway caravan of white camels crossing sand and heading for an oasis of green.

Other travellers exited their vehicles. One woman noticed a single animal on the very top silhouetted against the clear blue sky, then noticed another small herd to the right, once again on the very top of the mountain. With my lens-augmented eyesight I did manage to see them. It is nice to know that there are people who can still see distant objects without the use of glasses.

Later, as we were eating breakfast, a tour bus arrived. It parked and passengers disembarked, heading for the Interpretive Centre. Most didn't make it before one of our group pointed out those seven sheep which had almost traversed the slopes and were heading over the top. Five minutes later the sheep were gone. As with any event in nature, timing is everything.

So much depends on chance. Maybe we'll see a moose yet.

Burwash Landing

Travelling from Sheep Mountain to Beaver Creek was relatively uneventful, except for two incidents. We saw a moose. Finally!

In fact, we saw two moose. One was a male with velvet on its broad antlers, the other was a cow.

The male moose was eating leaves from bushes in the highway right-of-way, a mere couple of metres from the edge of asphalt. When we stopped to take his picture I had to honk the horn – the RV's four horns produce a unique sound – to get his attention and make him raise his head. After he looked up, he stared at us for a few seconds then unconcernedly dropped his head and continued to chew on leaves.

About five minutes later, we saw a female cow running across the highway. She was almost hit by a truck and camper but fortunately the driver slowed down quickly enough.

Interestingly enough, a receptionist at the Kluane Museum of Natural History in Burwash Landing was not especially happy about our finally seeing a moose.

The world's biggest gold pan.

We were taken aback. We had been searching for moose for seven weeks. We even made up in-jokes about the Loose Moose, the Missing Moose, the Masochistic Moose and, more generally, all those Stupid Moose.

Although she feels sorry for those hundreds of tourists who don't see any animals as they drive along the highway, she pointed out that having such large animals living so close to the highway is actually dangerous. Of course, she is correct. Vehicles, drivers and passengers travelling at high speed are easily damaged by animals weighing more than half a ton, when they suddenly and unexpectedly appear on any highway. Let's face it. All animals are not cute and cuddly, and animal behaviour is not as friendly and benign as often depicted in family TV and movies.

On a different topic, after visiting the excellent museum in Burwash Landing, which is being continually upgraded, I suggest you visit "Your Place" cafeteria. It is only a couple hundred of metres down the side road next to the museum. The quality and selection of food are good and the prices, when we were there, were reasonable. They served raisin pie, my favourite!

I wish I had bought gasoline at 64.9 ¢/L at Edith Creek, a mere 123 km from the Canada-USA border. I had expected prices to keep dropping as we neared Alaska, supposedly the source of this fuel. But I forgot about "Border Mentality". Prices always seem to be higher near international borders, and 70.9, 73.9 and 73.9 ¢/L at three different service stations in Bear Creek once again confirms that concept.

Even with the USA dollar climbing astronomically we decided to drive past the border in the hope of buying cheaper fuel. On June 15, 1998 CAN $1.00 equalled USA $0.68, and CAN 70.9¢/L equalled US $ 1.82/gal.

Tomorrow we'll find out if we made the correct monetary decision. (You, the reader, can find out by checking the prices in Appendix C.)

I almost forgot. Somewhere on the Alaska Highway, you'll think you saw an animal but you won't be sure. These rocks - Yukon location unspecified - were painted to look like bears. They certainly fooled me as I sped along the pavement. We both love a good joke. Painter, thanks for the laughs.

Saga of an Oil Leak

Yes. You too can make an emergency gasket from a writing pad that has a thin sheet of non-corrugated cardboard behind all those pages. And you can have fun installing it too.

Our 1979 Ford engine has a moveable connector on the engine block for its oil filter, which allows different sizes of filters to be positioned to avoid contact with hoses or frames. This connector is held in place by a single hollow bolt, which is actually part of the oil distribution system. Previously I'd changed oil and air filters somewhere in BC, tightened the almost inaccessible bolt and congratulated myself on saving a few dollars.

Weeks later, while stopping for gasoline at Scottie's, I noticed a puddle of oil under our RV. (I had begun checking because Liz and I could smell oil whenever we drove slowly.) We finished filling both wallet-draining tanks and moved away to a reasonably level piece of ground.

I put the transmission in Park, applied the parking brake, crawled under the frame, and Liz started the engine. I was so surprised at the sudden appearance of a river of hot black oil that I started pounding on the bumper, then got mad at Liz for not turning off the engine. I hollered in an uncomplimentary manner, Liz turned the key, and we could hear each other talk. She commented about my sky-colour vocabulary. I apologized.

Because I was only going to look under the engine, I hadn't changed clothes. Several days later the pants came clean but the sweater hung onto those oil stains like a ship-wrecked sailor hugs a floating mizzen mast. Weeks later the sweater is in a garbage dump somewhere and I'm still inhabiting canine accommodations.

I replaced the oil filter because it could have been cracked or punctured by my oil wrench. Unfortunately, black gold still gushed forth like an artesian well. After a couple more starts and stops, using paper towel to wipe off engine and frame parts, I finally deduced that the moveable connection was at fault. Maybe that hollow bolt had worked itself loose, allowing oil to pour past its gasket. No, darn it. I couldn't make it any tighter.

We weren't going to drive anywhere. I couldn't carry enough 175-litre oil drums to get me to the next town.

Reaching into my wallet for a card with an 800 phone number, I called BCAA. AAA answered because I was calling from Alaska. I really wasn't in the mood to try to tell and retell an over-zealous teenager in Missouri (who probably had never been north of the Mason-Dixon Line) where the Alaska Highway was, or why there was no name for the settlement of seventeen people where I was stranded, or why I needed a heavy duty truck that could tow a five-ton motorhome 92 miles, yes that's right 92 miles (150 km), to a town with a garage. Eventually we understood each other — Tok is not spelled with an 'e', Beaver Creek is in Yukon, Canada, Yukon is next to and east of Alaska, both are way up north, and there is no snow on the paved highway — and he promised he'd get back to me.

I walked back to our stranded motorhome. Rather than doing nothing for three hours waiting for a tow truck, I figured I might as well try to fix the oil leak. Whatever I did wasn't going to affect its being towed.

First a non-standard motorcycle mount, a leftover from our Central America trip, had to be unbolted from the frame and bumper to give me room to work. The new filter was removed, and more paper towel turned oily black. Finally I could get at the bolt.

Triple-A called back to tell me that they had no tow trucks available. But if I could find one myself, pay for the haul (about US $250) and send in a bill, they would reimburse me. Being partly covered in oil, itchy from sand and with dirt in my hair I politely replied "Thanks a lot." Or something like that.

That barely accessible bolt had to be turned 17 turns, one-sixth of a turn at a time. I think every automotive design engineer should come from the rank and file of trained and certified mechanics. That might bring an end to most of the foolishness that I've seen when forced to work on fully-assembled vehicles.

When the bolt eventually separated from the engine block and all pieces were lowered to a plastic sheet on the ground, the problem was obvious.

Little bits of 19-year-old gasket, once soft but now hard as brick, adhered to the bolt. Some was where it was supposed to be but most was elsewhere. No matter how tight I could have forced that hollow bolt, the disintegrated gasket would have prevented a decent seal.

Using gasoline, I cleaned all the pieces (engine pieces, not gasket bits) and was ready to put everything back together. But I needed a gasket. None was available. What could I do?

Scottie suggested cutting a piece of cardboard into the right shape. Even I can make a small paper doughnut, so I did. And forced it over those innumerable bolt threads, ensuring the hole was just big enough. Then I remembered that I had some blue silicon sealant and put some on top of the make-shift gasket. By the time I got all the pieces back together and managed to fit that bolt into its mating threads, much of the bolt was blue. But so was the gasket.

Turn rachet, back, turn, back, turn, back, turn. Ah, can't go much tighter. Uh oh. Is it positioned correctly for this filter? Attach filter. Can't. Frame is in the way. Loosen bolt, back, back. Change position. Tighten bolt, turn, back, turn. Attach filter. Can't. Radiator hose is in the way. Loosen bolt, back, back. Change position. Tighten bolt, turn, turn, turn. Attach filter. Yes!

Hand tighten. Then use the wrench to give the filter a quarter turn more. Add yet another litre of oil. Crawl onto oily plastic sheet and signal Liz to start engine for two seconds.

Almost unbelievably, no oil leaks out. Signal again, still no oil leak. Yes!

Gather up black paper towel sheets and stuff into a grocery bag. Collect five empty plastic oil containers. Wipe down the plastic ground sheet. Use towels to soak up oil that flowed onto gravel. Get rid of sludge on hands and arms using oily paper towels. Use more dry paper towels. Use spade to scrape oil-soaked ground and shovel gravel on top of towels in plastic bag. Place oil-filled, perfectly-good filter in same bag. Rub down all tools and store away.

Wash hands with soap and water. Use more paper towels to clean sink. Change smelly workclothes and put them in another plastic bag and tie it to back bumper. Shower and shampoo. Clean bathtub with paper towel. Comb hair. Take all paper and plastic to garbage can. Smile.

Ah yes. You too can experience the satisfaction of solving a problem all by yourself. You too can have fun making and installing cardboard gaskets. Maybe you should try it sometime.

Yeah. Sure. And maybe you should try running down the vertical gravel face of Dawson City's ancient Moosehide Slide without a parachute. When you see the Slide you'll know what I mean.

Note. Many weeks later the gasket is still keeping oil inside the engine. Although I bought proper gasket paper, I'm not going to replace it. I can't afford the cost of more paper towels.

P. S. I cancelled my request for roadside assistance. One never knows. I might need BCAA's help again.

Taylor Highway to Eagle, Alaska

We were approaching Wade's Junction as a light mist was falling, and we pondered the wisdom of travelling to Eagle, Alaska. How dirty would our motorhome get? But we'd travelled this far already, why not go all the way? Would the 100 km (60 mi) trip be worth it in the rain? Even in the sunshine, would this trip live up to its billing as an exciting drive?

Suddenly there was the junction just ahead. A narrow dirt road was approaching rapidly off to our left. What will we do? We turned left and continued on the Taylor Highway.

What a great decision.

Lots of mountain tops, but not as good as Top of the World

The scenery was wonderful, in rain or in sunshine. Riding on damp sandy roads meant no dust. Riding on top of mountains and looking down into valleys of green — new-life green, mature green, deciduous green, coniferous green, sunny green, shadow green, forest green, meadow-glade green, dusty green, freshly washed green — was captivating. Row upon rows of hill tops, one behind the other behind another behind yet another stretched to the horizon. We looked down on rivers and creeks that sparkled and foamed over rapids. We saw sections

82

of our highway disappear behind hills so far away that the road seemed to continue on to infinity.

And we had time to enjoy it all. Our speed never got above 65 km/hr (40 mph) because dozens of sharp curves and hairpin turns might have hidden an oncoming vehicle, or a short stretch of washboard would set our teeth to rattling, or we'd slow for an oncoming truck or fifthwheel or a moose (twice!), or we'd slow down for a stretch of construction or grading, or we'd drive slowly because of the scenery. We took two and a half hours to go 100 km, and enjoyed every minute of the drive.

Based upon clichés like "I survived the Alaska Highway", this was the kind of road I expected the Alaska Highway to be, a challenge but not frightening.

The Alaska Highway had been so simple to drive. After I set cruise control to 80 or 85 km/hr I could have left my driver's seat and gone back to the kitchen and perked a cup of coffee while making a sandwich. (Don't do it.) Even the scenic Taylor Highway from Tok to Wade's junction, especially the initial seal-coated 50 km (23 mi), was almost as dull.

But not the road to Eagle. Oh, it was slow, it was curvy, it was narrow in places, it was muddy (it could have been dusty), but it was fun.

Except for the Alder Creek bridge at mile 21, which Liz had read about in the Milestone.

We had already driven over one bridge without incident, so she didn't warn me. We fell into a puddle then slammed into a 15 cm leading edge of that concrete bridge. Fortunately, all tires held onto their air and no apparent damage was done to them or their wheel rims.

Near the end of our trip, within twenty minutes of Eagle, we stopped by a pipe sticking out of the side of a rock slide, and drank safe, cool, delicious water. Then I proceeded to use clear water in the ditch to wash parts of our motorhome: stop lights, signal lights, licence plate, rear window, and the name of our motorhome, Security. I wasn't going to wash the entire vehicle, but I did want us to look a little more presentable.

(Security. It is a great name. Some people actually think that we are in the security business. We've gone places and done things other RV's couldn't. I don't lie, but if people don't ask ...)

Gold Cleaning

Previously, we'd stopped by Mile 125 House, also known as O'Brien Creek Lodge, and found out that they charged US $1.65/gal, which was seven cents less than the lowest price in Eagle. Even if the price had been the same or a couple of pennies more, I would have used that pump, that restored relic from antiquity. Such opportunities don't happen very often.

Gasoline was provided from an old fashioned gas pump. You know, the kind with a large glass tub on the top and a scale displaying zero to ten gallons. After telling the operator how many gallons we wanted, he turned on the pump, liquid petroleum flowed into the glass tub, and the level of plum-coloured liquid slowly rose up to the number we'd said. Then he turned off the pump, slipped a hose into our gas tank, opened a valve and, subject to the law of gravity, gasoline flowed into our vehicle while air bubbles gurgled into the glass tub. Quaint.

While at the Lodge we talked to an ex-law enforcement officer from Texas who had had enough of protecting others from gun fights, knife fights, drugs and all of those activities most of us don't want to think about and don't have to because our police do such a good job. He moved to Alaska to start a freer life.

He introduced us to Dave and Scott, a couple of gold miners who were washing their gold.

Washing their gold? That's right.

These two young men are divers and underwater dredgers. Eight hours a day, seven days a week for almost three and a half months, using a large hose hooked up to a suction pump, they vacuum the bottom of a creek. Rocks, clay, silt, white sand, magnetic black sand and gold are fed into their sluices. Only a very tiny percentage of sand and gold stay behind in the sluice traps while the rest is passed through and discarded.

They stored this mixture of black and brass-coloured flakes in a large plastic bucket and a couple of tightly sealed plastic containers, which they had next to their gold washer.

Slowly — one tablespoon at a time — the mixture was passed through a cleaning machine, so advanced it was simplicity itself. The sandy mixture was poured into a nearly vertical, rotating plastic dish. The sides were about 8 cm high; the bottom was formed with a raised spiralling ridge. An aquarium pump forced water up from a bucket which then spilled onto the top of the plate and flowed down to the bottom over the slowly spinning spiral ridges, where it overflowed the bottom edge and was collected in the pail being used by the pump. The sand and gold mixture was constantly being lifted up on the spiral ridges then flushed back down by the water.

But gold is 19 times heavier than water, and black sand is 11 times heavier. These two elements stayed trapped in the spiral while everything else was washed away. Gradually a concentration of gold flakes and some sand moved to the centre of the plate and disappeared into a hole.

And into a rusty tin can. A used soup can. To hold gold!

Hardly high tech. But effective. The cost of the cleaning equipment couldn't be worth more than a couple of hundred dollars. A soup can full of gold fines, flakes and nuggets would be worth about $ 50,000. Of course, this can wasn't full. Yet.

These men had worked eighteen days of active dredging, which probably yielded only 60-65 ounces. As providers of a raw product, this gold would be sold to buyers at wholesale, perhaps 70-75% of the market value, yielding about $11,000. Because each was entitled to equal shares, each would get $5,500, which would almost cover their expenses for half a summer. They still had a lot of work to do, but by the end of the summer each man might clear $20-25,000. If the price of gold increased, they could make much more. Gold mining is a tough job but somebody has to do it.

You and I could do it.

It only costs $35 a year to stake and register a claim. And at least that much again for insect repellent to ward off mosquitos, moosquitoes (the really big ones), black flies and no-see-ums (also known as 'flying jaws'). We'd even get to eat our own cooking, lovingly prepared after 12-14 hours of bone-weary, back-breaking labour. Of course, mining equipment would cost a whole lot more, and then we'd have to pay to get it shipped to our claim. Then we'd have to set it up. Then learn how to use it. Then ...

Ah. The heck with it. You stake a claim.

Liz and I have to get to Dawson City for the June 21st Solstice Celebrations on the Midnight Dome, also simply known as the Dome.

But first we'll go to Eagle then retrace the road back to Wade's Junction and turn east onto the Top of the World Highway.

Eagle

Eagle is a pleasant small community of 137 persons, with a reasonably stocked small library. There are a general store, a laundromat, a restaurant and RV campgrounds, one of which is a few kilometres off on a side road.

But we parked overnight beside the library, after watching a home video about a spectacular spring breakup on the Yukon River. Some of those ice blocks almost could have qualified as icebergs. They were bigger than many modern houses in BC. No wonder much of the high river bank frontage of Eagle disappeared that year.

86

Before that, we had a pleasant and informative visit with Pat at the Yukon Charley Rivers Wildlife Preserve. To get there we drove over a small airplane runway (an elongated pasture) that is beside Fort Egbert, which closed in 1911. In season, look for small, delicious strawberries. This was followed by an evening stroll along the river, where we met and chatted with people from Florida USA, Germany and South Africa.

Returning from Eagle

Sadly, the trip back from Eagle was disappointing. All the really good scenery was behind us, visible only in our mirrors. It was almost like driving a different road, except this time we knew enough to slow down before crossing bridges.

We ended up behind a tanker truck for a short time, and talked to him on our CB. He's been travelling this highway at least twice a week for over a decade and doesn't think it's dangerous. However, one winter he did cut one corner too sharply and his trailer's left wheels slid into the ditch. As he got out to inspect the situation, the trailer started sliding again. It and the tank truck slid and crashed down through a couple hundred metres of snow and grass and shrubs. But all was recovered within three days, even the gasoline.

We stopped again at Mile 125 House (aka O'Brien Creek Lodge) , and talked some more with the new owner, who dabbles in flour, and his brother, who dabbles in gold. Both have had some interesting experiences. He treated us to cauldron-cooked biscuits made from his own recipe over a smouldering wood fire. Delicious. I hope you'll be lucky enough to taste them. You won't need butter if they come right out of the hot cast iron pot.

As we neared Wade's Junction, we met several men racing toward us riding Beemers, BMW motorcycles. They were usually solo or in pairs, several kilometres apart. We had driven through precipitation, sometimes a light sprinkle, sometimes a little heavier rain, and thus we commented that those guys had better slow down or they might run into something hidden by a sharp corner or lose traction in a slippery spot.

When we looked back, watching the dust raised by the Beemers, the overhead clouds started to look really dark. We had got out of there just in time. Within an hour the skies opened up and rained for two or three days. The highway was almost impassable for awhile.

Later in Dawson City, sad to say, we found out that one rider had lost control and crashed on the road. His face plate had shattered and his bloodied face was badly cut. He also cracked some ribs, broke an arm and suffered scrapes and contusions. When one of his buddies arrived on the accident scene, the fellow was still lying face-down in mud. But he had been taken to a hospital and would be alright. His bike could be repaired.

While at the Lodge we should have got more fuel than we did. Either I estimated incorrectly or travelling at high altitudes or climbing up and down hills consumed more gasoline than usual. We were forced to buy fuel at Boundary, just before the Alaska-Yukon border. The price was a wallet-emptying $1.95 per gallon .... the same price as in Dawson City.

We had a great time driving to Eagle and back. Other people didn't, either because of dust or mud and potholes or driving too fast. Pleasures or annoyances of a vacation are so dependent upon weather and attitude.

*At many places along Yukon highways, you will see peoples'
names written with stones. Why not put yours there too?*

Dawson City, Yukon

It had to happen. We ran out of money.

Because of the cost of flying to and from our son's wedding and payment for brake repairs, we're forced to stay in Dawson City until the end of the month. Then we can once again dip into our monthly allotted funds. But there are worse places than Dawson City, lots of them. It's not raining and cold, we are warm and getting sun tanned.

Afternoon view of Dawson from the "Midnight Dome"

Fortunately my repair — a hand-cut, writing-pad cardboard gasket and a layer of silicone putty — to our motorhome engine's oil system continues to work well. We no longer drip oil when we stop for more than thirty seconds. Unfortunately, until I get a chance to clean off all the oil and kilograms of sludge that collected on the engine, transmission and frame, the aroma of hot oil continues to waft around our heads as we drive.

As we prepare and eat breakfast, we're parked on the riverside of the town dike, next to the ferry terminal, watching 14 RV's and 3 cars trying to get on a ferry designed for about a third of that number. By the time one load is ferried across the Yukon River, and a second load is brought back to this side, the number of waiting vehicles is the same as it was before. Using this ferry promises to be more fun than driving over a bridge, and we'll get to meet more interesting people.

Here we can watch films at the Visitor Reception Centre and the Northwest Tourism Centre, for free. On Tuesday in the Museum, we watched three free "cheesy" movies about the Yukon as presented by uninformed directors and playwrights. They were almost as enjoyably-bad as the film "The Killer Tomato." Surprisingly, once I got past the terrible acting in the slow-moving Russian-made silent movie I enjoyed it the most.

Thank Heavens for CBC Radio. As usual the hourly news reports are dismal (why *do* we listen to bad news?) but their informative talk shows and humorous shows keep bringing us back to CBC.

A victim of permafrost and too much stove heat.

Generally, Dawson City is considerably more expensive than Whitehorse. Much more so than would seem to be dictated by being 300 km closer to the Arctic Circle.

Perishable foodstuffs and pop are really costly. Soft pulp fruit and vegetables bought in Dawson don't keep well. Perhaps they get bruised when trucked from warehouses to stores.

Stopped in the Golden Nugget and Ivory store to get a watch battery. While waiting I entered my name in a contest, the prize being a chest of flatware for eight people. And I won. I got the word weeks later when in Yellowknife, NWT. Of course, Liz and I had to wait a month to see it because the package was delivered to our hometown address. It is a beautiful set, all with gold-plated handles, and nuggets on the handles of eight serving pieces. Thank you.

We discovered a gravel pit about 2 km away from residences in Dawson (but still inside the city limits) where we can park overnight. We and three other rigs have done so for four nights. Night before last there were 14 rigs, and last night there were over 18 rigs in the level area and another half dozen haphazardly positioned on almost-roads and heaps of tailings. I fear that the owners of this claim will soon revoke the privilege of our staying here.

With that many motorhomes in one area, somebody is bound to turn on their generator first thing in the morning.

Liz and I drove up to the Dome near midnight on June 20th to watch the sun set then rise a couple of hours later. Although the sun did disappear behind the mountains, it never got dark. It resembled an early morning sky, which of course it was.

We and a couple from North Carolina debated about where the sun would rise, even though common sense kept reminding us that the sun rises in the east. Not here at Summer Solstice. It rises in the North, actually North Northeast. It takes awhile to adjust to that idea even knowing that we are seeing the sun from the 'other' side of our spherical earth.

PHONE:
1-403-667-1472
(CELLULAR 400)

Next evening was heavily overcast, cloudy with occasional heavenly moisture. We'd made a good decision to go to the Dome one day before Solstice. I had hoped to golf — using my five, nine, putter and five balls — under the midnight sun on June 21st. I still haven't tried my evening luck on that nine hole course, but will do so before we leave Dawson.

Note. The night of our midnight golf game with another couple we returned at 2 am. Five hours later a Class A next to us ran its generator for over an hour. Ye gods, how long does it take to make coffee and toast? We exchanged a few words.

The Dyea to Dawson Race is a gruelling marathon requiring pairs of contestants to carry at least fifty pounds up and over the 35 mile Chilkoot Pass, to eat and sleep while paddling their canoes more than 500 miles to Dawson City and then, finally, to pan for a salted gold nugget. In June 1998, gold was worth about US$ 300 per ounce. Depending upon its purity and size, a gold nugget is worth 115% to 175% of the wholesale price of gold flakes and fines. The competitors get to keep the large nugget as a souvenir. Having completed her marathon, one exhausted and befuddled contestant didn't realize the nugget was real, and she threw her nugget into the Yukon River. (This is an unconfirmed but probably true story told to us by her young daughter.)

Dawson Dollar

When in Dawson, see if you can buy or get a Dawson Dollar. They were printed as part of a marketing endeavour that failed a couple of years ago, but a few are still hiding in one Parks Canada location. You might have to mention you read about it in this book, almost no one knows about them. Good luck in getting a unique souvenir.

Failing that, you will be able to buy an authentic Yukon licence plate at the gift shop in the Museum.

Dawson City

Forget the Canada-Alaska Highway, Dawson City is where you want to go.

OK. OK. I know you have to drive part of the Alaska Highway to get to Dawson City. And that highway does offer some pretty and interesting sights. But Dawson offers a whole lot more, if you have the time to enjoy them.

We came to Dawson City for two or three days, to get a break from daily driving. Thanks to the excellent facilities and tours provided by Parks Canada, we've stayed eight days and have yet to rest our sore feet and overloaded brains. Sleep occurs the moment our heads hit soft pillows, which is usually just before the sun sets, sometime after midnight.

This week has been an extended version of night-before-exam cramming. I've learned more history than I can remember. Which is a shame, because it is so very interesting. The Klondike Gold Rush was really a flash in the pan. It was over almost as soon as it began. Only afterwards, with the vision and investment of a few, did Dawson City become a real city with family residences.

Dawson was the second city in Canada to have electricity, Montréal was the first.

When inside a bank during a walking tour through the town, check out a deposit slip then ask your knowledgeable guide about Canada's four dollar bills. You should get a quick answer, I had to wait for more than a month while the topic was researched.

Thank you Parks Canada. I believe you have admirably fulfilled your mandate, your mission statement, of "Preserve, Protect and Present."

The conversion from gold extraction by manual labour to construction of huge dredges occurred very quickly and pre-

Start of the Canada Day "Klunker" race ... already I'm in third place.

vented Dawson from becoming a ghost town when hundreds left for a new strike in Nome.

Nevertheless, by using gold pans for exploration, using pick and shovel and fire to dig vertical shafts and drifts to get to the paydirt, using pulleys and rope to haul it back to the surface tens of feet above then using rocker boxes and sluices to separate a few ounces of gold from tons of gravel, those hundreds of hard working, always cold, often hungry miners extracted more gold in six months than was taken out by all the dredges in the following five decades.

More miners died of scurvy — no vegetables and fruit — and dysentery — no sewage system — than by accidents or starvation or freezing.

The Northwest Mounted Police were the real unsung heroes. They were paid $1.25 per day when miners would work for $10.00 a day, which was just about the daily cost of living. When gold strikes were announced, none left the NWMP to stake a claim, even though some lucky miners were making $200 and more a day. They collected taxes and import/export duties, organized an interesting medicare plan that kept badly needed hospitals operating, showed the Canadian Flag and Canadian Presence, ran mail service, and ... and so on and so on.

And they kept law and order. Part of an article by Doug Bell in The Yukon News, June 24 1998 reads 'Wyatt Earp, reflecting on his career, said "If I'd had a couple of those red-coated fellers behind me, we'd have kept Tombstone clean for sure."'

Come to Dawson City and stay awhile. Don't be like one tourist who rushed up behind me in the Visitor Reception Area and, over my shoulder, interrupted me and a busy but still cheerful staff member by asking "What can I see in three hours?" That Parks Canada person had much more tact than I could have mustered.

And I feel sorry for visitors on some bus tours. They just don't allow time in their busy schedules for their passengers to see much more than a museum (you should too), a humongous dredge (ditto), or a single stage show (ditto, ditto). Even if they did find time to sit on Dawson City's dike and watch the boats speed or drift by, or to observe a front-end loader daily rebuilding the ferry wharf, they'd probably fall into road-weary sleep under a warm sun.

Time. You need time to enjoy this unique community, to begin to understand why students come for a summer and stay a decade or why the streets will never be paved or to marvel at a Victorian building that has withstood the relentless ravages of permafrost for almost a century.

We just heard that the Dempster Highway suffered 17 washouts and one mud slide during yesterday's storm. The highway is impassable for at least five days. Why didn't we leave earlier?

Why? Because Liz and I are having too much fun.

Canadian Four Dollar Bill, Eh?

Dear Mr. Plaxton;

I am responding to the query which you posed during your visit to Dawson City. You asked about the $4 denomination listed on the deposit slip at the BNA Bank in Dawson City.

I investigated the matter in a Canadian numismatic reference and determined that in the mid 1800's, there were at least

45 banks in Canada which produced a $4 bill, including the BNA Bank. In addition, I determined that this bill appears to have been equivalent in value to the British pound. This may explain why the $4 bill was in circulation in Dawson City during the gold rush.

I hope that this information answers your question satisfactorily.

Sincerely,

Michael Gates, Cultural Integrity Specialist

Yukon Field Unit, Parks Canada

Dear John & Liz,

Just a quick note to say hi! and to prove I wasn't crazy:

I've enclosed photocopies of the actual $4.00 which was legal tender in Canada.

'... The 1900 $4 notes were delivered to the Finance Department from December 1900 to February 1902, at which time the 1902-dated issue became available. The initial 1902-dated notes have large "4" counters in the upper corners and "FOUR's" in the lower corners. The last notes of this type were delivered in January, 1903.

The 1900 issue, as well as the 1902 notes with the "4" counters on top, bear the engraved signature of J. M. Courtney at the right. The 1902-dated notes (actually printed in 1911) with the "FOUR" counters on top have the engraved signature of T. C. Boville. All received manuscript countersignatures on the left at the Department of Finance prior to issue. ...'

Hope you find this info as interesting as I did. Enjoy your travels and good luck in your publication.

Best Wishes,

Linda P Thompson

Gift Shop Manager, Dawson City Museum

Letter to Sun Newspaper

The following is a letter that I sent to Jocelyn Bell of The Sun, a Dawson City newspaper. This article was included on a

MAC disk to make her job easier. Even though I use an IBM I can convert many files to MAC formats, and vice versa.

Please note that I have purposely not mentioned the names of businesses. Many stores, hotels, tour companies, etc. offer goods and services that don't appeal to us, or which we never used, or we chose to spend our limited supply of money elsewhere. I don't think it fair to single out only the businesses we visited. Besides, ownership changes quickly and what was true for me might not be true for someone else a year later.

Forget the Canadian Alaska Highway. Dawson City is where you want to go. Dawson offers a whole lot more attractions, when you take time to enjoy them.

We came to Dawson City for two or three days to rest our road-weary bones. Thanks to the excellent facilities and tours provided by Parks Canada and the friendliness of Dawsonites (even summer Dawsonwannabees), we've stayed fifteen days and have yet to rest our sore feet and overloaded brains. Sleep occurs the moment our heads hit soft pillows, which is usually just before the sun sets, sometime after midnight.

Robert Service's Cabin[2]

[2]Drawn by Bob Heinrich, who parked beside us in the gravel pit. He travels North America but exhibits locally at 3259 Calder Avenue, North Vancouver, BC V7N 3R6   (604) 985-6077

Midnight Golf, and Liz didn't use a flash to take this picture.

These two weeks have been an extended version of night-before-exam cramming. I've learned more history than I can remember. Which is a shame, because it is so very interesting.

Time. Visitors need time to enjoy this unique community, to begin to understand why students come for a summer and stay a decade; or why the streets will never be paved; or to marvel at two tipsy Victorian buildings that have withstood the relentless ravages of permafrost for almost a century. (It's too bad Dawson Sourdoughs hadn't been asked how to build roads and a high-way in 1942.)

Airborne. In Snowshoes!!

98

I need more time to write about: the view of worm-like tailings below Midnight Dome; what we saw and marvelled at during our excursion to King Solomon Dome; how a sunrise can be seen by looking north; about an unexpected ice cream treat made with two cones; the opulence of Yukon's Commissioner's residence; why a rusty gold pan costs more than a shiny new pan; our vial of gold dust and one small nugget; a toe "ice cube" in

CAPT. BILL'S WORLD FAMOUS

Member *John Plaxton*

N°: *1923*

SOURTOE COCKTAIL

Box 1, Dawson City, Yukon, Y0B 1G0

a little bit of Yukon Jack; where a watch battery can be found next to Woolly Mammoth ivory; a sad walk amongst three rotting hulls and rusted machinery of once majestic paddle-wheelers; the unexpected pleasure of enjoying "Gertie's Girls" a second time; the discovery that last Wednesday's 7:30 supper was being eaten outside at eleven o'clock at night; CBC Radio; how 3,000-ton floating dredges can move up a narrow creek; why Gyro is pronounced Delicious Hero; where to buy new multilingual magazines and used books; why RVers enjoy an inexpensive campground across the river; where to dump tanks for free, where to get potable water for a single loonie; how one company built a city, hydro-electric dams, water system and a plant to manufacture oxygen and acetylene, all without computers; where and when to get each of three informative newspapers; why part of one large hotel looks like four store fronts; when grocery shelves and produce were restocked; why there was need for a business named Klondyke Thawing Machine Co.; Internet access; the unsuspected location of inexpensive fuel; how a gambling casino can be non-profit; where we met Tom Byrne; our feelings while standing on the infamous ninth golf green at 1:30 AM; comparing stabilized Dredge #4 with the remains of #11; all dressed up in Red and White and proudly singing 'O Canada'; why ...

I don't have enough time to write about all that. We've

only got another day here. We've got to get out there and par-
ticipate, to talk to Yukon characters, to see more, to listen more,
to ask ignorant questions, to buy a log cabin, to ...??? Ye gods,
the first symptom of Sourdough-itis has appeared.
   Dang you Dawson City. Dang you Parks Canada. While
enriching my soul you are stealing it.
   Please. Please. If you let me drive to Inuvik, I'll come back.

Canoeing the Klondike

It's morning of July 2nd and we are finally, reluctantly leaving the town of the city of Dawson. Or is it the city of Dawson,
or Dawson City, or just plain Dawson (as indicated on Canada's federal Post Office building)? Yesterday's Canada Day
celebrations were excellent, well organized, and a lot of fun.

It really is time to leave. In fifteen days and nights we have
seen much, yet some things are still unseen. But if we stay to
see it all, we might become bored as we push the limit of diminishing returns.

Or at least that is what we thought last night, before we
met Father Tim down at the wharf.

He and four others had just come back from rescuing a
canoe that had become lodged under a sweeper (a tree with roots
on land and branches in water) which extended from the banks
of the Klondike River. The canoe had become trapped during a
race over a week ago, too much water had continued to flow too
fast for salvage operations.

Fr. Tim and his visitor from Ottawa waxed eloquent about
their river sojourn.

"We have a canoe, can we do it?" I asked one of the others,
he who takes novice canoeists on the Klondike. "Sure. You can
access the river just south of Rock Creek. Don't fret about leaving your motorhome, it'll be safe there. Stay in the fastest flowing water. Remember to stay in the middle of the river. The river
is only classed as a one or two. Don't worry, you can do it."

It's the morning of July 2nd and we are not leaving Dawson.
We are going to float and paddle 20 km of river back to Dawson.
Then we'll leave. Right? Right.

Breakfast consisted of fried eggs, turkey-imitation bacon, toast and decaffeinated coffee.

In preparation for our trip to Inuvik, we dumped our holding tanks, filled our water tank, ensured that all tires (spare too) were properly inflated, then headed for Callison Industrial Park to fill gasoline and propane tanks and buy 12 litres of 10-30 oil.

We were on our way to ... where, exactly? My beloved navigator wasn't quite sure, but there would probably be a sign.

There wasn't.

But we found a place three kilometres past Klondike River Campground where we could park our Class C and launch our canoe. So we did.

We took it and paddles and life-jackets off the roof, attached an empty 2 L milk container we could use as a bailer, and put in three stones weighing about 70 Kg (155 pounds) for ballast. After we struggled to scrape ourselves off a submerged rock, we were on our way.

The canoe was slightly tail heavy, because I sat back there. I weigh almost twice what Liz weighs. It must be my height and big bones. Tummy and waist fat don't weigh very much, do they?

Fearlessly Liz and I faced the unknown perils of Klondike River. Truthfully, we were fearful, not fearless, but once launched we were committed. The water was flowing too fast for us novices to turn around and go back, or even to beach ourselves on a rocky bank.

We, who are nervous on a lake that is smoother than most mirrors, were going to challenge a fast moving river complete with islands, backwater, white water, roaring rapids, rocky shallows and grasping trees.

And we did. And we made it.

Only once did I have to yell "Keep your hands off the gunwales. Paddle!" And Liz did. I was and am proud of her.

Did you ever see a bumper sticker that blares "Sit down. Strap in. Hang on. And shut up.?" That's what we did through several stretches of white water. Except once when torrents of cold water splashed up and over the bow and soaked Liz from the neck down. I thought she was going to expire right there, the way she was gasping for breath while hooting and hollering.

The bailer came in handy.

With a mere ten centimetres (four inches) of free board, water found several ways to get inside our canoe. My feet were soaked after zipping through the first stretch of rough water and stayed that way. After our next turbulent passage, my cotton pant legs sopped up a lot of chilly liquid. I must have bailed a dozen times. For what it is worth, Fr. Tim et al. were dry from heads to toenails when they arrived at Dawson.

One time we misjudged which river-fork to take and by the time we turned in the correct direction, the fast water was to our right and thousands of rounded rocks were rippling shallow water right in front of us. Bump, scrape, bump, tip left, bump, bang, bounce left, bump, scrape, tip right, scrape, scrape, silence. We were back in deep water and still floating.

Probably time for a paint job for our trusty canoe, though.

But all the river wasn't white water or funnels of turbulent, converging water. Almost two thirds was fast flowing but fairly smooth. Watching submerged rocks speed beneath us made us realize how difficult it would be to swim ashore if we ever had to. We didn't get to see as much of the surrounding scenery as we would have liked because we had to keep alert for hidden patches of white water.

Oh, I almost forgot to mention this. The Klondike River joins the silty Yukon River a few hundred metres (yards) above Dawson's downtown wharf. So ... Liz and I have canoed in both rivers.

Relaxing as we slowly drifted the last few metres towards the Yukon River, we saw some children walking along the river bank and talked with them for a short time. Suddenly seeing fast water to our right we realized we weren't paying attention to the river. We were floating towards a very wide arc of stones and pebbles and very shallow water.

Once again, it was scrape, bump, tilt, scrape. Only this time we ground to a halt, majestically stranded in the mouth of a river. Who saw us? The kids? No. Nobody. Phew!

But grounded we were. I got out, the rear of the canoe rose significantly. I held onto the stern as it bumped forward another few metres then again came to rest on stones. The canoe rose only a couple of centimetres when Liz got out. We dragged and carried it downstream several more metres before Liz got in. The canoe slid forward into deep water. Nervously Liz was saying "Don't leave me. Don't let go. Get in. Get in." Laughingly, chest extended, I did so.

(No wonder we've been married for 33 years. How could I not love a woman who lets me know that she needs me.)

Leaving the clear waters of the Klondike we paddled into the murky, silty-grey Yukon River. Suddenly that 25 m (80 ft) deep river seemed to be flowing awfully fast, swirling and forming miniscule spirals. We quickly turned to starboard and stayed in slower water. We weren't going to be swept past the wharf and maybe end up in Forty Mile.

We paddled over clouds of silt that slowly, ever so slowly, encroached on the clear water from the Klondike. Eventually the waters of both rivers would become one, but not here. It was like being in an airplane flying over Cumulus clouds. It was like watching a pastry chef mix dough for a marble cake. It was beautiful. What a shame we'd wisely left our cameras safely dry in the motorhome.

Once inside the wharf we chose to beach ourselves next to a parking lot.

The canoe was out of the water, paddles and life jackets were stored under the canoe and our RV was 20 km (12 mi) away!

Back to the Visitors Centre for info on taxis. $23.00 dollars ... ouch. That's a fair price, but maybe we could hitch hike. Of course, hitch hike.

Who could resist picking up a bewhiskered man of fifty-seven years wearing a battered and soiled Tilley hat, a damp shirt, and wet and rumpled, paint-stained, dirty-green pants. Who could resist a grey-haired woman wearing a bright Hot Pink sun hat above a faded print blouse and water-darkened shorts with frayed legs? Lots of people, that's who.

But eventually Tina stopped and took us as far as the Callison Industrial Subdivision. Fifteen minutes later, Marc and a co-worker picked us up and said they could take us half way to our destination. As we continued to chat I suddenly realized they had passed their turn off. We were dropped off beside our Class C, even though it meant they would be late for supper. This is just another example of Northern friendliness.

Our motorhome was very hot and stuffy. Quickly we opened vents and windows. I did a quick walk around, found a fish hook still in its packaging lying on the ground, leapt into the cab, started the engine, backed up, and once again we were on asphalt with wind whistling past our ears. Our cab's 2x80 air-conditioning (two open windows moving at eighty kilometres per hour) still worked.

Five minutes later, a piece of wood flew off our roof. Luckily, there were no vehicles ahead or behind us. Whoa, stop. I forgot to tie down some things when I unloaded our canoe. Our tent was jammed against the unused 110V roof-mounted air conditioner. All we lost was a metre of tie-down rope. Very lucky indeed. I wonder if I would have been sued if the board had hit someone or someone's vehicle?

Back in Dawson we parked as close as we could next to our overturned canoe. Everything had to go on the roof of our mobile home, our high-tech turtle shell that contains almost everything we own.

As Liz and I balanced the canoe on its pointed prow while resting the gunwales against the back of our RV, we heard gurgling. Water was flowing down the sun-dried hull. There, about two-thirds up, was a trickle of water, a miniature spring, issuing forth from behind a piece of torn fibre glass. We must have hit one rock too many, too hard.

We wanted to be on our way, so we loaded the canoe, water and all, on the roof. Everything was tied down securely, everything.

Just as I was about to clamber down, a man on the wharf shouted something.

I looked around and saw two canoeists in the river beside their overturned canoe. Apparently, their canoe had been spun around by a large swirling whirlpool. When both men tried to correct the problem they tipped over.

One fellow was wearing his red life jacket, the other was not. The first wisely stayed with the canoe, the other foolishly tried to swim to shore. Within a very few minutes "Help" boomed across the cold water. Two boats were on a rescue mission within seconds. From where I was it seemed as if drivers of the motorboats had been waiting for that call, as if giving those men a chance to save themselves and their pride before they acted. Manly but dangerous.

Two men, boat, paddles and other flotsam were collected and taken safely to shore. But I wonder what sank to the bottom.

Liz and I have canoed the Klondike and Yukon rivers, but watching those two canoeists floundering in the water reminded us that we were still novices, still greenhorns, still chechakos when it comes to using a canoe. We were prepared, but we were lucky as well.

But that's life. (People die in their beds. People fall off mountains. An uninjured child survives a three-car crash that destroyed everybody else. A woman falls three storeys from her apartment window and rips through an awning and sprains her ankle on the concrete sidewalk.) Liz and I have decided that a little risk is worth the worry. We don't want to die in front of a TV set, watching summer reruns.

"Take a risk, carefully. It really is more fun." is still our motto.

Dempster Highway: Km 0 to 116

We're finally on our way north, and it feels great to be travelling again.

We've decided to try to drive at least half the distance during evening hours. It should be cool and we might see some birds and animals.

We expect the Dempster Highway Travelogue, a photocopied handout that we got from Dawson's Visitor Reception Centre, will provide much greater or at least different detail than our other references.

Dempster Highway, Kilometre 0.0

The Dempster Highway is 734 kilometres or 456 miles long. With full gasoline tanks our ancient 1979 motorhome, with its reliable large engine and four-barrel carburetor, can travel about 450 km. The first fuel stop is Eagle Plains at Km 369, a second at Ft. McPherson at Km 550. Having a reserve of 20% there should be no need for us to carry extra fuel in plastic containers.

But we drive slowly. We stop at most lookouts, drive through campgrounds, visit interpretive centres, and go wherever we fancy. And we even backtrack short distances if we think we've missed a special view or a photographic opportunity. In addition we would be travelling a significant distance at an altitude of 1000 m (3300 ft) or greater, where fuel consumption is higher than at sea level. Therefore we stopped at Klondike River Lodge at Km 0 to top up our tanks. We would need all the fuel we could carry.

As I walked to the office to pay I looked back and saw antifreeze dripping beneath our motorhome. Ye gods. I've never had this problem before, now what? At least it happened before we got onto the Dempster.

After pulling off to one side and letting the engine cool down, I checked engine oil, transmission oil, belts, and hoses for leaks. Nothing was amiss. So why did the radiator boil over?

As you read this, I still have no idea. We've gone 116 km, and not once did the temperature gauge indicate a temperature above normal; in fact it was usually on the cool side. Strange things happen under the midnight sun.

The Dempster Highway is in remarkably good shape, considering all the horror stories we've heard. Of course we seldom drive above 90 km/hr (55 m/h) and usually about 75 km/hr so we don't miss something. Our rear dual tires ride over small potholes that single tires might fall into. Faster drivers, and especially those with long vehicles or trailers, might have a different idea of how good this gravel road is. Some places were dusty, a few very dusty, but the first 80 km were relatively dust free.

Mountains to our right still showed bands of white near the top, with some of the mountain showing above them. I suspect these are remains of hooded snowbanks formed when wind whips over the mountain tops. Huge lips of snow are formed, extending for several metres into space above the near vertical walls of snow.

Liz and I stopped at a trapper's cabin at Km 51 and parked by a creek, which is 500 m (1600 ft) higher than Dawson City's airport. The cabin is still occupied occasionally by grandchildren and great grandchildren, both for relaxation and as headquarters for working their winter traplines.

Liz finished putting together a cold crab and pasta salad — with temperatures of high-thirties we didn't need anything hot — while I set up our chairs next to rushing water and far enough away from bushes and trees to enjoy a cool breeze. A few mauve fireweeds and grey, thistle-seeded dandelions were the only flowers in sight.

It was marvellous. As much as we enjoyed the benefits and sociability of civilized Dawson City, we were so glad to be back camping amongst the quiet pleasures of nature. No AM/FM radio reception meant no unhappy news.

We did have to tolerate several flies but surprisingly no mosquitoes. Having been told that black flies, horse flies, deer flies and mosquitoes can be thick enough to cause caribou herds to stampede, I'm not looking forward to walking among hundreds of flying jaws and sneaky probiscises.

At Km 73, we turned left into the Tombstone Interpretive Centre parking lot. With lingering traces of Canada Day patriotism I observed that there was no Canadian Flag flying. Pity.

While trying to identify the various types of fur stuck on a poster, I inadvertently stood beneath a specific ceiling tile. Melted snow from last week's storm dripped on my head. Yes, it was still cold. And I failed the fur test miserably whereas my darling spouse got all but one correct. Show off!

There were so many other interesting displays set up in this tiny building that Liz, with her insatiable curiosity, wandered about for twenty minutes. Sylvia, daughter of a botanist, could answer all our questions but one, which was "Because there are many ravens but no crows this far north, why is Old Crow called Old Crow?" Hopefully I'll get an answer in Inuvik.

After Liz finally let herself be dragged outside, we toured 31 large and well spaced campsites. We saw this bumper sticker "Happiness is a level campground" on a camper and truck with all four wheels on the ground. Even though I choose to carry eight pieces of 2x10 board, I certainly appreciate that comment.

Having stopped at the largest lake to be seen from the Dempster Highway — Chapman Lake at Km 116 — to watch circular ripples magically appear on its calm surface, we decided to spend the night here. We didn't hear those two loons until next morning, I guess they too were sleepy .

This morning we remembered to read our Dempster Travelogue. Drat. We missed several points of interest. Make sure you get a copy, and read it as soon as you start to travel North America's only public highway that crosses the Arctic Circle.

Dempster Highway - Km 116 - Arctic Circle

Visit the Dempster Highway in summer. There is no road like it. None.

It winds through valleys closed-in by rocky and crumbling mountains, through flat plateaus, under hot midday sun, beside paths made by sheep and goats, up and over hill after hill in imitation of the Top of the World Highway, through miles of nothing but marvellous miles, alongside round-topped mountains completely covered with gravel and scree, through blackened, burned-out forests blanketed with brilliant purple fireweed, under never-setting midnight sun surrounded by orange and pink clouds, past empty treeless tundra waiting for thousands of munching Caribou to return, past ghostly-grey pingos, over unnamed creeks, past grey hills used as ready-made gravel pits, beside gophers scurrying into ditches, through hummocks covered in spring-green wool, past gravel mudboils encircled by sparse vegetation, and beside muddy ground capturing the print of some animal.

And it crosses the Arctic Circle.

It winds past charcoal-grey cliffs of shale, lime-green new growth, dull and dying grey spruce trees with twisted limbs, dark-green living trees, silver-white undersides of poplar leaves blown by wind. And it winds past iron oxide blushing the blazing colour of slapped cheeks, salt deposits so thick they remind me of melting snowdrifts, real snowdrifts hidden in crevices, and dark blue lakes surrounded by smooth ebony, tannin-brown creeks, or by rapids-white creeks.

Sometimes heading for infinity it twists past purple fireweed everywhere, rare white fireweed and common fluffy-white Arc-

tic Cotton that smells like baby powder, rocks as speckled as a Ptarmigan's egg, wet shale as black as the blackest coal, golden splashes of growth on a stagnant pond, and fading pink wild roses.

It winds under feathery Cirrus and cotton-ball Cumulus clouds and pastel blue sky (so washed out compared to the royal blue skies of Guatemala). It temporarily disappears under clouds of opaque or translucent dust behind trucks seen kilometres away.

It winds up and down hills, through valleys and plains, over plateaus, into gorges, constantly varying up and down between altitudes of 900 m (3000 ft) and 300 m. It climbs up and down hills, some so gradual as to be almost unnoticed, some so steep I have to gear down into second, around curves, and into yet another different artist's painting.

It skims by marten traps made from multi-hued pails and buckets set astride a sloping log. The only other sign of civilization is the road itself and an occasional microwave tower on some far faraway summit.

There is no drive like it. None.

But Mother Nature is not always benevolent.

This year, several areas were under remedial reconstruction, filling in huge chunks of road that were washed away in late-June by twenty-five centimetres (ten inches) of snow followed by heavy rain followed by blazing, cloudless, twenty-four-hour days that rapidly melted the snow. On June 25th at 3 am two metre high roadside markers in this portion of the Dempster were under raging water. Trees were ripped out with soil and vegetation still attached to their roots. At least one heavy bear-proof garbage can was washed into a river. Oversized culverts were inadequate, and they too were washed away when floods trenched through their road beds.

Highways Canada personnel are to be congratulated on quickly realizing the danger and evacuating, at midnight or shortly thereafter, all the travellers in Engineer Creek campground. No one was injured anywhere in the flood's path. And within four days, the highway was passable (barely) for all vehicles. Stranded campers, some with overflowing holding tanks and diminishing food supplies, were able to escape the Dempster.

And yet as we drive by a week later, the soil looks parched. Where did all that water go? Surely it couldn't have soaked into the solid permafrost?

We have to take the bad with the good.

This highway can be and usually is dusty. Travellers are warned to slow down when meeting another vehicle, ostensibly to prevent damage due to flying rocks. I slow down because often I can't see beyond a few metres in a man-made dust storm.

Which reminds me. "Travelling together" is an oxymoron on the Dempster. Caravans of two or more vehicles do not travel together, unless you consider 3 km spacing between vehicles being together. Even when dust clouds are blown off the highway, invisible dust particles hover over the gravel, waiting for unsuspecting drivers to pass by with all windows down.

I have to give credit to the fellow from Alberta who came up right behind me, waited until I saw his faint bronze headlights, then zoomed past us after I pulled over. I would not have got that close, buried in roiling dust and bombarded by sharp-edged stones, nor would I even attempt to pass anybody on that gravel road. Of course, I travel so slowly that I'll probably never get an opportunity to pass another vehicle.

At least that is what I was thinking as I closed the distance between myself and a fully-loaded dual-tanker fuel truck labouring up a steep hill, heavy black smoke roaring out of its two exhaust stacks. At the top of the hill, I quickly accelerated from 15 k/hr to my usual 70 k/hr, passing as far to the left as possible, *on an emergency airstrip for small airplanes.* What timing. I've yet to pass another vehicle on the real Dempster Highway on our way past the Arctic Circle.

I wonder why the trees and shrubs don't look dustier than they do. Maybe the Nisga'a Highway really was something special after all. Thick dust coated every deciduous leaf and coniferous needle as high as three metres (ten feet) above *that* road.

Long rooster-tails of dust behind trucks and RVs do provide one advantage. Being easily seen kilometres away, there's ample time to roll up windows and close no-drafts. (Does any body under thirty know what no-drafts are?) That doesn't keep the dust out, but at least my skull won't act as a side cushion for a caroming stone.

A few sections of the Dempster Highway haven't seen a grader for months, and are badly rutted. Not deep ruts, but deep enough to cause my motorhome to wander sideways a half metre or so. Of course, the first time it happened was just after I filled both gasoline tanks — one centre-mounted, the other behind the rear axle — which took some of the weight off the front tires and accentuated the problem. Sometimes unexpected mountainous windy gusts would cause our RV to wander as well.

It doesn't pay to drive too fast on Canada's wonderful Dempster Highway. Besides, with so much to see, why hurry?

Dempster Highway - Frog Creek

As usual after waking up, I pulled down a curtain to look at the sky to determine if it was cloudy or clear. What a pleasant surprise to look out onto a garden of mauve fireweed that almost stretched across my limited field of view.

We have camped in Frog creek, next to Lou and Colleen from Ontario. Last night we were invited over for an enjoyable hour or two of conversation and coffee.

This morning, things were not quite so cheerful. One of their inside tires had gone flat, hopefully during the night and not before driving many kilometres on sun-basted gravel. This is Lou's second flat in two days.

But to make matters really bad, he could not get at his spare tire. The tire is mounted on a storage tray which pulls out when the rear bumper is extended manually. Enough rocks, stones, pebbles and dust seemingly had collected on the tray's sliding mechanism that the tray would open only a few inches.

Being a firm believer in the cliché 'What goes around comes around' I offered to help and to stay with him until the problem was solved, or not. We both ended up staying an extra day and night.

After hooking up his air compressor and blowing away a lot of dust and some stones the spare tire was still locked away.

113

This man had tools, boxes of tools, compartments of tools, hundred weights
of tools. He could have travelled around the world and fixed anything.
I hope he does, and invites me (and my pliers and screwdriver) along.

After hooking up his half horsepower water pump and dropping its input hose into Frog Creek then washing out more dust and stones, it was still non-accessible. Lou finally determined his problem was with a small compartment getting caught on a bent power connector. It had been pushed up when he scraped his way onto the Peel River ferry. That was easy to fix, he merely tore off part of the compartment.

Thereafter, it was a simple although time-consuming effort to change his flat tire. To ensure both tires in a pair were the same tire brand (hence same sidewall height and flexibility) he had to put the tag axle tire on the inside dual and put his brand new spare on the tag axle.

I have seldom seen a man with as many tools and gadgets as Lou has, but many of them did come in handy today. How many people carry a torque wrench, a mini-welder and an external water pump?

Using his example, I'm going to buy a water pump. I can use it for power washing the dusty or muddy outside of my motorhome whenever I'm parked next to a creek, a river or a large rain puddle.

There has been so much dust on this road that we've found dust where we've never had dust before, and we've travelled to dusty Nicaragua and sandy Baja California, Mexico.

For the first time dust has shown up in my large storage compartment as well as inside my tool box. And dust has filtered into our bathroom cupboard and clothes closet. Dishes are covered in a thick layer of dust, cans and plastic containers of food under the sink are buried in brown-grey silt. There is even a small pile on one end of our over-the-cab bed.

Liz is disgusted and discouraged! Today she cleaned only what she had to. A major cleanup must take place after we get into Inuvik and before we settle down for a couple of weeks.

The Nisga'a Highway north of the Memorial Lava Beds in BC was a much dustier road but it is only 100 km long, not 734.

A couple in a camper drove in and parked next to our motorhomes. Sylvie told us of another woman who broke down and cried because there was so much thick dust over everything in her Class A. She and her husband would have worn medical masks if they had them because their throats were sore from breathing so much airborne dust.

Question. What should we call a sunset when the sun doesn't set?

Mid-day was so hot, 33.5^0C or 92^0F by our bedroom thermometer, 37^0C by Lou's outside thermometer.

Frog Creek is both a creek and large pool. That pool of clear but dark brown water beckoned irresistibly. Liz and I changed into bathing suits and went for a swim. The water was warmer than in some heated pools. Imagine. We swam in Arctic waters and thoroughly enjoyed it. We didn't stay in long because we didn't have any floatation gear such as Noodles but it was long enough to wash off most of the dust and perspiration.

We are out of shape, no doubt about that. We've got to get more exercise.

Later, as I walked along the high berm separating creek and pool I looked down into the pool and saw four fish, all at least 30 cm (a foot) long. Time to go fishing!

But I don't have any fishing gear. I had kept putting off buying some.

But I did have that hook I found by the Klondike River. Searching in my box of what-nots I found a few metres (yds) of 30-pound-test nylon line I had bought a couple of years ago for something or other. I didn't need anything else.

Liz came back with me to the fishing hole; I no longer considered it to be a pool. Her job was to hold that spool of nylon and rewind it as I drew in the hook. She stood at least two metres from where I cast the hook by twirling it around and around my head like a lasso and releasing it at just the right moment. It was surprisingly easy to do accurately, unless it tangled itself in nearby bushes.

Of course, I knew enough to go to the hook and untangle it rather than pulling the hook free then, hopefully, ducking in time as those nasty barbs flew towards me.

My very first cast soared out about seven metres. The line unwrapped from the spool in Liz's hands as freely as from any spinner reel. As I hauled in the line, Liz rewound the spool. I could do it faster than she, and line quickly accumulated at my feet. But I didn't even notice. An unseen jack fish had taken the hook within micro-seconds of its hitting the water.

I caught a fish on my very first toss of my low-tech fishing equipment!

Only after I brought it ashore did I realize I had no way to kill the fish nor to remove the hook. Back to our RV for my jack knife and a pair of needle-nose pliers. Back to the fish and I did what I had to do, while Liz looked elsewhere. (I've discovered the quickest way to kill a fish is to strike it behind its head and eyes, with a sharp edged rock or a heavy knife. I think it breaks the spinal cord.)

That done, I swung the line around and around again, released it. It took only minutes to untangle it and the hook from a bunch of leaves and branches.

That done, I swung the line again, and the hook soared out just as before. As I removed the line from a different shrub, the hook sank to the bottom. As I hauled it in, a second northern pike (jack) grabbed the hook as it neared the surface. Unbelievable. It too was dragged onto shore but this time it was readily dispatched. This was too easy.

I could see one 60 cm fish close by the shore. I dragged that hook right in front of it three or four times, but he (or she) wasn't interested. Twice I managed to pull the line over its back in hopes of snagging a fin or gill, but without success.

It wouldn't go away. It slowly moved its fins and tail, almost as if it were daring me to catch it. If I'd had a long stick I could have speared it. Or I'd have made a snare and caught it that way. If I'd used a rifle I could have shot it. But I didn't.

I also saw a half-dozen smaller fish. More casts quickly followed; all I succeeded in catching were reeds, weeds, branches, and my sandals. Once my thumb was pricked without spilling any blood. I had several nibbles and almost-catches, but all for naught. But I really didn't mind. I had two fresh kilogram (two pound) fish waiting to be cleaned and cooked for tomorrow's barbeque supper.

That was enough for Liz and me. Sure I would have liked to catch the big one, but we really didn't need it. In a strange way I'm glad I didn't catch it, and I'm not talking sour grapes either. There will be other opportunities for me to fish. They should be a little more exciting, a little more challenging, a little more work, a little more fun.

While studying my fishing technique, Lou was often seen shaking his head. Eventually he walked back to his Class A, opened an outside compartment and returned with a collapsible fishing rod and spinner, which he gave to me. He said he'd found it by some creek but never used it and wasn't likely to do so. [Thank you Lou. I've had a lot of fun with it.]

Evenings are as hot or hotter than midday. Once again we went for a swim, but this time on the other side of the berm in the swiftly flowing creek. For ten minutes we swam up the back water then floated down the middle of the creek to a real swimming hole then swam up the back water, etc. We would have stayed longer but for the horse flies which constantly swarmed around our heads.

We should have worn our bee-keepers' hats. Now that would have been quite a sight. Two khaki-green mesh hats floating and moving about above tannin-brown water with yellow body-like protuberances below.

But even those few minutes were marvellous. I wonder how many travellers and visitors think Arctic waters are so cold that going for a swim is a prelude to frostbite. I know we were pleasantly surprised to discover how warm the creek was.

Strange isn't it. 450 km to the south, the Klondike and Yukon rivers are much colder. I must check out Mackenzie River before we cross over on the second ferry.

Tomorrow we'll follow several dust-free minutes behind Lou and Colleen as they make their way to Inuvik without a spare. We'll both set our CB's to Channel 19, the truckers' channel, in the unlikely event he needs help.

Hopefully we'll get away early enough to beat the afternoon heat. Maybe we'll get to Inuvik before noon.

Letter to Editor of the Tsiigehtchic Journal

Following is a letter I wrote. You can write, or better yet, visit Tsiigehtchic by ferry to get a copy of this Journal. It makes for an interesting souvenir Although he doesn't expect payment, I'm sure he would accept something to cover mailing costs, perhaps a small bank note from your country that he can put in his bank account or mount on a wall.

July 7th, 1998

Mr. James Cardinal, Editor, Tsiigehtchic Journal
Tsiigehtchic (Arctic Red River), NWT Canada
Good Day Mr. Cardinal,

I am saddened to hear of the death of elder Joe Vittrekwa on the Mighty MacKenzie. May his family remember most of the good times and very few of the bad.

My wife I and visited Tsiigehtchic two days ago. Although we could not get any dried fish from Rose — highly recommended by another motorhome owner heading south — we did obtain a copy of the June 1st issue of the Tsiigehtchic Journal. I thoroughly enjoyed it and your quiet but not always subtle humour.

I look forward to hearing the Lonesome Indian Tsiigehtchic Country and Western Band at the Great Northern Arts Festival in Inuvik.

Our short visit prompted both Liz and I to remark that we thought Tsiigehtchic looked better (more greenery, better look-

ing houses, generally more prosperous) than Fort McPherson, which seemed very dusty. Although we spent more time in Tsiigehtchic than in McPherson, neither visit was long enough to draw valid comparisons. Feelings, yes; comparisons, no.

If you are in Inuvik in mid-July, look for a 23' "Security" motorhome with a pale green canoe on top, and stop by for a cup of coffee.

Sincerely yours,
John Plaxton

Dempster Highway: Frog Creek - Inuvik

As usual since the sun has refused to set, we awoke sometime after 9:30 am having had about eight hours sleep. Our bodies have acclimatized themselves to nature's time, not man's. The northern Northwest Territories (where we are now) are west of Vancouver Island but local time is set to Alberta time which is east and one hour ahead of BC. NWT time is askew by two hours. However it is very convenient for the people of and near Inuvik because almost all their dealings are with Yellowknife and Edmonton.

Lou and Colleen were just pulling out. As agreed, we would travel behind them, a long way behind them and their dust cloud. So much for CB contact en route.

Travelling to Tsiigehtchic (formerly Arctic Red River) was uneventful, as was the monotonous trip to Inuvik. Being in the MacKenzie River Delta means that the land is level, trees are short and skinny, and shrub and scrub bushes, sky-blue lakes and large puddles are everywhere. Early-July scenery is definitely green, many shades of green, with little of other colours to relieve the sameness.

As we approached our second ferry, we saw a sign indicating Inuvik straight ahead and Tsiigehtchic — Mouth of the Iron River — to the right. We kept looking for a road but we never saw one even though we stopped by the river. So we turned around, went back to the sign, turned around again, and again made it to the Mighty MacKenzie without finding a side road. A truck hauling a flatbed loaded with a big yellow Caterpillar was parked ahead of us, so I got out, strolled up to the driver

Trees in the Arctic are very short and have tiny trunks, especially when growing above permafrost.

and asked "How can I drive to Arctic Red?" Smilingly, he said "Ask the men on the ferry."

Minutes later I followed the truck onto the ferry then asked how to get to Arctic Red. They said "You want to go to Tsiigehtchic? Really? OK. We'll take you there." The noise of the diesels increased slightly, the ferry shuddered and backed away from its gravel ramp, swung ninety degrees starboard and headed up river. There, located on the V-shaped land on the other sides of MacKenzie River and Arctic Red River, inaccessible by summer roads, was our destination. No wonder that driver smiled.

"Tsiigehnjik" or "Tsiigehtchic" in Gwichya Gwich'in means "people of flat land." Their oral language is often times difficult to convert to the English written word. We've come across several words that sounded the same to us but were spelled slightly differently.

Tsiigehtchic is a very small community, but usually a source of well prepared dried fish, whitefish and inconnu or conney. The families of Rose and Annie hadn't been fishing because of the unusually high temperatures during the last ten days, and so we got no dried fish. Maybe we'll get some on the way back.

The owner, or at least the manager, of the only store in this community hails from Israel. How people do travel.

When in Tsiigehtchic, take time to watch the ravens play in breezes sweeping up the river banks. They put on quite a show for us. By the way, ravens are extremely intelligent — they are known as The Trickster in many local myths — and reportedly have 72 to 80 distinctive sequences of sound and music. That's a fair vocabulary.

An hour after leaving, the ferry returned for us. We made sure we were parked on the launch about ten minutes before sailing time so the Captain would see us. It wasn't necessary because three trucks and a taxi lined up behind us at the last minute.

After Tsiigehtchic, the only disruption to travel was a series of culverts that were being torn up and replaced. Because the old ones didn't look too rusty or full of holes we wondered why they were being replaced. The answer is that the middle of those culverts slowly sink into the permafrost and these steel tubes become quite bowed. The centre portion can sink so low that the top of the middle of the culvert is below the ends, and spring runoff cannot pass through snow and ice-choked culverts.

You should see plenty of grouse on the side of the highway, perhaps even some smaller ptarmigans, because they pick up gravel there for their gizzards. If you are into eating wild fowl, stop beside a group and you might get one or two by throwing sharp rocks at them. A simple bow and arrow outfit should be good for a half dozen. I tried to convince Liz to open her door as we drove by some on the side of the road, in the hopes of knocking them on their heads, but all she would do is open her window and shout "Run, run. Fly away."

About 20 km from Inuvik, we crossed over Campbell Creek and past nearby day-use facilities. Jackfish float in wait inside two culverts, attacking smaller fish that attempt to swim upriver. We heard them lunge several times. They occasionally chomp on a Red Devil that is dragged by close to the culverts. Although a boney fish, they do taste good when steamed in tin foil on a barbeque, cooled, broken into tiny chunks while removing bones, then fried in butter. I call these pieces Fish Crisps.

Cook them outside. The aroma of fish stays inside a motor-home, or any RV, for a long time.

I've heard of one man that can fillet jackfish and northern pike (two names, one fish) and leave behind only one or two small bones for every half dozen fish he fillets. How I would like to meet that fellow!

Liz and I are still waiting to taste arctic char and lake trout.

A pleasant surprise awaited us as we drove past the airport. There are ten kilometres of unbroken asphalt between the airport turnoff and Inuvik. I can only assume that this is a test track to determine if asphalt roads are feasible over permafrost, and not some federally-funded project used to provide a smooth, dust free ride for Members of Parliament to Inuvik. Whatever the reason, it works. The years-old road displays very few repairs, even though it has been subjected to many, many big trucks hauling tons of freight in all seasons.

Maybe, some day, all of the Dempster will be paved. And maybe the Circle Road along the Mackenzie River to Yellowknife will be started and finished soon. What would we humans be like without hope?

Inuvik

Inuvik is a small community, getting smaller. Last year twenty families left, and this year a similar exodus is expected.

Inuvik will not disappear, but it might become a hamlet. Recreational facilities such as a bowling alley and miniature golf have been closed. On the positive side, the public library is well stocked and a friendly place in which to read or access the Internet's Web and e-mail. And there is delicious ice-cream across the street from the library.

There is no need to bring a toad (towed vehicle) behind your motorhome. I encourage you not to, even if it is protected from sharp stones and rocks by a plastic sheet or cloth cover or a plywood deflector. Inuvik is small enough that you can walk almost everywhere.

We were surprised to see so many taxis in Inuvik. But maybe it's cheaper to drive around a small town in a taxi in the summer than it is to own a vehicle, or cheaper than replacing a windshield or a paint job to patch up a dozen stone chips. I wonder how many use snowmobiles in the winter.

If you get a fishing licence ensure that it allows you to fish in Gwich'in and Inuvialuit territories and in Territorial areas.

Most people stay one to three days in Inuvik, there isn't that much to see and do. We will be staying for most of the ten days of this year's Great Northern Art Festival. In fact, we might even become volunteer helpers and gophers. How involved we get will depend upon when or if we can barge ourselves and our RV to Tuktoyaktuk, or Tuk, and when we can return.

A dump station, fresh water and a laundromat are available just outside the entrance to Happy Valley Campground in Inuvik. The fee for a campsite is inexpensive, but occasionally none are available. At really busy times, Chuk Territorial Park (Chuk) about 5 km outside of town could be full also.

While there we met Hugh Dempster, son of RCMP Cpl Dempster who found the four men of the Lost Patrol, and who are buried in Fort McPherson. We chatted for a few minutes before he, his daughter and granddaughter flew to Tuk. I wonder how it feels to be known as the son of Cpl Dempster instead of as Mr. Hugh Dempster?

The huge **Inukshuk** on the corner by the MacKenzie Hotel is difficult to photograph because of power lines overhead, but

To me, this is the symbol of the NWT.

it can be done. Just stand in the middle of the side street, and hope no vehicles run over you.

Chuk is wonderful and breezy when temperatures are in the mid 30's (80's). A climb to the top of its lookout tower is rewarded by a horizon to horizon view of the Delta.

Do visit the Visitors Information Centre. Enjoy a cup of coffee or tea while taking time to look around. You will receive excellent service, even if you are as rude as one demanding European couple who thought they were owed whatever they wanted just because they were travelling around the world. You might even get picked for 'Tourist of the Week' if you are there at the right time. I know what that is, or was, but I'm not telling.

There is a truck and car wash in front of a gasoline station in the industrial end of town. It would have cost us $9.00. I have buckets, a squeegee and dry rags available whenever we camp near lakes and creeks. Another station, Esso, had cheaper gas prices.

The liquor store has sipping Yukon Jack plus an assortment of other beverages. There was no dust on the bottles of overproof rum, unlike on some of the unusual liqueurs.

Having been built without any architect plans, the Igloo church is unique and well worth a visit. Being an active church it is usually open during business hours. (I can't write 'during the day' because now the summer sun doesn't set until after midnight.)

Taking pictures of the Igloo church is easy. But how I

The story behind some of the paintings inside is remarkable.

wished I had a tripod to take several manual, time-exposure shots at night. Capturing a necklace of eight or nine midnight suns behind that brushed-aluminum dome would have been exciting.

(Author's note. The real name of that metal is aluminium. In the 1800's, due to the cost of replacing millions of letter-heads and forms printed with a typographical error by a North American business, the error was not corrected. We colonials didn't know any better and now we North Americans spell it as aluminum.)

Liz and I thoroughly enjoyed the dinner show at the Finto Hotel. We ate from an arctic buffet, watched the show, ate desert, watched, and participated. We laughed a lot, met a couple of locals who often come, and enjoyed the arctic delights of caribou, musk ox, and arctic char and other tastily prepared goodies. Unfortunately one vegetarian (because of health problems) could not pay to see only the show and thus she and her husband didn't attend.

Check out the premises of the insurance broker, whose name I can't remember, to see if he has any of his cuddly white polar bears left. My favourite was Cranberry although Cloud Berry – those are really tasty northern berries – is more apropos for an

125

arctic souvenir for grandchildren. Occasionally Diamond Willow walking sticks are also available.

Check out the local book store and its eclectic assortment of northern books, including this one (I hope).

Local fast food stores, coffee shops and restaurants offer reasonable to excellent selections of snacks and meals. The hospital cafeteria provides nourishing food at good prices.

The Northern Store can supply most food stuff required to cook your own meals although, being heavy and costly to ship, canned goods and pop are expensive. Fresh fruit and vegetables don't last long after being purchased; it seems to be better to buy only what you need for each day. Other smaller food stores are available when Northern is closed.

Good road but with lots of gravel, and dust or mud. Towed vehicles can be stone-chipped or damaged. Some kind of frontal protection is essential. The second best protection is to drive slowly. Plan on an overnight en route.

The Great Northern Arts Festival

The Great Northern Arts Festival is worth designating as an event to see and plan for.

I understand that this fabulous festival is usually scheduled for the third week in July of each year, including weekends on both sides. In 1998 the Great Northern Arts Festival (GNAF) was held from Friday July 17th to Sunday July 26th.

Drum dancing on outside stage. On cool days drums must be heated over fires to keep the skins taut. Drummers use an interesting technique.

Liz and I had communicated with Tanya, co-co-ordinator of GNAF, several times via e-mail long before we left on this summer's adventure. But it seemed as if our nebulous travelling schedule was such that we would not be in Inuvik during GNAF.

Our being delayed a week in Dawson because a storm washed out parts of the Dempster Highway was indeed lucky.

Our having painted a map of Mexico and Central America on the side of our Class C was also fortunate. The first evening we were parked in Inuvik, Tanya walked by our motorhome, noticed the map, figured out that there could be only one RV like that, knocked on our door, came in and drank coffee and talked about GNAF for almost an hour. That's how we found out about the volunteer opportunity, and decided to stay in Inuvik longer than we'd planned. Much longer as it turned out.

I suggest planning on staying two to four days at the GNAF. Artists arrive at all times, and their work can be displayed for the very first time on day three, or five, etc. although most are available during the first two days.

When you see something you want, buy it. These are one-of-a-kind art objects. Don't walk about thinking about it or you'll probably go back to get it and find that it is already owned by somebody else. I missed my chance at a carved cribbage board which had been on display for an hour. I've talked to two people who had a similar experience with their pre-empted choice, and I heard several similar stories while working there. Of course,Tanya and Marilyn, GNAF co-ordinators, loved to hear me say "Buy now." to visitors, but it is true.

Liz and I had an absolutely marvellous time, working as volunteers several hours a day as well as wandering about looking at very unusual and very, very professional works of art. We even bought some. Although I don't usually promote a specific event, this one I will.

Confirm your plans, get the latest information on this Canadian festival. Phone (867)-777-3536, Fax (867) 777-4445. Surf its website at http://greatart.nt.ca . Email to greatart@permafrost.com . Write to GNAF, PO Box 2921, Inuvik, NT, Canada.

During the GNAF, hotel and bed & breakfast accommodations could be filled. Both campgrounds could be full. Airlines might not be flying every day. Once you have decided to go to Inuvik, make reservations if you don't want to spend days and nights parked in the boondocks.

Parking motorhomes and vans on town streets really is not an option. Look for parking lots, there are some.

There is no need to pull a vehicle behind a motorhome because you can walk anywhere you want to go or hire a taxi. Windows, paint, under-carriage and even tires of towed vehicles, or 'toads', could be damaged by flying stones and will be covered in dust or mud. Park your 'toad' somewhere before driving the Dempster. If you *must* bring a towed vehicle – fifthwheel, trailer, car or truck – cover it well with thick blankets or build a plywood deflector in front of it.

Most tourists would not spend two weeks in Inuvik. We did. There isn't a lot to see except GNAF.

Inuvik is also a great place to arrange to fly to Tuktoyaktuk or, better yet, to Herschel Island or Sachs Harbour. Such tours are not cheap but are often worth the expense simply because of the flight over land, tundra, the MacKenzie River delta and Arctic Ocean. But be aware that weather can change extremely quickly. Your scheduled flight could be cancelled as you are driven to the airport, or made available if you can be available in minutes. Man has little control over the whims of Northern Nature.

But the drive over the Dempster Highway to get to GNAF is worth the dust and mud that will cover your RV. Most travellers wouldn't take four days like we did. Two days is usual.

We arrived a couple of days before the GNAF, discovered we could work as volunteers, and stayed for the entire festival. I wish we could go back and do it again.

Volunteers are expected to work at least one shift per day, each shift being four hours, for however many days you wish. Work two shifts in a day, and you should qualify for a free meal, possibly of arctic char, muktuk or my favourite, caribou. Until you've had spaghetti with caribou meat sauce, you have missed another unique Canadian dish. I can say the same about muktuk.

But what did we do?

Liz and I helped to set up and organize for two full days before GNAF officially opened. Once it opened, Liz spent most time doing inventory of new items as they arrived, working one of the cash registers, carefully wrapping purchases, or helping to enter data into the computerized inventory control system. Artists, equipment and art items come and go any time during the GNAF because of scheduled and unscheduled flights. They don't always arrive at the expected time. Accurate inventory and sales and commission control is an amazingly complex and time-consuming activity.

I was a gopher. Go for this, go for that.

I carried refuse barrels painted by children, cut caribou meat, put together two display cases, painted dozens of items, helped build a frame-and-plastic protection for outside band concerts, looked for lost equipment, picked up garbage, hung balloons and banners, evaluated the inventory control system and made suggestions for improved machine-user interfaces, made hundreds of photocopies, conducted visitor surveys, acted as day and night security guard for several hours for a couple of days, drank coffee, helped musical bands setup and take down their equipment, and smiled a lot. But most important, like all the other volunteers, we offered support to the overworked and occasionally exhausted organizers.

The Great Northern Arts Festival could not be without the help of volunteers, even two or three day volunteers.

What did we get out of it? We have new friends and acquaintances. We got to see beautiful works of art, got to meet world-class artists, worked with many fine people from Canada, USA and Europe, earned a credit of $1/hour credited against the purchase of GNAF objets d'art and used it all, and we have many, many heart-warming memories.

The best was when Liz and I were named as Super Volunteers for 1998 and each given a gift of appreciation. We were so surprised and very touched. When I was given what I had seen being made by a first-time GNAF artist and which I wanted very much and which I had tried very hard to buy, I cried for the first time since my father died twenty-three year ago. I was almost speechless and made some incoherent, irrelevant comment while struggling to say Thank You.

But volunteering at GNAF didn't take up all our time.

We had time to take in the Dinner Theatre at the Finto Motor Inn, featuring "East Three, the story of Inuvik." Great food, good performances, humorous script, unexpected audience participation and friendly company made for a pleasant and very enjoyable evening.

I managed to acquire one of those very rare outdated and de-registered Polar Bear licence plates. It proudly sits above the others, my Yukon, Mexican and Honduran plates. All are securely fastened and locked to our RV's bumper.

I had time to take part in a native activity called a Blanket Toss.

That's where one person gets onto the centre of a circular, tanned hide while several men grab its edge. Then they all pull at once and the person in the middle shoots straight up into the air and falls back onto the hide now held at shoulder level. If everybody does everything correctly, the person in the middle can be rocketed three to four metres into the air. It is very important that all men yank at the same time with a quick but steady pull. The jumper must keep his knees locked and his legs straight and he must maintain his balance. If anything is done incorrectly, the blanket could painfully drive the jumper's knees into

This you should try. Don't jump. Keep your legs straight.

his chin, or the jumper barely rises above the blanket, or he's thrown sideways. The only good thing about a failed attempt are the jokes and laughter that ensue.

And the jumper better have strong legs. I made four attempts before my legs became too weak for another try. Others had the same experience. I got airborne only once, and it was perfect. I felt like an astronaut or a cosmonaut might feel, effortlessly floating. The other three times I instinctively bent my knees trying to help by jumping and flopped around like a fish out of water.

Of course I helped launch several other people. The best was a young native girl. Every one of her six flights sent her high over the heads of the dozen of us pulling on the hide and she came down in the middle of it. Once she did a back flip. For most other persons we had to quickly shift sideways to catch them in the hide, or they'd bend their knees and go nowhere.

Although a GNAF volunteer, I made time to try to get our RV to Tuk.

Barging an RV to Tuktoyaktuk

No vehicle can drive to Tuk in the summer; there are no roads. Vehicles can drive there in the winter, on a surprisingly smooth ice-road that is mostly on the frozen MacKenzie River.

Many RVers want to have Northern Transportation Company Limited (NTCL) barge their motorhome to and from Tuk, *with them in it*. This **cannot** be done.

NTCL has neither the licence nor the authority nor the financial incentive to do so. Besides, RV's would be securely tied down on deck, sitting above millions of litres of diesel fuel, gasoline or propane. All their barges always carry fuel. Under a hot summer sun and subjected to sloshing due to wave motion, these petroleum products generate flammable vapours and fumes which could be ignited by propane-fired water heaters and furnaces. Being inside a huge fire ball would be an interesting story to tell, if you survived. Please don't waste your time and NTCL's time by trying to get yourself (inside your vehicle) to Tuk on one of their barges.

We tried very hard to have our RV shipped to Tuktoyaktuk on a barge.

We had hoped to be the first RV to drive into Tuk in the summer. We also wanted to attend the Summer Games and use our RV as accommodation. The cost of shipping was almost the same as a week's accommodation for two in a hotel. And fuel prices are 10¢/L cheaper!

And we wanted to drive the RV into the Arctic Ocean. Its wheels have been in the Gulf of Mexico and when in Panamá, the Atlantic and Pacific Oceans.

We actually had a small barge arranged . But at departure time the company's tug was inoperative because of an engine failure.

Liz and I had planned on stowing away inside our RV so we could see the scenery in and along the mighty MacKenzie Delta. It would also have saved the cost of flying to Tuk. But the backlog of scheduled barge deliveries precluded our trying again so we never found out if we could have got away with breaking the law. Maybe we were lucky after all, we weren't put in jail.

When we enquired of a second barging business, the cost was going to be $8,000 to make an unscheduled trip with only a two day layover in Tuk. That's out of our price range. Perhaps, if Liz and I had had time to organize such a trip with two or three other RVers long before we got to Inuvik, the cost for each RV might have been half or less.

However, *you* might be able to get a small barge company to ship you and your RV to Tuktoyaktuk. They might even ship it and you back to Inuvik when you want. But check that out. That would depend on weather and whether you would be willing to travel within their schedule. If interested try to contact Brian Turner or Bob Gully. Don't be sad if it can't be done.

If it could be scheduled, and if the barging business could get a license to do so, and if you would be willing to pay the price, you'd probably be required to sign an iron-clad contract that relieved the company of any responsibility for damages of any sort for any reason. Such a contract is remarkably difficult to write to make it hold up in a court of law, and might not even exist in the Northwest Territories. Also you would have to provide your own insurance, life, damage and third party liability.

We never made it to Tuktoyaktuk with our RV.

(If we had known earlier about MV Norweta, which makes one trip per year down and up the MacKenzie River, we might have been able to make a reservation for that unique cruise.)

However we did manage to fly there.

Tuktoyaktuk (Tuk)

The day we planned to leave Inuvik overcast clouds suddenly disappeared, instantly, completely. We quickly checked with a tour company and learned that they had an airplane available now but needed two more people. As we talked a man walked into the office and asked about seats for three. A flight was arranged. And yes I could bring along a 20 kg package.

Liz and I briskly walked to our RV, undid two bolts and got the package, then walked back to the office. All of us were driven to the airport.

With five passengers our aircraft could not take the package. A second airplane was scheduled to go at the same time as ours, and it could carry it behind one of the seats. I loaded it aboard. Pilots and passengers looked at me, wondering what I was doing.

Remember to bring along something warm if you get to visit the Ice House.

Both airplanes flew to Tuk, landing minutes apart. The package came along with us in the van that toured Tuk.

Two hours was enough. Even with a pingo visible on the horizon, there was even less to see than in Inuvik.

We did manage to go down into the Ice House. I wish we had brought a flashlight of our own. After going into a shed, passing through a 1 m² hatch, climbing 10 m vertically down into frozen-solid permafrost, walking along tunnels carved out of ice and frozen mud by pick and shovel, and entering small storage rooms, there is very little light to activate the cones and rods of retinas. In other words, it's pitch black dark. We were given one flashlight, but ours would have been brighter. Still, we're glad we managed to visit the Ice House. I know of one other in Canada, this small example is behind the Visitors Centre in Inuvik. There are probably others somewhere.

Back in the van, we drove along the few roads of Tuk. Total length might exceed seven kilometres. Gasoline prices are ten cents a litre lower here than in Inuvik. The price is reduced by the portion of taxes usually paid for road and highways maintenance. Think of the money I could have saved by filling up both RV tanks in Tuk.

One of the roads led us to the Arctic Ocean. Liz and I took off our shoes and waded in. We didn't go very far, not because the water was cold – it wasn't – but because the stones were hard on our bare feet.

We've been in all oceans surrounding Canada!

We dried our feet, put our socks and shoes back on, and returned to the van. Liz got her camera, I got what I brought with us.

Together we walked back to the shore. Liz readied her camera while I again waded into the Arctic Ocean. And I threw the package, the spare wheel from our motorhome, into the Arctic Ocean.

I couldn't get our motorhome to Tuktoyaktuk and the Arctic Ocean. But by god, I got one of its wheels there.

One 16.5 inch rim and 8.75 inch tire from our Class C has bathed in three oceans – Atlantic (including Gulf of Mexico), Pacific (including Sea of Cortez) and Arctic – and has travelled from way down south inside the Tropic of Cancer to way up north inside the Arctic Circle. Yea!

Stick Gambling

While at the fabulous Great Northern Arts Festival in Inuvik I learned an ancient game called Stick Gambling. I don't know if it was originated by Indians or the Inuit people.

The game can be much more complicated than was explained to me, but at least the basics were explained. After I typed up the rules as I learned them, I asked a couple of locals to see if I had them written correctly. I did. Experience can sometimes be a good teacher.

2nd from right, a German lad. Other side of sticks, a woman's team who defeated us soundly. It's hard to believe that one person could be so good.

Two teams attempt to capture all available sticks, about a dozen or so. They do so by correctly guessing where stones are in the opposing players' hands.

To start the game, choose an equal number of players for each team, perhaps women versus men, or children versus adults, or family versus in-laws. Each person must have one pebble which they can transfer easily and secretly from hand to hand, and a jacket, hat, apron, etc. behind which to hide their hands.

Flip a coin, or toss a pointed or marked stick, to determine which side will begin. The beginning team is the "hiding" team.

Place all gambling sticks in a central location. Form two lines of players, facing each other.

The hiding team places their closed hands under their jackets. Each player transfers his/her stone hand to hand, then brings their hands into public viewing while holding the pebble without indicating which hand has the pebble. The hands may be held straight out in front of the body, or arms may be crossed to place hands on shoulders.

After all players have 'gone public', one member of the opposing (or "calling") team makes a call. A caller indicates whether opposition stones are held in either their right hands or their left hands. Each hiding player extends his arms and opens the hand indicated by the caller. Those players who have rocks in the indicated hand are eliminated, those who do not, win.

One stick for each winner is taken from the central pile and placed in front of the "hiding" team.

Only non-eliminated "hiding" players continue to play. The opposing caller can always be the same person, or any player on the calling team can become the caller at any time.

Action in the previous three paragraphs is repeated until all 'hiding' players are eliminated, which is the end of one round.

Play now switches sides. The calling team becomes the hiding team and the hiding team becomes the calling team. Teams continue to hide and call and transfer sticks until all "hiding" players are eliminated and the end of another round is reached. Each winner gets a stick from the hiding team.

If all the hiding team's sticks are gone, then sticks are taken from the central pile.

Play continues, round by round, until all available sticks are placed in front of one team. The game is over and the team with every stick wins.

But how does a caller indicate which hands — left or right, and whose left or right — might have the pebbles? The caller's thumb determines the call.

When a caller extends either hand and points his thumb to his right then members of the hiding team, which is facing the caller, will see the thumb as pointing to their left. Those of the hiding team with pebbles in their left hand are losers and are eliminated. When a caller points his thumb to his left those of the hiding team with pebbles in their right hand are losers and are eliminated.

For a more lively game, bystanders and watchers can chant, clap their hands in unison, beat on drums, or all of the above to add a rhythm to the handling of the pebbles. This is usually done, and I suspect the drum beat is an important part of the game.

Stick Gambling can be played using only the rules above, and should be until all players understand how the game is played.

An interesting option is to allow hiding players to "lock their choice." After moving a pebble from hand to hand but before exposing them to view, a player strikes both hands on the ground or table then crosses his arms and places them on his/her shoulders. By crossing arms, the player's right hand is on the left side of his body, and left hand on right side. Now when a call is made, the hiding player who struck the ground is not allowed to extend his arms, but must keep them crossed, and opens the hand on the side of the body indicated by the caller. By locking his choice a player reverses his choice by making left right and right left.

This game can be made even more challenging by also using and watching a caller's fingers.

When all fingers are closed or curled into a palm, every hiding player is subject to the direction of the caller's thumb.

If one finger is extended, then only one person is affected by the direction of the caller's thumb; all other eligible players are affected by the direction opposite to the thumb. The affected person is the last person in the indicated direction.

For example, assume a hiding team has four eligible players. When a caller extends one finger and points his thumb to his right, the eligible player to the caller's extreme right is affected by a right-direction but the other three players are affected by a left-direction. Another way to describe this situation is to assume the teams are lined up East-West. When a caller extends one finger and points his thumb to the East, then the eastmost player is affected by an East call and all the other three players are affected by a West call.

Similarly, if two fingers are extended with a thumb pointing East, the two eastmost eligible players are affected by an East call, and the other players are affected by a West call.

Similar situations exist for three or four extended fingers, or if the caller's thumb was pointed Left or West.

Why bother with fingers? Well. If you know certain people have demonstrated a tendency to hold their pebble in a particular hand, you can increase your odds of winning by the use of fingers to determine which direction affects which persons. It's subtle, but very effective.

Cheating is possible and quite easy in this game, especially for those who are manually dexterous. Although not common, some players will accept that and determine team penalties if a cheater is caught, making it a part of the game. Other players will outlaw cheating, usually when money is involved. How the game is played is up to the players, but all players must know and abide by the decision reached before a game begins.

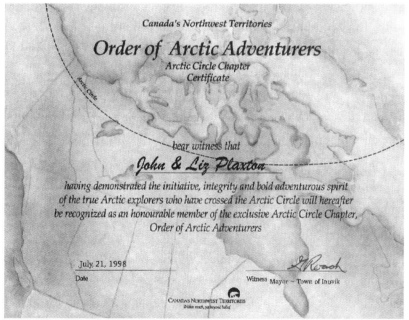

*Remember to get **your** (one of two) free "Arctic Adventurers" Certificates, available in Inuvik or NWT Campground immediately after Perry Crossing.*

Inuvik to Dawson City

Well. The Festival is over, neither barge was available to take us to Tuktoyaktuk, and we've flown to and from Tuk, so it is time to head back Up South.

I'll have to start rethinking my directions again. After I get to asphalt highways, I can return to saying up north and down south and stop worrying about in which direction the MacKenzie River flows.

As we were doing a last minute dump and fill of water and gasoline, Abraham came by and asked if we would take him to Fort McPherson, so we said "Sure, we leave in about an hour from the Igloo Church. Meet you there." He sat patiently in the hot sun as we did last minute grocery shopping, credit card payments, checked e-mail at the Inuvik Research Centre – home of the Aurora Research Institute – and visited a (related?) feminine Plaxton in Trappers' Inn, one of the few places that are dark at 10 am in July.

When we were finally ready to leave, he gratefully came inside and immediately drank two glasses of water after declining a beer. If we who are used to months of summer heat find 30^0C+ hot, how do people who spend a great majority of their time at temperatures below 0^0C feel?

Finally we were off, memories intact but looking forward to being on the road again.

Although we tried to include Abraham in our conversations while he was sitting back at the dinette, wind and road noise and motor noise made that difficult. Sadly he spent most of the time thinking his own thoughts, and we missed an opportunity to learn more about himself and the Gwich'in. We parted company at the first ferry.

We missed the hourly, on-the-hour ferry departure by ten minutes, even though I had been driving faster than usual. Several times we sped along at 90+ k/hr before I realized that our rig was harder to control than usual and slowed down to our usual 70-75 k/hr. We were on the road again and anxious to explore new territory. We had Destination Fever! Even if we didn't know exactly where we were going, we two gypsies were on the move, with wind in our faces and scrunching gravel beneath our turning wheels.

Fortunately, the roads were only slightly damp. We had *no* dust and *no* mud.

We stopped at fish camps on both sides of both ferries, but we were unable to buy dried and smoked fish strips. If white fish hadn't been so large we would have bought one just extracted from a net, but we didn't want to be eating fillets for a week.

When the monotony of the northern, flat delta-land and short trees and scrub bushes was suddenly broken by the Richardson Mountains appearing on the horizon, we both cheered, looked at each other, and self-consciously laughed at our feelings.

You can take a BC'er away from mountains, but you can't take the love of mountains from a BC'er. It feels so good to be away from the flat, boring MacKenzie Delta.

Moosehide Gathering

Moosehide is more a bi-annual gathering than a gathering place.

A jigging contest, with amazing foot work.

Moosehide is three kilometres down river from Dawson, or Dawson City, and is on uninhabited land owned by First Nations People. (But are they the first? They too have myths of giants — possibly similar to two biblical references — who lived in their lands before they did.) Every two years all Indians and others are invited to come and celebrate together.

A Moosehide Gathering was a truly unique experience for ourselves. I encourage all who can to join in the alcohol- and drug-free summer festivities and activities in 2000, 2002 and beyond.

They will be more than a picnic, more than good food, more than a learning activity, more than spiritual, theological and psychological discussions, more than drum-making and hide tanning, more than listening to jokes and stories and history, more than just fun and games, more than just sitting around a fire, more than music and dancing and jigging contests, more than a give-away, more than all those things together. It could be a four day renewal and re-creation.

A maker of Caribou-skin drums.

It could also be boring unless you are able to slow down your pace of life. The choice is yours.

A free boat service runs on demand and will take you quickly to and from the site. It is available virtually any time from 10 am to 1 am daily. Or one can take an hour hike from Dawson over a ridge and through the Moosehide Slide along a narrow but not especially dangerous trail. You cannot drive to Moosehide.

On the second day Liz and I proudly canoed down the Yukon River — several times almost suffering the ignominity of being turned around by gentle but persistent swirling water — and arrived like those brave voyageurs of old. That evening we loaded our canoe and ourselves in a motorboat for the return journey to Dawson's water front. We were told that the far side of this river flowed slowly but we both realized that by the time we novices got to the other side, we would be halfway down to Forty-Mile.

Visitors may camp overnight during the Gathering if they bring their own tents and eating utensils. Some chairs are always available but much of your time could be spent on blankets or on grass. You can also bring your own food or buy meals and snacks. Supper is provided at no cost although a few volunteers will be asked to do many dishes.

If you manage to get a schedule of events, take its listings of activities with a grain of salt, or better yet, with warm, deep-fried bannock and home-made blueberry jam from a pickle jar. Many of the 1998 activities didn't happen because the persons who were to organize or lead the activities never made it to Moosehide. And if activities do occur, they probably won't happen when scheduled.

But so what? Do you want to eat at exactly 6:00 pm or when you are hungry? Take time to smell the roses, relax and float along with the flow. After all you could be there for one, two, three or four days and there is ample time to get involved, or not, as you wish.

Moosehide Gathering is an unhurried and entertaining way to learn more of the customs of Indian Tribes from across Canada. It is certainly different.

A lone cook deep-frying delicious Bannock on a wood-fired stove.

Imitation Bannock

Following is a recipe for genuine Bannock.

Get up in the morning, realize that you forgot to bring your cookbook, then proceed to make pancakes from scratch from memory. Let's see, you'll need flour, salt, sugar, egg and milk. Baking powder? Remember to use at least twice as much flour and half as much water as you think the recipe called for.

When you realize that your pancakes are not quite what you expected, add some bacon fat or a drop of cooking oil and enough water so that the mixture will at least flow off your spoon. Ladle the mixture onto a hot cast iron frying pan; "hot" means that water droplets perform a frenzied dance before they evaporate. Brown both sides. If in doubt about the middle being cooked, slice your two-inch thick bannock into two slices then fry them with the insides down.

Depending on how much oil is in the Bannock batter, you might have to pour a little more oil into the frying pan. Carefully! Or you could use butter.

Pour a warm cup of coffee from your blackened coffee pot. You know, the kind where you scoop regular grind coffee into a metal basket sitting on top of a hollow pole immersed in cold water, which boils after a few minutes of sitting above a propane flame. Add nothing, sugar, whale-oil powder, milk, cream, black rum or whatever suits your taste.

Slide your bannock onto your plate; don't drop it or it might crack the dish. Lather on gobs of butter and spoonfuls of jam. Sharpen you knife. Eat heartily.

Aahh, oomm, so good. Once again you've snatched victory from the jaws of defeat.

Seriously, bannock is made many different ways in different parts of Canada. It all depends where it is made and by whom.

Some are exceptionally dry and heavy, some are moist and light, some are in-between. Some are deep-fried, some are baked in an oven, some are fried in a frying pan or directly on the top of a wood stove. (No no. Not a stove made out of wood. They don't last too long and you can't use them more than once. I meant a metal stove that burns wood for fuel.)

If you follow the recipe above, you will have created genuine Bannock, not an imitation. Remember, no matter how yours turns out, you can say a Canadian told you how to make it.

Klondike Highway -Stewart Crossing to Carmacks

Sign warns of danger of hitting mountain sheep/goats on the highway.

Two pairs of kayakers of oriental background touring Canada's wilderness.

The campground at Minto Landing on the Yukon River is no longer part of Parks Canada. It has become merely a large field in which to park. There are no services available and there is no charge.

Yukon means Big River. Our Big River boat tour to Fort Selkirk, which began and ended near Minto Resorts, was wonderfully calming.

Four hours of someone else driving a twenty-four foot skiff along a scenic river on a sunny day has to be relaxing. Listening to our knowledgeable sharp-eyed guide, and Tim from Tennessee, we idled quietly down the Yukon, walked among and into the many buildings of the fort for a couple of hours, then sped back upriver wrapped up in our own thoughts and the noise of two 40 HP outboards at full throttle.

Water levels in all rivers are lower than usual this year. Our captain made twice as many turns as there are bends in shallow Yukon River. How he could tell where the deep (2 - 3 m) channels were amazed me, until I realized that he probably does this trip at least twice a week. Three times he slipped the engines' transmissions into neutral and coasted over gravel bars.

We never saw any bears, moose or mosquitoes, but we did see a young porcupine struggling its way back up a crumbling river bank, a peregrine falcon, three mature bald eagles and one nest, three small herds of Dall sheep, several marsh hawks (northern harriers), a few ravens of course, a gaggle of straggling, spread-out canoeists, and at least two oriental kayakers. (Why are they called kayakers and not kayakists?)

We also saw clouds of dust wheeling and reeling above a very long sand bar in the river.

The restored log buildings of Fort Selkirk look great from the outside. But on the inside they looked deserted, forlorn and messily empty. Disappointing and sad.

But the real shocker came when Liz and I discovered that some of the construction techniques and types of material had also been used in our parents' houses.

Yukon's history of its white settlers is so very recent. Imagine building and living in log houses in 1939. Building of the Alaska Highway, 80% in British Columbia and Yukon, a mere fifty-five years ago really was a major turning point in Yukon affairs. It led to more roads and highways, which eventually caused the demise of steam-driven river boats and paddlewheelers in the mid 1950's. Dawson didn't have highway access to Whitehorse until thirty some years ago, which was four years after we were happily married.

Fortunately Yukon still has lots and lots of pristine land, lakes, rivers and creeks to which tourists cannot drive, and many where tourists and businesses have never even been.

A thin layer of white ash dated at 700 AD lies beneath an even thinner layer of twelve hundred years of soil. Amazing. This white layer really feels like damp ash from a camp fire a day after water was poured on it to ensure that it was out. (I'm going by memory because we have had no campfires for several weeks due to hot weather and extreme fire hazard, as evidenced by fires such as the ones at Mayo and Stewart Crossing.)

Five Fingers Rapids was a disappointment for us because we didn't walk down the stairs to the lookout beside the rapids. Today we felt lazy, and not even the reward of hot dogs and ice cream could tempt us down and down to riverside, then back up and up those many steps. The early evening sun was reflecting off the rippling surface and masking the tumbling white water. Although the water looked benign, the author of "Yukon" strongly warns that canoeists and kayakers MUST use the safe and easy East channel. Both experienced and novice boaters and rafters have lost their lives in the other channels.

These firefighters were in Stewart Crossing before and while forest fires raged around their home town.They wanted to go home.

Faro

Faro may be a live ghost town, but it was deserted when we visited it on Sunday.

Katie at the Interpretive Centre deserves Employee of the Month or an Outstanding Host Award ... she answered completely all of my many questions but one, always with a smile. She also went out of her way to find enough different sizes of T-shirts and sweatshirts for all our children, in-laws and their children. Later we received a letter answering the question "What is the difference between sternwheelers and paddlewheelers?"

Faro's dump (land fill) used to be known as The Place to go to view Grizzly bears. No longer. Federal regulations now require that the dump has to be encircled with an electric fence to keep animals out, thereby preventing destruction of animals that had become dependent on, and possibly aggressive about, that particular food source.

Both the Public Library — closed Sundays and Mondays — and the Faro Campus of Yukon College have free Internet access.

Talking with a mechanic (no, I don't need his services but I sure do need his fishing expertise) I discovered why I was not catching any grayling. Unlike jack and pike and pickerel, grayling have tiny wee mouths. I need a very small hook on a #0 spinner. I'll visit the hardware store and buy appropriate fishing tackle.

I'll even get some plain #4 or #8 hooks and some bait, then arrange to have them float a half metre (20") above lake bottom and wait for hungry rainbow trout to swim by and be tempted. This seems like a lazy way to fish, something like Ron Englishtuk sleeping on a river bank with a string tied around his big toe. But if it works, butter will be sizzling in a cast iron frying pan before the gills stop moving.

It was suggested that at any time of the day fishing off the second bridge on Faro's Blind Creek, or from nearby creek sides, would yield a grayling or two. We drove down the described gravel narrow road past the first bridge, came to a T-junction and turned to the right which took us past a dozen brown pigs then a farm entrance (No Trespassing. Keep Out). We never did find the second bridge nor any grayling.

We did see several salmon. But we weren't allowed to fish for them. We could only look at them in a weir set up by Canada's Wildlife personnel to count the number of fish returning to spawn. Two weeks earlier someone had sneaked in at night and netted at least three dozen. Now that's a great way to reduce the quantity of future fingerlings and fish. Somebody is really, really stupid!

On the way back, we detoured to another road and went to a lookout with a view of where some Fanin sheep might be. None were. "This cross between Dall and rock sheep might be there in the winter." said another local Faro-ite later.

"Whiskers" (a name not found in any book or on any map we've read) is supposed to be a large lake just before Ross River. We were guaranteed it would produce some tasty trout, even when fishing close to shore. Another local told me that there were no fish of any kind in Whiskers this year. Being unable to find Whiskers, we'll never know who was correct.

Of the two restaurants still in town, we choose Sally's Roadhouse for an afternoon lunch because there were more vehicles there than at "Cranky Frank's." The owner's daughter, home from studying pre-med in Queens University, served us lots of good Chinese food for a reasonable price. If we hadn't been warned that the Roadhouse would look as if it were closed, we wouldn't have gone in. Notwithstanding the lack of ambiance, that would have been a shame.

Campbell Highway - Eagle Bluff

We'd topped up with gasoline at Carmacks, drove back up to a road-side sign to find out what the Tantulus Butte was all about, then headed south-east on the Campbell Highway.

Both Liz and I were surprised how quickly the scenery changed. Every highway seems to have its own style of beauty.

We remarked that the Alaska Highway - from Junction 37 (Stewart-Cassiar and Alaska Highways) to Whitehorse and from Beaver Creek to Tok - is probably the least exciting and certainly the least spectacular of northern highways we've seen.

Reading more of the descriptions in the Milepost, we both think that publication is *much too cautious in its descriptions of roads*. For example, "Steep, narrow, winding road south to Little Salmon Lake campground" could easily be navigated by underpowered 40' buses or Class A's. Once there, drivers would find several sites large enough for vehicles with three slides or tip-outs. We met a couple from Germany (she was Spanish) there in their rented Class C, enjoying the solitude and the fishing. Unfortunately, temperatures were low enough to require woollen sweaters and jackets when outside.

The north is a truly vast expanse of scenery. All highways have fair to good to fantastic scenery separated by kilometres and kilometres of "the same old thing" or long stretches of "can't see the landscape because of the trees." And yet, even if it is monotonous at times, driving north of 60 is so much more enjoyable than driving from crowded cities to nearby towns.

Green leaves are starting to turn to yellow, orange and red and hills are becoming a Joseph's Coat of many colours. This is

150

Eagle Bluff - how would you like your home with this as a front yard view?

a very pleasant change from previously unlimited vistas of greens and blues. These changes have been brought about by colder temperatures and very dry conditions. Liz thinks that August might be the best (that is, most colourful) month to visit north of 60. Maybe so, but warm autumn clothing becomes essential.

We have started to dread going south.

Lordie, lordie! After places like Tsiigehtchic, Fort McPherson, Pelly Landing, Mayo and Keno, we now think of Carmacks with its population of 489 as a big community. After all, it has two service stations and two restaurants.

We have heard each other comment on coming back next year, and the heck with our plans to start a five-year, one-way, coast-to-coast trek across Canada. Blasphemy of blasphemies, we are even wondering how beautiful a sub-arctic winter would be, and could we survive one.

After listening to the 7 pm news on CBC as we drove on an extremely well maintained asphalt, gravel and chip-seal highway to Ross River, my stomach informed me that it was getting empty. When I checked, Liz's stomach was sending out the same message. So we parked in dust-free Eagle Bluff pullout, overlooking a bend in the green (not silty-white) Yukon River with a sandbar surrounded by sparkles of scintillating sunlight, and began preparing a simple supper of hot dogs and noodle soup.

I opened the driver's-side outside storage compartment, took out levelling blocks, water hose, box of nuts and bolts, a wayward leather glove, and, finally, our cast-iron barbeque. Leaving all that on the ground, I went back inside our motorhome and extracted the folding picnic table given to us by a friend and set it up behind our RV, out of a cool wind.

Then I went and got our propane bottle from behind the passenger's seat and set it on one end of that strong but frail-looking table. Then back to the other side to get our barbeque. Once again back inside to get safety matches then back to the barbeque and, voilá, orange and blue flames roared up and around a dusty grill.

Back inside once more to get some paper towel to clean a warm grill, I was handed four frozen wieners. Using full propane flow through an enlarged jet and maximum heat, those 'chiens chaudes' were almost instantly black on the outside and still frozen-white on the inside.

Turning the flame down to a mere whisper of its previous self, I slowly turned and heated each of those wieners until all of them were at the same tongue-tingling temperature.

I might be inefficient, but I am effective.

Liz arrived with a tray full of condiments, cheese, tomatoes, fried onions, warm buns, boiling soup, and cutlery. We ate like a king and queen sitting on their balcony overlooking the pristine land of their private holdings.

Hunger really is the best sauce. So too is having lots of time to spend with one's Dearest Love surrounded by spectacular scenery under a warm golden sun. That has got to be one of the better ways to truly enjoy a royal repast of hot dogs.

For entertainment during our supper, a raven spread its unmoving wings and slowly soared higher and higher on the breeze blowing up the valley wall. It then circled us three times before performing four barrel rolls looking for eagles and hawks above before it flew away in search of other sources of food. A hawk did soar by minutes later and it too left empty-taloned.

Also, a couple of helicopters and one water bomber flew overhead and onto yet another forest fire.

(Never let fear of forest fires keep you from driving through nature. Even if you're not as out of shape as I nor as rounded, it is extremely unlikely you would be stopped and asked to help. If there is real danger, roads will be closed. If there is no danger, you could collect some interesting pictures and maybe have a few exciting stories to tell your stay-at-home friends.)

With supper done, I opened the RV's large rear compartment and got out our folding chairs while Liz got our paperbacks and readied insulated cups of hot coffee. We ignored bemused or startled looks by occasional drivers passing by as we sat and read. Eventually the sun set and turned white clouds to pumpkin-orange then wild-rose pink while blue sky changed to purple then black.

No doubt about it. This is a young Caribou.
But check the size of its feet!

After putting everything back except for a few dishes in the sink, we closed curtains, climbed into bed, and turned off the overhead light.

Liz is a woman who had no trouble sleeping in later-afternoon or early-morning sunlight when the sun never set. In this almost-dark, she immediately reached over and turned off the dull display of our wall-mounted digital clock because it was too bright. Fall has arrived.

Muncho Lake

I must continue to check those long paragraphs in the Milepost for [advertisement]. Generally speaking if the description of services seem exceptionally good, the last word probably is [advertisement]. This means it is a paid commercial written by or for the business owners.

Gasoline was considerably cheaper in service stations at the north end of Muncho Lake.

It's great to be camping again and not just travelling miles and miles of highway. We'll be staying here in the provincial park for at least two days. (Province or Territory, British Columbia or Yukon? The Alaska Highway weaves its way through both so often we have trouble knowing where we are.) Yukon's Campbell Highway had some great places for camping, fishing and canoeing, but the weather was overcast with intermittent rain, windy and bone-chilling cold. Which is a pity, because we would have liked to have spent more time where travellers were few and the land, beaches and lakes were almost undisturbed except for campgrounds. Ah well, we have to take the bad with the good. What an wonderful time we've had so far!

Right now, it is hot and sunny, almost sun-tanning weather.

Liz and I saw a female Stone Sheep, but we both thought it was a Mountain Goat because of her short horns. Sheep live in the Sentinel mountains, goats live across the lake in the Terminal mountains.

Muncho Lake is said to be 500 ft (160 m) deep in one place, and is fed from underwater rivers from the Sentinel Mountains. All those seemingly dry river beds of stone and rock we've seen from the highway are actually rivers of flowing water covered by stones.

Today there are few fish in Muncho Lake. Possibly, probably, years ago one or more fishermen used live sucker bait to entice those huge trophy fish we've heard about, but some of those suckers got away. Now they scavenge the eggs of all the other fish, which effectively have been wiped out in this lake and in adjoining lakes and rivers. Too bad. But if the suckers weren't there, I wonder if thousands of visiting fisher-persons would have done the same thing?

We took a forty-five minute boat tour, but it really was more of a narrative about the history and geology of the area. We'd already seen the same mountains and shores from our canoe. I enjoyed the descriptions and discussion, but a young German honeymooning couple didn't know enough English to follow along.

Adventurous? Hike or drive to the microwave tower above Summit Lake.

They were camped at the same provincial park as we but they never lit a fire. It wasn't until they left that I realized that they might not have had an axe or hatchet in their rental motor-home. I should have gone over and asked them if they wanted some kindling and split logs. Hindsight is wonderful, bah.

Smith River Falls

Smith River Falls, BC was a great spot to visit, even if we had to drive three or four kilometres of good dirt road and had to plod up and down stairs and saunter along a kilometre-long walk in the woods.

We camped overnight in a small inclined parking lot. Another vehicle was parked near a break in the trees that over-looked the falls. A roar of falling water was barely discernible.

While we were there, several people came, fished and left. Using barbless hooks, fish that were caught could be returned with little injury. The ones we saw were quite small.

Smith River Falls is also a great spot for pictures, especially when the afternoon sun shines into the canyon and on the mist from the falls to produce a colourful rainbow. The first day I tried to get a picture of Liz with her fishing pole pointing at the 'pot at the end of the rainbow', but by the time she was ready the sun was behind clouds. Or when the rainbow was there, her rod was in the wrong position. I didn't get a picture before the sun moved out of the chasm, leaving us in shadows.

However, next day we were a bit more prepared. We arrived earlier than before, tied a stone to Liz's fishing line so she could pull and bend the fibre-glass fishing pole, and positioned ourselves up to take pictures.

An abandoned service station, another victim of the smooth, paved, two(sometimes four) lane Alaska Highway.

Being completely automatic, Liz's camera produced pictures with matte-black shadows and a rainbow, or bright, colourful pictures of her and the falls but no rainbow. I used my decades-old manual camera – no batteries, no electronics, a dusty view finder, and a lens and shutter assembly that had been boiled in Central American water and dried in a propane oven to remove dust and oil – and managed to set the f-stop and shutter speed just right to get a reasonable picture.

Having a fishing pole and hooks handy, we were tempted to cast a few times into the pool at the bottom of the falls. But I didn't have a BC fishing licence.

Liard Hot Springs, BC

Today is the first time in a month of cool overcast that Liz and I have been "summer warm" when getting out bed. Our furnace didn't turn itself on in the early morning and a golden sun is shining in a nearly cloudless sky.

If you want gasoline, drive a couple of kilometres to the Lower Liard Resort by the Liard River bridge and save two or three cents a litre. Also stop in at the restaurant which was built during the 1940's and dragged to its present location in the 50's. Rustic and charming, with great cookies and good coffee.

After parking in the large lot of the Liard Hot Springs Provincial Park, or setting up in the nearby campground, just slip into or bring along your bathing gear and head for those two pools with a towel over your arm or shoulder. Don't even bother going to check out the Hot Springs first, as we did. Unless you like to walk for exercise, you'll be wasting your time because the water will look so steamingly inviting you'll merely walk back along that half kilometre of boardwalk and get your swimming gear anyway. Mind you, the walk does pass through some interesting land and, sometimes, by intriguing birds.

We never got to see the prettier Upper Pool because a bear was wandering about in the area. That walkway gate was locked and a Park Ranger was patrolling the area with a rifle and "bangers" (no, not British sausages, but very loud noise makers) to scare away any nearby animals. We were told that sometimes the bear would play and soak in the pool. Whoever said animals are stupid has never watched or studied them very much. In a similar train of thought, I suspect the 'bangers' are only effective two or three times.

Another ranger wanted to use dogs – dogs and bears seem to be natural enemies – instead of bangers because he figured that the sharp retort might actually attract bears from some distance away. Hunters' rifles make noise, and after hunters leave animal remains are often left on the ground, which makes for easy scavenging. Animals, like humans, are basically lazy and always looking for a free lunch.

When I put on my bathing suit I realized that my skin was ghostly white, no tan anywhere. At least I wouldn't be the only one of that colour in the pool. Mind you, most of the people actually in the water were red.

The geothermally-heated water is wonderfully hot, or warm, depending upon where you go in the pool. When you arrive at the Lower Pool you are near the spring where almost boiling water drips and flows out of the rock. Trying to get into the pool at the first set of stairs might be a bit of a shock. Even at the second it took us a long time to get in. Later on we realized that we could have slipped in easily by the little dam, then worked our way into hotter water as our bodies acclimatized to the heat. Young children gravitate to the cool waters below the dam.

You've read it here first. I'm about to explain a trick or a technique to get you right into the hottest water without being boiled red like a delicious Prince Edward Island lobster.

We all know that hot water, like hot air, rises. At Liard this means the hottest water is on the top and the coolest is near the bottom. So ... when you get in the water, bend down and stir up the water near the sandy bottom and stand in the disturbed cooler water. With that technique, arms moving in vertical circles, you should be able to slowly work your way into hotter and hotter water without feeling it. I made it to the very hottest spot immediately next to the source of the surface water, and next to the eighty-two year old man who had told me how to do it.

We were the only two in that part of the Lower Pool. If there had been more people in the pool there would probably have been a few more at the hot end. All those arms and legs would have stirred and mixed the top and bottom waters and more people would have ventured into the area of hot, but not scalding hot, water.

By the way, Liz and I stayed only one afternoon, then went on our way. However, we came back a couple of days later. Our first visit had been so enjoyable, we wanted to repeat the experience. We're really glad we did. Muscles relax and the troubles of the world and the dust of highways disappear like the mist above the hot water when soaking in soothing warm water.

Mineral Lick

We almost missed the turnoff which leads to a huge, level parking lot and the circular or loop walk to the Mineral Lick. If a car hadn't been parked (abandoned?) at the turnoff we probably would have driven by. Glad we didn't.

This was another great spot for photographs just before and during sunset. Three pink and charcoal and mauve clouds, multi-hued deciduous and coniferous greens, deep blue sky and azure river, cliffs of sharply delineated, startlingly-white rock flour, all these were waiting to be photographed. Sadly, neither of us had brought a camera.

Supposedly animals come to this area for a taste of salty minerals. We saw one squirrel.

But we returned another day and took a picture or two. I missed a really fabulous shot waiting for the clouds to get even brighter and redder from an iron-smelter sun setting behind a ridge of gun-metal-blue mountains. But by the time I realized they were getting greyer and snapped a quick picture, all that was left was the promise of what could-have-been. Darn.

Ah well, maybe I can buy a postcard.

Fort Nelson

A really good day is one when you can help a bicyclist who had pushed his bike on a flat tire for 10 km (6 mi) under a hot afternoon sun, and also provide gasoline for a grubby old converted bus whose driver miscalculated distances by 5 km under the incorrect impression that gas would be cheaper in a city.

You know you've been away from civilization for a long time when you look forward with mixed emotions — dread and anticipation — to getting to a big city of 4,000 people.

Fort Nelson has two large grocery stores, several service centres, RV parks, an excellent and inexpensive private museum, a golf course, several RV dump locations, a public library with a paperback book exchange and Internet access, three fast food outlets, two automotive parts' dealers, and an auto wrecker. Prices are definitely lower than what we have been experiencing in the last few weeks, except for gasoline which was cheaper at the northwest end of Muncho Lake.

Fort Nelson has a lot of traffic, stop signs, a few concrete triangles at intersections, and two frontage roads next to the highway. I have had to remind myself not to stop in the middle of a road or street to ask directions, and always to use my signal lights when turning onto another road or into a parking space.

Liz walked into one grocery store and proceeded to spend twice as much as expected. The produce section was filled with so many fresh vegetables and fruits, the bakery had so many kinds of bread, and the rows of shelves were filled with so many cans and boxes. When she went into the second grocery store, she again proceeded to spend twice as much as expected. Same reasons.

We'll have to come back and visit Fort Nelson. We left for the Northwest Territories — since there is only one, why is the name pluralized? — immediately after I spent two windy days in a paved lot rewiring our motorhome.

The first problem was a noisy heater fan that stopped turning just because a groaning bearing seized. This phenomenon seems peculiar to older Ford vehicles. I searched through a couple of dozen wrecked and salvaged trucks and cars before I found one that still had its fan motor. That van had been dragged in three days earlier. Actually, I had found another fan partially removed, but the vehicle was so badly damaged that the fan could not be extracted from its twisted plastic and metal housing.

The second problem was our headlights. (You might recall that I'd had this problem months ago, at the beginning of our trip, but because we never drove at night and days got longer and longer until nights were non-existent, I never got around to fixing the lights. There was too much else to do and see, which is a standard excuse for a procrastinator extraordinaire.) If both were connected and/or high beams were selected, the alternator went into overdrive immediately prior to a 15 Amp fuse blowing. I solved that problem by tearing out two electrical relays

160

and a tangled mouse nest or drunken spider web of at least 10 m (30 ft) of blue, yellow, green, black, white, striped, plastic, cloth-covered, 10 A, 30 A and 60 A wire, five metres of black electrical tape, two fuse holders, and a damaged trailer-connecting plug. (Why did anything electrical work at all? The person who owned this motorhome before us might have done good work, but it was sloppy.) I rewired four horns, backup lights, yellow fog lights, and high intensity halogen driving lights. The halogens worked independently of the headlights after that, which was useful. In fact, everything works well.

[Wrong. Four days later, driving at dusk for the first time in many months, I realized that several minutes after selecting high beams both headlights systematically began turning themselves off, then briefly on, then off, etc. I eventually diagnosed the problem as an over-heated dashboard switch with some type of automatically resetting circuit breaker. I replaced the switch and *now* the headlights work fine.]

After fixing the lights, I added a second 30 A connection from our deep cycle RV27 battery directly to the distribution panel under the dinette. This is in parallel with the original 5 m of wiring, which allows the alternator to charge an RV battery located some 3 m away and which supplies power via a very circuitous (pardon the pun) route through the engine compartment and up and back along the frame. Voilá. The overhead lights shine twice as bright as before, and now both water pump and furnace fan can kick in without dimming the lights.

Liz did manage to drag me away from my fun, my break from days of driving.

The tourist information centre, housed in the town's curling rink this year, will be shutting down at the end of August. This seems to be unseasonably early, but then again, I haven't spent an autumn this far north. Maybe enough tourists don't travel here in September to warrant the expense of providing excellent service to visitors.

The main building of the Museum — if it has a name I was not made aware of it — is a marvellous collection of mid-to-late forties and early fifties highway and military equipment.

Another building is filled with working antique and vintage cars, and yet another imitates an old logger's cabin, except that it is too big, too full, and too tidy.

Initially Fort Nelson was Mile Zero of the Alcan (Alaska Canadian) Project, which produced both the Alaska Highway (80% in Canada) and the Canol pipeline from Norman Wells. Later, Mile 0 was relocated to Dawson Creek. To find out why, you'll have to visit the museum or read about the history of the Alcan.

You can buy postcards containing a four-line verse about travellers on the Alaska Highway, written by Anonymous. If you want to read all of that poem, and discover the intriguing modern story of when and why it was written and the name of the author, visit The Museum.

Even when 16 mm 1940's films extolling building the Alaska Highway are colourised and transferred to video, they still have terrible music. My, my. How some of the techniques of propaganda have changed. So much for "the truth, the whole truth, etc."

For me the really unnerving part of the museum was seeing equipment that I have used as a child and as a teenager. I've driven mates to one of those old caterpillars and that Cockshutt tractor, used gas lanterns, even played with an old non-superhetrodyne radio. My Gosh, at fifty-seven, am I an antique too?

I offered to buy a dilapidated, incomplete 1941 Johnson 5 HP outboard — with its own gas tank surrounding its magneto and started by pulling on a rope wrapped around a pulley — to use as spare parts for the one that I own. Mine still runs even after resting on the bottom of Waskiseu Lake three times. I own it because it was manufactured in the same year that I was born, and because I could use it when I could carry it. I used it a lot. I particularly wanted that three-bladed propeller and its shear pin. My offer was refused, twice, graciously.

At the edge of The Museum parking lot, there is a dump station and, when we were there, fresh drinking water. I strongly encourage you to fill your minds and empty your RV at the same place. Plan on spending at least two hours in The Museum and get a feeling for what happened there in the 1940's.

Sadly, we will not be going south on the Alaska Highway to Dawson Creek. I hear that portion is beautiful but under repair, which doesn't bother us as much as it does some others. However, even with so much time we can't see everything. Instead, we're heading for the Northwest Territories via the Liard Trail, an appropriately named highway.

Liard Trail

The first 40 km of the Liard Trail in BC is a difficult stretch of pot-rattling washboard and potholed gravel highway — it appears to be minimally maintained — that contains several "sand traps." Sand traps are breaks in the highway surface that contain soft sand and are usually spring-and-shock-testing holes if entered at speeds greater than 50 km/hr (30 mph). After that first hour of tortuous driving, the rest of this highway is fair to excellent gravel, especially in the Northwest Territories.

Dyed porcupine quill weaving

But as always a driver must be ready to slow down. There is one spot marked "DIP" which could be bone crushing at high speed in a long motorhome. Nonetheless, there were several moments when I had to force myself to slow down to below 80 km/h. We were the slowest vehicle on the highway. We were passed by at least four trucks and one car pulling a trailer.

Now I know at least one reason why Territorial law says you must travel with headlights on. After a spell of hot, dry weather logging trucks can kick up so much dust that you would never see another vehicle coming at you unless they had their lights on. And its driver wouldn't see you buried in thick clouds of dust if your lights weren't on.

After a spell of heavy rain you might have trouble seeing a mud-camouflaged vehicle that blends into a dirty-brown background.

There is little picturesque scenery on this highway, although one does get to drive on the world's longest Acrow (Bailey) bridge over the Nelson River.

But it is an inexpensive way for us to get into the NWT from the BC Hwy 97 portion of the Alaska Highway. Because we want to drive most of the NWT highways and roads, the Liard Trail saves us a lot of backtracking. The distance from Fort Nelson to Fort Simpson and Yellowknife is 1270 km, and via Dawson Creek and Peace River is 2843 km. Our record keeping indicates that our old motorhome with its huge and powerful 7.5 L engine manages to eke out 2.83 km/L of regular gasoline. Because average fuel cost on this part of the Deh Cho Connection was 0.70/L we saved $390.

Fort Liard has an interesting and well stocked craft shop. A visit there is worthwhile, even if you are just looking.

Blackstone River Territorial Campground is certainly worth a visit, and possibly an overnight stay. See if you can figure out how to turn on the showers-without-taps in the late-1980's technological marvel of a washroom, without getting your head wet. Do visit the interpretive centre, and plan to spend at least a half hour there. We spent an hour reading slowly and asking lots of questions about what was in the various drawers. From pictures we've seen, visitors can get a beautiful view of Nahanni Butte if it isn't hidden by overcast or low clouds.

MacKenzie Highway - Fort Simpson

We miscalculated our travelling time and our remaining funds.

We could have spent more time in those wonderful, frequently tourist-free, lakeside campgrounds on the Campbell Highway in southeast Yukon. If we had parked a couple of more days, that period of cold, grey overcast and generally unpleasant weather we were experiencing would have passed. Ah well.

As it is, we are in Fort Simpson marking time, until next month's budget lets us travel again. Not that being in Fort Simpson is bad, it's not, but we would have preferred being by a lake instead of a river. The treed territorial campground is pleasant, but we choose to park on the river bank overlooking both MacKenzie and Liard rivers and bask in warm sunlight.

The footpath on the left as you drive into the village will eventually extend all the way to the subdivision 3 ½. (It's 3 1/2 miles from the village centre.) It is being built to provide an alternative to dangerous highway pedestrian traffic.

Driving east on the highway from the Visitor Information Centre, take the very first left turn, then right turn about 200 m later, to get to the Territorial Campground. In addition to at least 20 roomy sites, drinking water and sewage disposal are available. Also the village of Fort Simpson subsidizes drinking water at Yanny's (Esso Gasoline and tire repair). This water is very soft, use only a little soap when doing your dishes.

People here use abbreviations to describe locations. JMR is Jean Marie River, RBTM is River Between Two Mountains, Willy is the small settlement immediately on the left after the bridge crossing over Willow Lake River.

This Sunday was the 140th anniversary of the introduction of Christianity to this area. A small ecumenical celebration was held in the Papal Grounds, followed by a potluck lunch. Liz and I were made to feel very welcome by those we talked and ate with.

Good weather prevails, so I was talked into playing on a six-hole golf curse with sand-greens. [A previous word was either a typographical error or a Freudian slip, I meant to write "course".] I think Liz wanted some time to herself. But I had a great game anyway.

I brought only a five, a nine and a putter with me because of space constraints in our motorhome. Every swing of my two irons was perfect. I learned quickly how to putt on sand. I was relaxed. For a time I played with John M. who began playing only last year and was already blasting drives beyond 300 yards, and I didn't even care. Almost all my long shots were straight down the fairway and my approach shots were on or near the green. It was a great afternoon.

That evening Liz joined me, and she asked if she could hit a ball or two. This from a woman who had spent a year and a half driving balls into the ground because she was afraid she might hit the grass with her club, who once managed to hit a ball farther than 50 yds (m), who once managed to putt less than three times on a green, and who finally got so frustrated she gave away her clubs.

She too did alright, especially considering she was using my clubs which are much too long for her. The majority of her shots rose into the air and landed on fairways at least sixty yards away. Her approach shots were in the general direction of the greens (sands?). She also enjoyed herself.

Next day I was playing a second round when the rain started. Playing as well or better than yesterday I continued to golf even as the rain become a downpour. But I had to quit on the 11th tee when my five iron and its slippery leather grip flew out of my wet hands and went almost as far as the golf ball. Between rivulets of water running off the peak of my cap, I watched both land on the fairway. Fortunately both were several yards closer to our parked motorhome. Stupid rain!

Fort Simpson does not yet have public access to the Internet. However, I did manage to convince a government employee to let me use his computer. There was no e-mail of consequence.

There are two craft shops in Fort Simpson. Lynx River Craft Shop retails local leather and birchbark crafts and video rentals after 5 pm, Nats'enelu manufactures handmade crafts for distribution locally, nationally and internationally.

Cooper Barging Service was unable to ship us and our motorhome to Wrigley (they seldom go there any more), Norman Wells or Hay River. Their time schedules and ours weren't even close. Besides, people are not allowed to travel on barges, and they didn't need another deck hand or qualified line handler or roustabout, nor a cook or nurse on the tug. Darn.

We discovered that over the years many, many people have asked about barging motorhomes and trailers up or down the MacKenzie River. But no Canadian business seems to want to investigate this source of income and/or spend the money necessary to make such travel safe. Can you imagine what some people would pay to be part of a caravan of 24 rigs on the inaugural barge trip from Hay River to Fort Simpson to Inuvik, or Inuvik to Fort Simpson to Hay River?!! Or to be one of the select few each year who were chosen to experience a once-a-summer barge sailing up and down the MacKenzie?! Maybe tour operators of Mississippi River excursions would be interested in organizing a MacKenzie River adventure. Who'll do it?

A tree-cleared route for next winter's snow and ice road that allows locals to drive north to Norman Wells.

Upon our return to Fort Simpson from Wrigley, we were picked as "Tourists of the Week" and our picture now graces Fort Simpson's web site. I wonder if we'll still be there when our book is published?

Both Liz and I eagerly returned to the golf course. Sadly, our skills had evaporated. Our two balls hemstitched their way to distant greens, often followed by displaced clumps of dirt and grass. Time was spent in wilderness seldom visited by man or woman. Sand greens were covered with dozens of lines and ball tracks. By the time we finished, there were more burrs on our socks than there were patterns. And to add icing to the cake, so to speak, mosquitoes flew in from the four corners of the earth to sample our blood lines. It was not a good evening.

A Song

Words by Reverend David Lehmann, Anglican Minister, Fort Simpson -- sung to tune of Barrett's Privateers.

O, the year was 1848. I'm so glad to be on Simpson Isle! When a letter of request came from the Chief, To come to the most beautiful place I've seen.

Chorus: God bless us all! We are called to share the news of Jesus Christ, Our Lord God, He's our friend. We've made Him known throughout the Deh Cho, And pray we may continue so.

The answer came in 1858. I'm so glad to be on Simpson Isle! An Anglican named Hunter left The Pas, to journey to met this Slavey Chief.

Chorus

He made a quick stop at Fort Res. I'm so glad to be on Simpson Isle! There Hunter met Father Gollier, And asked him to come and share the news.

Chorus

After five short days they reached their goal. I'm so glad to be on Simpson Isle! There they began to tell of Jesus And help the people make a choice for Him.

Chorus

Today we celebrate this our history. I'm so glad to be on Simpson Isle! We praise God for His faithfulness, And to be in His continued grace.

Chorus

Wrigley, NWT

We are not sure that the drive to Wrigley is worth the time and expense, especially under a grey overcast sky. The gravel road was in good shape, certainly as good as Yukon's Dempster and Campbell Highways, but there isn't a lot to see except trees and side roads that invariably lead to gravel pits. However, if you want to see a neat and spacious hamlet with community pride in cleanliness, close to a shallow lake ideally suited for brand new novice canoeists, perhaps during an aboriginal gathering, visit cheerful and welcoming Wrigley.

Their municipal campground, with two pull-through and other large sites, can handle a dozen motorhomes, fifthwheels and/or trailers.

Driving north from Fort Simpson, approximately one-half kilometre before the "Wrigley 100 km" sign (at Km 587.7 on the MacKenzie Highway aka Highway 1) are two well maintained roads leading to the left. Both lead to the same gravel pit, which offers a superb view of a wall of towering rock faces called the MacKenzie Mountains. A panoramic lens and distance-filter should produce an adequate picture. [Author's note. My wife thinks they were the Franklin Mountains. Since we don't know in which direction we were facing, the dispute remains unsettled.]

Liz's electronic point-and-shoot camera refused to operate on an expired battery, so I had to use my thirty-year-old camera with manual focus, shutter speed and lens opening. Hopefully both of my pictures can be scanned and combined digitally to produce one panoramic image.

Almost always, when you see a microwave tower close to a highway you can safely bet that you are nearing some kind of summit. This summit provides very clear views of the Mighty MacKenzie; mighty as in wide with a large volume of slowly moving water, not as in roaring and tumbling ferocity.

Smith Creek never freezes. Somewhere there are hot springs, possibly close enough to explore. Ask personnel at Fort Simpson's Information Centre, or check out their website.

Although fishing near to the two bridges is reported to be excellent — jack fish and pike under NWT's longest bridge, grayling at "river between two mountains" — don't bother when river and creek levels are as low as they were in August 1998.

Which reminds me of a story I heard about friends of one of the ferry personnel. These two boaters had gone up river to Trout Lake and were returning after a week of fishing. Unexpectedly ..... of course it wasn't on purpose, they're not masochists. Unexpectedly, they struck a rock, bruised shins and shoulders and almost broke one nose on a suddenly stationary boat windshield. Then they had to spend four exhausting hours grumbling, walking and dragging their boat over rocks and sandbars. A month earlier than usual, river water levels had dropped more than 30 cm (one foot) in one week.

Last night, during three-quarters of an hour while we were playing a word game called Boggle, five or six cars came down the back road to isolated Airport Lake, discovered us and immediately left. An exasperated John finally remarked "Why don't these techno-teenagers drive to the local airport and watch stealth bombers fly by and leave us old timers to watch the submarine races?"

As we snuggled under the comforter and settled into bed, Liz asked "Is there a full moon shining outside? It is so bright." After pulling back the side window curtain, it quickly became obvious that there was no moon. Rather, the sky was filled with three-dimensional gossamer strands of luminescent green that arched from horizon to horizon. Finally! Clear skies and Aurora Borealis.

Quickly we dressed and went outside for a better view. Three then four beautiful ribbons and one planet were so bright that they produced clear reflections on the lake. I tried to take a picture, but could only guess at what setting and time exposure to use.

I wonder how much we missed. Why didn't any of those drivers or passengers knock on our door and tell of the marvellous spectacle. Why did we close all curtains, especially the ones for the window overlooking the lake? Habit and the desire to sleep in next morning, that's why.

Why am I complaining? We saw Canada's spectacular Northern Lights crossing the heavens in a place where no man-made lights diminished their beauty.

Wrigley-Airport Lake

Sitting at our yellow fold-away table on a little-used wharf on the edge of Airport Lake, with a still warm barbeque beside my computer and a T-bone steak inside me, I'm looking over water so calm that I can see leafy-fern and grass-like water weeds a metre below the surface. The sun is just starting to go behind the hill to my left. Three ducks are flying low over the far side of the lake, their reflections following directly below them. Birds and reflections merge just before white water foams as they slide, glide on their watery runwa...

Phwoosh. Phwoosh. A hawk just flew overhead, low enough to startle me. As I look up all I can see is a huge grey and brown egg, then immediately I realize that it has wings. It lands fifty metres away, high in a black spruce next to the water. I think it is watching two nearby ducks diving for their supper in this shallow lake, perhaps with the intent of getting its own evening meal.

The sun continues to disappear. No longer is the far shore basking in yellow sunlight, no longer do old birch trees look like desiccated white bones. The tall grasses behind them are light brown now, not bright gold. Far away green reeds are no longer florescent, but ducks continue to paddle amid their pea-pod-green reflection. Off to my right, sun shining on grey dolomite of the Franklin Mountains spotlights them against the dark green of white spruce in shadow.

The surface reminds me of a mirror of the 19th century with slight imperfections and waves. Small circles are constantly appearing and disappearing as hundreds of water beetles magically walk on this lake's greenish-black and multi-hued-blue and charcoal-grey and pumpkin-pink and dark green surface. The reflected scenery reminds me of a digital bit-map picture that is blown up so large discrete squares and rectangles of colour are discernable.

Sadly there are no large circles caused by pike rushing up out of the lake to feed on those water beetles and other flying insects that have been trapped by surface tension, some drowned and others still fluttering madly to no avail. There are no fish in this lake. At least I didn't catch any while casting from our drifting canoe which always turned slowly to point to my submerged hook. In one spot the shallow bottom might be three metres deep but is probably closer to two; the sand is covered completely with carpets of green, some of which floats its leaves above water.

The sun continues to set. Clouds overhead are darkening in the middle while their westerly edges are painted ivory with hints of dusty rose. Rings around a pair of ducks fifteen metres to the west are silver bangles.

The only sound, besides the clicking of computer keys, is a rare squawk or quiet pop as ducks surface or dive. Even rarer are sounds of beating wings as different pairs of ducks take to flight, leaving behind a line of effervescent bubbles that gradually disappears. The solitary raven has left, taking its seventy-sounds vocabulary with it. Was there really a frog in the far reeds or was the raven pretending to be one? Wait. Did I hear a squirrel or a chipmunk chittering in the trees?

Liz has finished baking. Following her approach which was announced by jarring clomps of wooden sandals on a wooden wharf, she's distracted me by holding a hot chocolate-banana-bran muffin, partially iced with sour cream, in front of my nose. My mouth has started to water.

The sun is below the horizon and I feel the beginnings of a cool damp dusk. Excuse me while I go and get a jacket from inside our warm RV that is currently an aromatic bakery. I think I'll turn on the propane burner beneath our half-full blackened aluminum coffee pot. If Liz doesn't catch me I'll be back with a cookie. If she does catch me I'll be back with two. I might as well be hung for a lion as for a lamb.

Until we meet again, good night from the southern shore of tiny Airport Lake near Wrigley in Canada's Northwest Territories.

MacKenzie Highway- Km 370

370. Exactly.

Kilometre 370 on the MacKenzie Highway is the entrance to Ekali (often pronounced Kelly) Lake, which is a great place to visit if you want peace and quiet, and you have a small boat and like to fish. It's much better than Airport Lake and even more isolated. No radio or TV signals are available unless, perhaps, via satellite.

[Liz just burst out laughing again and was forced to hold her stomach. She thinks it's so funny how I fell into the lake while trying to get into our canoe. You can read about it in her diary, not mine. Drat, it's hard to stay mad, she does have an infectious laugh.]

Any size RV can traverse the half-kilometre road and park and turn around by the lake. There are no services except two log outhouses, one imitating the Tower of Pisa.

On the west end of this lake, about 200 m up a creek, resides a one metre (at least!) jack fish with a #4 Five of Diamonds hook and a few centimetres of 12# line hanging from its lower lip. I forgot to release the ratchet on my spinner so when 'Jack' did a quick about face as he came near our canoe, the rod jerked into the water then sprung back with nothing but line attached. I'm going back today with a Red Devil and see if I can retrieve my hook.

All my hooks are barbless. I'll release 'Jack' once I get my hook back because we can't eat more fish.

Beginning at 4 pm, after two hours of paddling with maybe a half hour of casting and trolling, we caught seven fish and had at least two serious nibbles. Most were shorter than a half metre so I loosened the line and let them shake themselves off the hook, two swallowed the hook and I had to kill them to retrieve them, and three had to be brought in, hook removed, then thrown back into the lake. Liz caught the biggest of the ones we kept.

It turns out that my beloved Liz doesn't like pike. And by the time I've picked out all their tiny y-bones my supper is cold. So I created 'Fish Crisps'.

Fry or steam the meat — filleted or gutted and in the skin — then slowly, painstakingly, carefully remove all the bones. Take those hundreds of small chunks of meat, wet them in a little milk, roll them in cracker crumbs using various crackers for different flavours, brown lots of butter in a very hot frying pan, add the fish and crumbs, stir until butter covers all the meat, then flatten and brown the mixture. Using a spatula or fork, turn the fish over (as best you can) and brown the other side of the pieces. Repeat until all or almost all of the fish is whole-wheat-toast-brown or darker.

Remove your plate (or plates if you have company, spouse, or significant other) from the oven, scoop on the Fish Crisps, add a touch of lemon juice if you wish, put your plate on the table next to a glass of water or white wine, sit down and feast yourself on warm crispy jack fish. Kernel corn and pasta-in-sauce can round out your meal. Say. This sounds so good I'd better go out and get some more pike tomorrow.

After supper we paddled out to the middle of the lake to watch a colourful sunset. We did see it, but only after listening to a loon I saw dive, after watching an eagle fly to a tree close to where a fish was creating huge silvery splashes, and after trying unsuccessfully to sneak up on two beavers swimming in front of their lodge. We have yet to see any ducks on this water, which seems unusual. Liz's camera needs a battery, no pictures for her for awhile.

Wispy, cream-coloured Northern Lights were visible again against a clear sky filled with stars, but not nearly as bright as those Aurora Borealis we saw a couple of nights ago. Oh how we want to see layer upon layer of multi-coloured curtains writhing, waving and dancing like those we saw years ago. I went inside and to bed, and was asleep by the time Liz joined me.

Today we spent 3 then another 3 ½ hours paddling the entire length of Ekali Lake. I caught so many jackfish or pike that the fun stopped. They bit on red and white, florescent orange, and blue and silver hooks and a deep-running green plug. If I'd

174

had others they probably would have chomped on them too. Finally all I could think about was how I was hurting them before releasing them so I stopped casting. All fish being less than 40 cm long, none were big enough to keep.

Our day on the water took us past sunset, which occurred in a nearly cloudless sky. I was more impressed by that globe of melted gold dropping behind black trees followed by the vividness of three flame-and-coal clouds standing out from a pastel blue sky than Liz was by a sky full of colourful clouds.

As we paddled past the beaver lodge under a bright but sunless sky, three beavers were swimming around and around. Even though they dove each time our canoe squeaked or a paddle bumped into the gunwales, two of them came right back up and continued swimming. We had the impression that Momma was teaching her offspring to react to her loud and energetic tail slaps. Dive. Dive. When I slammed my paddle on the water these two beavers placidly continued with their swim. We enjoyed fifteen, maybe twenty, unique minutes of watching this pair of aquatic rodents which were not the least bit frightened of us in our nearby canoe.

We didn't see an eagle tonight, but several ducks unexpectedly flew out of reeds and grass as we silently (we thought) slipped by. We saw only one diaphanous strand of Aurora Borealis shortly after midnight. My hook still adorns Jack beneath the wide leaves of thousands of water lilies in the distant creek.

Good night.

MacKenzie Highway - Sambaa Deh Falls

No hunting is allowed in any provincial and territorial parks, even from the highway.

This is another NWT territorial park that we think you should take an hour or two to visit with your camera.

Of course, if you are in a hurry you can park on the side of the highway, walk down to Trout River then along the top of its rocky ravine, look back to view one of the two waterfalls, and return to your vehicle and depart, all within twenty minutes.

But when you drive in to Sambaa Deh Falls Park drive a little past the tourist centre with its unique birch tree planters, then go in. You'll find hot coffee and a pleasant couple who have lots of information, including the location of a fishing hole with a truly unique entrance way.

Make sure your footwear has good tread, and take your camera. Head for Coral Falls, about 1 ½ km (1 mi) of easy walking. Only if the water level is low, leave the footpath amongst the pine and walk part way on the river bank. If you are as lucky as we were, you might even get out to a rock — carefully — that allows you to take a picture looking up at the falls.

Once back at your RV pick up your fishing pole if you have one, go under the bridge and look at the fossils there, head back up and over the bridge and along the river-side path to the fishing hole. Even if you don't fish take the walk and enjoy the view and fresh air. You'll see a hand-lettered triangular sign tacked on a tree and pointing down into a metre-wide (maybe) crevice. If you look carefully enough, you see a hawser or rope lying on the damp earth (no sun shines directly into this narrow break in the rocks) that slopes not-so-gently towards the river far below. Jump or climb down and proceed downwards. Whoever gets down first should take a picture of the others hanging onto the rope with their shoulders almost brushing against the rock walls.

When you are at the end of your rope, turn right and take the easy walk to the right, which will take you down to the river.

If you go left, you'll still be several metres above the river, but you can cast from there. I did, using a very small Five of Diamonds in hopes of catching small-mouth grayling, but caught another pike which I had to lift up on my nylon elevator, released it from my barbless hook, and throw it back. I think it survived the shock of a 10 m dive.

To the right I wandered to three promising slow-water or backwater bays and cast with abandon, while the Love of My Life read her book. Within thirty minutes I had caught and released eight pike, all much smaller than the ones I got at Ekali Lake. Graylings were non-existent in late August, but are supposedly there in spring and early summer.

When we got back to the campground, stopping to admire the Sambaa Deh Falls and vertical-walled gorge, Liz discovered that the campground hosts love pike but had never managed to catch any in this part of Trout River. I wager they'll be there tomorrow with a tiny spinner instead of flies.

Perhaps you'll be able to give them some freshly-caught fish next time you stop by.

Fort Providence

Although we've been to the mammoth MacKenzie Delta, it took a stop at the Territorial Campground outside of Fort Providence to get a feeling for the immensity of the MacKenzie River. And we saw it at low water level. And we saw it near its beginning, before other NWT rivers emptied into it. The campground is pleasant, with large sites and clean washrooms. Drinking water is available although powered by gravity not an electric pump.

Fort Providence is the administrative headquarters for the MacKenzie Bison Sanctuary. Twice we saw a lone bull on the side of the road, and once a herd of 27 females, calves and yearlings, all near Fort Providence. Swarms and clouds of black flies constantly tormented those bison. Keep your vehicle windows closed when not taking pictures, or have a good fly-swatter handy.

This herd must have created a half dozen sand wallows, in their attempts to scratch their backs and get rid of thousands of pesky black flies.

Black flies also bother people in Fort Providence and surrounding area, including tourists. Question. Are those black flies here because the bison are, or for other reasons?

The price of gasoline was considerably cheaper at the grocery store Yamori near the centre of town than it was close to the highway. And we used their pay phone to check our voice mail.

I visited the computer store and training centre in the new Snow Shoe Inn mall. During conversation I mentioned that I had taught computers and the next thing I knew I was being considered for employment. Liz and I have enjoyed being in Yukon and NWT so much that we talked about spending a winter here, driving on ice roads, and then watching spring breakup on the MacKenzie River. The job was tempting, but eventually I felt I was too much out-of-date on modern computer software, and the offer was mutually declined.

I got stuck leaving the side parking lot of the Snow Shoe Inn. It had rained the night before and the ditch, a dip, between the road and the parking lot had softened. When backing out, the RV's rear wheels dropped in and kept on going down into the mud until the rear bumper rested on the road. Sheesh. I've driven on back roads and trails and never got stuck. Why here, in town?!

Fortunately a local came by with a 4x4 and pulled me out. He was heading to a hospital in far away Edmonton, Alberta because his daughter had just been admitted, yet he took valuable time to help a stranger. That is the kind of people many northerners are. Many thanks to my unknown benefactor.

Yellowknife

Our first impression of Yellowknife is that this is a real city. It has a vertical skyline, good and wide asphalt streets, stop lights, an historical "Old Town", a modern downtown commercial section, large malls with stores that look like they really do a lot of business, and several people who never smile as they rush to or from work.

What a pleasure it is to shop in large retail and well stocked grocery stores!

It also has a Fred Henne Campground — $5 for day use and $12 for overnight camping — within the city limits. As with all NWT campgrounds, it is tastefully constructed and beautifully maintained. Although we could park and walk down to the picnic area, vehicular access to the day use area is only through the campground entrance, which is another kilometre towards the city.

We missed the Old Airport Road driving on Highway 3 into Yellowknife. If you want to take it, turn right at the Ford car dealership, about 0.7 km after the parking lot outside the Fred Henne day use area and before you get to the campground entrance.

The knowledgeable staff at Northern Frontier Country Tourist Information Centre will be able to answer most of your questions. In addition, they sell local newspapers, and there are two phones one of which allows free local calls. If they don't have an informative copy of Coffee News, I suggest you get one from other establishments. The staff sells passes for Ingraham Trail.

When we were there they also swapped pins, in our case, an Inuvik pin for a miniature yellow knife.

After you turn onto the access road for the Legislative Building, make an immediate turn to your left and left again to find the tourist centre. Unfortunately, you have to exit into the city centre. Because you cannot go back out the way you came in, you might want to visit the Museum and Legislative buildings first, even though it is only a couple of left turns and blocks to get back to them.

The Prince of Wales Northern Heritage Centre is worth at least two hours of exploration in, and possibly even a return visit to, this superb recognition of native and non-native pioneers. Unlike many of the explorers of The North there is no need for you to experience hardship and starvation. The museum provides comfortable seats and a coffee/snack shop.

A working RV dump and water refill station is located at the corner of the Old Airport Road and Kam Lake Road. Here also water is chlorinated and pumped into trucks for house delivery to Old Town and the occasional modern building which

A superb example of Moose-hair Tufting.

cannot be supplied economically with water and sewer services because of this area's unique geological conditions.

I was told the following. City Hall is built on sandy soil using standard "southern" construction techniques. The adjacent RCMP building is built on bedrock and cost almost twice as much as city hall because of the blasting required. The military building next to it cost about three times as much as city hall because it sits on muskeg, permafrost and 23 m (75 ft) pilings.

Propane was available in only two locations: at Sam's Monkey Tree Payless Gas on Range Lake Road, three kilometres (2 mi) along Old Airport Road; and at an ICG location which I didn't look for. If you have some nuts with you, you might be able to feed the pet squirrel at the Monkey Tree.

I've noticed that the most common street or road name is "No Thru Road".

During our week in Yellowknife all gas stations offered the same price for regular unleaded gasoline, which struck me as being a bit unusual. What ever happened to entrepreneurial competition and gas wars?

Although I could have sent and received Web-mail, I could not send e-mail on the public library's computer nor on a local coffee shop's computer. I don't like the continuous barrage of banners and advertisements on Web-mail. But I expect these commercials eventually will allow Internet Service Providers to offer free Internet access in the very near future, maybe even by the time you read this book.

Please take time to walk about Old Town, maybe even stopping for a snack at some of the more interesting old buildings. Climb the Rock for a spectacular view, even in windy overcast conditions.

There seem to be as many planes as houseboats in the bay near Yellowknife. If the houses stay there all winter encased in ice, how do the residents travel to and fro: by car, truck or snowmobiles?

I believe that Bruce of Kingland Ford has finally solved the brake problem that has plagued us during our entire summer adventure. Now if only the other dealers will stand by their guarantees we might get some of our money back.

Liz and I were interviewed on CBC about our trip and forthcoming book. A professional interviewer certainly makes it easy for us novices. Afterwards we received a souvenir fishing hook and a taped copy of the interview. Liz is still the more eloquent speaker.

A view of 'Old Town' taken from top of "The Rock".

When I publish my CD Browser Book ™, with two books in four languages, maybe I'll include that six-minute interview as an audio file.

Ingraham Trail

It seems we arrived in NWT at the end of their summer, although we've heard locals say that their end of summer happened in early August this year. We are both sick — John literally, with a cold and sore throat — and tired of dull or dark and gloomy overcast skies, and tired of staying inside our RV to keep out of drizzle and rain showers. If we didn't have to wait for forwarded mail, we both agree that we'd be heading south right now. It is a pity that we are so influenced by the weather.

General Delivery at the main post office in Yellowknife will keep mail for two weeks, not a month as I had expected, and our forwarded mail was returned two days before we got there. If I had known I could have phoned ahead and the mail would have been waiting for me.

If you want to know why the last 100 km of highway to Yellowknife is unpaved, you should travel the first paved twenty kilometres of the Ingraham Trail.

Riding a roller coaster is less exciting than driving the Ingraham Trail at 80 km/hr. Our Class C swayed left and right, springs and shocks bounced up and down, and our home tilted and righted itself constantly. We quickly slowed down to 60 km/hr, and sometimes even to 50 km/hr.

The Trail is built on rock and muskeg and permafrost. Thus it is easier and cheaper and better to maintain a gravel road than it is to dig up then repair a frost-damaged asphalt surface. It must be. The gravel portion is smoother than the asphalt.

As you drive by the active gold mine on your right, still within the city limits but in the middle of nowhere, see if you can see how locals have solved the sub-arctic problem of providing electricity to engine block heaters and battery warmers, using a minimum of posts driven into solid bedrock in a snow-covered parking lot.

The Ingraham Trail is a recreational area. As such it cost us $10 to be allowed to travel the road and use the picnic areas. This is a fair price for three or more days (it is an annual pass) but a trifle expensive for a single day of driving. Ah well. We encourage you to get your pass at the Tourist Information Centre rather than spending time driving around and looking for other vendors.

Although we were told that the Trail was worth driving for its scenery, we didn't notice it being much different than the rest of southern NWT except for the many outcroppings of igneous and often pink rock. But it does have several pleasant campgrounds — visiting NWT Territorial Campgrounds has been a pleasure always — and small lakes, which are ideal for small and large boats.

These stirations were created by ancient ice fields sliding over these rocks.

As you drive the Ingraham Trail, do drive the access roads to various locations that you can't see from the road. We think you'll be pleasantly surprised at one or two of them. Be careful though. Most *good* side roads without a sign lead to highway maintenance yards or gravel pits.

By fishing from the shore at the very end of the Trail I managed to get a jack fish in the creek flowing out of Tibbett

Lake. (We were saddened to see four cottages on the lake which had been destroyed by fire, one owned by the man who first reported the blaze.) I cleaned it on one of the flat rocks next to the water, which I used to wash off the rock after I was finished. As recommended, head, entrails and fins went into a nearby garbage pail.

The easy hike to, and the Cameron Falls itself, were interesting. The 4-6 km trail crosses many metres of solid rock many times and so direction markers are needed. Small blue markers on top of steel rods hammered into the rock were usually easy to see so we never got lost for long.

On our way back we met a wedding party heading to the falls. The minister who was going to preform the rites wore hiking boots but the men wore shoes or sneakers. The bride wore high heels and bridesmaids also wore high heels or runners under their dresses.

Did you know that most mud puddles, if undisturbed, have a layer of clear water above their muddy bottoms? This water can be used with a squeegie to wash off tail lights, windows and even sides of a motorhome if you are careful to avoid scratching the finish. In really deep puddles, reasonably clean water can be gathered in a bucket and thrown on muddy (actually silty) sides and rear of vehicles that have travelled on wet gravel roads. This summer I have used puddle-water many times to clean our back window and several times to clean the entire motorhome, all at no expense, coutesy of Mother Nature.

Canada's Labour Day weekend finally turned sunny at Monday noon. Liz and I happened to be in the Hidden Lake (Small Cameron Falls) access parking lot, so we decided to canoe and portage to that lake. We wanted to see the grandeur of places not easily accessible by cars, campers and recreational vehicles, and thus not overrun with refuse from weekend visitors. And we wanted to fish where there was a reasonable chance to catch something besides northern pike. [Oh oh. I've gone into tourist-brochure mode. I've used the more exotic sounding name Northern Pike instead of commonly used jack fish.]

We chatted with a young couple who beached their canoe beside us and learned that it should take us about an hour to get to Hidden Lake. We must be out of shape. It took us two hours of paddling on smooth lakes and climbing up and down four slippery, muddy or rocky trails to get there.

When Liz and I returned to the last lake, these two men were ahead of us.

Our canoe continues to absorb water in the hole or holes which resulted from our Klondike River adventure. We can get about half of it out, but it takes several to many minutes to do so. Our 30 kg (65 lb) canoe probably weighed ten kilograms more at the end of the day than it should have.

It took us just as long to get back. By this time we had learned how to carry our canoe properly and we made better time during the portages. But this was offset by our spending a few minutes to cast in each lake. And that was for naught as hook after hook remained untasted.

Next morning, both Liz and I were stiff in places we expected and some we didn't. But overall we weren't too sore, which makes me think we late-fifties couple are in better shape than we thought we were. I was particularly proud of the effort of my dear wife who never complained. At least not out loud.

Oh, by the way. We did catch one lake trout while paddling and casting on Hidden Lake. My fishing line got tangled after one particularly good cast, and as I worked out the knots the

CBC's "Hooked on Radio" spinner sank down and down into deep water. As I was bringing it back up for another cast, the tip of the rod started to vibrate then was pulled into the water. Out went more line, then slowly it was brought back in, seemingly straight up out of the depths, then out again, then in, etc. It took about five minutes to land a one kilo (2 pound) trout. Fried in butter and crumbs it was delicious!

Sun makes such a difference. We truly enjoyed the day. We especially enjoyed the red sunset — red because of smoke in the air — and the playful antics of two curious loons who came close to us to see what kind of strange animal we were.

Letter Concerning Nunavut's Logo

I sent this letter to several newspapers and the Up Here magazine after a married couple we had met in Yellowknife suggested I do so. They forwarded a copy to a Member of the Legislature, as well as to others. I wonder if it had any impact on the decision for a NWT logo.

......

Dear Editor

During our two months of motorhome travels on all eight "Roads to Adventure" in the Northwest Territories we learned of several challenges related to the creation of the territory of Nunavut on April 1, 1999. Interestingly enough the questions "Who gets to keep the polar bear licence plate?" and "What will we call the Northwest Territories?" were heard the most often.

I think that the Canadians in Nunavut should adopt a traditional yet modern symbol for their own, the Inukshuk. The outline of the Inukshuk is known and recognizable both nationally and internationally. It is truly an old-yet-new unique symbol, a marketable logo, that has already been established in the consciousness of millions. (Check out the NavCanada advertisement in Up Here, July/August 1998, pages 2-3.)

The reason for choosing an Inukshuk is that was and is used to indicate a trail to follow, a direction to go, a reassurance that a traveller is on the right path. It is confirmation for any one who sees an Inukshuk that what appears to be a new and challenging route has been travelled by others before him/ her. It is indeed an appropriate symbol for those daring to create a new-to-them government and infrastructure.

Why limit the Inukshuk design to use by automobiles, which most definitely are not the main means of transportation in Nunavut? Boats, barges, snowmobiles, ATV's and airplanes also need to be licensed. What a powerful and definitive symbol to have painted on the tail of airplanes and on the sides of ocean-going containers! And on mushers' parkas, and Holman golfballs, and ...

Any good graphic artist could easily adapt the outline to dimensions required for a logo or licence plate. Would aurora-borealis-green numbers and letters on a soap-stone background be practical?

As an aside, thousands of extra plates would need to be manufactured. They would probably become more desirable than those time-worn "polar bear" plates.

With the widespread use of Yukon instead of Yukon Territory, with the disappearance of the Districts of MacKenzie and Keewatin, why keep the now inappropriate name Northwest Territories? Why not call it what it is now, merely another northern territory, but one that still evokes the remembrance of legend and history.

Yukon, Northwest Territory, Nunavut. Sounds good to me.

That name still evokes all proud and political and marketable associations that Northwest Territories evokes, but eliminates the question "Why Territories when there is only one?".

Northwest Territory is geographically correct on a map of Canada.

Northwest Territory is a practical name.

It would also be easy and inexpensive to change old sign names, merely paint over the 'IES' and then add a 'Y'. Simple. And the design of these signs would still appear balanced.

Letterhead and logos can be updated just as easily, and old stocks of paper could be used up as is without too much confusion. Updates to all computerized legal (and other) documents could be done quickly, merely search for and replace 'Territories' with 'Territory'.

These are my suggestions. Rename Northwest Territories to the more accurate Northwest Territory while keeping its polar bear logo, and let Nunavut meet and overcome their new challenges under the ancient guidance of an Inukshuk.

Yours sincerely,
John & Liz Plaxton

Edzo-Rae

Edzo is, to us, a bleak sub-community of Rae, and located 15 km south of it. Edzo is built on good soil which allows for underground services and a planned community layout. Rae sits on unyielding rock.

Challenges concerning sewage disposal and fresh water in Rae led to the creation of Edzo. But it seems most of the people wouldn't leave their homes. They are still in Rae.

Rae straddles solid bedrock on the shore of the North Arm of Great Slave Lake. Houses and streets and bridges exist haphazardly wherever they can, on rock and between rock and above (most of the time) the lake's high water mark. This community reminds us of a Newfoundland outport except for the difference in the shapes of the buildings.

The decorated street signs are written in native language.

Having visited Rae during cloudy, windy and drizzly weather, we returned several days later to get some better pictures. Because the clouds were thicker and darker than before we decided to take none. Pity. Rae is quite picturesque, at least in our sun-filled imaginings.

Look for the wind sock in the middle of the bay. I presume float planes land there, perhaps belonging to people in Rac.

Look for the three small graves in someone's back yard.

Look for a house where the entire front yard is a dome of pinkish granite-like stone.

Look for the play of sunlight on the colourful homes, blue waters, green reeds, and multi-hued rock. You will probably be luckier than we were.

Look for a gallery displaying the work of Archie Bealieu. He's an artist who was asked to display his work at the annual Great Northern Arts Festival in Inuvik inside the Arctic Circle.

Fort Smith and area

We think this is probably the nicest town in NWT. Residential lots are spacious, most houses and yards are clean and neat, and the people we met were exceedingly friendly. So friendly they reminded us of Newfoundlanders, which some of them are. We even discussed buying a town lot here on which to park our motorhome when we return.

While grocery shopping in Fort Smith, it occurred to me that if we'd had two walkie-talkies with us, we could have saved enough money to pay for them. Every store had its specials and some stores were so close that they were within RF range. We could have determined which products in which store had the better price. Ah well. Maybe someday I'll remember to get another walkie-talkie and remember to use it when shopping.

For those so inclined, visit the liquor store. You don't have to go in, just walk around the outside and enjoy the landscaping. Very pleasant. It's too bad more stores couldn't look so good when approaching them.

One townsman gave us a book of NWT images and several kilograms of frozen white fish he caught himself. They were

Mushing, or sled dogs, waiting for winter and some excitement.

delicious but are only a pleasant memory now. However, "**Our Forgotten North**, a glimpse of the subarctic in Canada's North" by Leslie Leong is still with us and still being enjoyed. It has particular meaning for us because we've seen about a third of the places she photographed so beautifully. I suggest you buy this coffee-table book as a souvenir of your visit to NWT, and western Nunavut which comes into existence on April 1st, 1999.

Lewis Beck of the Fort Smith Tourist Information Centre also exemplifies friendliness and helpfulness. If you get the opportunity to attend one of his bi-weekly evening Tea and Bannock gatherings, go. Bring along a musical instrument (no, not a CD player) and play alongside him and his mandolin.

But if he gives you a pamphlet describing nearby rapids and mentions the Cassette Rapids, ignore the latter. When we arrived by following directions we were met by an irate homeowner who really didn't want to see us on his land, and mumbled something about a lawyer. However you can get to the Cassette Rapids without trespassing on private land by taking and returning via the deserted Yanick Farm. Both Liz and I figure the walk and the view aren't worth the exercise. Note. We have since talked with a local man who is familiar with all NWT rivers, and he said that there is an excellent view on the first line of rapids. If so, the trail definitely does not indicate a side trail to them.

The Mountain Portage Rapids and the Pelican Rapids definitely are worth the time to drive there and the minimal effort and walking needed to get to them.

The individual rapids are not exceptional in themselves, but when you look over hundreds of hectares (acres) of water flowing around rocks and boulders and ridges and islands, then the view is spectacular. When we saw butterscotch-coloured water turned into roiling ridges of whipped cream, we had to wonder how voyageurs of the previous century felt as they grounded their canoes and York boats above such awe and fear inspiring sights. Where would they go? Which channel was least deadly? Would they have to portage, and how far?

Pelicans are Liz's favourite water bird. Two are airborne behind the trees.

These rapids, including the Rapids of the Drowned, are world-class white water challenges for experienced kayakers. International competitions have been and will be held here. But less dangerous rapids also exist and every summer many kayakers come to practice and increase their skills.

Also worth seeing are the Karstland Trail, starting at the Pine Lake Road Day Use area, and 2.5 km farther on, the martian-

This rabbit was completely snow-white on his underbelly and lower legs. What a contrast! This is a sign that fall is here and winter soon will be.

like scene at Grosbeak Lake. Liz and I have been to Yucatan, Mexico and seen cenotes, not knowing that similar although smaller sinkholes plus caves and underground rivers, exist right here in NWT. But the Yucatan does not have fields of crumbling and misshapen stones being corroded and dissolved by salt water and sub-arctic frost. Take a hike to Grosbeak Lake.

Pine Lake Campground is in Alberta, not the NWT. It is rustic but does have wood, boil-before-using water and sewage disposal. From your canoe or boat, clear water should let you see way down into one or more of the five sinkholes that form this lake, and the shallow beach and swimming areas are great for parents and young children.

Two black bears were sighted eating berries next to the highway. We stopped and watched, but neither seemed to care about our being close by. Although tempted to get really close for a close-up picture, I didn't. These are wild and unpredictable animals, and they can move a lot faster than I can run.

We drove along Parson Road, which was easy to do in our smallish motorhome because the narrow trail was barely damp or dry. We might not have been able to do so after a heavy rain.

We drove slowly because we were looking for buffalo in the trees. After seeing dozens of sand wallows created by bison rolling around trying to get rid of mosquitoes and black flies, we finally spotted two young bulls off to our left. We stopped. We looked at them, they looked at us. Then the pair silently trotted through the trees, across the road, and disappeared into the spruce and poplar to our right.

Later, we were surprised to hear a rifle shot. Ancient hunting was part of the history of this area and local natives have maintained the right to hunt here. On the other hand, anyone can shoot a bison if it wanders so much as a metre (a yard) outside of the Wood Buffalo National Park.

Liz and I had a great view of fall colours from Parson Lake Fire Tower hill. I wish I had been allowed to climb half way up the fire-lookout tower and see the salt flats about two kilometres behind the surrounding trees.

An immature eagle flew over head. A flock of grouse took flight right in front of us. They had gorgeous gold and black bands on the edges of their wings.

While visiting the museum in Fort Smith, an 1874-78 map of the area in Upper Canada where my great-great-grandparents lived was on display. One never knows when good luck will come his or her way. I'm still trying to track down this map to help with my genealogical research.

During our last day here, I wanted ice cream, but all I could find in the stores was a four litre container. My initial thought was "How would we store it, it is too big for our tiny freezer compartment." Then I realized that I could buy all that ice cream for the same price as two large cones at Northern DeLight. Even if we had to throw half of it away I was still getting a bargain, although not the quality. I bought the four litres and Liz and I had two huge bowls of Butterscotch Ripple for supper's dessert.

We parked at the Queen Elizabeth Campground. That night was so cold that by hanging the container outside on the RV's antenna the ice cream didn't melt. But it was softened by early morning sunshine sneaking in between the spires of black spruces while we slept. Under the tolerant, head-shaking gaze of my beloved wife – this was the same look she had when I created the delicacy Tunanana, also called Banuna, which is a tuna and banana sandwich on whole wheat bread – I had another bowlful after breakfast then scooped the remainder into a large plastic bottle and stored it inside the fridge, to be used later as coffee flavouring.

We've driven every highway in NWT from end to end except for the short one from the Alberta border to Hay River, which is our last destination. It's been a lot of driving, much of it boring because we couldn't see the scenery because of the trees, and many times in damp and cool and even cold temperatures. It's mid-September and fall has definitely arrived. I'd like to come back sometime when it's warm or hot and use our canoe to explore more lakes and catch many huge fish. That visit would be more of a series of camping and fishing explorations than an RV-on-the-road experience.

Driving back towards Hay River we again camped overnight in the parking lot beside a big sink hole below Angus Tower. We heard an owl but never saw it. The Canada Jays were still there and ate all the breadcrumbs and seeds we put out. This is one advantage of travelling off-season when few tourists are about; we can get away with camping in places which would be off-limits in the summer.

The Little Buffalo Falls park and picnic area is graced with two falls, although it is easy to miss the second unless you walk upriver along the river bank. It's naturally terraced and different enough to warrant a five minute stroll. I wish there had been some way to get down to the river's edge and look up at the first set of falls.

Polar Lake, NWT

Only 86 km from Hay River and 50 km from Enterprise, on asphalt except for the 2 km gravel road into the lake, is tiny, shallow, fishless Polar Lake. There are about six lakeside campsites and the same number on the other side of the road.

In 1998, day use was $3.00 and overnight camping with all the fire wood you reasonably need was $5.00. This campsite is

A beautiful golden sunset taken from our canoe in the middle of the lake.

privately run by a volunteer group but visitors are certainly welcome. However, I expect summer weekends might be very crowded so arrive early, perhaps Tuesday morning.

On Saturday and Sunday in mid-September, Liz and I enjoyed the friendly company of one couple our age, two young couples with three pre-schoolers and two dogs, and a father camping with his daughter. Unless you count twelve ducks, two beaver and their two kits, a half-dozen grey jays (also known as camp robbers for obvious reasons), at least one northern harrier or hawk, and one loon as company, Sunday evening we spent by ourselves.

Liz couldn't resist saying it. ... Resist what? Read on.

Twenty metres to our right, our canoe was tied up to a small wooden wharf, with our life-jackets, paddles and fishing gear exposed to Indian Summer weather. Sitting in our lawn chairs with warm supper on our laps and cool, clear, un-chlorinated water in our glasses, with the only sound coming from our crackling spruce fire, with flames masking the darkening blue of the lake only partially hidden behind a few trees as stars magically began to appear above them, with our own queen-sized bed parked but a metre away, she just had to ask one more time "I wonder what the rich folks are doing?"

An hour later we marvelled at Aurora Borealis that spanned horizon to horizon to horizon to horizon, in all four directions. Three then five then four then two then six curtains of phosphorescent green and pale purple ribbons wavered and whipped in front of the Big Dipper (Ursa Major, or the Plow), Cassiopeia, the twins Castor and Pollux, searchlight-Venus, and hundreds of the other bright celestial diamonds glistening on a black velvet sky. For almost a minute we spied a satellite sneaking along its polar orbit. My oh my. When there are no city or town lights to lighten the sky, there is so much to see.

The sandy beach to our left displayed several day-old paw prints of a wolf (big feet!), an older single black bear print, and brushed sand where a beaver hauled branches from a large poplar it had felled the night before we arrived.

Before supper Liz and I got some rope, tied it to a large log and dragged it twice over much of the beach. Actually, I dragged it and Liz used our broom to smooth out sandal and running-shoe prints in dips and depressions. Sadly, our work was for naught. No prints were available next morning for our cameras.

An interesting sidetrip from Hay River is a visit to the Hay River Dene Reserve. Although just across the river, one must drive 20 km to get there.

But happy hours of magical and mystical moments can't last forever. This morning we're off to Hay River to visit to a laundromat, gas and propane stations, telephones and an e-mail provider.

Solitude will never be permanent for us. But it can be so relaxing.

Highway 1, Twin Falls, NWT

Today is September 22, 1998. As we get close to the Northwest Territories-Alberta border at 60°N Liz and I realize that out adventure is coming to an end.

The end of our adventure, and summer, is rapidly approaching.

It has been a long one; we left Kelowna, BC on April 19th. It's really not over yet. We still have to travel Alberta's Northern Woods and Lakes route. But somehow this border seems to signal the end of our summer travels.

The Territories seem sad to see us leave as well. At kilometre 8 a light rain – heaven's tears – dampens the blacktop and forces me to use the wipers. On the other hand, all campgrounds have been closed since September 15th so maybe the parks are glad we are finally leaving and those rain drops are tears of joy.

... Is it my imagination, or is the road to the border blocked by a huge dike? No. No it's not. This is the first time in NWT that I've had to look *up* at a distant hill.

Twin Falls and the Hay River Gorge are definitely worth a visit. Although wheel chair accessible, there are places on the 2.5 km trail where really unusual views can only be seen by wandering a few metres off the gravel path. Six interpretive panels are easily read from the path.

I wonder if the two small but obviously well-used paths where animals walk to a shallow sinkhole for a drink will be evident a year or two later.

Speaking of unusual views, I suspect that there would be one from the Department of Highways's woodpile cache that is accessible about one-half kilometre north of the entrance to Louise Falls. Unfortunately a "No Trespassing" sign eliminates the possibility of a telescopic photograph, from the top edge of the gorge, of the caramel-golden falls and the churning river below.

For those who can, I encourage everyone to get a close up view of the Louise Falls. You'll have to descend 43 or 44 circular stairs and 96 wooden steps and that additional steep ten metres while hanging onto a rope. Otherwise, you might never notice the terraced staircase over which the water flows. Even in September and with low water levels, they are worth seeing up close.

Broken Brakes No More

As you've read, our motorhome has been having a lot of rear-brake problems. They started while we were in Mexico and heading for Central America. Finally, after many thousands of kilometres of worrisome driving, and several unwanted withdrawals from our bank account, I think the problem has been solved by Bruce, a technician at Kingland Ford, Yellowknife.

The cause of all our problems was such a small thing. I suppose that makes sense because a big and obvious problem would have been discovered months ago.

Our brake system employs a small cable inside the brake. This cable, which wraps around a tiny metal guide or arc, is used to automatically adjust the spacing between brake pads and brake drum and thus compensate for wear.

The arc was bent slightly out of shape and effectively shortened the cable by less than a centimetre. Being that much shorter caused the adjusting mechanism to be offset by the tiniest fraction, but enough to prevent it from working properly. Although everything looked correct, it didn't work at all. In fact it worked against the brake design. Rather than automatically adjusting a star wheel, it allowed it to completely unwind then disconnect from other components and fall to the bottom of the brake, usually accompanied with other pieces of metal that also got chewed up and bent into barely recognizable shapes.

Looking at the metal clip, or cable guide, it was impossible to see the problem. If it had been placed beside another, then the difference in shape might have been seen. But it never was.

It took almost three hours to discover the bent guide, which was easily corrected by one small hammer blow. It might not have been found if I hadn't been allowed in the shop. While working with the technician I asked lots of ignorant questions and twice insisted that the brakes did not function properly. Eventually he agreed with me and we tried many, many different procedures and parts replacements.

He found the problem, not I.

The sad part is that the other garages - Yukon Tire & Mechanical in Whitehorse and Northern Superior in Dawson - did good work, used quality replacement parts and charged an hourly rate that was less than I would have been charged farther south. You must realize that these businesses were very busy but that they kindly fitted me into their schedule. They ordered parts and, after they arrived, immediately worked on my vehicle. They worked efficiently. In Dawson, they even worked a couple of hours of overtime so Liz and I could sleep in our motorhome. They did the best they could, which would have been more than sufficient in 99 and 9/10ths percent of jobs. Unfortunately luck was against them this time.

The business in Whitehorse was subcontracted by Whitehorse Subaru, owned by Mr. Raman Grewal. The General Manager of Northern Superior is Mr. Boyd Gillis. Although these gentlemen did not believe that the technicians had done anything wrong, they paid me back for the costs of their repairs within days of receiving my request.

I think the words of Mr. Gillis in his last letter to me should be repeated because it conveys the attitude of most quality garages and dealerships -- "... I have been in business in Dawson City for 14 years and sincerely try to go the extra mile for the tourist traffic which travels in our area, the local people and the community. ..." When in their communities I'd go back to these garages immediately if I had another problem with my RV, or any vehicle for that matter. I know of no stronger recommendation than to return to a business as a satisfied customer.

Our motorhome has now travelled twice as far as it had previously before a failure re-occurred, and we've had no brake failure. Even adjusting the rear drum brakes has been unnecessary. I believe the problem has been solved, at last, at long last.

Thank you, Bruce!

Epilogue

Liz and I have been very fortunate. We've had months to travel in northern British Columbia, Yukon and Northwest Territories. We've seen many things that most tourists won't because they lack the time to travel.

We've seen so much, and enjoyed so much, that it is difficult to determine which was the best. Remember, every part of the world has something worthwhile to see and visit. Rather than try to summarize the many, many adventures and varied scenery and make suggestions to our readers, I'm going to suggest you re-read this travelogue and all the diaries.

Then I'm going to encourage you to travel to the beautiful areas around and above 60°N in Canada. Barring accident or ill-health, you will never regret what you'll see or experience.

If you have only a month or if you are lucky enough to have several weeks, drive your recreational vehicle into Canada's wonderful and warm north lands. You really should experience

RVing into Canada's Arctic.

Appendix A: April-September 1998 Daily Journal

Author's Note: Although I wrote articles when the mood was upon me or when a particularly interesting event occurred, my wonderful wife kept a daily account of what happened. Liz has slightly expanded some of the original entries for this travelogue. It is an excellent reference. Her diary duplicates some of my articles, briefly, but her opinions are hers and they do not necessarily agree with mine. For over thirty years Liz and I have agreed to disagree on a few things.

Sunday, April 19-22, 1998
Finally, after a two year delay, we are starting on our northern adventure. It is already 7 pm but we're leaving anyway. Even if we go only 50 km tonight, at least we're on the way.

We slept the night in a parking lot at O'Keefe Ranch, because our headlights were systematically going off then coming back on. Stopped in Kamloops to do laundry, then on to Steelhead Provincial Park (Sk'emqin) just past pretty Savona. We were the only ones there on April 21ˢᵗ ; it was so quiet and peaceful.

John's old 286 portable computer — the one used to draft articles which eventually ended up in our first book "RVing into Mexico, Central America and Panamá" — quit working. Its ten year-old hard drive had failed. A replacement that small (10 Mb) would be impossible to find. What to do? Since all of his programs were back in Kelowna, we decided to drive back there, buy a new laptop and get all of his programs loaded on the new machine. It was more economical than buying elsewhere and having to purchase new software.

April 23-24 Juniper Provincial Park, BC
We finally got away again at 1 pm - with a new computer - taking a very scenic section of the old highway beside Kalamalka Lake. Had supper at Savona Restaurant, an old truck stop with

average food but large servings. Stayed two days at Juniper Provincial Park on the Thompson River, which was much nicer than Steelhead. A few other units were there. Trains rumble and rattle by on both sides of the river all day. It was nice to have a slow day after the hectic pace of the last three days.

<u>April 25-May 2 Lac La Hache, BC</u>

Clinton is an appealing looking town of 700 people. It is very clean and neat, has a campground in town, and lots of different little windmills and wood products for sale. Although we didn't know it until after we had passed through, there is a place accessible from the highway where we could have put our names on a wooden slab and added it to a forest of signposts.

After Clinton we seemed to be on a plateau, no more driving along the bottoms of valleys.

We took a 5 km side trip to the Chasm lookout. Worth the trip but with the wind it was very cold. The road in is paved, and layers of lava can be seen on the road sides. Saw a raven flying upside down, which they do when looking for eagles in the area. Creeks are high, snow on mountains, no bird nests on the poles. Saw a black bear (finished hibernating?) peering through a fence at vehicles going by on the highway below.

One of North America's largest pair of skis, at 100 Mile House

Arrived at Fir Crest Resort, 6 km north of the stores and post office of Lac La Hache. We'll stay for a week. Twelve other campers here, some just overnighting.

The smoke from another fire drifted slowly across the lake.

Beautiful sunsets over the lake. Had a campfire every night, lots of free slab pine. John lent his new axe to a university professor on exchange from Ireland. Inexperienced. Axe handle has been slightly damaged where it, instead of the metal head, struck wood.

Took our canoe down when we arrived, canoed daily. Being so quiet, we could get within three metres of some birds. There's a marsh a few hundred metres away, with lots of geese, ducks, loons and a near-sighted muskrat who almost swam into the side of our canoe. Watched loons do a splashing routine - wonder if it has anything to do with mating?

Got a ride into Lac La Hache with one of the locals and walked the 6 km back. It was a warm sunny day and when we returned we were both ready to put our feet up and have a cool one.

A few mosquitos have shown up, as well as flying ants. On May 1st we both got sunburned.

May 2-4 Williams Lake, BC

Drove to Williams Lake, about 65 km. away. There are lots of log cabin-style houses along the highway. They are mass-manufactured near here.

Ducks Unlimited conservation area doesn't seem to have an access road directly from the highway. Where is it?

Visited Scout Island Nature Centre. Very hot, didn't see any animals or birds. All the birch trees were dead for some reason.

Laundromat was dirty and noisy. Parking lot was gravel and was part of an alley. Wind came up and we were obliterated in dust. Unfortunately motorhome windows were open. Everything needed to be wiped off. Seems to be a dry dusty town.

The firemen were having a car wash fundraiser. Vehicles were washed by driving under the big ladder truck where they were sprayed - similar to having a shower. The fund raiser was called the Boot Drive and you put your donation into a pair of firemen's boots. No roof leaks thank goodness. Had picture taken by local newspaper, Tribune. Don't know if it will be published.

Spent the afternoon parked on a bluff on the other side of the lake. Quiet, sunny, peaceful, relaxing.

On Sunday went to Mass at Sacred Heart. Singer-guitar player was lively, western with a deep voice.

Stayed overnight in order to get information on PLAXTON family tree.

May 4 Barkerville, BC

Unfortunately museum and library are closed on Mondays and City Hall couldn't help regarding family tree info. Left empty-handed.

Tried to take the gravel back road to Soda Creek but a bridge was out. Saw a big coyote.

Stopped at Marguerite. Took ferry across the Fraser River, then came back immediately. Steep access will prevent longer motorhomes or RVs from accessing ferry landing. This was the first day ferry was running this year. Martin, the boat operator/ captain, said last spring a huge log with a massive root system came floating down the river. It had a STOP sign sticking out of it. So he stopped the ferry and let it pass by. Said he wasn't going to argue with something that big.

About 10 km south of Quesnel is a new mall, Maple Park.

Mohawk gasoline station has a sani-dump and propane, we used both. Very friendly.

Turned east on paved Highway 26 to Barkerville. Saw a black bear. He stood there for quite a while looking at us before ambling off into the bush.

Stopped at Cottonwood House, one of the few original road houses remaining in BC. Original buildings, telegraph poles and part of the Caribou Wagon Trail are there. This historic site wasn't open yet for the season, but we were allowed to come in for a photo-op and a self-guided visit. Being authors has some advantages.

At Barkerville, signs indicate no overnight camping in parking lots. Three motorhomes and one car left before dark. We are parked in a small daytime overflow parking area next to fast-

Rules are to be obeyed by computers and offer guidance to wisemen, and pre-season travellers.

flowing and noisy Williams Creek. Patches of snow still on its banks and the nearby hillside. We are the only ones here. Couldn't do this in tourist season.

May 5 Barkerville & Hush Lake, BC

Toured Barkerville - rather chilly. Of course nothing is open yet so we could only walk around and look in the windows.

This would be a fun place to visit during the summer. Met Tonie and Martin from Holland. They were walking around Barkerville also. Had coffee with them in our RV. After lunch we walked 1.5 km to Richfield to see courthouse of Hanging Judge Begbie. Path was uphill and covered in snow. Our feet were soaked from the wet snow and the rest of us was soaked with perspiration. It was sunny and warm and hard work slogging through the wet snow. There wasn't much to see once we got there. The only building was the courthouse and the windows were boarded up for the winter. This would be a very pleasant walk in the summer.

En route to Quesnel we stopped to see Wells, and Stanley Loop Road and cemetery. Many Chinese have been exhumed and returned to China. You can see the hollows in the ground where they had been buried. In town, Ceal Tingley Park has excellent drinking water and a sani-dump, and is close to a 5 km paved walkway around town. We did the walk but should have changed clothes first as it is much warmer in town than in Barkerville because of the lower altitude.

Wanted to go to Pinnacles Provincial Park to see the Hoodoos, but we couldn't find it. Continued on through 10 Mile Prov. Park — beautiful, $12/night — and into Hush Lake Rest Area, where we camped down next to the lake. Mosquitos here. Had supper on the roof, (bugs aren't so bad up high) watched a loon and some ducks. Hoped to see a moose, but none appeared. Saw a deer. Joined by a couple in a van.

May 6 Vanderhoof, BC
On to Prince George: lots of parks, shopping centres, live theatres and campgrounds. Big sign advertising "Gateway to Alaska", why not "Gateway to Yukon"? Did our banking, made airline reservations to attend Robert and Teresa's wedding. Usual frustration driving about in an unfamiliar city. Left for Vanderhoof on Hwy 16.

At Dave's RV Park (FMCA-affiliate) we met a couple from Alaska with two pet wolves. Female was dark and pure wolf, male was white and husky mix. Both beautiful animals.

Parked at tourist info for the night, windy and cool.

Like all wolves, this one was extremely shy, even though raised by humans.

May 7 Burns Lake, BC

60 km north to Fort St. James on Stuart Lake. About 200 people but spread out. National historic site is still closed but we walked the grounds. Met Brian, a knowledgeable history buff and maintenance man, who took us through two of the buildings. Officers' quarters or factor house has big rooms and two eagles on the walls. Walked to Our Lady of Good Hope church, but it was locked. It's the oldest Catholic church in BC.

Took loop road at Fraser Lake down to Francis Lake, coming back to Highway 16 at Endako. Gas station here is defunct, so had to drive back to Fraser Lake for fuel.

En route to Burns Lake we saw a dead moose in a ditch. Probably hit in the dark last night. Many roadside lakes have beaver lodges in them.

Planned to go to forestry site near opal and agate beds but couldn't find our way on narrow dirt roads. Probably didn't go far enough.

Parked at free municipal park on the lake - 10 sites with lots of room for overflow. While we were gone for a long walk — hilly town — local youths took all the wood John had cut and laid in our firepit.

<u>May 8 Driftwood Canyon Provincial Park, near Smithers, BC</u>
Slow start today. In Houston we phoned the son of friends but no one was home.

Bought locally-made ice cream in Telkwa. Very creamy and tasty. They also sell home-made bread. Yum!

Smithers is a small town with many Dutch families. It seemed to have a lot of traffic for its size. There is a laundromat and two grocery stores where you can stock up. It is a pictur-esque community surrounded by snow-capped mountains.

Couldn't go to Twin Falls and Glacier Gulch (Hudson Bay Glacier) because there is too much snow still on the road. Drove 11 km to Driftwood Canyon Prov. Park to see fossils in the shale cliff. Found two, one of a mosquito(?). This is a day park, but we'll stay the night anyway. This time of year there's not too much going on. Young couple arrived in a car and saw a black bear on the walking path. They left immediately.

<u>May 9 Kleanza Creek Provincial Park, BC</u>
Very cold during the night. Furnace not working properly. John up several times turning it on and off. Up at 6:00 am.

All animals were posed naturally.
Look at the Lynx reaching for a bird.
Once inside, will you be able to find the smallest creature?

Stopped at Adam's Igloo just west of Smithers. Well worth the $4 entrance fee. Ted Moon is a taxidermist and displays his animals, birds and insects in natural settings and sounds. A must see.

From parking lot we had a good view of Hudson Bay Glacier and the falls, which appeared (through binoculars) to be still frozen.

Hazelton tourist info was closed, but it displays three big carved statues, very well done. Hazelton is the northern-most community on Hwy 16.

A lot of native heritage here, advertised but not well marked. Hard to find some of the places. Went to 'Ksan (Gitksan) Village: 7 buildings, several totem poles (good condition) a small museum and gift shop. $2 to walk the grounds, $7 for a guided

tour of buildings. Can't go into buildings unattended. This place is worth a stop. In summer, there is native singing and dancing on Fridays. Sorry we missed that, one of the disadvantages of travelling early in the season. There is also a well-kept RV park here.

Good stands of totem poles are supposed to be in different villages which we drove to but, years ago, the ones at Alert on Vancouver Island were more impressive. The most we saw in one village was 20. Saw a fox while returning from Kitwancool.

There is a Hands of History tour in the area, which no one seems to know anything about. Finally got a photocopy of an old brochure at the museum. There were 19 sites, we saw/found 11. They're not well marked on the hwy. A lot, but not all, of the sites pertain to native history. They were interesting to see.

The Seven Sisters — mountain peaks — are awesome!

At Usk there is a tiny pioneer church that looks like a dollhouse on the side of the hwy. It is unlocked so visitors can stop in, say a prayer and read about this very unusual church and its miracle.

Stopped at Cedarvale Grille for supper - Prime Rib and Yorkshire pudding. Delicious meal and tender meat.

Stayed at Kleanza Creek Prov Park for $9.50. Jim & Carol keep it exceptionally clean. Our site was next to fast-flowing creek. Enjoyed campfire tonight and the sounds of the water. At our site there was a small mouse grave made by a child.

Sunday, May 10 Terrace, BC

Slow casual day in this park. John caught up on his writing after enjoying another campfire. Left at 3 pm.

Made our way to Terrace. Downtown was a bit dirty-looking, as were the two grocery stores. Parked at the Catholic church for the night. Hoped to find some information regarding mass times but there was nothing posted. Walked around the area, a mix of old and new.

May 11-13 Kitimat, BC

Rained during night. Travel centre has lots of info about Yukon. Sani-dump here plus three others in town, propane available.

Went to Heritage Park, but it is closed Mondays. Went to Northern Lights, a Japanese Garden no longer open to the public. Mat & Kay retired last year, but they generously let us walk through the small, well done area. It has a stream, bridges, miniature pagoda, goldfish, jade sidewalk and jade benches. The largest jade slab weighs nearly a ton. Jade comes from Dease Lake region. Hopefully this place will re-open sometime in the future, under new management. A charming, restful setting.

Waited in Terrace for library to open so John could get/send e-mail. Couldn't make connection.

En route to Kitimat stopped to see Lakelse Lake Furlong Bay Prov Park. Campground has 156 sites @ $14.50/night. Beautiful spot, nice beach, old growth forest, massive trees (need four people to encircle one of them).

Drove 1 ½ km on unmarked logging road, then walked a trail close to edge of canyon and finally came to spectacular Humphrey Falls. Great volumes of water rushing and tumbling over 16 m drop. Impressive.

Kitimat is a planned industrial town of 12,000. Some parts are pretty shabby and others are quite nice. Has two malls and no downtown or main street. Kitimat has 2 grocery stores, 4 banks, hospital, a big recreation complex, and a library where we finally got on the Internet. Had 41 messages, mostly junk. Overcast and periods of light rain all day. Parked at a mall for the night.

May 12

Same weather today. Basically killed time waiting for Alcan tour at 1 pm. We, one other couple and a dozen kindergarten kids and teachers were driven by bus through the complex. At least the explanations were at a level I could understand. Afterwards went to see the giant Sitka Spruce, about 53m high and 11m in circumference. 500 years old. Massive.

May 13 Terrace, BC

Did laundry. On the way back to Terrace we stopped at Layton Hot Springs. Wednesday is 2 for 1 which is good because they charge $6.75 to use their pools. They even gave us the Seniors' rate, maybe we looked tired. Air was cold — life guards wore winter jackets — but the water was hot. Just as we returned to the RV Tonie and Martin pulled in, so we had coffee and delicious European biscuits in their motorhome.

Saw a deer on the way back to Terrace. Filled up with inexpensive gasoline at the Superstore, which they call a wholesale club. Parked at Canadian Tire outside of town, where John changed the engine's oil and filter. Another wet, damp day.

May 14 Prince Rupert, BC

Took 13 km gravel side road trip to Shames Mountain Ski area. Beautiful drive, saw a bear cub.

Lots of sunny periods today, trip to Prince Rupert was enjoyable. Saw an osprey. Prince Rupert has sudden heavy rain squalls and there were several this afternoon while we were sight-seeing. The totem poles here are more attractive, probably because they are painted.

This city of 20,000 has much more appeal than Terrace or Kitimat. A beginning tourist spot is in the Cow Bay area. Fire hydrants, benches, and light standards are painted black and white, some in shapes of cows. There is even a "cow-pacino" café, and by the yacht club 3 or 4 big fuel tanks display cow faces. We went to Smile's Café for supper and had delicious fish and chips. We shared the order, it was huge.

Stayed at Park Avenue campground for the night. The campground is soaked with all the rain that has fallen. We need electricity to charge the battery, which doesn't seem to be charging as we travel. Tonie & Martin are here. This is the last time we will see them as they are taking a ferry from here in the morning.

May 15 Kitsumkalum Lake, Nisga'a Hwy, BC

More rain during night but sunny today. Stopped and hiked in to see Butze Rapids. Hike is through old growth forest, with some 'banzai-type' trees further on. Muskeg path is covered with chips between plank boardwalks. Took one left-hand path which almost got us lost, but it was fun because we got down to the river right beside the rapids.

Drove to Ridley Island which is a powdered coal and grain shipping area. Huge piles of powdered coal were being watered to keep the dust down. Watched BC ferry leave, coastal view is quite scenic.

On to cannery at Port Edward. Tour is $6 and there was an hour wait until the next one. We walked a bit, had clam chowder in a tiny restaurant, and left. $4 seemed expensive for what we got. At this end of the Skeena River there are many little islands in the river, very picturesque.

Saw an eagle, and watched a bear munching grass for five minutes before ambling off into the woods.

In Terrace we shopped, gassed up, got propane. We are ready for the Stewart-Cassiar Highway (Hwy 37) via the Nisga'a Hwy.

Parked next to highway at Kitsumkalum Lake for the night, overlooking lake which is about 50 m below. We are about 30 km along the Nisga'a Hwy/Nass Road. Watched a gorgeous sunset behind snow-capped mountains. Saw a beaver swimming and climbing rocks along the edge of the lake below.

May 16 Kelly Lake, Cassiar Hwy (37), BC

At Rosswood there is a "water tree", a living tree providing cool drinking water. Natural springs were piped into the tree by Don Parmeter, who powers his home with a small hydroelectric generator he built beside a waterfall. A fox trotted down the paved highway, coming quite close to our RV. Very bushy tail.

By Lava Lake a young brown bear ran across the road. We stopped at beginning of lava beds and did a two-hour hike trying unsuccessfully to find the source crater. On returning to the beginning we noticed people reading a sign that indicated we were supposed to travel these sacred lands only with a native guide, for $12 per person. Oops.

Travelled 160 km on the Nisga'a Hwy to where it meets the Cassiar Hwy. 60 km paved, 100 km of fine gravel and *very* dusty. Not worth it, there is nothing to see after the lava beds which are just at the beginning of the gravel. The beds extend for about 15 km but because of lichen growing on them, the lava beds look like dirty rocks. Very extensive. Ancient stories tell of the destruction wrought by the lava as it flowed through a deep valley now filled with lava, with (lots of air bubbles.

I don't think we were ever this dusty and dirty before. I couldn't see through my glasses and our hair felt like straw. Looking out the back window of the RV, we could see clouds of dust motes inside our motorhome. We do not recommend the Nisga'a Hwy, especially past the pavement!

We passed a few small emerald lakes and stopped at Beaupre Falls for lunch. There is a pleasant spot here beside the river where the road leaves the lava bed and climbs a hill. Today for the first time we used the fold-away picnic table our friends Jack and June gave us before we left Kelowna.

Pulled in at Kelly Lake on Hwy 37 for the night. Another family here for the weekend. Washed the inside of RV, had a shower, took the canoe off the roof and paddled around this small lake. Ate supper outside, had a fire. Lots of blackflies and a few mosquitos.

Saw a total of five bears today, plus a fox and a gartersnake in the lava bed.

Sunday, May 17 Bear Glacier, Hwy 37A, BC

Saw a groundhog. Ahead of us the coastal mountains rise above everything else, all white, majestic and dominating the scenery - they *are* the scenery. The glaciers we can see are part of the Cambrian Ice Field. Surprised at how many deciduous trees are up here.

At Meziadin Junction (elevation 260 m), the turn off for Stewart and Hyder, lots of snow patches are along the side of the road. For 2 km the hwy was lined with a carpet of bright yellow dandelions. Meziadin Prov Park is very nice ($9.50). Terraced sites with higher ones giving a better view.

Gas prices take quite a jump here, 10 cents a litre and more. We turned off here to take paved Hwy 37A to Stewart, BC and Hyder, AK. Bear Glacier comes almost right down to the hwy. It calves its icebergs into ice-blue Bear River. It's cold here from the air flowing down over the glacier. Partially overcast. Several small waterfalls on north side of hwy.

Talked with John and Dolores who have lived here for 16 years. She is a lab/x-ray tech for the health centre and he drives heavy equipment for the town. Stewart was a logging/mining town. Now logging is slow, the mine is shut down, and population is down to 450. There's an awful lot of empty houses, windows boarded up, due to almost. 400 families leaving in the past 1 ½ years after the mine closed.

Al and Sheri Lindsay (retired RCMP) run the Lion's Rainey Creek Municipal Campground, which is clean and neat. $12 dry, $15 with electricity. Sani-dump and washrooms with showers. Al told us about an episode he had last year with a grizzly bear. He chased it through the campground and then shot it 4 or 5 times - with a Paint-Ball gun!

John went to the Museum, I didn't because they couldn't make change. Talked with the cashier and her husband, both history buffs. They came in 1990 for two years government work and are still here and loving it.

Drove to Hyder. This is the only entrance to Alaska from BC, the others are in Yukon. Pavement stops at Canada-USA border. What a depressed community. Maybe 200 people here. Most houses are pretty shabby-looking. There is good salmon candy at a small processing plant, also some excellent vacuum packed salmon. Hyder uses Canadian currency. There is no bank in Hyder. The folks there come to Stewart to do their banking. The Hyder Post Office requires US funds though. Couldn't drive the 32 km to Salmon Glacier lookout because snow blocked the highway near its summit.

Customs are only on Canadian side of border. Declaration of purchases must be made; unloaded rifles pass after an inspection, at least for Canadians and locals.

Eagle soared overhead, then rested on tree. Saw three bear today and one beaver tonight.

We heard Bear Glacier glowed in the moonlight so we have driven back here for the night. Doubtful what we'll see because there is a light cloud cover.

May 18 Tanzilla River, Cassiar Hwy, BC

Set the alarm for 1 am. Sky was clear and full of stars. Could see glacier but it doesn't 'glow in the dark'. Very windy & cold here in the parking lot. Cloud right down to tree line at 7:30 am.

Back at Meziadin Junction there is supposed to be an RV park with 48 full service sites - in your dreams! A big gravel area looks like it might have 8 sites with electricity. They advertise a sani-dump but charge $5 if you don't camp there. We didn't see it. Did we miss it?

Light overcast all day with patches of blue sky. Clouds sitting on top of mtns to west. In front of us the mountains appear as a wall of translucent ice.

Travelled 50 km of well-packed gravel and intermittent pavement. Stopped at Hodder Lake for lunch. Not much to see today, should cover some good mileage (kilometrage?).

Stopped to check out Willow Ridge Resort at km 353. Lovely clean campground run by Jay & Andy Andersen. *Big* sites, 8 with full hookups for $15, five dry sites for $10 and six tent sites. $2 for showers. We paid $3 to use their sani-dump and fill up with water. Surprised to see hummingbirds here, thought it would be too cold for them. Apparently in June this place turns purple with flowers called lupins.

Leaves are now starting to come out, even with snow patches here and there.

Kinaskan Lake Prov Park ($9.50) is nice and clean. 50 sites, all on the lake. In fact all BC provincial parks have improved greatly since their maintenance has been privatized.

Trees along highway are getting shorter and thinner.

Passed a Class A motorhome from Utah that we saw in Stewart. He burned out his distributor cap. Again. Wife pleased to have someone to talk to and break monotony of waiting while husband was driving 50 km north to Bell II for help and repairs. It's not likely they'll have the needed part, he should have brought his own. Of course it had been fixed so who would have expected it to fail once more?

Hey, Billy! We got an oscillatable fulcrum bar for a Bluebird Wanderlodge?[1]

Llamas at Tenajon Lodge.

Met cyclist Sven Tuft from Vancouver, BC with his dog on a cart. He says his dog runs about 30 km/day. Has already biked

The dog runs about 30 km per day, then rides the rest.

to Valdez, Alaska and is on his way home. Been on the road two months.

50 km south of Dease Lake, there is ice on another lake.

Gnat Summit, 1240 m (3900'). We were going to spend the night at Gnat Lake — nice camping area next to lake, does name mean anything? — but it is frozen. Carried on to Tanzilla River. Free camping here, about 10 sites, clean, treed and on the river. Lots of bear scat.

Travelled 360 km. 1 groundhog, 2 porcupines and 1 bear sighted. Lovely sunset at 10 pm but still light at 11 pm. Talked with Frieda and Charles from Kentucky, USA. They are already on their way home after visiting Alaska.

Passed several wilderness lodges ranging from rustic to luxurious. These are jumping off points for back country experiences - flight-seeing, horseback riding, hiking, canoeing, kayaking, fishing, etc.

Three Provincial Parks, Mount Edziza, Spatsizi (meaning Red Goat, and accessible only by hiking or air) and Stikine River are connected. One starts where the other stops. Mt. Edziza is an old volcanic crater visible at a distance from Hwy 37. Campsite at Kinaskin Lake also views the crater.

217

May 19 Telegraph Creek, BC

Dease Lake has a fair-sized Superstore, with competitive prices. Of course everything costs more the further north we go and in smaller communities.

Decided to take the 112 km dirt road to Telegraph Creek. Road is in good repair, very hard packed but occasionally dusty. Nothing to see in the first 60 km but the rest of the way is spectacular. The "Grand Canyon" of the Stikine River and Tahltan Canyon. Steep grades — 18 to 20% — and gorges, narrow roads, hairpin turns and layer on layer of solid-rock lava beds. During this drive the pickles and olives tipped over in the fridge. Of course the lids had loosened. I had to empty and clean the fridge of sticky juice.

Walked 100 m where we could see over a huge green valley with a plateau on the other side. Coastal mtns in the distance.

So far, this road is better than the Nisga'a Hwy by far, and even better than Hwy 37. However everything is covered in dust but I'm not cleaning because we have to drive over it again tomorrow.

No minister home. Good thing.
John's language was very colourful.

In Telegraph Creek, if there are 400 people here they must be back a kilometre and on the Reserve. Except for the houses on the main street by the Stikine River, all houses and buildings seem deserted. Like stepping back in time. Very picturesque here, glad we came.

Got so frustrated with my hair feeling like straw after we travel a dirt road that I chopped it off. John will have to trim the back for me. It probably looks worse than before but it will be easier to clean and keep neat.

The only animals seen today were some horses.

John sensed the back brakes hadn't been working properly so after we walked a bit, bought ice cream, talked with a few people (including 'Pete the Heat', an RCMP constable) he took off the rear wheels and sure enough there was a mess inside the brake drums. Decided to call it a day and fix it tomorrow.

May 20 Cottonwood River, Cassiar Hwy, BC

John cut the back of my hair, then spent an hour on the brakes. Fortunately he had a spare brake shoe and was able to implement a temporary fix. Hope it holds till we get to Whitehorse. Talked with Ann and Francis Gleason. Francis is a retired heavy-duty mechanic. He does some river tours and wants to convert his old, overstuffed garage-machine shop into a museum. He helped John by giving advice, which was needed. Francis' grandfather was born here. Francis lives 100 m from where he was born 70+ years ago.

En route to Dease Lake we saw 3 groups of horses and 2 rabbits. We gassed up. We do that a lot. Was going to do a laundry but they charged $4 just for the wash. Hopefully Watson Lake will be more reasonable.

Nice rest area at Cottonwood River. Decided to stay the night. I did a major cleanup, including washing the floor.

An Australian family pulled in. 3 adults and 3 children in a station wagon packed to the rafters. The right rear tire was low and he had no spare tire so we lent him a pump that plugs into the cigarette lighter. Purposely overfilled the tire. Hope he makes it to the next garage.

Dull overcast day with very slight sprinkle of rain. Tonight a beautiful wine-coloured bird and one with a gold head plus several whiskey jacks -also known as camp robbers and Canada Jays - came by. They are grey and white birds about the size of

Just a pretty swamp on side of the highway.

a pigeon. Another couple from Florida, USA pulled in. We all used binoculars to see mountain goats on mtn.

It's 10:30 pm and we don't need the lights.

May 21-23 Boya Lake, Cassiar Hwy, BC

Beautiful sunshine this morning.

What the mosquitos lack in number they make up for in size!

We are just about out of water, the brakes are scraping again, and the tail pipe is loose. John is wiring it up with a coat hanger.

Canadian Jays joined us for breakfast. They are quite tame and fearless.

Despite all my cleaning our RV still smells dusty. When we drive the motion shakes everything up. Dumped at Jade City where we visited the well stocked gift shop. They had no potable water.

Missed the turnoff to Cassiar, not well marked.

Good Hope Lake is a beautiful blue/green colour. Indian community of about 100.

Pulled in at Boya Lake Prov Park, $9.50/night. The lake is amethyst blue and jade green. Potable water comes from a hand pump, so we put 20 potfuls in by funnel. That gives us more than ½ tank full.

Took the canoe out, it's like paddling in a swimming pool. Water is so clear and blue. We found an artesian spring and another large hole nearby.

Fred and Ann from Australia are camped here, a return visit for her.

Wind came up quite strong while we were canoeing and also a bit of rain. We were in a bay and took shelter by the shore then headed home when the wind let up. Clouds from 3 pm on.

John did lots of fixing, the big job being trying to seal any openings that allowed the dust to come in under both sinks.

Mostly cloudy but no rain. Went for a long walk, then a long canoe ride even though it was windy. Saw a loon and beaver lodge, several ducks, a cormorant, and a grouse but still no moose, although I saw moose droppings/scat during my walk. The wild flowers are coming into bloom.

There is a really big beaver across the lake chewing on a stick. We were watching with binoculars at 10 pm. Finally he swam away and disappeared into tall grass.

May 23 Watson Lake, Yukon

Boya Lake is fairly large with lots of islands and bays. We canoed for two hours this morning. Cool and light overcast. A lot of beaver lodges, many abandoned. 2 loons. A 'must stay' campground especially if you have a boat.

The remaining 80 km drive to Alaska Highway is paved but boring. Not even the mtns are in view. Tall thin trees on either side of hwy.

At the junction of Stewart-Cassiar and Alaska hwys there is a gas station with store, restaurant & motel made out of ATCO trailers, and an RV park on gravel. Also a laundromat with regular machines inside another trailer. Washers $1.50, dryers $0.50 for 10-30 minutes. By this time I needed two washers. I washed my hair in a big sink in the laundry trailer. It sure felt good to get the dust out.

Driving into Watson Lake the highway ditches were full of plastic bags and other garbage. Watson Lake is very dusty. Has a nice park, Wye Lake, in the centre of the village. 2 RV parks in the community and several along the highway.

Tonight we parked at the end of a little used street right next to the water of Second Wye Lake. We couldn't have walked around the RV without getting wet.

Sunday, May 24 Morely Lake, Alaska Hwy, Yukon

This morning we went to mass at St. Ann's church in Watson Lake. About 18 people in attendance. Priest was an older man with quite an accent, guitarist has hint of Irish brogue. Many of the clergy here in the north serve more than one congregation and spend a lot of time travelling to remote or isolated communities.

Went to Northern Lights Centre and saw an hour-long animated visual display. $16 and so-so. We'd hope to see more pictures and videos of actual Northern Lights. A lot of 'dead time' was filled with images of falling snow instead of the aurora borealis. We mentioned this to them, I wonder if they will make any changes.

Visited the Signpost Forest with over 20,000 signs and a one-third scale wartime plane.

Visitor Reception Centre was close by. It shows a 20 minute slide show about the Alaska Highway. This wartime effort by Canada and the USA was called the Alcan Project but later the road they built together became known as the Alaska Highway even though only 474 km (300 miles) of this 2446 km (1520 mile) highway are in Alaska. The other 1972 km (1220 miles) are in Canada. The presentation and gallery were both well done. At the Visitors Centre we plugged in so John could print a couple of letters, one to the Mayor complaining about the litter at the entrance to town immediately after passing a sign stating "This is a litter-free Community". The staff at the Visitors Centre said that area was adjacent to the village dump and always poses a problem in the spring because of the high winds. Watson Lake is subject to frequent small dust storms, Whitehorse is worse, they say.

Stopped at Walkers at the Continental Divide for rhubarb pie. This seems to be a big thing up here. That and cinnamon buns. The pie was good but I make better.

Drove 210 km. Pulled off by a lake at 9 pm. It was after 4 pm when we left Watson Lake. En route we talked on CB with a

222

An abandoned miner's cabin ... and we thought we lived in a small house!

trucker and his wife from Seattle, Washington, USA who are going on to Whitehorse tonight. Told us about McCrae's Restaurant outside of Whitehorse that has great Chinese food.

May 25-28 Atlin, BC

John washed the RV this morning before we left.

Teslin is a neat community of about 500 people, mostly native. Many nice log houses. Different design for the church, Immaculate Heart of Mary. It's round. Inside are hide banners and a copper tabernacle shaped like a teepee.

Nisutlin Bridge, 584 m (1917 ft) is the longest one on Alaska Highway. Nisutlin Trading Post in the village a little way off the hwy has good selection of groceries at very reasonable prices. Best we've seen for a while.

Mukluk Annie's has 'Jesus is Lord' on ad in Milepost and on menus. Huge servings, delicious food, reasonable prices. Difficult to get one plate and share with spouse/partner because of 'all you can eat' salad bar. We ordered a huge Mukluk Annie Burger and shared that. There is a one-hour river boat trip in the evening for folks who order from their "Salmon Bake" menu. The boat isn't ready yet (will be day after tomorrow). This is one of the problems of travelling early in the season, a lot of things aren't ready yet. On the other hand, it's not crowded. Free sani-dump, dry camping and water. Free RV wash also if you order from "Salmon Bake" menu. Because we couldn't do the river boat trip we decided to drive a bit farther.

Johnson Crossing. Friendly people. Caroline Smith is owner and baker. Enjoyed cinnamon bun. John took photo of handmade arrow, including hand-chipped arrowhead.

At km 1335 there is an abandoned airstrip with a deserted tower and bare windsock. Giant eagle's nest in the tower, with occupants. Could hear the babies but not see them. One adult eagle on nest, one on windsock.

The road to Atlin, BC is 70 km of dirt and 30 km paved. Light rain so no dust, but lots of mud. Stopped by a creek after we were back on pavement and washed the RV. We had tried to get to another creek and almost got stuck. The RV was brown all over. Couldn't see out the back window. I had about a pound of mud on each running shoe. Used a potato brush to clean them in the creek.

The drive to Atlin was beautiful, even though clouds and fog blocked some of the mountain views. They swirled around

We promised to put his picture in our book - how could we not with scenery like that? - but we've lost his name.

the mtns and just above the lake giving it an ethereal beauty. Lots of squirrels and rabbits.

Atlin is a unique little town in many ways: 1) streets are paved; 2) appears to be thriving; 3) pleasing mix of log homes and new homes with siding; 4) clean; 5) colour here, not all buildings are natural wood or stained, some are painted blue, green, pink, white; 6) restoration in progress; 7) at least a dozen buildings have historical plaques; 8) several small buildings —

224

Atlin homes have character, whatever that means.

play house size — abandoned but not falling apart; 9) a couple of intriguing birdhouses; 10) idyllic setting. We walked around from 9 - 10:30 pm. Sun set at 10, still light at 11 pm.

Museum has an outside display of several pieces of mining equipment including 2 'donkeys' which are so heavy they have sunk into the ground.

May 26

Stayed in Atlin until 4 pm. Walked around taking pictures, talking to people. Chatted with Marion who moved here 8 years ago. She gave us a lot of info and helped us to get a feel for this place.

Atlin is unincorporated so has no rules or by-laws. This can sometimes be a problem, as for example, if someone wants to build a home or other edifice whose design does not blend in with the existing structures. They are hoping to have the whole village declared an historical site. This would preserve the atmosphere and harmony of the community. Went into St. Stephen's Anglican Church, nice, and St. Anne's Catholic Mission, bare. At St. Anne's, a lay couple do Eucharistic services on Sundays. A priest comes occasionally.

Drove 10 km on Discovery Road to the deserted and non-existent town of Discovery, not much remaining. There are some placer mining operations on Spruce Creek & Pine Falls. Pioneer cemetery has some interesting epitaphs: "Accidentally killed by gunshot, mistaken for a bear"; "Killed in mining accident at Spruce Creek"; "Pilot died of starvation"; etc. Two pilots have propellers over their graves.

Went to end of Warm Bay Road, then back to Palmer Lake. Free camping, 3 or 4 sites. Two units are here from California, USA. En route to Palmer Lake a moose (finally!) ran across the road in front of us. A yearling, I think.

Two loons playing, cavorting or courting on Palmer Lake. They would "fly" with their feet in the water and their wings flinging spray everywhere.

When we went canoeing, the same moose was in the lake in front of us. It scrambled ashore and we paddled along beside it until it headed inland and into the woods. We saw two pike about a half-metre (18") long and a swimming beaver. Couldn't get close to it. A bald eagle sat in a tree, too far away for a picture.

Supper at midnight! Into bed at 1 am, still light.

May 27

Slept 'til 9:30 am. Wonderful sunny, warm day. I read and John did a lot of typing. Canoed tonight for two hours, saw the beaver again, a really big one. He was on shore but entered the water when we drifted within 3 m of him. Slapped his tail twice and swam across the lake.

This morning 2 loons were scooting back and forth across the water. Courting ritual? They were flapping their wings and skimming the surface. Quite a sight to see these birds zooming across the water.

We are the only people here tonight.

May 28-June 2 Whitehorse, Yukon

Stayed at Palmer Lake 'til noon, soaking up sunshine. Went into Atlin and returned library books. We donated one of our self-published travelogues to the library. Many houses and drive-way entrances have moose antlers arched across the top. We dumped in a cesspool/lagoon about 15 km outside of the village along Discovery Road. Headed back to Alaska Highway.

On the way to Whitehorse, thought we had a flat but when we pulled over and John checked the pressure they were all good. Drove slowly, but we could still hear a flapping sound. At the junction to Carcross we pulled into a service centre at 5 pm. On closer inspection, the inside tire on John's side had a strip of rubber missing from the tread. He's not happy with one of the rear tires on my side either - bulging - but hopefully it will last until we get to Whitehorse.

Foam from theWhitehorse Rapids, painted on the side of the MacBride Museum.

227

Changed the bad tire. Had soup and sandwich for supper, we'd been planning on Chinese in Whitehorse but I couldn't wait any longer.

Whitehorse, population of 20,000. Drove 2nd, 3rd and 4th streets (downtown) then up the hill to the airport. It will cost only $9 to leave the motorhome here for a week while we fly back to Kelowna, BC for Rob & Teresa's wedding.

There is a big forest fire burning in the vicinity, the city is shrouded in thick smoke. Visibility is poor.

Stayed in an RV park in centre of town, $21 for full hook-ups including cable TV which we don't want. We didn't come here to watch TV. There are 4-5 good campgrounds along the hwy as well. Being outside the city they are a bit cheaper. Nice to have a really long shower.

Windy and dusty here, but not as bad as Watson Lake.

A modern residence but in historic style and bright colours and trim.

RV battery needs to be charged but it needs water before we can charge it. John bought four litres of distilled water and the big battery took almost half.

Spent an afternoon at a tourism meeting, asking or suggesting that BC businesses and cities should advertise BC and

Yukon, not Alaska. Or maybe all three. You can't get to Alaska without driving through Yukon but many people don't know that. Went to airport to pick up tickets.

Very hot- 31^{0}C, in truck cab it's 84^{0}F. All the windows open trying for a breeze.

Engine leaking oil a little, and John thinks the brakes are starting to fail again. Checked e-mail at library.

While in Whitehorse we visited with our niece and her family. They have lived in Whitehorse for quite a few years and love it here. We can see why. We stayed in their driveway for a night and were able to charge the battery. It still doesn't seem to be charging when we drive. John worked on the RV trying to discover and fix the source of the oil leak.

Sunny and windy. A lot of yellow pollen floating around. Great for my allergies!! Parked for a night or two beside Schwatka Lake on Miles Canyon Road, at a small pull out across from floatplane docks.

On Sunday, after Mass at the cathedral, we walked around part of the city. Drove out to Miles Canyon and hiked to Canyon City. Nothing remains of this once vibrant sternwheeler river stop. We followed the river on the way back, (very green water). About 4 km round trip. Very scenic. Pleasant afternoon. Mix of sun, cloud and wind today.

We have a MOUSE. I saw it run into the opening for the furnace this morning.

Bought a new battery for my camera. Missed a couple of pictures yesterday.

Mural commemorating construction of the AlCan Project on the side of the Yukon Transportation Museum, up near the airport.

Bought two new tires and had them balanced, $321. Had to rotate tires to ensure each type of tire was on only one side of rear axle. Now we have a spare again. The brakes will be done while we are at the wedding.

We parked at the airport (told security the RV would be gone for mechanical repairs, then returned) and went to see Beringia and the Yukon Transportation Museum. Both very enjoyable and intriguing. Combination passes for $6 each, an excellent deal.

John thinks he fixed oil leak. Another glorious sunset.

June 9-11 Whitehorse, Yukon

Returned from a very enjoyable week in Kelowna attending Robert and Teresa's wedding. Arrived back in Whitehorse at 1:30 pm. Brakes were fixed while we were gone, $273. Got gas, water, groceries and dumped our tanks. Went to see the Fish Ladder next to the dam on Yukon River. No fish using the ladder right now.

Drove 8 km on dirt road to Chadburn Lake and parked for the night. Thought we might canoe but it was too windy. There must be beavers here because a lot of trees have been felled by them. Temperature today was only 14^{0}C. By 8 pm wind had died down so we canoed for an hour. Some big beaver lodges, but no beavers, only a few ducks.

June 10

Slept ten hours, very quiet. No furnace last night, for first time. Cool when we got up.

We were going to leave Whitehorse today but ended up staying. John not satisfied with brakes. He'd asked to have one piece replaced and it wasn't. We have another appointment tomorrow at 8 am.

He toured the SS Klondike ($3.50) while I walked to the Log Church museum, which was closed because they were working on the displays. It's an Anglican church built in 1900. McBride Museum ($4) has a lot of outdoor exhibits.

Government building has a beautiful stained glass window depicting history of Yukon. John spent a couple of hours at the archives researching family tree. Got one reference. Went to the library to hear CBC's writer and humorist Arthur Black do some readings from his new book. Got some ideas about how we could do same. Talked with producer who asked us to call him in the fall and maybe we can do an interview. Parked at Yukon Tire for the night, because they'll be doing the brakes.

June 11 Tutshi Lake, BC

Mainly sunny, very windy and cool, no animals.

Brakes fixed at no charge to us. Breakfast at Subway, deli sandwich was really tasty. We're on our way once more.

Picked up Rob Horne and gave him a ride to Carcross. He's a student in Thunder Bay, Ontario, working in Whitehorse for the summer. Very pleasant young man. Stopped to see Emerald Lake, which was a bit disappointing, probably due to the wind and its small size. Boya Lake is better in our opinion. Brief stop at Carcross Desert which is the world's smallest desert. This highway is very windy! At least it is today.

Stopped for cinnamon buns along the way and met Teya(?) and Andy who were cycling to Skagway.

Spent two hours at Carcross, community of 400. Matthew Watson General Store, established at the turn of the century, is one of the oldest stores still in operation in Yukon. It is now a gift store. Behind the Post Office is a bridge spanning the narrows joining Nares Lake and Bennet Lake. Fast moving water. Windy. The old blue and white Anglican church was built in 1904. Has a lovely stained-glass window behind the altar.

Carcross Barracks is now a souvenir and ice cream shop. Very busy, lots of signs and soft mannequins. In the back is the NWMP 'office' with Sgt. Pringle at a desk. There is also an original jail cell, and at the drop of a hat you get thrown into the cell and locked in. Of course John got himself 'arrested' and locked up. After his release he bought an autographed T-shirt.

Met Teya and Andy again at Carcross then later at a viewpoint overlooking an old mine building. The wind was really strong and against them. At this point they were willing to accept a ride and loaded their gear and bikes into the RV. They came with us to Tutshi Lake, about 30 km farther along. We all set up camp for the cool and windy night.

June 12 Skagway, AK

Cloudy, cold (4⁰C), very windy. Saw 1 rabbit, 3 eagles.

Seems so cold this morning, the wind makes it feel like winter. We drove the cyclists to the White Pass Summit, 3290 ft. We'll see them on the ferry to Haines tomorrow. Carried on to Skagway, stopping at viewpoints along the way. Deadhorse Gulch was quite poignant. There are many beautiful scenic photo opportunities en route. One very different scene is "Tormented Valley", a large area of rocks, lakes and stunted growth. A very desolate area. Low grey cloud sitting on the mountain tops added to the effect.

Skagway is one big colourful tourist trap. Broadway, the main tourist thoroughfare is 12 blocks long with boardwalks, false-fronted stores, all brightly painted and nicely done. Each store is a souvenir shop, tour office, jewellery store or restaurant. The town is 4 or 5 streets wide and 23 blocks long. A huge tourist ship was parked in the marina.

Drove to Dyea, now an abandoned town, at the beginning of the 53 km Chilkoot Trail. Walked around the "Slide Cemetery" which is the final resting place of the avalanche victims. Every marker has the same date of death, April 3, 1898.

After supper we walked to Gold Rush Cemetery then to Reid Falls which are beautiful. We were gone 3 hours and had sore feet when we returned to our RV. Saw the White Pass and Yukon Route Railway train and maintenance station. People were preparing the old steam locomotive for its first trip of the summer.

Spent night in Skagway ferry terminal parking lot.

June 13 Haines, AK

Cloudy and cool, saw several eagles

In parking lot we were lined up according to destination. Loading seemed to be done randomly with some of the standby vehicles going on first. Most disorganized on and off loading of any ferry we've been on. Because now there are only two cross-

232

ings a week, it was packed. The last fifth-wheel was squeezed in with barely centimetres to spare. It was such a tight fit an employee had to back it in. Crossing from Skagway to Haines on ferry MV Malaspina took about an hour.

Unfortunately it was cold outside with low lying cloud and drizzling rain. We wanted to be outside to see as much as we could but it wasn't pleasant and the low cloud hid a lot of the view. On a warm sunny day this would be a lovely trip. The rain stopped when we reached Haines.

While unloading the ferry, the driver of the last-on fifthwheel bumped into his friend's fiver next to it. He ripped his awning and broke his neighbour's water inlet and slightly damaged one of his window frames. The employee should have driven it off. Staff had to use chains and a winch to move each RV over to get clearance. That provided 45 minutes of entertainment to everybody on the lower deck. No vehicle could get off until that one did. It is a drive on, back off ferry and it was quite the show watching the big 35' and 40' motorhomes backing up and turning around. One fellow was so upset at the delay he roared up the ramp, almost tearing his bumper off when it scraped.

When we left the ferry people from Haines were handing out red plastic bags with maps and info about the town. A nice gesture and much appreciated.

We were very low on gasoline, waiting to buy in Haines where prices were lower, so we headed straight for a gas station. Petro Marine gives 5¢/US gallon off if you have Canadian (probably non-USA) licence plates. We got propane there as well. Petro Marine also has a sani-dump so we'll stop there again tomorrow when we're leaving.

Had poor halibut and chips for supper for Can$10 at Dockside Express. Win some, lose some. No comparison with fish and chips meal we had in Prince Rupert (Cow Bay) for same price.

Went to Mass at Sacred Heart. Talked afterwards with guitar player Dick, his wife Caroline, and Fr. Jerry who was filling in. He knows the priest in Dawson City, Yukon and asked us to say hello when we get there. Very pleasant people.

Haines is not nearly the tourist trap that Skagway is. Real people live and work here. It's a little bigger but prices are about the same. Bought some smoked salmon — $14/pound — and a small piece of delicious fudge.

Went to the Eagle Foundation, only $2 each. Most enjoyable. It is set up like Adam's Igloo but not as crowded nor extensive. Displayed lots of eagles in various stages of maturity. Saw several eagles in trees around Haines. Raining tonight.

There is a lot of snow on the mountains here and a few small glaciers. Had six layers of clothes — undershirt, flannel shirt, fleece sweater, fleece vest, wind breaker, and jacket — on today, will wear socks to bed tonight. Furnace is on already. Sure wish I had a toque to cover my head.

The Chilkat Dancers perform only on Sunday-Thursday ($10) so we missed them. The Chilkat Potlatch Salmon Bake at Fort Seward is nightly from 5 - 9 pm but US $21.75 each was too steep for our budget. That would be about $55 Can.

Stayed at Mud Bay Road right next to beach on almost private road. Saw some distant glaciers.

Sunday, June 14 Rock Glacier, Kluane National Park, YT

Overcast, periodic light rain, 1 eagle, rabbits and gophers.

Stopped at Chilkoot State Park and visited with camp host for half an hour. Very pleasant couple. He used to teach at Whitman University and Gonzaga University, Washington; she wrote an illustrated book on tropical birds.

Left Haines at noon. Travelled slowly through Eagle Preserve but saw only one eagle. Fall and winter is time to be here if you want to see eagles en masse.

Went over Three Guardsman Pass (3215 ft) and Chilkat Pass (3493 ft). Some awesome scenery today even though clouds were low. Lots of snow up here, mountains are almost all white. Feels warm now that we are away from the coast but it looks like February.

Mt Elias Range is tall, white and rugged.

More deciduous trees near USA-Canada (Alaska-British Columbia) border. They get 20-30 ft of snow here in the winter. After Customs, elevation is 2500 ft. Lots of snow but no trees for 50 km.

Interesting landscape. We seem to be driving on top of mtns. Wild flowers are starting to appear. Pale mauve and a deeper purple which I think is the fireweed and it turns red in autumn.

Drove to Klukshu which is a native summer fish camp. Nothing happening now but there are several small homes, caches, drying racks and a few people inside log cabins. Fishing restricted by government.

Some deserted buildings have character, others are just old falling-down wrecks. What makes the difference?

Walked to Million Dollar Falls, 20 m angled drop. Pretty but not exciting.

Parked at Rock Glacier and walked 1 km up the glacier. We didn't know there was such a thing. It is huge, all broken pieces of rock! It formed in waves and moved with an ice glacier. When the ice was melted the rocks were in place. It moved like lava down the mountain, covering everything in its path. Amazing to see from up here, so far from parking lot. Excellent view of Desadeash Lake.

Stayed night in Rock Glacier parking lot, Kluane National Park, Yukon.

June 15 Sheep Mountain, Km 1706.8, Alaska Hwy, Yukon
Predominantly sunny, occasional large cloud patches.

235

Cloud is lifting this morning, big patches of blue. Nice to be warm again. Late departure-noon.

Climbed the Rock Glacier again before leaving to get photos. Stopped in at Kathleen Lake in Kluane National Park. Very pretty, $10 to camp. At Haines Junction, Yukon picked up some groceries. Did laundry, after 3 quarters in dryer I finally hung them up in RV to dry. Wrote postcards, got gas. Bread is expensive, a loaf of 7-grain in a bakery costs $3.50.

Visitor Centre has a good slide show for $3. We saw most of it for free because two of twelve projectors weren't working.

Our Lady of the Way church, built in 1954 from a left-over Quonset hut, is very different, small, cosy and bright. It is one of three Catholic mission churches built on Canada's Alaska Hwy. The other two are at Burwash Landing and Beaver Creek.

Mosquitos are starting to arrive.

Short detour to Silver City, a deserted trading post with actual buildings that haven't fallen down yet. It's on the shore of Kluane Lake and there is a bed and breakfast here. Very idyllic and serene. One of the prettier places we've come to.

The wild flowers are out and splashes of yellow, purple and white dot the roadsides and meadows. Also the pink of wild roses, the blues and violets of bluebells and harebells.

The highway follows Kluane Lake for 63 km. There are large mud and sand flats. Very impressive drive with the lake on one side and the ranges of the Kluane Mtns. on the other. Is this normal or is the water level down?

Spent night in Sheep Mountain Info Centre parking lot, right below that mtn. Seven RVs are here, but no sheep.

June 16 Alaska Hwy, near Canada-US border, Yukon

Mainly sunny, several sheep, 2 moose, 1 fox.

A herd/group of seven sheep traversed the side of the mountain while we breakfasted. Another group was spotted on the crest, they looked like small puffy white clouds.

I hiked to Soldiers' Summit — easy 10 minute walk — where Alcan dedication was held in 1942. Beautiful vistas of Kluane Lake.

We finally saw a full-antlered moose on the side of the road. He nicely lifted his head for a photo.

236

Kluane Lake, from Soldiers' Summit

Burwash Landing has the Kluane Museum of Natural History and it is the best museum we've seen to date. Wonderful animal displays behind glass with a short write-up on each, and in some cases a sample of fur or a footprint. Our Lady of the Rosary log mission church was closed so I had to content myself with looking in the window. A single schoolroom is attached. It was built in 1944

The lovely purple wildflower on the sides of the road is called vetch.

As we crossed White River — so called because of the volcanic ash which has given it a muddy grey colour — there were several wild(?) horses on the flats.

100 km of travelling brought us to 5 km of dirt then alternating pavement and gravel the rest of the day.

Drove through a heavy but short rain fall which kept the dust down without making the road muddy or slick.

Beaver Creek Yukon has Our Lady of Grace mission church built in 1961. It is the third one. It is also an old Quonset hut but smaller than the one in Haines Junction, without a row of windows on the very top. It must be dark inside but door was locked so I'll never know.

While we were in Beaver Creek we met a friendly couple from Australia who are on 23-day bus tour. This village has only 400 people but has a big Westmark Inn — log style — which hosts a dinner theatre every evening ($28) or just the show for $11. We drove another 25 km west and parked for the night in a small side road (lots of mosquitos).

A multi-coloured fox came by the RV sniffing around and leaving his mark. He looked so very thin and hungry.

<u>June 17 Chicken, AK</u>

Grey day, sun up at 4:30 am, cloud at 6:30, rain at 7:00 am. Saw a wolf or coyote on side of road. Got a good photo, I hope.

Crossed border into Alaska, USA and stopped for gas at Scottie's about 6 km from customs. We are leaking oil badly and John can't fix it. Called AAA, not much help. We talked with someone in Missouri who doesn't have a clue where we are; we are 132 Km east of Tok (pop 1405) but he hasn't heard of that either. Doesn't seem to understand that up here you don't get a tow-truck that easy. No idea of the distances between settlements up here. Left it up to us to find a tow truck and send them the bill. Yeah, sure. John made an O-ring from the cardboard back of my writing pad. That worked and we are back on the road shortly after noon hour.

Not a lot to see en route so we're in Tok, Alaska about 3:30 pm. We both showered before we dumped and got more fresh

238

water because it seems that there are no dump stations between here and Dawson City, Yukon. Got gas too because it'll be more expensive in Chicken. Most folks up here are very friendly and trusting. Wild sweet peas growing on side of road. One campground has a salmon bake ($16) with free day camping, sanidump and water but we're not staying. Want to drive a bit farther.

Back about 20 km to Tetlin Junction, then northeast on Taylor Hwy. There are some big cracks in the shoulders of the Taylor Highway, looks like a mini-earthquake. Wonder how long before the shoulder drops away?

First part of road is sealcoat or chipseal and is in good condition. The rest is gravel or dirt. Earlier rain kept dust down but the road wasn't muddy or slippery. Some very pretty areas. We seem to be riding on the top of the mountains and looking down into vast green valleys. The mtns look like the foothills- gently rolling green hills. We drove through a 5-10 minute rain storm about 4 km before Chicken. There is free camping at The Goldpanner and lots of RVs are there. Some are covered in mud, especially their toads (towed vehicles, cars or trucks).

This is NOT downtown Chicken, which is only a five-minute walk away. Probably more people stay here than there. We did.

Chicken's population is 39 so there's not much here. Both Alaska's Taylor Highway and Yukon's Top of the World Highway are closed in the winter. What do these folks do then?

After supper we walked over to 'beautiful downtown Chicken' which consists of a General Mercantile (gifts and souvenirs) Saloon and Café. Saloon is small and every inch of dusty ceiling and wall space is decorated with calling cards, caps and T-shirts from all over the world. Worth a visit.

One woman working in the gift shop does so only one day a week, on her day off. She is a miner and a diver; she vacuums river and creek beds. In winter she trains horses. In the bar we met Linda who was very friendly (fabulous laugh) and a part-time palaeontologist, well-read and informed. Goes on digs in July and August in the Colville River area.

Stayed in Goldpanner's parking area.

June 18 Eagle, AK

Lots of sun, some cloud & rain. Saw 2 moose and a rabbit.

Went to café to watch bus tour arrive at 9:00 am, and had a fresh, hot, huge, light, delicious cinnamon bun before the bus arrived. We couldn't travel that way, too rushed for us slowpokes.

Walked to "old Chicken' which is now private property. A young blacksmith was working there tearing down old buildings which are unsafe. He gave us a bit of a tour and took us into the old cook house which they are attempting to restore. All in all, Chicken has been a pleasant, social time.

Before we left, we met Darrel Goldsmith from Indiana, USA, who pulled in with a modified VW van. He had cut the front off one van and welded it onto the back of another, making for a very elongated vehicle. Unique. Took a picture but it was over exposed.

We thought of driving right to Dawson City, then taking a boat down the Yukon River to Eagle, AK. It would be a pretty trip. But at US $200 each return, we decided it was out of our price range.

We decided to drive the 180 km to Eagle, AK and we're glad we did. A fantastic drive. The scenery is incredible and

These huge machines float up tiny creeks by continuously dredging and building their own deep pools in front of themselves.

goes on and on. It's amazing how many shades of green there are. Rivers and creeks are brown from tannin.

On the way we stopped to see a mining dredge abandoned in a creek beside the road. It's huge. How did it get there? There's lots of mica in the area, at first I thought it was silver.

As we came around a curve we startled a cow moose who was standing in a marsh beside the road. She ran into the woods. We stopped, turned around, coasted back quietly, and there she was again. After a few minutes she ambled back into the brush. Later another cow moose ran out in front of us and crossed to the woods on the other side. They have an awkward looking gait. Glad we didn't hit her.

At O'Brien Creek Lodge we stopped for 1 ½ hours. Met Scott and Dave, mining partners, who were cleaning their gold. They had a lot of fines and small nuggets.

At 3200 ft we were suddenly in pasture land and there were patches of snow.

Eagle's population is 137 but it looks larger. Pat Saunders of the Yukon Charley Rivers Wildlife Preserve showed us a 10 minute video on the area. While we watched she checked out our home page, then bought one of our "RVing in Mexico, Central America and Panama" - now called "Mexico and Central

America by Campervan" - books. We had some good laughs together.

At Eagle's library we watched a 45-minute home video on the 1990 spring breakup and the flooding of the 'village', a native settlement down the road. The Yukon River in full spate with blocks of ice the size of a house is a very powerful entity.

Most homes here are log. Some are very nice.

After supper we went for a walk and met couples from Germany, South Africa and southern USA. I walked about Fort Egbert; only 5 of the 45 buildings remain from 1911 when the fort was closed.

Laundry is $6 for a large load, $4 for small, and 25¢ for three minutes of drying. It is now 12:30 am and still light, but it is bedtime. The sled dogs were howling tonight.

Tonight we slept next to library in Eagle, AK.

June 19-July 2 Dawson City, Yukon
Sunny, one cloudburst, saw a bear.

Stopped at O'Brien Lodge to get gas from old-fashioned glass bubble pump. A couple from Texas own the place. One

 was a federal law enforcement officer in the Attorney General's office. He just had enough and it was time to quit. He makes great sour dough biscuits. His brother is a miner and during the winter he designs and makes jewellery with some of the nuggets he finds in summer.

Got a photo of Scott cleaning his gold with the green plastic cleaning-wheel in the background.

Came across a brown bear standing on the road, but it ran off as soon as we rounded a curve.

Scott is pre-cleaning his gold in a well-used gold pan before using the spiral-wheel behind him. Note the $10,000+ soup can on the table.

Met fifteen bikers on the road to Eagle. It's just starting to rain so it won't be a pleasant trip for them.

Went through quite a downpour on the Top of the World Highway but it still was a spectacular view. A vast sweep of land in every direction. At some points we were above the tree line and there were large patches of snow. The summit near the Alaska-Yukon border is 4515 ft.

At Boundary on the USA side, gasoline is US$1.99/gallon. But what can you do if your tanks are empty? We bought $5 worth. Thank heavens the last few kilometres were downhill, we coasted and idled in neutral. We slid into a gas station in Dawson City, Yukon on our fumes.

The Canadian side of this highway is paved. The George Black ferry takes you across the Yukon River in about 5 min. It carries only 7-8 cars, trucks or RVs. The river flows very quickly. Because it was raining when we arrived, we picked up two young women who were getting soaked while waiting for the ferry.

In Dawson we made a quick stop at the Visitors Centre, got gas, did a short drive around the town, then parked in a gravel pull-out south of the town with four others. Had coffee etc. with Diane and Mike, Bert and Hank in the latter's fifth-wheel. We had been talking outside for some time but the mosquitos were getting pesky. Stayed the night here.

At the campground near the Esso station, laundromat has regular machines. Washer is $2 and dryer is $1 but you usually have to run the dryer twice. Camping fees are $11 dry or $16 for full hookup.

June 20

Sun, cloud, rain.

Spent all day walking the streets of Dawson City, often called just Dawson. Pleasantly warm today, wearing shorts at last. Buildings which are not log are all brightly painted with contrasting trim. Very colourful. All streets except Front St. are dirt/gravel and the walkways are boardwalks. Most buildings are elevated a foot or so off the ground so as not to melt the permafrost below. Several old buildings built right on the ground are at quite an angle.

Later met up with Bert and Hank and went for ice cream,

The shade was almost as enjoyable as the company.

after which we all drove up to the Dome (930 m) to watch the Midnight Sun. It set from 12 to 1 am, cruised along behind the Ogilvie Mountains and rose again at 4 am. The sky was the most beautiful shades of pink from the dark rosiness of sunset to the lighter hues of the rising sun. The mosquitos were out in force and really bothered Hank. We sat inside and played a game of dominoes called Mexican Train — without need of lights — with periodic breaks to 'ooh' and 'aah' at the constantly changing cloud patterns and to take photos. They are a lovely couple and we had a fun evening.

Got to bed around 5 am. Surprisingly we didn't start to feel tired until 3:30 am. Parked at gravel pit again.

Sunday, June 21

Up about 11 am. Said good-bye to Bert and Hank who are off to Tok today. Drove into town to dump and to get water so we could shower. Ended up doing a major cleanup which finished at 9:30 pm when John discovered water under a seat. He tried to fix it and broke a plastic connector to the water pump. Water was gushing out everywhere. Turned off pump and now we are without water until we get a new connector tomorrow. He filled a pot of water from the outside tank drain and heated it up to bathe with.

June 22

Started raining during night. We got up at 10 am, had coffee and headed for RV repair. The guy said he only gets asked for that connector twice a year, always for different pumps, so he doesn't stock any. On to Dawson Hardware Company - big name, small store. Ended up replacing plastic piece with galvanized steel and copper and a piece of Teflon tape. It worked.

Went on tour of the Palace Grand and the Commissioner's Residence. Watched some films at the Visitors Centre, each about forty-five minutes long and well done.

Went for supper at Klondike Kate's. The food was excellent. Unfortunately John had his mind set on Arctic Char and they didn't have any that night. His second choice wasn't available either so he ended up sharing my pita platter- gyro, Greek salad and fries. Delicious. We shared Tin Roof Pie for dessert. Then back to the pit for another night. No more water on the floor so his 'fix' seems to have worked.

Rained nearly all day today.

June 23

Temp of 7⁰C...Brrr! Still raining, rain alert for Dempster Hwy continues. Rain stopped around noon but clouds remained until 7 pm when the sky finally cleared and sun shone. The Dempster Highway has been closed because of slides, washouts and flooding. A campground had to be evacuated in a hurry at midnight.

Walked to and toured the sternwheeler graveyard. These were huge boats, beached and left to rot, often after just one trip. The Julia B, Seattle No. 3 and another whose name was

A derelict boat, crushed by river ice.

gone have been pushed against each other by the pressure of river ice. A big barge is rotting there also. After the tour, John and I stayed to poke around and take some pictures. We walked back via the river's shoreline and arrived just as the ferry was leaving for Dawson. The rest of the tour group was on the same ferry, I guess they walked slowly.

We arrived just in time for the free movie night at the museum-Cheesy Movie Night. Three old movies: "Call of the Wild", "Klondike" by Jack London, and a Russian silent movie called "Yukon", which I thought was terrible but which John enjoyed although it did drag on. Acting was stilted and facial expressions very much over-dramatized. Good for the times, I guess. Condition of film was good. Stayed in museum parking lot for the night.

June 24

Did a laundry in the morning at the Dawson City RV Park next to Esso gas station. Cold water only, but at least it was clean. Ones in town are either out-of-order or dirty or both. All the tenters and backpackers use them so they get a lot of heavy traffic.

Lovely sunshine this morning. After breakfast John went to the library to try to get our e-mail. Visitors can use the only computer from 9-10 am, no reservations accepted. Will try tomorrow.

Visited gold fields and took the tour of Dredge #4, biggest dredge in North America. Carrie Ann led the hour-long tour (she led yesterday's tour of sternwheeler graveyard). Very interesting. People of the early 1900's had brains and ingenuity, and they built BIG. The Parks Canada staff certainly know their stuff and can be very entertaining in their presentation of it.

After that we went gold panning at "Claim 33." That was fun, to my surprise, and we each found some flakes in our pans. John found a small nugget in his pan. If it clinks when dropped, it's considered a nugget.

Went to see the Gaslight Follies at the Palace Grand. Very good performance. We were in second row of the balcony. First row has best seats. I couldn't see over the head of the woman in front of me, so moved to an empty seat in front row for most of first act. Unfortunately the person who had bought a ticket for that seat showed up after intermission so I had to go back to the second row.

All of the entertaining troupe but one-can you spot the dancers and singers?

Parked behind museum again, but under trees some distance away.

June 25

Another beautiful day. At 9:30 am we joined a walking tour of the town. John discovered that the British North America Bank had a deposit slip with a place for $4 bills. Tour guide was surprised. Suggested checking with Parks Canada.

When we returned to RV, Bert and Hank were in the parking lot! They went as far as Chicken, then came back because they enjoyed Dawson so much. We were so glad to see them again.

We couldn't stay and talk because we had to get to the Discovery Claim for the presentation at 12:30 pm. Following that, John panned for gold for ½ hour at Claim 6, no luck using cast iron frying pan. Then we drove/raced to Bear Creek for a 3:00 pm presentation. Both were given by Myriam and were very interesting and informative.

Back in town we walked along the dike and saw where the clear Klondike River and murky Yukon River meet. Water looked like the swirls in a marble cake.

Returned to gravel pit and stayed up talking with Hank and Bert until 1:30 am. Three other fifth-wheels were here as well.

June 26

Rained a little during the night. Dempster Highway is closed until July 2nd which is next Thursday. Hwy suffered 17 washouts and one slide; one of the two ferries isn't running. Also had snow.

Today was partial cloud, cool in the morning, warm in afternoon. Spent morning at the museum. After lunch we wandered around town separately for a few hours. I took more pictures and bought a T-shirt. John got a battery for his watch and entered our name in a draw to win a chest of silver at Klondike Nugget and Ivory Shop. NOTE: We won - 8 place-settings plus 9 serving pieces.

This evening went with Frank & Sharon to Diamond Tooth Gertie's gambling hall to watch the performances - three ½ hour shows each night. We went for walks between shows — $5 admission for the night. Shows, with audience participation, are at 8:30, 10:30 pm and 12:30 am. Each show is different. An-

We could have used high speed film and a good camera in here!

other late night. When we got back to the pit there were 16 rigs parked there. Getting crowded.

June 27

Cloudy and cool today. We are staying here most of the day so John can get caught up with his writing. I annotated and sorted photos and put them in an album. Sky cleared up somewhat this afternoon and got warmer.

We had an early supper then drove up on the old Dome road to see the cemeteries. Quite extensive but generally unkempt except for the NWMP/ RNWMP/ RCMP section which has a fence around fourteen graves.

After 7 pm mass we went back to Gertie's with Hank and Bert and had another enjoyable time. The midnight show was different and better than last night's. We sat upstairs for the first show, then down by the stage for the next two. Gertie sang to John and Hank, big firehouse-red lipstick mark on John's forehead. Another late but fun night.

16 rigs (fivers, trailers, motorhomes, campervans) parked in pit plus 4 or 5 more on the tailings behind. This is okay now as friendly owner is not hydraulically mining here because of low gold prices. Space probably won't be available next year.

<u>Sunday, June 28</u>

Lovely and sunny this morning. Stayed here all day. John did more writing and I wrote postcards then baked a cake. Borrowed Hank's portable generator and charged the big RV battery. Sharon and Frank had us and Hank and Bert over for dinner tonight. We started to play chicken (dominoes game) when a man from a truck camper came over to return some papers and didn't leave. We made conversation, finally returned to our own units at 11:30 pm. (I need to write am and pm to remind me of the time, there's too much sunlight.) Beautiful sky, clouds are pink and grey. We had a downpour of heavy rain during the evening, had to shut some windows for awhile.

Several units here again tonight, lots of truck campers.

<u>June 29</u>

Some cloud but mostly sunny. Hot in the afternoon, and humid. Banking day today. Back to museum to see second floor and the train museum outside.

Hank & Bert came with us to the Downtown Hotel where John had a "Sour-Toe" cocktail from 'Captain' Alf and his wife Carol (who are from Merritt, BC). John had Yukon Jack ($5, a liqueur made from Canadian whiskey, very smooth, very tasty) and selected the biggest, blackest toe available (all toes are $5)

to put in his glass. These are real human toes, lost by accident, illness or frost, which are preserved in salt. If the toe touches your lips when you drink you get a certificate and a membership card. You can also buy a pin ($5), a book, and other mementos. John bartered, selling one of our books at less than full price.

Went to Klondike Kate's for another pita wrap and gyro (pronounced hero). Still delicious.

Went golfing with Frank and Sharon at 10:30 pm. Played 9 holes of Midnight Golf, returned at 1 am. Bugs were bothersome, sky beautiful, course mediocre — work being done — until last treacherous green. $18.

As you can see, another ball is right down the middle. Well done Frank.

June 30

Drove up to King Solomon Dome on the Ridge Road Heritage Trail with Hank, Bert, Frank & Sharon in Hank's truck. Gone 5 enjoyable hours.

Lots of evidence of mining - rusting equipment of long ago and present day activities of hydraulic mining and sluicing. Came across Dredge # 11 rotting away on Hunker Creek. Spent an hour roaming over the dredge. 70 years old and still in reasonable shape. (Dredge # 4 on Bonanza Creek Road is restored and stabilized.) Hot, muggy and buggy in mountains.

*This surrounding view makes one realize how difficult it must have been to find and prospect for gold on a specific creek. In **which** valley?!*

Did a major grocery shop, got wine (cheaper than in BC), cleaned fridge. Bread expensive, up to $5 for a specialty loaf. Parked in Visitor Centre parking lot while John wrote an article for local newspaper and I prepared supper.

It is so hot it feels like it did when we were RVing in Mexico and Central America in May. Very little shade, even my eyeballs are sweating. It is so dusty here I wonder if we'll ever be clean again. Table is always gritty no matter how many times I wipe it. The floor has a fine coating of dust too.

Haven't seen any crows here, lots of ravens though. They are quite vocal.

At midnight we sat outside and I cut John's hair. Parked behind and across the street from Commissioner's Residence because we want to be here for early morning ceremonies.

July 1, 1998

Canada Day!

Up at 7:30 for flag raising at 8 am in Victory Gardens, followed by coffee and muffins in museum. We assisted in carrying a huge Canadian flag in the parade from Visitors Centre to Commissioner's Residence where, for the first time in Dawson's

252

Liz re-affirming and receiving certificate of Canadian Citizenship.

history, citizenship court was held. Fourteen people, we included, reaffirmed our Canadian citizenship or became new Canadians. We wore our red and white *"We're Canadian, eh!"* T-shirts. Received many comments and compliments all day.

Next was the official opening of the new Han Cultural Centre, which had to take place outside because of an electrical fire in the building last night. The scheduled performances took place in the old Han Hall across the road. Some performers wore intricately beaded dresses and jackets. They had a fabulous cold food buffet, smoked salmon, caribou, etc.

Walked a kilometre to watch a professional gold-panning competition but couldn't see much as we weren't allowed to get close to the panners. John took part in the "Clunker" bike race along the dike. Out of shape, but not last.

At the Nugget and Ivory Shop I had our gold fines and nugget put into a locket and bought a complementary bow broach.

Got in line early for a delicious Salmon Barbeque ($10/plate) in grassy area next to dike. This was followed by a lively show of the "Stave Falls Scottish Dancers", 23 of them touring from BC. Especially entertaining was their Yukon version of the can-can, four girls dressed in one-piece long blue underwear, red net mini-skirts, toques and, believe it or not, snowshoes. Hilarious!

More Scottish music followed, then a band played enjoyable Irish music (marvellous harp solo) for an hour or so.

A wonderful, fun day. The best Canada Day we've had for quite a while. Thank you Dawson City for all the effort that went into making this a very successful day.

Laundry at City RV Park. Showers, filled-up with water downtown, dumped, then back to gravel pit for one more night.

Bert and Hank left for Alaska today. We sure enjoyed the time together with them.

NOTE: We had a marvellous time in Dawson City and think it deserves a minimum 3 day visit. There is so much to see and do here. At the Visitors Centre you can buy passes to the various Parks Canada attractions. You can purchase them singly or in books. There are 2 different size books. If you have the time buy the larger one and see everything, you won't regret it.

July 2 Km 116, Dempster Hwy, Yukon

Hot. Sunny! Finally left for Inuvik, Northwest Territories.

Filled up with gasoline and propane at Callison Industrial Park. Gas is 10¢/L cheaper there, propane 2¢/L cheaper than in town. Drove 21 km to Rock Creek, put canoe in Klondike River and took only two hours to get back to Dawson. Some white water, we got wet a few times, scraped bottom on canoe once. Fast current. Where it joins Yukon River, we weren't paying

254

attention and grounded on rocks in the middle of the river. Had to get out and lift canoe into deeper water. Cold water! At Dawson we beached the canoe and left everything on shore of Yukon River while we hitch-hiked back to our motorhome. Tina drove us to the Industrial Park turnoff, then half-hour later Mark and a woman co-worker gave us a lift in a truck. They weren't going that far, but drove us all the way anyway. Forced $5 on them for ice cream or beer. Then we had to drive back to Dawson City to get our canoe.

While we were loading canoe on RV roof, two other canoeists overturned in swirling Yukon River. One stayed with canoe, other wasn't wearing a life-jacket and tried to swim to get it, couldn't, tried for shore, couldn't make it against the current, finally called for help. Three boats zoomed out to rescue them, their canoe, their paddles and one life-jacket. Except for lost equipment, this incident ended happily.

Stopped at junction of Klondike & Dempster hwys to top up the gas tanks and the radiator boiled over. First and last time all summer, never did find out why. Finally we are on the Dempster Highway!

We are driving along the tree-line and tundra. We'll pass through three mountain ranges -Tombstone, Ogilvie and Richardson. Quite cool at night. Surprised by the amount of traf-

Several burn areas and lots of purple fireweed among the small black trunks.

fic on this well-gravelled highway. It isn't bad at all so far. After 30 km there is hardly any dust. But lots of bugs.

Stopped at Tombstone Mountain Campground to look around. Good sized lots. All Yukon territorial parks are $8 for dry camping. The small Interpretive Centre was interesting.

Drove on to km 116, Chapman Lake, and a sign commemorating the RCMP and the Lost Patrol of 1910-1911. They were lost in December 1910 and found in March 1911 by Cpl Dempster. After that incident a native guide always accompanied the patrols. Stayed for the night. Beautiful sight.

Saw a dozen 'wild' horses, at least one with a horse bell on neck - can't be too wild. Passed a ranch or outfitters a little farther on. Guess he lets his horses roam free. Glimpsed a wolverine!! At Sheep Mountain an eagle soared overhead. Later we saw an arctic owl sitting on a post.

We have decided to travel at night (still daylight) because it might be cooler. It was 35C today. Hopefully we can avoid some if not most of the traffic and increase our chances of seeing wildlife.

July 3 Arctic Circle, Dempster Hwy, Yukon

Leisurely morning. I made pot of soup, John caught up on his writing. Lots of vehicles stop to read the 'Lost Patrol' sign and enjoy the scenery. Some ducks on Chapman Lake, Tombstone Mtns behind us, Ogilvie Mtns ahead.

Big transport trucks go so fast they raise a lot of dust. Most tourists travel at a more leisurely pace, with less dust. Screen door covered with mosquitos and flies.

In pullout next to Ogilvie River, John painted/traced a map of our journey on the side of our RV. Met Carole and Bill from California, USA. She has crippling arthritis and is in a wheelchair much of the time. But still they travel. That's great.

The Ogilvie-Peel Rivers viewpoint is a nice place to stop. Large parking lot and a great view of the valley and mountains. A little further on at km 263, we started to see small stands of arctic cotton. Little white balls of individual threads, soft as rabbit fur, and smells faintly of baby powder.

Dust is terrible today, and we have lots of it. The construction areas where crews are repairing the washouts are good because the road has been watered. Any time we stop the bugs move right in- mosquitos, flies, horseflies and the smaller deer flies.

The Ogilvie Mountains are huge, bare, smooth and gray. Look like pale giant sand dunes.

Parts of this highway are like driving the Top of the World Hwy. We are on top of everything and look over vistas that seem to go on forever. We can see the ribbon of our hwy winding off in the distance. Row after row of mountains. Awesome!

Passed an area of old forest fire and it was alive with colour from the fireweed that is growing amongst the charred-black tree trunks. km 302.

Farther on, about km 356, the road was thickly lined with fireweed for 4-5 km, making it a blaze of colour in the distance.

We pulled into the Arctic Circle parking lot about 11 pm. Two other units were already there. Very windy. We cleaned the RV, showered, washed our straw-like hair, and took a picture of us at midnight (just made it on time!).

July 4-5 Frog Creek, Dempster Hwy, Yukon

Sunny but hazy due to forest fire 100 km away. Very windy.

All of us here at the Arctic Circle are Canadians. One couple, Shirley and Ralph from Moosimin, Saskatchewan are go-

Bad news and bad news. When it rains, it's muddy. When it's dry, it's dusty.

ing to Inuvik, NWT to visit Ralph's sister who happens to be Judith Venaas, the Federal Government Officer we have been writing to and talking with since we met her at an RV show in Vancouver, BC in January. Small world.

Stopped at Rock Creek Territorial Park, the water was bright orange - rust. Flies and mosquitos were awful, we were covered almost as soon as we stepped out of our RV. Good thing we didn't have to use a campground toilet.

The soft hills look like a desert covered in green velvet.

Still windy today, blowing the dust to our left which works well for us when we meet oncoming traffic.

Took some photos of the NWT border sign. Yukon has prettier signs. John tried to get me to pose like the model did, photographed by Mike Beedell for NWT's 1998 brochure "Explorer's Guide to Road Touring" but I kept sliding off the sign. John did too. Wonder how the model managed to stay on?

Richardson Mountains seem to have a red soil base. Just past the Yukon-NWT border there were chasms and gorges, and an occasional snow patch.

Seems to be even dustier today. Road has huge storm drains and culverts.

Took ferry across Peel River, didn't have to wait more than a few minutes.

Fort McPherson, now called native name of Teetl'it Zheh, looks like a depressing place to live. No grass, just dust. Indian village of about 800 people. Saw a fox here, slinking around between buildings. Photographed burial place of the "Lost Patrol" of 1910-1911 in cemetery next to Anglican church which is on a cliff overlooking the Peel River. The cemetery does not appear to be cared for. Quite overgrown with weeds.

Went back to Natainlai Campground to get water then drove on to Frog Creek about 30 km past Teetl'it Zheh. (Natainlai is also spelled Nutuiluie. Different brochures use different spellings. The native word means 'fast flowing waters'.) Lou and Colleen whom we first met in Dawson City are parked here also.

37°C. Had coffee with them in air-conditioned comfort after clean up and showers.

Dust is starting to get me down. It is everywhere, even in dishes and cutlery. John's taping job at Boya Lake probably helps but dust still gets in all cupboards.

To bed at 1:30 am, still bright.

<u>Sunday, July 5</u>

Beautiful big patch of fireweed where we parked last night. We are about 1/4 km off the highway so are away from the dust. Water flows into a rectangular pond -- man-made water source for spraying highway to control dust -- which flows into Frog Creek. Very peaceful.

This morning Lou discovered his 38 ft rig has a flat tire. His spare is in a slide-out drawer which won't slide out because it seems to be jammed with small rocks kicked up from the highway. He has extra hoses and a small water pump (to wash his RV when muddy) so now he's moved closer to the pond to pressure wash the drawer. Didn't work, still jammed. We decided to wait until he got his tire changed to make sure he wouldn't be stranded here. Eventually got it open, after discovering that one small piece of metal had got bent when he drove onto the ferry and dragged his bumper in the bulldozed dirt ramp.

I'm enjoying the break from all that dust. Went for a swim in the pond about 3:30 pm. Very refreshing, not too cold. Horseflies are so big and so numerous that we can't sit outside for long. Today put RV's awning out for the first time.

33.5^0C (93^0F) in our over-the-cab bedroom. Not much breeze. Just like Yucatan, Mexico in May.

Went fishing after supper. John had found a hook when we launched our canoe into Klondike River. He used it and some heavy fishing line we had used for clothesline, twirled it in circles over his head before throwing the hook. He caught two jack fish.

Had another swim, This time in the flowing creek. It feels so good! Had coffee with Lou and Colleen. Still bright when we went to bed.

July 6-28 Inuvik, NWT

Ferried across the MacKenzie River to the native village of Arctic Red River (Tsiigehtchic) which is at the confluence of the MacKenzie and Arctic Red Rivers. Walked around town for 1 ½ hours. The churches were locked, the larger one no longer in use. Both are on a bluff overlooking the Arctic Red River. Grocery store and post office are run by a man from Israel whose father was a ship's captain. He's also been to Panama. Tried to buy some dried fish but none available, too hot for fishing. Ferry came by and took us back to Dempster Highway. Each trip about ten minutes.

Saw a wolf trot across road ahead of us, also three grouse.

The territorial parks/campgrounds have their signs, outhouses and shelters painted blue and white, which are the colours of the territorial flag, and the Polar Bear logo. Trees are very scraggly.

Stopped about 40 km before Inuvik at Caribou Creek and barbequed our fish that we caught yesterday. It was good, whatever it was. Northern pike or jack fish or pickerel? I think they're all the same. Obviously we're not serious fishermen.

Finally, we're here. We've reached our goal, Inuvik. Population of 3200. Pavement starts 10 km south of town, at airport turnoff. Some of the town streets are paved.

Went to Happy Valley campground to dump and fill up with water. This town doesn't seem to be bigger than Dawson though it has a larger population. It isn't attractive either. It's mainly a government town. A lot of residences look like military PMQ duplexes or quads, which they are. The military used to be here. Some are shabby looking while others are brightly painted. They are referred to as 'Smarties' because of their many colours. Streets are laid out at odd angles. MacKenzie Road is the main street with most of the shopping and attractions on it.

Chuk Park territorial campground, 2 km south of town, is a nice clean park located on a hill overlooking the town and the

This truck is used to transport dog teams and sleds. Notice openings in the sides for the dogs to poke their heads through.

delta. Happy Valley Park is in town. Both have electrical hook-ups only with a water tap for filling up. Happy Valley has the only laundromat and sani-dump. Both are $12 for dry camping or $15 with electricity.

July 7

Heavy rain and thunder during the night. Raining today. John used the rain to wash the RV.

These utilidores are well insulated. Water is always flowing through the pipes.

Water, heat and sewage is carried to and from houses by insulated above ground pipes called utiladores.

Went to the Inuvik (Aurora?) Research Station to see a slide presentation about the fauna of the north. It's amazing the variety of plant life that thrives up here and has adapted to the harsh conditions that prevail in the north. Spent the rest of the afternoon tracking down leads to barge the RV to Tuk.

This afternoon we met Tanya Van Valkenburg who is one of the coordinators of the Great Northern Arts Festival (GNAF). John had been communicating with her via e-mail so it was nice to meet her in person. We will be volunteers throughout the 10 days of the festival.

Walked over to Happy Valley Campground and visited with some folks we met coming up on the Dempster.

Stores here close at 6 pm.

Went to the library to get our e-mail. The library here is new and staff are very accommodating.

July 8

Raining, cold and windy. Furnace not working properly, fridge light flickering. Battery reading very low. Will have to go to a campground and plug in for a day or two. Passed the afternoon at the Visitors Centre watching short videos about life in the north. Quite interesting. They let us plug in to charge our battery so we will stay here the night.

Tonight we went to the dinner theatre at the Finto Motor Inn. Performances are Sunday and Wednesday evenings and cost about $40.00 each. Dinner was a smorgasbord and the food was great: white fish, arctic char, caribou and muskox. For the non-adventurous there was also chicken, potato, rice, green beans and lots of salads. The play was about the beginnings of Inuvik and the move from Aklavik. It was an amateur production but very well done. One scene called for audience participation: 4 men and 1 woman. John was one of the men and he played 'Bubbles' the Newfie bartender. Apparently there are quite a few Newfoundlanders living here. Inuvik is jokingly called 'Inewfik'! As we walked back to the RV it was still pouring down rain. The Dempster Hwy must be a sea of mud.

July 9

Still raining. Had an interview with Blake Lambert of CBC Radio re our trip, the upcoming book on the north and our attempt to barge the RV to Tuktoyaktuk, or Tuk.

At noon we went to Ingamoo Hall which is the native Friendship Centre. Every Thursday there is lunch with the elders. We arrived late and there were no seats left. Another table and chairs were set up but we didn't get to sit and talk with the elders. The meal today was spaghetti, salad, bun and dessert. You pay by donation. There is a small gift shop there also.

In the afternoon we had an interview with Glen Korstrom for the local paper, the 'Inuvik Drum'. We covered the same topics as this morning.

This evening we returned to the Visitors Centre for another video and then for a walk. Handwritten sign now posted saying "no overnight parking." Now that the rain is finally over the mosquitoes are out. Stopped at the 'Carving Corner' and watched a few local artists working in ivory and soapstone.

Inuvik is one of many communities that had residential schools. These buildings are now empty and for the most part unused. One residence is called Grollier Hall. It has a big parking lot and is a good place to park for the night.

People are quite friendly here but unfortunately this town is dying. Each year they lose something else. This year the mini-golf went under.

The Catholic church here is quite unique, it is shaped like an igloo. Beautifully built, without plans. Some lovely local art work inside and melodic chimes.

<u>July 10</u>

Walked around town a bit this morning. Things aren't going well regarding barging the RV to Tuk but we're still working on it. There's already been a blurb on the radio about what we are trying to do.

Nora Dixon from the library tracked us down to say the library would be interested in having us do a reading/talk about our book 'RVing in Mexico, Central America and Panama.' We booked in for Tues. the 21st at 7:30.

Northern Images gift shop has some beautiful merchandise. Mostly high quality items.

We drove 20 km to Campbell Creek for the weekend. Will do some canoeing and fishing. Tonight we canoed for a couple of hours, the fish didn't cooperate. The mosquitoes are terrible out here and they get inside the RV so easily. Thank goodness our Kelowna friends Pat & Gene loaned us their mesh hats. The bugs were buzzing all around our heads but they couldn't get at us. Reminded me of that old song "I Hear You Knocking But You Can't Come In."

John decided we should set up our mesh tent. What a fiasco. One hour and many bites later it was up but it would only stay up if we tied it to the RV. We had set it up at home to make sure we had all the pieces and had no problem. But that was on nice soft grass. We are on rocky ground here so we can't use the pegs as they are plastic and bend under pressure.

264

John saw a fox tonight.

<u>July 11</u>
Terrible night's sleep because of the mosquitoes. Canoed down the creek and across the lake which was rough going as the wind came up. Saw 10 tundra swans on the far side of the lake.

This is a popular spot, cars in and out of here all day. We never did catch a fish but a family was here this evening doing catch and release fishing. They caught several and gave us a big one, a pike, which we cooked on the barbeque. There are as many mosquitoes inside the RV as outside.

<u>Sunday, July 12</u>
Good sleep last night. I guess we got rid of most of the mosquitoes when we sprayed last night. This afternoon we canoed through the culvert and up the creek in the other direction. We didn't get far before it became too shallow and we had to turn around. Saw some ducks and ducklings and an eagle.

I've decided I don't like the taste of pike. Today I used the rest of it to make fish cakes and with sour cream on them they were good.

Late this evening we gave the fish one more chance then packed up, showered and returned to town at midnight. There's no sense of time with the 24 hour sunlight. It's great. At Happy Valley we dumped our tanks and got fresh water. While there we met Mr. Dempster, son of Corp. Dempster who found the 'Lost Patrol' that is buried in Fort McPherson. He was travelling with his daughter and granddaughter who is one of the Scottish dancers we saw in Dawson City on Canada Day. Small world.

We parked at Grollier Hall tonight. It is quite cool outside with a bit of wind.

<u>July 13</u>
Last few days have been sunny but cool. There is a big forest fire in the Carmacks, Yukon area. We can see the smoky haze on the horizon all the way up here. Went to Happy Valley and did a laundry. Their laundromat is very clean. Two washers

and two dryers. The dryer runs for about 45 min. and has lots of heat.

Tonight we helped paint the panels and shelves for the arts festival. Afterwards we went for a walk and ice cream at the news stand across the street from the library. Best ice cream in town and the best prices too. Tonight we parked behind the SAM school on MacKenzie Road. (SAM = Sir Alexander MacKenzie. GNAF is being held here.)

July 14

Did preparation jobs for the festival till supper time. John vacuumed the hall and helped set up tents while I folded T-shirts, cleaned acrylic sign holders and put the artist's name inside. After supper we went to the library to get our e-mail and then crossed the street for ice cream. They have lots of flavours.

July 15

John spent most of the day helping to get things ready for the festival. I worked only 3 hours. I'll be a volunteer salesperson so today I learned how to operate the computerized cash register & credit card machine. Back in the RV I did some baking in the afternoon. There is no breeze today so the RV is very hot. It's 25°C outside and since I've had the oven on its about 30°C inside. Following supper we went for ice cream and then painted shelves for an hour.

July 16

John and I spent all afternoon assembling 2 display cases with glass sides and fronts. We went to the hospital for supper, the cafeteria is open to the public. Today was roast turkey but it was all gone when we got there. I was so disappointed. Tonight there was a short meeting for volunteers. After that I pre-stamped invoice and credit card forms.

July 17

We were busy all day. John was a 'gopher' plus helping on the computer. I helped inventory the artists's things as they ar-

GNAF's most photographed 'two-rist'.

rived. There is a lot of beautiful work here: ivory and soapstone carving, jewellery, painting in many different mediums - wood, bone, metal, ivory; also silk screening, clothing - seal skin, caribou, knitted beaver. And much more.

Festival opened tonight at 7 pm with its attendant ceremonies. There was a blanket toss which John participated in. He did quite well for a first attempt. Some of them really get airborne! Only T-shirts, posters and bags were on sale tonight and they went like hot cakes.

July 18

A casual day. I didn't work till 5:30 so had the day to take a leisurely look around at all the art work. The gym has been transformed. The artwork and talent on display here is incredible. Tonight Frank Cockney from Tuktoyaktuk played the fiddle followed by the Inuvialuit Drum Dancers who performed outside. I think they are trying to revitalize a dying tradition. The dances used to have meaning but the younger dancers don't know it and their heart isn't in it. For the observers the moves are very repetitive and meaningless. It would be helpful to understand the meaning of the different movements of the dance. Nevertheless it was different and interesting. John did surveys tonight.

Met Steve & Laura Gasaway from Oregon. They are volunteers too. This is their second time in Inuvik and their fourth time north of 60. They came as many others do, especially for the festival.

Lots of opportunity to learn native crafts from knowledgeable instructors.

Sunday, July 19

Church this morning and a few hours of volunteer work in the afternoon. Had an early supper and worked 4 hours this evening. Living in a motorhome, space is limited therefore shopping is restricted. Good thing, because there is plenty here I would like to buy.

July 20

Off to dump our tanks and get water, gas and propane. Volunteered most of the day then went to the hospital for a roast pork supper. Supper time is the hottest part of the day. Inuvik is 800 km west of Vancouver yet it, being in the NWT, is on Alberta time so that supper time here is 3 pm solar/sun time. That explains why it is so hot in the evening.

After closing time tonight we went for a walk. Some people here have beautiful gardens, both vegetable and flower. Because of the 24 hour daylight you can almost watch the plants grow.

We have met a number of people who are in favour of our barging to Tuk and who gave us suggestions and names of people to contact. Everyone agrees that it would be great for NWT tourism because of the publicity we could give them in our book but no one seems capable of helping us achieve it. It's like banging your head against a stone wall.

July 21

We both worked all afternoon then went to the hospital for chicken supper. Sat with two medical students one of whom has Plaxton connections so we talked family tree for awhile.

Tonight we did our presentation at the library. Unfortunately the festival schedule changed, or we misread it, so we were in conflict with the superb northern fashion show which I also wanted to see. However, although the group was small it was lively and we sold some books. Six of us went out for ice cream afterwards.

Gorgeous outfits from head to toe, fantastic beadwork and trim.

July 22

Tonight there was a jam session in the gallery (gym) so the sales continued for an extra half hour. John & I were there till 11 pm cleaning up. John vacuumed the hall. It gets pretty messy with all the people coming in and out, plus the bits and pieces

269

that fall from the craft tables. Went for ice cream and then to 'the zoo', a pub at the MacKenzie Hotel. Staff, volunteers and artists were there tonight.

Didn't stay long. The flashing lights are hard on the eyes and the music is too loud for us. Our age is showing!

Met a man who is *getting paid* to talk about the local scenery and history on a boat trip up the MacKenzie River. Why didn't we hear about this earlier? He's getting paid and we'd do it for free - except we wouldn't know what we're talking about and he does.

Two native women working outside on fresh (odorous) caribou hides.

July 23

Did a laundry this morning and worked in the afternoon. Some really big sales today. Salmon supper at the hospital. Tonight John learned how to do 'stick gambling'. About 10 people participated, 5 men on one side and 5 women on the other. The Dene taught them how to play and beat the drums continuously during the game. Lots of laughter as the beginners tried to figure out the strategy of the game.

We went back to the RV to get our jackets and have a cup of tea and missed the Dene Drum Dancers from Ft. Good Hope.

270

That was disappointing as we heard they are very good and we wanted to see them.

It has been quite cloudy and windy here the last few days. There was a big storm in Ft. McPherson yesterday - rain, thunder and lightning. Temperature here is 15^0C

A large percentage of the population in the north are smokers. I guess all the fuss, bother, government rules and regulations of the past year haven't reached the north. I don't care if they smoke, but why do they throw butts on the ground?!

July 24

Worked 1-7 pm today. Musical entertainment outside this evening but it is very cool and windy. Impromptu dancing. Drums made of animal skin had to be warmed up over a fire. A big sound system is set up on the outdoor stage for the band. John is one of the volunteers on all-night security for the sound equipment. We moved our 'Security' RV and parked it next to the stage which is in Jim Coe park in front of the SAM school.

July 25

I worked 11-5. John was up till 4 am so he slept most of the morning and came to work later. After work we were one of several people interviewed by CBC TV for a promotional video for the festival. We went to Arctic College for a turkey supper. The staff and artists have their meals at this college and volunteers who put in 6 hours or more a day can get one free meal there.

I bought some beaded earrings today and asked Antoine Mountain to make me a necklace to match. Antoine is a Dene artist from Yellowknife working to promote pride in the young native people. His bright and impressionist style paintings are hung in various galleries and shops in the city. Archie Beaulieu from Rae is another Dene artist whose work I like very much.

This evening's entertainment was supposed to be outside but the drum dancing was moved inside because it was so cool and windy. The Inuit drum dancers from Tuk performed first followed by the Tlingit Indian dancers from Teslin, Yukon. They were unprofessional but are also re-learning their culture and tradition. They were reminiscent of the Central American dancers we saw. Very little stage presence and because the younger ones don't understand the meaning of the dance and the gestures their heart isn't in it. The costumes were nice but not all the performers were wearing them. High top runners, baggy jeans and baseball caps just don't fit in with moccasins and traditional ceremonial clothing. Oh well, all in good time. Their performance, while entertaining, was too long. The band was outside waiting to play and they were frozen. We brought them all into the RV and made them coffee and hot chocolate to warm them up. The musicians needed to warm their hands so they could play their instruments, especially the guitarists.

It is midnight. I am writing by natural light though it is a bit darker tonight because of the cloud. Young children (about 10-12 years) are playing in the school grounds till 1-2 am. Everything is very laid back here. Things are on 'northern time'. Attitudes very different.

Bought a pair of walrus ivory 'ulu' earrings from Martin Goodlife who owns the 'Carving Corner' adjacent to the SAM school. He has some lovely pieces and does such delicate work.

Sunday, July 26
Cold and windy again today. After church we went back to the festival for our last day of volunteering. After sales closed, John did various jobs while I helped de-inventory and then assisted Josee enter data into the computer from the invoice forms. Closing ceremonies were good but brief as they should be.

The festival was very good to its 'full-time volunteers'. We were all given lovely gifts that will continue to remind us of this extraordinary event, the talented artists, the various coordinators and hard working folks who make something like this possible and successful. To all of you we take off our hat and say congratulations and thank you for letting us be a part of it all.

July 27
After 3 weeks of effort we are unable to barge the RV to Tuk which is 80 km north of Inuvik. If we are going to go, we

272

Tenth Anniversary Commemorative Sculpture, carved during GNAF, and Artists. Visitors were allowed to help by sanding and oiling this stone.

will have to fly. However, the cloud ceiling is very low today so we won't see anything from the air. If it clears up later we will take the evening flight. If not we'll head south. It's time to move on. Tuk has northern games this coming weekend which we would have stayed for if we could have barged there with the

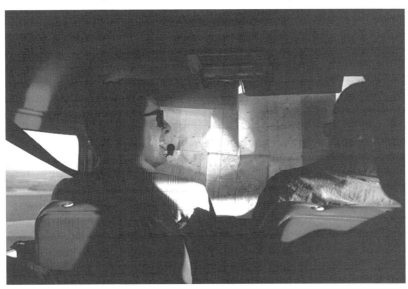

I tore my eyes from the scenery below and looked forward and was surprised to see our pilot reading this map. Thank Heaven's for an automatic pilot.

273

RV. They have missed a great opportunity for publicity and increased tourism by not having barge travel available for RVs. They just don't seem to care.

The weather cleared this afternoon around 4 pm. It seemed as if in a matter of minutes the sky went from gray to blue with bright sunshine. We flew to Tuk at 8 pm. It's a 45 minute trip and the aerial view of the MacKenzie River Delta is breathtaking. We flew at between 500 - 900 ft. Didn't see any seals, whales or land animals but we did see some Arctic swans in the lakes below.

Because we couldn't barge the RV up here, John brought the spare tire along and dumped it in the Arctic Ocean so at least part of the RV has been here. When we walked into the water we were surprised. It wasn't as cold as we expected. It wasn't painful to stand in it, as some rivers were.

We saw the pingos (large frozen land pimples covered with moss) and the ice house which is built 25 ft down into the permafrost. People rent ice rooms for their food which is raised and lowered in a barrel on a rope. The ladder is not on an angle but goes straight down. From outside it is a very small building - looks like an outhouse.

We were taken to one craft shop which is a room in a private home and which had very little to sell. That surprised us as

Is this the multi-lake Mackenzie River Delta or treeless tundra? Find out.

we had previously met some tourists who purchased some unique items on their trip here. It has been a busy summer for them so maybe they have already sold most of their stock, or maybe this was the only one open this evening.

The village of Tuk was a disappointment. It reminded us of some of the poorer Central American villages we have seen. The town is stagnating due to the capping of the oil wells. Flew back to Inuvik at midnight.

The ½ hour flight over the MacKenzie Delta was awesome. You can't imagine how big this river is and how the delta fans out for miles as it prepares to enter the Arctic Ocean.

A trip to Herschel Island would be more rewarding visually and you would likely see caribou and/or muskox. There or Sachs Harbour would be our choice on a second visit although both of those cost considerably more.

We are now having brief sunsets at about 1:30 am

July 28 Km 340, Dempster Hwy, Yukon
This morning we dumped our tanks, got fresh water & groceries, wrote some postcards and headed south about noon. Gave a Dene man a lift to Ft. McPherson.

A lot of the lakes have pumps run by generator so that the trucks can fill up and water the roads, especially in the construction areas.

At Ft. McPherson we went to see the canvas factory which was very clean. They have some very attractive and useful items at reasonable prices. It is advertised that they give tours of the factory which isn't very big - one big room where the work is done plus a small shop. The woman who was there the day we arrived was a grouch of the first order. I can't see them making too many sales while she is there. She should take a course in customer relations. Oh well, maybe she was having a bad day.

Re-visited the church (locked) and cemetery where the Lost Patrol of 1910-11 is buried. John spoke with Neil Colin, a Dene, who is building a replica of the 'Mad Trapper's' cabin. Apparently he was shot in this area.

This replica will show how the cabin was designed and built as a fortress ...
when the "Mad Trapper" moved into the area.

We got a tiny stone chip in the windshield today. Storm clouds, thunder and lightning all around us. By the time we reached the NWT-Yukon border the storm had passed. The roads were wet so no more dust. There were two animal hides on the muskeg. One was long-haired like a wolf, the other short. Both were old hides and there were no bones around. The muskeg is funny stuff to walk on - very spongy. You feel as if you are sinking but really you aren't.

There are a lot of side roads off the Dempster but they are short and most lead to gravel pits used to maintain the highway.

The fireweed is almost finished. It is going to seed. The stems and seed pods are a deep purple and it is very pretty with the foxtails waving in front. They say when the fireweed goes to seed the winter isn't far off. The caribou have started moving south already. They are migrating a month early.

The fireweed's purple colour formed a kilometres-long border to the highway.

At 10:30 pm we pulled into a gravel pit about 20 km south of Eagle Plains. Stayed up to watch the sunset at midnight. Saw the green flash tonight. It's 12:30 am and I am writing by natural light but it is not a bright light as it was in June. Saw the moon tonight for the first time in a long time.

The gyrfalcon is the bird of the NWT and the mountain avens is the flower. We haven't seen either. The fireweed, which is the flower of the Yukon, is as prevalent in NWT as it is in the Yukon. It is the first growth to come up after a forest fire, hence its name. It also grows along the roadside with vetch, larkspur, delphinium and lupins. Away from the roadside there seems to be very few wild flowers, at least not that you can see from your vehicle. Off-road walking or hiking will reveal a variety of tiny delicate flowers that aren't visible from the road.

July 29 Km 139, Dempster Hwy, Yukon

Didn't get away till noon again today. It's nice not to have to rush. We made several stops - fishing, chatting with folks along the way, stopping to enjoy the magnificent views. Once again the fish did not cooperate so we had a delicious steak cooked on the barbeque by 'Chef John'.

Shallow Engineers' Creek did have a couple of [empty] fishing holes.

John says the brakes aren't working properly - again! Just the front ones are stopping us. Scary as we are about 600 km from Dawson City. We thought we had this problem repaired in Whitehorse.

Parked by a creek for the night. Lots of animal tracks in the mud - bear, moose and some type of cat. Got a fire going and it started to rain. Really came down hard for about 10 minutes then it passed on.

July 30 Tombstone Mtn Gov't Campground, Dempster Hwy, YT

After the rain last night there is no dust today for which we are grateful. There are patches of snow on the banks of the Blackstone River and on the Tombstone Mtns. These mountains are higher and more jagged than the Ogilvie Mtns which are rounded and quite smooth looking.

278

Stopped at Tombstone Mtn. Government Campground to-night. The Territorial & Yukon Gov't Parks are very well maintained. They are spacious, attractive & clean. We went on a guided hike tonight part way up the mountain. Saw some Dall sheep up there as well as a variety of mushrooms and wild flowers. The view was gorgeous.

Enjoyed a campfire and hot chocolate with Steve & Laura who were in the park also.

July 31 - August 4 Dawson City, Yukon

Went on a short hike this morning before leaving for Dawson City.

Went to the bank, got gas, propane, groceries, supper at Klondike Kate's, then checked into Guggieville RV Park. Great to have water and electricity. Major clean-up in the RV to get rid of most of the dust and then a nice long shower. Very refreshing.

Met a couple in town who were trying to park by the Palace Grande. There's quite a dip beside streets in some areas and he got hung up on his long overhang. John loaned him some of our boards to put under his wheels and he was able to back out. Fortunately he didn't damage anything.

Saturday morning I gave John a much needed hair cut and did some laundry. Went by boat to Moosehide Village, about 3 km down river (Yukon R) from Dawson City. The Han Tr'ondek Hwich'ih people are having a four day gathering. (Han = river; Tr'ondek = mouth; Hwich'in = dweller) Native people from the Yukon, British Columbia, Alaska and other areas get together to share and learn their native traditions. Moosehide is an old native village that is now used mainly in the summertime. The gathering is held every second year on the last weekend of July, Thur - Sun. Some of the people wore traditional dress. The hide dresses and jackets with the bead and/or quill decorations are very colourful and attractive. What a lot of work goes into the making of this clothing.

The public is invited and tours of the village are given. In the evening there is a free potlatch supper. This potlatch is a western (BC) native tradition. The line-up for the food was unbelievably long. We were standing at the wrong end of the table when the line formed. A woman came by and told us to go and sit with the elders where we would be served. Gray hair paid off!

We sat with Percy and Mabel Henry. He used to be a chief. They won the jigging contest. Also at our table was Winston Wuttunee, a Cree from Saskatchewan. He is a musician, sings and plays the guitar and drum. He held a healing workshop incorporating Christian and native traditions.

These two young comics were fabulous. CBC Radio should hire them.

During the four days there are workshops, games, music and craft sales. I bought some earrings - of course. Other items available include T-shirts with native design, baskets and moccasins.

At 10 pm we took the boat back to Dawson and parked behind the museum for the night. A beautiful midnight sky and 3/4 moon.

Sunday morning after mass we parked near the river and paddled our canoe down to Moosehide. Now we have canoed on both the Klondike and the Yukon Rivers even if only a short distance. We would like to canoe the Yukon from Whitehorse to Dawson and maybe even to Eagle but that will be another time.

A pretty Indian dancer in beautiful pure-white leather dress.

More of the same activities today. We watched one man making the wooden frame for a drum. Another man was making the bannock for tonight's supper. That is a hot job. Tonight's meal is turkey and ham.

We donated one of our second-print "Mexico and Central America by Campervan" travelogues to the daily raffle. A native couple from Alaska won it. They just bought an RV last year so were quite pleased to win the book.

Tonight at the close of the gathering they had a 'give-away'. Gifts are given to all guests and visitors of the gathering. Once everyone had received something there were still gifts left. We were asked to form a circle and gifts continued to be given out until they were all disposed of. The elders were all given blankets. Other items included: towels, CD holders, fishing rods, camping equipment, scarves, plastic tarps, thermos jugs, socks, toys and various other items.

Around supper time there was thunder & lightning and we could see a big storm building. We didn't want to be canoeing up-river in the rain so John put our canoe on one of the big boats and had it taken back to Dawson then returned to

Moosehide. The rain held off till after the meal but while we were helping to wash up the sky opened and it rained heavily for half an hour then cleared up again.

We sat in on the workshop on tribal drumming, singing and dancing then went over to the shelter where there was dancing and a band was playing western music.

It was 1:00 am when we took the boat back to Dawson. A very interesting and informative weekend. To the Han people we say Mahsi-cho. Thank You.

Monday morning we went to Northern Superior Mechanical to get the brakes fixed. They had to order some parts from Whitehorse which meant another day in Dawson. We spent the night in their parking lot.

August 4 Gravel Lake, Klondike Hwy, Yukon

While they were working on the RV we walked into town - about 3 km - for ice cream. Several hundred dollars later we are ready to travel again. We had supper and left Dawson at 7:30 pm. We passed a big beaver walking along the side of the road. Quite unusual.

We picked up five German Boy Scouts and gave them a lift to Gravel Lake where we stopped for the night. They had been waiting 6 hours for a ride! They set up camp 1/4 km down the

Four good voices, one quiet homesick young man.

road but first they sang a German folksong for us accompanied by guitar. Their voices blended very well together. Older than scouts in Canada. They range in age from 16-29.

We went canoeing in the lake and saw tundra swans and ducks. Bert and Hank had spent a few days here and saw several moose including a cow and her calf. No such luck for us even though it's ideal habitat for them. Lots of marsh and lily pads.

August 5 Mayo Lake, Silver Trail, Yukon

We left late this morning and the German scouts were already on the road. They had been there waiting for a lift for 3 hours. We picked them up again. They are heading for Whitehorse where they will spend a few days before catching a flight to Vancouver and then to Germany.

Down the road we stopped at Moose Creek Lodge to check out 'Max the Mosquito' and the tree phone. While there, two of the boys found a ride to Whitehorse. They will be travelling with their two backpacks plus two women and two dogs in a small compact car! We took the other three to Stewart Crossing where we turned off on the Silver Trail. We gave them some lunch and then headed east.

At Stewart Crossing the smoke from the forest fires was so thick the sun was a red ball and then it disappeared. You could see the smoke billowing over the mountains on the west. The area is under evacuation alert. Two new fires started near Whitehorse yesterday. We spoke with some of the firefighters who were taking a well-earned break. Some of them are up from

I have a laptop. What do you mean you don't have Internet access?

Kamloops, BC and are anxious to get back as fires are now blazing in that area.

The Silver Trail to Mayo is chipseal. While we were driving around a corner the fridge door opened and the stew fell out. Fortunately only a small amount spilled on the floor. Mayo has about 500 people and is a clean town with lawns and flowers. After visiting the information centre and museum at Binet and getting a few groceries we continued on. The road forks into the Old Silver Trail and is dirt surface and very dusty. We spent the night at Mayo Lake and parked by the dam. Went canoeing and fishing. The smoke is thick here. We can't see the east end of the lake or the mountains. You can smell it in the air. It's so quiet and peaceful. It will be hard to go back to urban living. There is a big nest in one of the trees - an eagle maybe? Watched another gorgeous sunset.

Yet another interesting old cabin - where someone is still living.

August 6 Keno, Yukon

The smoke is worse this morning and smells stronger. We have started using the furnace at night. It is set for 55°F (13°C) and it comes on occasionally.

Keno is a very small community - less than 50 people. It used to be a thriving mining town but the mines have shut down and only a handful of people have chosen to remain here. It has a remarkable mining museum which is worth the drive. It is in a renovated two storey hall and is very well done.

The most mouth-watering aromas were emanating from the snack bar. They are cooking a pot roast for a private party to-night. Too bad. The snack bar has only 3-4 tables and is full of antique signs, bottles, containers etc. The hamlet is in the mountains, nestled among the trees. Most of the buildings here are old, ramshackle, miner cabins that have been added on to. The effect is pleasing and restful.

We drove the 10 km to Keno Hill Summit which is at 6000 + ft. We took two hikes up there walking about 5 km. Breathtaking view on the Silver Basin Trail hike. Considering the smoke and haze in the air, the view was still impressive. There are a lot of abandoned cabins and mine sites up here. We walked around one mine entrance that had caved in.

We watched a marmot as he came right up to the RV, went under it , out the other side, climbed up on a rock and stretched out to enjoy the warmth of the sun.

The folks in Keno say they have lived with smoke since the first fires broke out in the Hanson Lakes area in mid-May. They've had only one rainfall since then and their tourism is way down because of the smoke. Their water is trucked in from Mayo. There is a nice campground near the creek. It has 10 sites with tables and wood. The leaves are already starting to turn colour here.

August 7 Minto, Klondike Hwy, Yukon

Exchanged a few books at the library, said goodbye to the folks we met and started back. We had planned to stay in the area 3-4 days, going to Hanson Lakes, McQuesten Lake, Minto Lake and climb Mt. Haldane. When we considered the distance we still have to travel and the short season that's left, we decided to cancel these stops and continue on. We are also concerned about the Klondike Hwy being closed because of the fires. There is a new fire burning about 10 km east of Mayo and we can see the smoke rising as we drive.

We drove into what is left of Elsa, another abandoned mining town. No one lives there now and several buildings have been sold and hauled away, some as far as Alaska. Mine shafts can be seen from the road. We stopped at Silver King claim and climbed down to the mine adit which is closed with wire fencing.

As we approached Stewart Crossing we could see and smell the smoke from the bigger fire across the Klondike Hwy. It is about 2 km from Stewart Crossing. The Highway was still open so we were able to go south. There is a sani-dump (filthy) at Pelly Crossing so we dumped our tanks and got fresh water.

At Minto we inquired about the river trip to Ft Selkirk. It is $50/person, 6 hours, 40km down river & back, bring your own lunch.

Today is our anniversary and we celebrated with barbequed steak. We would like to eat outside by the Yukon River but it is too windy. There is very fine sand here and when the wind is up you get quite a dust storm. There is a dirt airfield here and while we were eating a plane landed and shortly after took off again.

John took our mats down to the river and gave them a good scrubbing. Hung them in the trees to dry overnight. There are 3 - 4 others parked here tonight. This used to be a government campground but it is no longer maintained.

August 8 Campbell Hwy, Yukon

Tim from Tennessee came with John & I on the boat trip to Ft Selkirk. The trip was 1 ½ hours each way. We saw a porcupine, four eagles, some Dall sheep (with our binoculars) and some hawks.

We spent 2 hours at the fort which has 25 well preserved buildings. You can go inside them but nothing has been done to restore the interiors which is too bad. The native cemetery is interesting. The spirit houses are brightly painted in red, green,

yellow and blue. Some are fenced in. The cemetery is about a 5 min. walk into the woods. At the far end of the fort is another smaller cemetery with only a few headstones marking the resting place of some North West Mounted Police.

At 5 pm we left Minto and drove to Carmacks stopping to see the Five Fingers Rapids. The sun was hitting it the wrong way for a picture. From the cliff you can hardly tell there are rapids. You can take a one hour hike along a trail and down 192 steps that leads to another view point farther down.

We drove around Carmacks, a village of about 500 people. A boardwalk follows the Yukon River for 2 km with a few interpretive panels along the way. A park, gazebo and playground are at the end. There are a lot of log cabins with sod roofs and many buildings have moose antlers mounted over the door or on the roof.

At Carmacks we travelled 30 km east on the Campbell Hwy, stopping on the side of the road at Eagles Nest Bluff for the night. We sat in our lawnchairs overlooking the Yukon River, eating barbequed hot dogs, reading and watching another amazing sunset.

<u>Sunday, August 9 Faro, Yukon</u>

Slight smell of smoke this morning. Helicopters are in the area. One landed across the river so we stopped to watch. We thought he was coming for water for the fires but he was dropping off some men, picking up others, and moving equipment in a net slung beneath the craft. A bit farther down the road is the entrance to the fire-fighters camp. Still farther down on the north side of the road is evidence of the recent fire damage including a fire break made by a bulldozer.

Little Salmon Lake territorial campground is very pleasant. About half of the 15 sites are on the lake. If it was warmer we would stay a day or two but with this drizzle we may as well be driving.

This is getting monotonous.

Went as far as Faro. It has become a semi-ghost town since the lead/zinc mining operation shut down in the spring. The population dropped from 1500 to 500. A lot of nice looking company built apartment blocks are sitting empty and falling prey to vandalism. We went to Sally's Road House and had a belated anniversary dinner at Wong's restaurant. The food was delicious but the place was quite run down.

Kate at the interpretive centre was very pleasant, helpful and informative.

The laundromat is at one end of a house trailer. There are 3 washers and 3 dryers. Our clothes were still quite damp after three sessions in the dryer so we strung a line in the RV. This seems to be a common problem with laundromats. Either there's not enough heat or not enough time in the dryers.

August 10 Hoole River, Campbell Hwy, Yukon

Rained most of the night, gray & overcast, cold & damp today. During the night the temp. went down to 3^0C, now it's 9^0C. We can see fresh snow caps on the mountains. The trees are orange & yellow and the leaves are dropping.

We picked up our e-mail at Yukon College then drove to a lookout to see Fanin sheep but there weren't any. Drove about 25 km on back roads and came across 18 pigs on the road. Someone has a farm way out here. Stopped at a camp where they are monitoring the salmon going upstream. Spoke with a young native man who has been there for a month counting the salmon.

Coal seams are visible along the 10 km road that leads into the small community of Ross River. It is home to the Kaska Indians. There is a suspension foot bridge across the river and a path leading to an Indian village but because it was raining we didn't go there. After a quick drive around the area we gassed up and carried on another 70 km to Hoole River where we stopped for the night. Two men in a truck camper are also here. A good place to fish.

August 11 Watson Lake, Yukon

Stopped at a couple of places to fish but no luck. We saw three small animals on the road but couldn't tell if they were foxes or coyotes. As we drew nearer they ran off into the woods. We should have stopped and used our binoculars. A moose was standing on the side of the road, he crossed in front of us, ran in the ditch for awhile then crossed in front of us again and went into the woods.

At km 166 we drove through the charred remains of the fire that just recently burned through here and closed this highway for a few days. Even with the rain there is smoke off to the south where the fire is still smouldering.

At Francis Lake we stopped to fish and John saw 12 loons quite close. We drove through two sections of construction each about 3 km long. We went through a 10 km stretch where a water truck had been watering the road (in the rain!) and it was muddy. The RV was a mess. The upside of rain is there's no dust; the downside is there's lots of mud and most of it is on our rig. We stopped at a creek and John washed the worst of it off.

At Watson Lake the sun was shining and it was warm. What a treat. We bought gas and groceries, dumped our tanks, got fresh water, washed the rest of the mud off the RV and had refreshing showers. We are dust free for a few more days. This was reminiscent of cleaning up in Dawson after travelling the Dempster. All told we didn't feel the Campbell Hwy was worth the trip in this cool weather.

August 12 Smith River Falls, Alaska Hwy, BC

It rained all night and was overcast all morning, clearing up at noon. Did a laundry at the Good Sam Campground. The fan for the truck heater is broken so after we bought propane we went to an auto salvage dealer. They had one but the blade was just a bit too big.

On the Alaska Hwy we went through 20 km of construction starting at Ironside Creek and going east. They are using the big ore trucks from the mines to haul dirt and gravel. Stopped at a couple of places to view the Liard River and rapids. Very scenic.

Stopped at Smith River Falls for the night. It is 2 km off the hwy on a narrow dirt road. From the parking area there is a path through the woods and then 2 sets of stairs totalling 165 steps take you to the bottom. There is a small viewing area in the parking lot but it is becoming overgrown with trees. The falls aren't terribly high but they are two tiered and have a large volume of water. Several grouse here.

August 13 Km 730 Alaska Hwy, BC

Saw a bear cub crossing the hwy on the 30 km drive to the Liard Hot Springs. These springs are in a provincial park, the pools are natural (not developed) and free. There is a boardwalk through marshland connecting the two pools with the parking lot. The upper pool is the nicer one but it has been closed for the last five days because of bear activity.

The bear is a big black one with her cub and apparently she was right in the pool. We stayed here all day and it was so relaxing after all the continuous driving. This is the first day we've worn shorts in two weeks. The springs are very hot, 38 - 54^{0}C (100 - 129^{0}F). We talked with lots of fellow travellers and heard some interesting stories. One BC couple we met had canoed the Yukon River from Whitehorse to Dawson. It took them 2 weeks. What a trip that must have been.

The ranger said the bear usually shows up at the pool at 5 pm. Tonight he and another ranger are going to shoot her with

Great graphics! This is a Black/Brown bear outlined by a Grizzly.
These animals can be dangerous. Photograph them with a telephoto lens.

rubber bullets. They hurt and hopefully she will not come back. If she does they will tranquillize her and move her about 160 km away. We stayed to see the action but the bear didn't show up - at least not before we left.

We went about 20 km and pulled off for the night at a place marked 'Mineral Lick'. The rocks here contain a variety of minerals and the animals can sometimes be seen here licking them, hence the name. ½ km off the road there is a big clearing and a short trail that leads to a viewpoint of Trout River, the valley and the mountains. Lots of colour. At sunset the rocks turned different shades of red. Too bad we hadn't brought our cameras along.

August 14-15 Muncho Lake, Alaska Hwy, BC
Driving along the Alaska Hwy near Muncho Lake we saw one Stone sheep on the side of the road. The Stone sheep are a sub-species of the Dall sheep and are a reddish brown colour.

Muncho Lake is 12 km long and the water is a dark green. We are camped in a provincial park at the eastern end. We went canoeing a few times and took an hour cruise around the lake. The boat captain said there aren't many fish left in the lake because their eggs get eaten by sucker fish. Back at our site we enjoyed a fire and wieners. Our last campfire was at Tombstone on the Dempster. This park has 15 spaces, is $9.50/night and is usually full.

The Hwy follows the lake and there are several places where you can pull off to take photos or just enjoy the view. We are entering the Rockies and the mountains here are big and rugged.

Next morning we decided to go back to the Liard Hot Springs. Glad we did, another lovely relaxing day. The upper pool is still closed.

Went back a bit further to Smith Falls. John wanted to get a picture of the rainbow in the spray from the falls. On the way back to Muncho Lake we stopped again at the mineral lick to get a sunset picture. Unfortunately there was cloud over the rocks so we couldn't get a shot of the changing colours. It was perfect two nights ago but we hadn't carried our cameras with us then.

Sunday, August 16-17 Ft. Nelson, BC

It was cool and noisy last night. The furnace won't come on this morning. We decided to just have coffee and toast and move on. Passed through a couple of areas of construction.

Folded Mtn is interesting to see. The contours of the mountain are all pressed together. The postcard looks more impressive than the real thing. I guess you have to see it in the right light.

Saw a young caribou grazing on the side of the road and later two older ones. They don't have their winter coat yet so at first we thought they were small elk. They are a rusty brown with very big hooves. Their antlers are covered in velvet.

At Summit Lake, which is a small lake, there is an attractive and well-groomed park with 15 sites all overlooking the lake. We found this area more picturesque than Muncho Lake.

We drove the 7 km trail to the microwave tower which is at 5,400 ft. Stayed up here for an hour. What a majestic view! The last bit of the rough path was quite steep with loose gravel and big rocks. We bent the step brace somewhere along that stretch. John fixed it later.

Rest in Summit Lake Campground after driving or hiking to the summit.

Tetsa River outfitters and campground is a pleasant and clean looking place. As well as a gift shop they also sell very large and tasty cinnamon buns and sourdough bread.

Just east of Ft. Nelson we picked up a cyclist with a flat. He had already walked 9 km pushing his bike. We blew up his tire with our air pump but it went flat again immediately. We drove him to Ft. Nelson where he met up with his friend. They are biking from Prudhoe Bay, AK to South America.

At 8 pm it is 24⁰C. It is nice to be warm again. A lovely sunset at 9:30. Hard to believe just three weeks ago we were in 24 hour sunlight. Stayed here in Ft. Nelson tonight.

Monday was a stock-up, wash up and repair day. Ft. Nelson has two big grocery stores. It was so nice to shop in a 'real' store again with lots of selection and good produce. John bought 'guy stuff' including spare parts for the RV. He also found a fan for the truck heater.

They have a wonderful museum here with lots of information and artifacts from the building of the Alaska Hwy. The museum does not get any funding from the town. It is a private venture run by a local individual who loves this part of the country.

We had a delicious supper of fish, fresh veggies, new potatoes and ice cream. After supper John worked on the headlights.

He bought a new halogen bulb and now we have two halogen lights and two regular lights. Up till now we had one of each. Fortunately they were on opposite sides. We don't drive after dark anyway unless we absolutely have to.

August 18 Ft. Liard, Hwy 7, NWT

John spent most of the day continuing his repairs. He re-wired the battery and what a difference in the lights. Now they don't flicker when the pump is in use.

We left Ft. Nelson at 4 pm and started up the Liard Trail. Took 3 hours to go the 175 km to Ft. Liard. That was good time considering the first 40 km are horrendous. Lots of potholes and loose gravel. BC does not maintain their portion of the Liard Trail. It has heavy use from logging and transport trucks which continue to chew it up. And the DUST! So much for our big clean up in Watson Lake. We had to stop when big trucks passed. It was impossible to see. There were times we were choking on the dust and 3 times I had to clean my glasses. This is comparable to the Nisga'a Hwy outside of Terrace.

At the NWT border the road changed and so did the weather. No more dust and no more sun. NWT uses calcium chloride on the roads for dust control. We could have used the rain on the BC portion of the road! Considering how windy it was in Ft. Nelson when we left, we were surprised to find it very calm on the Liard Trail. As a result the dust just hung there. The clouds were so dark I would not have been surprised to see snow.

There is a free community-run campground just outside Ft. Liard at Hay Lake. We pulled in there for the night and visited with a couple we met earlier at the Visitors Centre in Ft. Nelson.

August 19 Liard ferry crossing, Hwy 1, NWT

We drove into Ft. Liard and dropped in at the Acho Dene craft shop. They sell baskets of all sizes decorated with porcupine quills or bead work. This area is known for its birch baskets. The work is exquisite and they should have been represented at the Arts Festival in Inuvik. If you're looking for baskets this is the place to go.

Today's drive was much more pleasant. No dust and better road surface. We stopped in at Blackstone Territorial Park which has 20 sites and costs $12/night. A very attractive and clean park with some sites on the river. They have a comfortable Visitors Centre in a log building with displays and a seating area overlooking the Liard River and Nahanni Butte which rises to 4579 ft. Today the top part of the Butte was hidden in cloud.

As we were driving a small black bear crossed the road in front of us and ran into the woods.

At the Liard Hwy and MacKenzie Highway junction, known as Checkpoint, we stopped for supper. There is nothing here but travelling services: a restaurant, motel, gas, diesel, propane and a 3000 ft airstrip. Major stop for all travellers. As we were eating, a helicopter landed across the road. It was still there when we left.

We drove to the Liard River ferry crossing. The ferries across the rivers are free and take about 10 min. We parked by the river in a free municipal campground with three sites. Another pretty sunset.

August 20 - Sunday, August 23 Ft. Simpson, NWT

Ferried across the Liard River and drove to Ft. Simpson a village of about 1200 people. John used the computer at the Visitors Centre to get our e-mail.

There is a golf course in the making. So far it has six holes and sand greens. It is always in use. John played here a few times over the weekend. Once he got caught in the rain and came back drenched.

We took a walk down the main street to the river and followed the river back to the site of the 1987 papal visit. The main street is all torn up as they are working on the pipes. There is a nice campground here with 20 sites at $12/night. It is in a stand of birch and diamond willow trees. The sites are big and there are several pull-throughs. There is also a dump station which was closed when we were here. We found another place to dump in town but you have to get the key for it at the Visitors Centre.

The craft store in town is also a video store and has more videos than crafts. It is open only from 5-8 pm. The crafts are baskets and some moccasins.

There is a Dene business here called Nats'enelu. They have a few items for sale but mainly they are a factory producing leather and beaded goods which they sell in cities across Canada.

We went to the end of main street and parked on the river bank for the night. Floatplanes were landing and taking off right in front of us. The sunset was reflected in the river.

Another thunderstorm on Friday and a short but heavy rain on Sunday. The weather sure has turned cool and miserable.

On Sunday there was an ecumenical service in the papal grounds celebrating 140 years of the gospel in Ft. Simpson. Catholic, Anglican and Pentecostal churches participated. About 50 people attended. It was followed by a potluck at the drum which gave us an opportunity to meet and talk with some of the local folks. We were also interviewed about our upcoming book by a reporter for the 'Drum'.

The electricity here, as in most of the communities, is diesel generated. Some of these communities have sewer lagoons and some have their water trucked in. Ft. Simpson takes its water from the river. It's very soft.

The laundromat here is in an apartment building. Once we found it, I did a laundry in preparation for our leaving in the morning.

Tonight we watched the barge returning from Wrigley.

August 24 Willowlake River, Hwy 1, NWT

Did several errands this morning and were on our way to Wrigley by noon. Ferry across the MacKenzie River. The road is good but dusty in areas where they haven't used calcium chloride. If the weekend rains reached this far you'd never know it from the roads. They're dry as a bone.

Some jerk was doing about 100 km/hr, didn't have the courtesy to slow down, sent gravel flying everywhere and put 2 chips in our windshield. That is so maddening. It's not a big deal up here for locals since most vehicles have damaged windshields.

The drive was boring as the trees grow fairly close to the road and block any view that might be there. As we neared Willowlake River the Franklin Mtns came into view in the distance.

We reached Willowlake River in the late afternoon. We stopped there and sat in the welcome sun enjoying its warmth. We had supper outside but once the sun set we moved inside as it became quite damp. John tried his hand at fishing but they weren't biting. There's a lot of bear tracks along the river bank.

John thinks the brakes are going again. If they are, we still have a lot of driving to do before we can get them fixed in Yellowknife.

August 25 Wrigley, Hwy 1, NWT

We think we have a mouse again. We've been hearing him the last few nights.

Wrigley is another small hamlet of 140. It is clean and spacious with big yards and nice homes - relatively speaking. There are some mobile homes here, I hope they have good insulation. We have heard that mobile homes going to the north must have the 'arctic package' installed.

The Dene here call Wrigley by its native name of Pehdzeh Ki. Gas is trucked in here to a pumping station and the cost is the same as in Ft. Simpson. The Co-op store also houses the bank and post office. The manager of this facility is from the Maritimes, Cape Breton if I remember correctly. At noon everything shuts down for an hour.

We drove down to the river to see where the barge docks when it comes with supplies. Met a young couple there with their two young sons. They were preparing to canoe to their camp down river and do some hunting and fishing for their winter supplies.

We parked at Airport Lake for the night. Had a wonderful paddle around the lake. Barbequed steak for supper and ate outside on the dock. It was clear and calm and the lake was like glass. John brought his computer outside so he could enjoy the weather while he worked. I was not so fortunate. I had some baking to do and that had to be done inside. It's 9 pm and I am writing this outside. Just a few mosquitoes of the large variety.

We are surprised at the lack of birds and their sounds. It is so quiet here. As the saying goes, the silence is deafening. There are a few ducks here but no fish in this lake. It is quite shallow.

A beautiful sunset tonight with the pink and gray clouds reflected in the lake.

After we went to bed it was so bright we thought there must be a full moon. We got up to check and the aurora borealis was arched across the sky from horizon to horizon!! A big silver band reflected in the lake. We watched as it faded, then intensified, subtly changing patterns as it stretched across the night sky. What a show and what a magnificent phenomenon!

August 26-27 Ft. Simpson, Hwy 1, NWT

It must have been really cold last night as there is a heavy dew this morning. We left our table and chairs out overnight and they are all wet. As we drove along we wondered if there was another fire burning somewhere. The mist was so heavy it looked like smoke.

The water level in the rivers is very low. At Camsell Bend crossing they are using a barge instead of the ferry to cross the MacKenzie River because the barge doesn't draw as much water. The barge companies are worried that they may not be able to make their last trip before freeze-up. They are increasing their loads in an attempt to get supplies to those communities that are isolated.

There are big sand dunes on both sides of the road just south of Willowlake River bridge which is the longest bridge in the NWT. There seems to be more yellow in the trees than there was a few days ago.

When we got back to Ft. Simpson we stopped at the Visitors Centre. They made us 'tourist of the week' and took our picture in front of the big sign outside. The photo was then put on their web page where it will stay for one year.

Went to play golf but there was a local tournament in progress. We did get a few holes in. The mosquitoes come out at sunset.

Another day of rain. I get the feeling rain is the norm in Ft. Simpson. We got our umbrellas and went for a walk ending up at the Nahanni Inn where we had coffee with some other tourists. The streets are a sea of mud.

The fire hydrants here are painted to look like Dalmatians with red hats. Also the garbage cans are housed in boxes which are also painted with flowers, cartoon characters & animals. A nice effect making these necessary parts of living pleasant to look at.

My camera battery died and I can't find lithium batteries here. I guess I'm without a camera till we get to Yellowknife.

August 28-29 Ekali Lake, Hwy 1, NWT

We got some water at the Esso station, did some shopping at the Northern store and left. The bank here does not have a cash machine so we will have to wait till Yellowknife to do our banking. Stopped at Checkpoint for gas and propane. There was a dead red fox on the side of the road.

At a pullout we met 2 units who were part of the caravan from Grimshaw to Hay River. There were over 100 units in the caravan which was part of the 50th anniversary celebration of the MacKenzie Hwy. A lot of the participants were retired truckers who travelled that route when it wasn't much more than a rough path. There were lots of stories and reminiscing going around.

We stopped at Ekali Lake for the night. It is bigger and deeper than Airport Lake. We put the canoe in and did some fishing. We each brought in a pike. Mine was bigger but John's broke his line. John cooked them outside. I love fish but have decided I do not care for pike. I don't like the texture. To me they're rubbery. Maybe we don't cook them the right way. They're also a very boney fish.

In the evening we went out on the lake again after a little setback. I'm not quite sure how this happened. The canoe was tied at a rickety little dock and I got in first. When John got in, he had one foot in the canoe and the other on the dock when the canoe started to move away. The foot in the canoe was tipping it over and I thought I was going to end up in the lake. However it was John who went in. He's standing there hip deep in the water on one leg with the other leg still in the canoe. I'm laughing so hard my stomach hurts and the tears are running down my cheeks. (No sympathy here.) I don't know why I didn't get wet. Even with all the water we took on I stayed dry including my feet. John sloshed his way back to the RV to change and we tried again - this time successfully. Oh, for my camera.

It was so still and quiet on the lake. We watched the sun set behind a band of cloud that turned pink & purple with tree tops jutting into the colour. Just beautiful. There was a loon on the lake which we could hear but not see. Their call is so haunting. As we paddled around we found three beaver lodges and saw the splashes of two beavers as they went under the water. An eagle flew overhead to a nearby tree. What a perfect evening.

Next morning I cleaned and defrosted the fridge and freezer. We spent six hours on the lake today, three in the afternoon and 3 in the evening. We did catch and release fishing, found another beaver lodge, listened to the loon and watched two beavers playing. Another colourful sunset with a few clouds catching the vibrant pinks.

Sunday, August 30 MacKenzie River, Hwy 3, NWT

A heavy rain and lots of wind during the night. Just before we got up this morning a vehicle drove to the lake then turned around and left.

Stopped at Sambaa Deh Territorial Park and walked upriver to Coral Falls. They're wide but not too deep. Lots of water. They're on the Trout River. Whittaker Falls can be seen from the road. They start just under the bridge down river from the Coral Falls. The river narrows and flows through a rock-walled gorge. A great volume of water rushes through here. We hiked about 1 km along and climbed down a ravine which was a deep narrow crack in the rock. There was a rope to hold on to as we made our way down the ravine to the river where we fished for awhile. The only fish we seem to catch are pike. John caught several which he released.

Back at the park we spoke with Phil and Mary Norwegian from Ft. Smith. They are the caretakers. She was surprised we'd caught some pike, which she loves. Mary had just made bannock with cranberries in it. She gave us some to try. It was delicious, still hot and very light.

While we were talking with Mary we heard a rifle shot. When we drove out to the road three young men were hurrying into a blue truck. One of them was carrying a rifle. When they saw us coming they drove quickly away. Mary said there's not supposed to be any shooting around the park.

Saw lots of animals today. Two porcupines, one on the side of the road walking towards the woods, the other in a big puddle of water. We stopped to watch as it came out on the other side of the puddle, stood on his hind legs and shook himself dry before waddling off. The wind was ruffling his hair which was blond at the tips.

A bear was walking down the side of the road. We got fairly close before it realized we were there and scampered off into the bush.

A crane flew by overhead.

Another short-legged animal was crossing the road. He had a black head and tail and a brown body. We think it was a muskrat.

It must have rained quite heavily here, there is a lot of water on the side of the road.

At the junction with Hwy 3 to Yellowknife, we finally have pavement. There are also power lines here.

We parked for the night just off the road in the parking lot of a picnic area. We are about 3 km from the MacKenzie River ferry crossing to Fort Providence and Yellowknife which is 400 km north. Still cool and windy. Quite cloudy, looks like snow! Lots of black flies in this area.

August 31 Ft. Providence, Hwy 3, NWT

Took the ferry across the MacKenzie River. On the ferry we met Joanne who is moving with her family from Hay River to Ft Providence. They have just bought the now defunct Target gas station, restaurant and campground which is on the highway just south of the ferry crossing. Ft Providence territorial campground is on the access road to Ft. Providence along the banks of the MacKenzie River. It has 30 spacious and bright sites, a sani-dump and pump water.

Ft. Providence is another small neat village of 700. Some nice homes, large lots and grass in the yards.

John was offered a job here teaching computers and while it was tempting we eventually decided against it. It would be quite an experience to winter here and witness spring break-up on the river.

September 1 Hwy 3, NWT

After we dumped our tanks we went to the pumping station in town. It's not open to the public but a man was there filling the water truck and he kindly let us fill our tank. Water is delivered to the homes on demand and costs .004¢/L. Septic is drained every second day. There is no bank here. They have a nursing station and a doctor comes once a week.

John saw two osprey this morning. One of them had a fish in its claws.

Just south of the junction of the access road and Hwy 3 is Bison Crossing Crafts. She has a large selection of items to choose from.

We left Ft. Providence at noon. The MacKenzie Bison Sanctuary extends 50 km along the Hwy and we saw only one bison. We did see a few hawks and a pheasant was sitting on the side of the road. The black flies are bad along here. We've been told it's because of the bison.

The brakes are definitely gone again. What a worry. We'll be glad to get to Yellowknife. This is getting ridiculous and expensive.

The road is paved or chipseal as far as Edzo. Edzo is a dismal government attempt to relocate a town. Across the bridge and 11 km down an access road is the Dene community of Rae, about 2000 people. Because it is built on rock and is right next to the water it has drainage problems. The gov't built a lovely big school in Edzo and wanted everyone to move there. The people didn't want to move so now they drive their children everyday over to Edzo (20 km) for their schooling. As far as we can see the only people living in Edzo are those connected with the school. It looks to us like a depressing place to live. There are no stores, no businesses of any kind, just the school and a handful of houses.

Rae, on the other hand, with its brightly coloured houses built on the rock of the Canadian Shield and its location on the water is very picturesque. It reminded us of the Newfoundland outports. All the street signs are in the native language and have a painted floral border. It has a motel, small store, church, and rec centre. It is a Dogrib community of the Slavey Nation and is the largest Dene community in the territories.

At this point the road reverts back to gravel for the last 100 km into Yellowknife. Apparently it can't be paved because of the permafrost & muskeg. We are now in the PreCambrian Shield and the scenery changes dramatically. Trees are more like shrubs, the area is very marshy, lots of small shallow lakes and channels and huge chunks of pink-tinged granite. We parked off the road in a big gravel pit for the night.

September 2-4 Yellowknife, NWT

In Yellowknife we stopped at the Visitors Centre and got lots of information on the area. They gave us each a 'Yellow knife' pin. Went to Tim Horton's for a doughnut and coffee then walked around Wal-Mart. Imagine finding a Wal-Mart here!

Went to Kingland Ford and have an appointment with them for 8 am tomorrow, so we'll park there tonight. The rest of the day was spent, doing laundry, banking, grocery shopping and then to Subway for supper. Tonight we went to the library to listen to author Tristan Rhodes do a reading from his book. The audience was mainly high school students, teachers and parents.

We offered to do a presentation for them but they are already booked for the time we will be here. The library is in Centre Mall which is a large modern shopping complex with some unique boutiques. There is some excellent art work here as well. Some of the artists who were at the Festival in Inuvik have their work on display here.

September 3

Light rain all day today. We need a new master cylinder and a star wheel for the left brake. They have to order the master cylinder. It should be here tomorrow. We drove carefully to 'Old Town' and parked at the Northwest Trading Company which is an excellent gift shop. From there we walked around with our umbrellas. Sure makes you think you are in Newfoundland. Very interesting place. It's on a narrow spit of land which is mainly rock. Some very exclusive homes here as well as some of the original shacks from the '30s.

We wanted to eat at the Wildcat Café which is in one of these original buildings but it was closed already. Most seasonal things in the territories shut down the middle of September. In the harbour there are a number of brightly painted houseboats which people live in year round. Having a floatplane seems to be as common as having a boat. They are parked side by side in the marina. We climbed 'The Rock' for an overall view of Old Town and New Town as the city proper is known.

This city is very different from Whitehorse. The population is less but the city appears larger because it is more spread out. It looks more like a city with its taller and more modern buildings whereas Whitehorse has chosen to retain the flavour of the past. With its false store fronts it has a small town atmosphere while being very up to date. We enjoyed both cities. Because of the rocky terrain, Yellowknife expands where it can and is a bit confusing to get around at first. Also permafrost is a problem here. City Hall, the RCMP headquarters and a military building are adjacent to each other. One sits on sand, another on rock and the last is on permafrost and muskeg. It is built on 70 ft pilings.

Tonight we went to the movies then back to Kingland Ford for the night.

September 4

They can't work on the RV until this afternoon. This morning we went to CBC radio and did a taped interview with Randy Henderson.

What a relief to have the brakes working again. Let's hope

they're really fixed this time. This recurring problem has put a lot of strain and worry in our trip, not to mention what it has done to our wallet.

We met Wendy & David Colpitts who, like us, are retired military. They invited us to join them for supper at the military complex. It was a most enjoyable evening and we had the opportunity to meet several delightful people including the mayor and his wife. Being part of a group is one of the things we miss in our nomadic life style, so thank you Wendy and David for including us in your circle of friends for an evening.

September 5-7 Ingraham Trail, Hwy 4, NWT

Frontier RV Sales was having a garage sale this morning. Took us a while to find it. They were selling parts - water pumps, vent lids, linen, cutlery, lawn chairs etc. We bought a few small items then headed for the Ingraham Trail which is the recreation area for the Yellowknife region. It is 70 km long and has many lakes and parks on either side. We stopped to hike in to picturesque Cameron Falls. It isn't much more than a 1 km hike but we were gone about 1 ½ hr. The 'trail' is over the rock of the Canadian Shield and metal markers have been pounded into the rock to show the way. Overcast all day and a fine rain while we were hiking. On our return we encountered several people who were going to the falls for a wedding. Most were appropriately dressed for a wedding but not for a hike, especially their footwear. A few wore hiking boots.

The first 1/3 of the Ingraham Trail is paved and is terrible. It's like being on a roller coaster, lots of heaves. The result of permafrost. No potholes, just very uneven. The dirt part was much smoother. The Ingraham Trail ends at Tibbett Lake. We wanted to put the canoe in but didn't want to get caught in a downpour so decided to wait till tomorrow. Remained overcast with occasional breaks in the clouds.

Sunday, September 6

Well, it didn't rain today but it was cool and cloudy with occasional sun. Nevertheless we spent most of the day on the lake. The temp was 18^0C (63^0F). Saw several loons and two eagles. John caught several pike one of which we had to keep. He couldn't get the hook out even though it was barbless. Those pike have big mouths.

Forest fires burned here also. Four cabins along the lake were demolished by the blaze. While out in the canoe we stopped at one cabin which had no damage and yet the ones on both sides were burned to the ground.

Clear this evening for an hour or so but clouded over again just in time to block the sunset. Later this evening the aurora borealis was faintly visible. A large full moon tonight. Cold.

September 7

Pouring rain today, it started during the night. We have the furnace set for 55^0F and it ran nearly all night. I think it's time to say good-bye to Yellowknife and head south. We've heard it's in the high twenties in southern AB. What are we doing here in the cold and rain? Every morning we have to wipe the condensation off the windows, especially the ones by the bed or the linen on John's side gets wet.

Left Tibbett Lake at noon and stopped to check out Reid Lake Territorial Park. As are most of the territorial parks, it is pleasant, spacious and clean. There are wooden platforms for tents. Several tenters are there now, it must be cool for them.

Farther along the Ingraham Trail there is a large sandy area which has an un-maintained camp with 12 cabins. It's quite a pretty area. A big brown eagle was sitting on the back of a sofa that had been left outside.

A lot of road signs in the north have bullet holes in them. Are they being used for target practice?

Stopped at Poplar Point on Prelude Lake and canoed/portaged to Hidden Lake. That canoe is heavy, 60 lbs plus about 25 lbs of water we've got between the hulls. There were three portages. The first one was short, the second a bit longer with a climb of 60 steps - at least there were steps - and the third longer still and over rock. The Canadian Shield again. My arms felt like they were hanging down to my feet! If I do this again it will be with a much lighter canoe. Unfortunately we didn't start till noon as the morning weather was poor. We weren't aware how long it would take us to get to Hidden Lake so that when we arrived we had only a couple of hours there before having to head back. We didn't want to make the return trip in the dark in case we couldn't find the entrances to the portages.

We did catch a three pound lake trout and it was delicious.

There was a brilliant sunset as we paddled across the lake, the deep reds reflected in the lake and silhouetted in the midst of this colour were two other canoeists. We were gone seven hours and saw a muskrat on the way back. Several loons were on the lake and one was quite vocal.

There was a full moon on the horizon and the northern lights were beautiful tonight. I am surprised we can see them with the moon being so bright.

September 8 Yellowknife, NWT
Used the lake to wash down the RV before leaving here this morning. On the way back to the city we checked out the east access to Prelude Lake. It is a residential area with a few very nice homes. The park on the lake is nice and large with an area for seasonal renters and a marina.

In Yellowknife we did grocery shopping, laundry, got gas, water, propane and emptied our holding tanks at the sani-station. Went to Fred Henne day park on Long Lake for supper. The sunset was the most spectacular so far. The hues of red, pink, mauve and purple were so intense and all reflected on the perfectly calm waters of the lake. I was so engrossed I forgot to take a picture until it was too late and the colour was gone.

I saw a young woman today wearing an amouti - an Inuit poncho - with a baby in the hood. I wish I'd had my camera with me.

It was sunny all day today. What a treat.

September 9 Hwy 3, NWT
After breakfast I bought some yarn while John did his price check then we headed for the Prince of Wales Museum. There is no admission fee but a box for donations is by the door. This is a large, new museum and very well appointed. Definitely worth a visit. We spent most of the day here. Went back to the 'Rock'

in Old Town to take a few photos, stopped at Wendy and David's to say good-bye and then we were on our way.

Even stuffed, this Polar Bear looks like a formidable carnivore.

Stayed at the gravel pit again tonight. At dusk two young men came in from across the barren land and fired and sighted their rifles at targets against the gravel piles. Were they showing off to the young lady with them? John joined them with his old .22 calibre rifle but they were better shots than he.

September 10 Ft. Providence, Hwy 3, NWT

It was so cold during the night that my watch, which hangs on the no draft window catch, stopped at 6 am. Three and a half hours later it started up again and is running fine. I guess it froze during the night. On the radio we heard the temperature in Ft Liard is only 1°C.

On the road early for a change. There was a lot of mist but it gradually cleared. We went into Rae again to get some pictures of the village for our book but the sky was all gray and ominous - not a nice background.

At the junction to Rae a couple about our age was stopped in their car. We got out and talked with them. They couldn't read, at least not English. She had a moosehide purse with beautiful beadwork on one side. She wanted to sell it to me for $125.

In the villages you often notice tepees in the yards. This is where the people smoke and/or dry their fish and sometimes do their cooking.

There are some interesting cloud formations here in the north, and more so here in the NWT than in the Yukon. At one point the clouds were so dark we felt we were driving into a snowstorm.

As we drove along we could see an eagle soaring overhead. They are so graceful.

Once we were back in the MacKenzie Bison Sanctuary, we saw one young bull bison but he ran into the trees as we drew near. Just before the turn into Ft. Providence we came upon a herd of 25-30. We stopped to watch them for about 20 min. Had to keep the windows closed because of the black flies. It was amazing to watch these enormous creatures rolling on their backs in the sand.

We stayed at Ft. Providence for the night. John did a couple of hours of writing and then we went for a long walk. Once the sun goes down it gets damp and chilly almost immediately.

September 11-12 Hay River, Hwy 2, NWT

Made several stops on the way to Hay River. Lady Evelyn Falls on the Kakisa River looks like a miniature Niagara Falls.

Down a rickety ladder to a small falls that disappeared into a stream of rocks and gravel.

It is very smooth and uniform with a considerable volume of water dropping 16 m (49 ft). We continued down the access road

311

to Kakisa village, a small Dene community at the mouth of the river and lake of the same name. It has about 20 homes, many of them log. It's neat, has grass and some gardens.

We met a trucker there who was hauling gas. He said three RVs had been to the village this morning and one of them took 300 L of gas. He was very interesting to talk to and told us some stories of hauling big rigs over the ice roads. They go as far as Fort Good Hope, then the diesel is hauled by cat and then by helicopter to the towers which generate electricity for the territories. Speaking with him gave us some insight into just how important the waterways are to the people of the north. It really is their lifeline.

Very few hydroelectric dams in the north. There is one in Whitehorse on the Yukon River. In NWT, Hay River, Ft. Resolution and Ft. Smith get their power from the Taltson Dam northeast of Slave River. The rest of the communities are dependent on the diesel generators.

At the falls we met Marty Brown. She's entertainment editor of a newspaper and was in Rankin Inlet for three years. She barged the MacKenzie River for two weeks and said it was the best experience she ever had. We were green with envy. (Could a tourist arrange a barge trip, sans RV?)

There is a cruise ship called the Norweta that plies Great Slave Lake and makes one trip from there to Inuvik and back, but by the time we found out about it, it was over. Tourism was not very helpful in that area as we had been in contact with them before leaving on this trip. Of course our big push was to barge the RV but still no mention was made of this boat trip for passengers only. Could be its just for VIPs and government officials.

Stopped at Hart Lake Fire Tower. If not for the Milepost and the Deh Cho book we would have missed it. The access road was closed so we walked in. It's less than 1 km. Magnificent view. It's called the Alberta Plateau. The land abruptly drops away 76 ft. leaving a solid rock escarpment. You can see all the way to Great Slave Lake, 100 km away. The escarpment has several large fissures in it.

Liz can look down a 25 m vertical wall and enjoy the view. I almost panic.

The fire warden's house was closed for the season. The remains of a vegetable garden and rose bushes indicate someone cares. Tiny carrots found in the garden were delicious. There is also a bird bath made with a garbage can lid. This has been a strange year all-right, the peas and strawberries are flowering a second time.

The next stop was McNally Creek Falls and Gorge which looks like a big punch bowl. It's part of the escarpment. You can't see it from the highway bridge but a short trail leads to it. The path crosses the creek by means of a foot bridge allowing you to view the falls from both sides.

We passed a few trappers' cabins along the way and there are also survival cabins offering basic shelter from the elements. They contain a wood burning stove and wood bunks.

Today we took the last of six ferry crossings here in the north. We have ferried across the Yukon River at Dawson City, the Peel River south of Ft. McPherson; the MacKenzie River at Tsiigehtchic (Arctic Red River), Wrigley and Ft. Providence; and the Liard River at Ft. Simpson.

Hay River looks like a real town. It also has Old Town, located on Vale Island, where the town began. Most of the industrial part of the town is located there now as well as Northern Transportation Company Ltd. (NTCL) headquarters. This is the barge company. The town has about 3000 people, paved streets and sidewalks, nicely maintained homes and yards. Vale Island also has a fine beach and territorial park with electrical hookups.

The island flooded several times over the years so as the town expanded and grew it moved onto the mainland. Hay River has a 17 storey apt. building which is the tallest building in the NWT.

There is a Trade Show at the Sports Complex this weekend so we spent the morning wandering through there. Walked around town this afternoon. Went to mass this evening but Fr. Felix is away in Yellowknife for a conference. Most of the villages in the NWT are mission communities and their spiritual needs are attended to by the priests and ministers of Ft. Simpson and Hay River. They spend a lot of time travelling.

We parked by the river for the night. It's not a very scenic spot but it's quiet. It was sunny all day and turned overcast in the evening.

Sunday, September 13 Wood Buffalo National Park, Hwy 5 NWT

Heavy rain during the night. In Hay River this morning we dumped our tanks, filled up with water, propane, gas, did a laundry (best price yet -$1.25 for the washer and $1.00 for the dryer which ran for 28 min.- and it was clean), mailed some letters, stopped at the Northern store for milk and left for Ft. Resolution by 1 pm.

As usual, not much to see on the highway except trees. Pine Point used to be a lead/zinc mine. It closed in 1988. We drove through the area that at one time housed 2000 people. All the buildings were destroyed or moved. There is absolutely nothing left except streets and overgrown sidewalks and driveways.

We drove in to see Little Buffalo River village located on the edge of the lake. It's very small and most of the houses/ cabins look deserted. Some are in use though as smoke was coming from a few chimneys.

314

Eidjercon Buffalo Ranch consists of one building probably used for storage, and about 24 buffalo inside one medium-sized muddy enclosure. Feel sorry for the animals not being able to roam and graze. The place looked deserted but there were several large bales of hay so assume the animals are being fed.

Ft. Resolution located on Resolution Bay is a Chipewyan community of 440. It has several big buildings - different halls -some brightly painted houses and a bright orange store/coffee shop/B&B/gas station which charges 79¢/L. That's almost as high as Inuvik.

Look carefully and you'll see several dogs, some on top of their houses.

Racing dogs are tied up on short leashes in fenced-in areas. Each dog has a dog house. The dogs race 10 to a team and run in pairs rather than fanned out.

Our nice clean RV is once again covered in mud as it rained all day.

We camped tonight at Angus Fire Tower in Wood Buffalo National Park. There is a sink hole here. It is similar to a cenote except it has very little water in it.

The sky began to clear this evening and the northern lights were awesome. I stayed out watching them until I got so chilled I had to come inside.

Everywhere in NWT postcards are $1 each. Why? That's ridiculous. All through northern BC and Yukon they were 3 for a $1.

Brrrr, it was a cold night. When we got up it was 10⁰C inside but at least the sun is shining. There is a picnic site here and the boards have frost on them.

Several of the hydro poles along the road have ravens' nests in them.

We didn't buy quite enough gas at Fort Resolution to get us to Ft. Smith. About 25 km north of the town we were able to buy some from a resident farmer. Although very inconvenient for him he was kind enough to sell us sufficient to get us to town.

Saw a black bear crossing the road ahead of us but no buffalo.

Ft. Smith, population 2100, is a pleasant town. It's very green here and known as the garden of the NWT. Like Hay River, it has paved streets and sidewalks and yards with grass. We preferred it to Hay River. The liquor store has a really charming flower garden in front planted and cared for by the owner's wife.

This area is a breeding and nesting site for the white pelican. There were lots of them in the waters of Slave River at the Rapids of the Drowned.

Tonight there is a big bonfire, tea, bannock and jam for the community at the river lookout. It was very cold but we went anyway. Only about a dozen people showed up and we had cake instead of bannock. The woman who was to make the bannock had a death in the family. These gatherings occur regularly during the summer and are opportunities for the elders in the community to tell stories about life styles in the past. Lewis, who runs the Visitors Centre, organizes these evenings and does a good job of it.

Parked in the church parking lot for the night. Northern lights out tonight. We awoke to a lovely sunny fall day. We headed out to see the rapids on the Slave River. There are four sets. The Rapids of the Drowned are here, then Mountain Portage Rapids 8 km south, followed by White Pelican Rapids and lastly the Cassette Rapids at Ft. Fitzgerald just inside the Alberta border. At Mountain Portage we drove in quite a distance then hiked about 20 min. The path had a steep descent. It is a pelican nesting ground and some of the birds were on the islands in the river. The whole set of rapids is part of the Pre-Cambrian Shield and the rock stretches across the river causing the rapids. We climbed over the rocks along the shoreline hoping to get to an outcropping but I had to stop. I was feeling uneasy as the path narrowed and became more difficult.

Pelican Rapids was awesome. We parked close to the road and a very pleasant 45 minute walk through the woods brought us to the rapids. The woods smelled fresh and the leaves are now all yellow and orange making it a very pretty walk. The rapids have a protrusion of granite extending almost to the middle of the river. We spent at least ½ hour walking over the rocks. The roar of the rapids is deafening. On the way back to the RV we saw a large bird which we think is a gyrfalcon. Also saw several grouse today.

A carver of Love's hearts and arrows-will someone think 'twas done in 1898?

Ft. Fitzgerald is a small hamlet of about 10 homes on the Slave River. Bucolic setting. In the winter it is linked to the rest of the province by an ice road. The rest of the time it is cut off.

The last set of rapids was poorly described in the brochure and instead of a 10 min walk it was more like 1 ½ hours. It was a bit unnerving as we were deep in the forest, the path was not well worn and had no markings, there were lots of bear droppings, and the sun was now at the tree line. We didn't know whether to turn back or continue. Being people who don't give up easily, we continued on. We came across a big white egg shell. I wonder what bird it belongs to? We eventually came out at the river and what we saw was the least impressive of all and not worth the trek. We have since been told that the Cassette Rapids are the best of the four so maybe we went too far or didn't go far enough. Until the way is better marked we won't be going back.

Also, according to the pamphlet, the start of the trail is through someone's private property. He wants the Visitors Centre to stop giving out those old brochures and create new ones, which they have done.

Returned to Fort Smith and went to the library to get our e-mail. Their computer link is down so we were out of luck.

September 16 Pine Lake Road, AB

It's really cold at night. This morning the bedside thermometer was reading 8^0C. We can't use the furnace at night because now it doesn't shut itself off. The fan keeps running, blowing out cold air. John's cold, which he's had for a week, seems to be on the mend.

The sky is totally gray this morning and there is a light fog. The sun is just barely visible so maybe this gray mist will burn off by noon.

Went to Parks Canada to watch their 18 minute audio-visual presentation on Wood Buffalo Park. It is a 9-projector affair and for the first time this season, some of them wouldn't work and slides were getting stuck. We'll come back tomorrow.

John's been having trouble with his computer almost since we left. Some old program he bought 'ate' his operating system; yesterday it went into DOS mode and stayed there. This

318

afternoon he took it to a computer shop here and they managed to get the Windows program running again.

We decided to do a loop trip of about 120 km through the park. We took the Parson Lake road for 50 km. It is more of a sand-based trail but easily travelled. We stopped to see the Salt Plains and mud flats. It was disappointing as we expected to see lots of salt as we did in Mexico. People harvested salt here in the past so maybe it used to be like that but there was very little salt to be seen today. We took the ½ km trail down from the viewing platform and then walked through mud and marsh in search of the 4 ft. salt mound but to no avail. Maybe it dissolved in all the rain we've had. We did come across one bit of salt, about 2x3 ft, flat on the ground.

From there we went to Parson Lake fire tower which is at the end of 1 ½ km path off the trail. A pretty view as the land drops away so you are above the tree line looking south. From about half way up the tower (closed to tourists) you would be able to see the Salt Plains to the north.

This trail has lots of indications of buffalo activity - fresh prints, wallows, the ground all pawed up. We drove 40 km before we finally saw two bulls standing in the trees. We stopped and watched as they came out, crossed the path and re-entered the forest on the other side. On this trail the trees grow right next to the road, just like a country lane. Very pretty with the autumn colours.

At the junction with Pine Lake road we went south 16 km to see the campground and the lake which is a karst (sink hole). Several of them are joined together to make Pine Lake. The park was very rustic but it did have a dump station which we used. We didn't get any drinking water as you have to boil it. On the way a black bear was eating berries on the side of the road. He went into the trees as we passed. We stopped and he came back out and resumed his meal. We observed him for 15 min. Other vehicles passed without disturbing him. He was still there when we returned from Pine Lake.

A lot of the wild flowers are blooming for the second time.

Tonight John rigged a set of wires from the thermostat to the bed so we can turn the furnace off and on from there. We'll see how it works. We're spending the night on the side of the road.

September 17 Ft. Smith, NWT

Better night last night. When the furnace fan wouldn't shut off on its own we used the bedside switch John rigged up. We had a warmer and more comfortable night thanks to John's ingenuity.

This morning we took an easy 1 ½ km hike to Grosbeak Lake. This is really worth seeing. The trail has bear droppings and evidence of anthills disturbed by bears. There is about ½ km stretch of mud flats with some salt and lots of erratics (rocks) which have been eroded into weird shapes by salt and frost. Much more interesting than the Salt Plains of yesterday.

Lots of buffalo prints and possibly wolf in the mud flats. A flock of trumpeter swans flew overhead.

The Karstland Trail has a long hike and a short one. We took the short one. The interpretive panels are very well done. The area is full of sink holes and the ground is unstable. The red-sided gartersnake has an hibernaculum here. A rabbit was sitting under a tree and was changing to his winter colour. His feet and belly were pristine white but his back and head were still gray.

This is the Salt River day use area and there is a lovely monument here for our war dead.

Across the road we walked the 1.3 km Salt River Meadows trail. A pleasant meandering path through predominantly birch forest. Lots of buffalo chips here.

A young golden eagle flew by and sat on top of a tree. We watched him for awhile with our binoculars before he flew off. What a sight! What a wingspan!

Back in Ft. Smith we went to the Gallery restaurant for a hot beef sandwich. It is a Vietnamese place so we also had a vegetable roll and dip. It was good but surprised us because it was cold and we were expecting it to be hot.

John bought some double-sided tape and tonight we covered the vent and bedroom windows with heavy plastic. It's so cold up there, maybe this will stop the draft and keep it warmer.

September 18 Angus Fire Tower, Hwy 5, NWT

Getting water and dumping tanks is a problem now since the territorial parks closed September 15th. However, the dump station at Queen Elizabeth park just north of Ft. Smith, is outside the park gates so we were able to dump there.

In Ft. Smith we were given a beautiful book, 'Our Forgotten North', by Leslie Leong. She's an award-winning photographer from Ft. Smith. Some of her photography was at the festival in Inuvik. This book protrays the north in pictures, with some interesting commentaries. A wonderful memento of our journey into this vast land.

We went to the Northern Lights Museum. It's a new building, well laid out with some good exhibits.

Back to Parks Canada to see the audio-visual presentation. The projectors were fixed and it was worth waiting for.

Said good-bye to Ft. Smith and started the journey to Hay River at 5 pm. Stopped at Little Buffalo River Falls which is 1 km off the road. There are two set of falls. One falls is terraced and is more appealing. Both are difficult to see well as the land is unstable and it is dangerous to walk near the edge of the cliff. Protuberances of cliff obstruct the view.

From the hwy, got a quick view of a bear running into the trees. A bit farther along another bear was munching grass. He backed off a bit as we approached but once we shut the motor off he continued eating & came fairly close to the RV. We stayed inside. Good photo op.

Pulled in at Angus Fire Tower again for the night. There's an owl hooting. Either he's far away or not very loud.

Southern Northwest Territories is full of sink holes and underground rivers.

The aurora borealis is so bright and beautiful tonight.

September 19 - Sunday, September 20 Polar Lake, Hwy 5

We chatted with three local couples who pulled in to see the sink hole. Finally got away at noon.

We stopped in to see Polar Lake, found out there is a small campground here and decided to stay a few days. There are 3-4 units here plus the camp hosts. Did some canoeing and fishing, not even a nibble. We enjoyed sitting around a campfire again. It's nice to have a day off from driving and just sit and soak up the sun. We were on the lake for both sunsets.

There are beavers in the lake, saw some of them swimming around. There is a new beaver lodge by our site. We found wolf tracks in the sand at the beach area. One night we smoothed out the sand so we could check for fresh tracks in the morning - there weren't any.

Northern lights were out both nights but Sunday night was better. They were everywhere, dancing and vibrating. Many shades of green could be seen.

September 21 near Louise Falls, Hwy 1, NWT

Problem: We have been carrying a mesh tent for bug protection - only used it once. We carried it on the roof and it kept the canoe in place. We sold the tent this weekend and now the canoe is moving around when we drive. Not good. John has had to devise a new means of keeping it secure.

322

Drove through the Dene Indian Village on the east side of Hay River. At the very end of the road is the old but well-maintained St. Peter's Anglican Mission church, an outdoor communal gathering area and the cemetery with traditional spirit houses.

Went to NTCL headquarters and spoke with Jeff Armistad about barging RVs on the MacKenzie River. NTCL is not licensed to transport people so that puts them out of the picture. RVs by themselves are not a problem as everything is shut off. Barging the MacKenzie River would be about a 10 day trip. He gave us some interesting information about the problems related to barging - cost, river water levels, weather, fog, water and sewer etc. However, I believe where there's a will there's a way. These problems have been surmounted in other places. I guess there just isn't the interest in developing this tourism niche. Nonetheless, don't bother NTCL. They can't do, won't do it, and really don't want to be bothered doing yet another feasibility investigation. My and your only hope for such a trip is with a small barging company. But even so, it won't be cheap.

But it sure would be nice to be able to drive the Dempster to Inuvik and barge up river to Hay River, or vice versa, rather than drive the Dempster both ways, beautiful as it is.

We can't use the library here in Hay River for e-mail but were able to pick it up from a private source for minimal cost. We bought a few groceries, gas, propane, filled up with water and headed south. At Enterprise there is a small community which we hadn't noticed our first time through. They have a 'cash n carry' store, like a small Costco. Big selection, good prices , but it's bulk buying which is not good for many RVers.

The territorial parks and day use areas are now closed for the season (as of September 15). We are parked for the night down river from Louise Falls. We are in a 'No Trespassing' area that at least gets us off the highway. Can't figure out what this clearing was used for but it doesn't look active now. As a matter of fact, it looks like it hasn't been used for a few years.

After a pretty sunset the sky clouded over. The past two nights have been warmer - maybe the plastic on the windows is helping. We've stopped being frozen at night.

September 22-23 High Level, Hwy 1, AB

We had sun, cloud, rain and more sun today.

At Louise Falls there is a spiral stairway of 44 steps plus a stairway of 96 steps that lead down to the falls which drop 14 m. One portion of the falls has no water because of the low water level in the Hay River.

The 2.5 km well-groomed trail between Louise Falls and Alexandra Falls has several round interpretive signs done by the Dene explaining their legends and the 6 km portage they would take around these falls. It is a pleasant and informative walk.

Alexandra Falls drops 34 m and has more water. It is hard to get a good photo as too many trees obstruct the view, unless one were to climb through grass and weeds to get next to one wall of the gorge. There is a viewing platform but you can't get all of the falls in a picture from there as it is too close.

The information centre at the Alberta-NWT border is supposed to have a good display but it was closed. We stopped to take some pictures there and then continued on into Alberta.

A short stop at Indian Cabins (pop 10). We talked with the family who are fixing up some of the buildings, putting in gas tanks and a restaurant and possibly a small liquor section. Hope they make a go of it. Prices are considerably cheaper in AB than in NWT.

We checked out Hutch Lake Provincial Park. The lake looks man-made with small dam at one end. The park tends to be dark because the trees are tall and thick.

On to High Level for the night. Two well-stocked grocery stores here. Did our price check. Population here is 3,000.

Went to the library tonight for a presentation by Georgia Graham who illustrates and writes children's books. It was very interesting.

September 23

Light rain all day.

Went to the small but very good museum at the Visitors Centre. Entrance is by donation.

Drove around the town and wandered through some of the stores. We need to plug in tonight and charge the battery and the UPS so we went to Aspen Ridge RV Park 3 km south of town. John hasn't been able to compute much lately because the UPS starts to beep shortly after he turns it on. The park fee is $20 for full hook-up and $15 for electricity only. It must be very pretty here in the summer as the park is in a stand of poplar trees. Right now there are only a few leaves on the trees and the ground

Even a roaring fire couldn't overpower the damp autumn chill.

is all orange and yellow with the fallen leaves. It's pretty now but would be more so if it was sunny instead of cold, windy and raining. The owners have a three-legged dog called Ginger who comes out to greet everyone.

Despite the light rain we had a fire but finally we got so chilled we had to give up and go inside.

September 24 Peace River, Hwy 55, AB

There is more traffic on the road today than we have seen in weeks. A lot of big transport trucks. A coyote trotted across the road but he was already in the trees when we got to where he had crossed.

Grimshaw is Mile 0 of the MacKenzie Highway. It is about the same size as High Level but the latter is more appealing, more modern and has better shopping.

The drive is more pleasant as we are not so enclosed in the trees as we were in the territories. The road and the ditches are wider giving an impression of space. Also there are a few hills which afford a wide-open view. The autumn colours are so visually rewarding.

The approach to Peace River is very attractive as you drive down a long hill and then cross the river. The town of 6,000 is located on both sides of the Peace River and surrounded by hills.

This Northern Woods and Waters Route (Hwy 55) across northern Alberta is very scenic and we would like to drive it again in the summer when it is warmer and we can enjoy the many lakes and campgrounds along the way. Can make very good time on this paved hwy.

Right now we are cold, most campgrounds are closed and we are "vacationed-out." We just want to get to our daughter and son-in-laws's new home in time for her birthday and the birth of our third grandchild.

In summary, this has been a fabulous six months. Travelling in the north has revealed to us the immense size and incredible beauty of Canada's north. It is truly magnificent. We can see why people keep going back. We want to.

Please refer to Page 342

A

B

C

D

E

F

G

H

Appendix B: Food Costs

This appendix summarizes the approximate costs of various grocery prices found in one or more stores in a town or city. The intent is to show how food costs varied as we travelled to Inuvik and return. Consequently, eighteen items were chosen for their probable availability in chain stores throughout our travel route. We neither recommend nor not recommend these particular items.

These costs are in Canadian dollars. Federal, provincial and state taxes could increase the costs, but they are not included because some items are taxed and others are not and we had no way of knowing which is which.

The cost of each item was recorded in each store; many communities had more than one store. If an item was on sale, that price was used. Similar but different brand name items were available for missing items but not used. If an item was unavailable at a specific location, then its cost was estimated based upon the average cost at all other locations. The number of items available in any community is indicated in brackets. The costs of recorded, and computed prices, for all items were averaged then totalled for each community.

The grocery items chosen were: a single roll of ASA-200 24-exposure film; four double rolls of 2-ply Purex toilet tissue; one litre container of V-8 juice; two litres of a brand name cola; one head of lettuce; 1 kilogram of carrots; one loaf of plain white bread not from an in-store bakery; one dozen large eggs; two litres of homogenized milk; one 425 gram box of Cheerios; 500 grams of medium cheddar cheese; three cans of tomato Soup; 300 grams of packaged coffee; one kilogram of whole chicken; 500 grams of lean ground beef; 500 grams of T-bone steak; one 200 ml bottle of HP or A-1 sauce; and four litres of vanilla ice cream.

In general, groceries (and fuel) in smaller communities cost more than in larger ones, and the farther goods are transported the more they cost. Heavy or dense items such as canned goods, bottled soft drinks and many fresh fruit are noticeably more expensive the further they are transported. For example, the cost of groceries (and fuel) in Inuvik, NT inside the Arctic Circle is almost 50% more than in Prince George or Prince Rupert in middle BC.

Location	# of items At location	Cost of Groceries Cdn Dollars
British Columbia (BC)		
100 Mile House, BC (Hwy 97)	18	$ 63.37
Williams Lake (Hwy 97)	18	$ 66.03
Prince George (Hwy 97 & Yellowhead)	18	$ 64.46
Smithers (Hwy 16 aka Yellowhead)	18	$ 66.13
Terrace (Hwy 16)	18	$ 67.10
Kitimat (Hwy 37S)	18	$ 64.06
Prince Rupert (Hwy 16)	18	$ 63.32
Stewart (Hwy 37 aka Stewart-Cassiar)	17	$ 80.51
Dease Lake, BC (Hwy 37)	17	$ 80.23
Yukon (YT)		
Watson Lake, YT (Alaska Hwy)	18	$ 83.10
Teslin, YT (Alaska Hwy)	18	$ 83.13
Atlin, BC (Atlin Road)	16	$ 88.23
Whitehorse, YT (Alaska Hwy)	18	$ 75.18
Haines, AK (Golden Circle Route)	15	$ 87.84
Haines Junction, YT (Alaska Hwy)	18	$ 76.85
Tok, AK (Alaska Hwy)	14	$ 85.75
Dawson City, YT (Klondike Hwy)	17	$ 79.51
Inuvik, NT (Hwy 8 aka Dempster Hwy)	17	$ 93.88
Faro, YT (Campbell Hwy)	17	$ 76.81
Fort Nelson, BC (Hwy 97 - Alaska Hwy)	18	64.64

Location	# of items At location	Cost of Groceries Cdn Dollars
<u>Northwest Territories</u> (NT)		
Fort Simpson, NT (Hwy 1)	18	$ 83.17
Fort Providence (Hwy 3)	18	$ 77.47
Yellowknife (Hwy 3)	18	$ 64.70
Hay River (Hwy 2)	18	$ 73.33
Fort Smith, NT (Hwy 5	17	$ 73.44
<u>Alberta (AB)</u>		
High Level, AB (Hwy 35)	18	$ 70.69
Peace River, AB (Hwy 2)	18	$ 66.46

Grimshaw, Alberta is kilometre 0.0 on the MacKenzie Highway. This was the starting point for the caravan that drove to Hay River in celebration of the Fiftieth Anniversary of the opening of the MacKenzie Highway, which now extends all the way to Wrigley, NWT.

Appendix C: Fuel Prices

As Liz and I travelled through cities, towns and villages we recorded the prices of fuels as we saw them at the gas stations we visited or on signs as we drove by. We recorded prices even if there was a price war and prices were temporarily lower than usual. If prices are blanks it means only that we did not see prices for that type of fuel. It might have been available and probably was, but not necessarily at every station.

Stores in two Canadian grocery chains – Canadian Super Store and Overwaitea – sometimes have a gasoline station, although I saw none with diesel. If so, they offer discount coupons for use inside their stores.

Gasoline usually comes in three grades: Octane 87 (Low); Octane 89-90 (Med); and Octane 91-94 (High). All Canadian gasoline is unleaded. Most vehicles can safely use gasoline of any octane rating. Why pay more for gasoline than you have to?

Prices are cents per litre. One hundred cents equals a dollar. A Canadian dollar was equal to about US $0.70 (or US$1.00 = CDN$ 1.42). 1 US gallon = 3.78 litres. USA prices ($/Gal) were converted to Canadian prices.

These prices were only valid at the time they were recorded. There was a general slow decrease in gasoline prices during the summer of 1998. What the prices are as you read this is anybody's guess. But the trend in price increase or decrease should be similar as you travel the same highways and roads we did.

Location	Low Cents/litre	Med ¢/L	High ¢/L	Diesel ¢/L	Propane ¢/L
British Columbia					
Kelowna	51.9	55.9	59.9	49.7	25.9
Kamloops	48.9	---	---	46.9	29.9
100 Mile House	49.9	55.9	58.9	51.9	24.9
Kokanee Bay	49.5	---	---	48.9	24.9
150 Mile House	48.9	---	---	46.9	24.9
Williams Lake	49.9	---	---	-	24.9
Quesnel	49.9	56.9	60.9	46.9	24.9
Prince George	51.5	55.5	59.5	48.9	30.9
Vanderhoof	53.9	59.9	63.9	-	30.9
Fraser Lake	57.9	67.9	69.9	51.5	-
Burns Lake	58.9	64.9	70.9	50.9	-

Location	Low	Med	High Diesel	Propane
Houston	54.9	62.9	66.9	
			51.0	36.9
Smithers	54.9	61.4	66.4	
			56.9	34.9
Hazelton	54.9	60.9	69.9	
			53.9	37.9
Kitwanga	56.9	64.8	66.9	
			-	-
Terrace	54.9	59.9	64.9	
			54.9	35.9
Kitimat	58.9	63.9	68.9	
			53.9	37.9
Prince Rupert	56.9	62.9	66.9	
			55.4	39.9
Meziadin Lake	65.9	---	---	
			60.1	44.8
Meziadin Junction	69.9	---	---	
			65.9	39.9
Stewart	62.9	---	69.9	
			-	39.3
Bell II	71.0	---	---	
			65.0	53.0
Tatogga Lake Resort	73.5	---	---	
			66.5	-

Location	Low Cents/litre	Med ¢/L	High ¢/L	Diesel ¢/L	Propane ¢/L
Iskut	69.9	---	---	62.9	-
Deasc Lake	68.9	---	77.9	64.9	62.4
Jade City	70.9	---	---	61.9	-
Good Hope Lake	70.9	---	---	66.9	-
Junction 37	69.9	---	77.9	59.9	54.9
Yukon					
Watson Lake	65.5	---	74.0	59.0	43.0
Watson Lake	67.9	---	74.9	59.9	-
Rancheria	63.9	---	65.9	58.9	49.9
Walker's	62.9	---	---	64.9	-
Morley River Lodge	62.9	---	---	53.9	-
Teslin	68.9	---	---	62.9	-

Location	Low	Med	High	Diesel	Propane
Johnson's Crossing	66.9	---	74.9	59.9	-
Jake's Corner	64.9	---	77.9	54.9	54.0
Atlin, BC	72.9	---	78.8	-	-
905 km Alaska Hwy	67.9	---	---	62.9	46.9
Whitehorse	66.9	---	75.9	59.9	46.9
Whitehorse	64.9	---	71.9	-	-
Carcross	66.7	---	75.6	64.9	49.9
Haines (AK, USA)	57.7	---	---	59.6	-
Haines	59.2	---	---	60.0	-
Haines	58.5	---	63.7	60.0	87.4
Haines Junction, YT	69.9	---	78.9	64.9	-
Haines Junction	67.0	---	76.9	58.9	-

Location	Low Cents/litre	Med ¢/L	High ¢/L	Diesel ¢/L	Propane ¢/L
Destruction Bay	66.9	--	81.9	68.5	-
Destruction Bay	69.9	--	--	59.9	
Burwash Landing	67.9	--	--	65.9	-
Kluane Landing	68.9	--	--	67.9	67.5
Edith Creek	64.9	--	--	-	59.9
Kaidern River	65.9	--	--	64.9	
Beaver Creek	73.9	--	--	67.9	
Beaver Creek	70.9	--	--	65.9	
Alaska, USA					
Scotties Texaco	54.0	--	--	54.0	-
Tok	55.5	57.7	59.2	55.1	72.2
Tok	54.8	--	--	58.5	-

335

Location	Low	Med	High	Diesel	Propane
Tok	55.5	---	59.2	55.1	-
Chicken	66.6	---	---	64.8	-
O'Brien Lodge	61.1	---	---	-	-
Eagle	63.7	---	---	-	-
Boundary	73.7	---	---	-	-
Yukon					
Dawson City	77.9	---	81.9	69.9	-
Dawson	76.9	---	80.0	69.9	67.0
Dawson	76.9	---	80.0	69.9	-
Dawson (Callison)	66.3	---	---	-	52.0
Dempster Junction	78.9	---	---	71.9	58.0
Eagle Plains	81.9	---	---	71.9	75.0
Fort McPherson	82.9	---	---	70.9	-

Location	Low Cents/litre	Med ¢/L	High ¢/L	Diesel ¢/L	Propane ¢/L
Northwest Territories					
Inuvik	81.9	---	---	74.9	-
Inuvik	81.5	---	83.5	71.0	-
Inuvik- 4 km South	---	---	---	-	76.0
Yukon					
Stewart Crossing	74.9	---	82.9	66.9	-
Mayo	72.9	---	82.9	71.9	-
Pelly Crossing	70.9	---	---	66.9	-
Carmacks	71.9	---	78.9	62.6	-
Carmacks	69.5	---	78.5	62.5	-
Faro	71.5	---	78.5	64.9	57.0
Ross River	74.0	---	79.0	67.0	-
Watson Lake	64.3	---	73.5	56.4	44.0

Location	Low	Med	High	Diesel	Propane
British Columbia					
Ironside Creek	64.9	---	---	-	-
Contact Creek	64.0	---	---	-	-
Fireside	78.9	---	83.9	77.9	-
Coal River	69.9	---	76.9	66.9	-
Liard River Lodge	67.9	---	---	-	-
Liard - Mad Trapper	69.9	---	76.0	67.9	-
Muncho Lake(NNW)	---	---	65.8	63.9	-
Muncho Lake(NNW)	63.9	---	68.9	-	-
Muncho Lake(SSE)	71.9	---	---	67.9	-
Muncho Lake(SSE)	75.5	---	---	68.0	-
Hwy Marker 426	69.9	---	---	64.9	-
Toad River	72.9	---	---	72.9	48.9

Location	Low Cents/litre	Med ¢/L	High ¢/L	
			Diesel ¢/L	Propane ¢/L
Summit Lodge	73.9	---	---	
			-	-
Tetsa River	78.5	---	---	
			67.8	-
Fort Nelson	68.7	---	71.6	
			64.9	38.9
Fort Nelson	68.7	---	75.7	
			-	-
Fort Nelson	67.0	---	73.5	
			-	-
Fort Nelson	68.7	---	---	
			64.5	37.9
Northwest Territories				
Fort Liard	72.9	---	---	
			61.5	45.9
Checkpoint	69.8	---	---	
			64.9	50.0
Fort Simpson (Esso)	72.9	---	82.9	
			66.9	54.0
Fort Simpson (TJs)	71.9	---	---	
			-	-
Wrigley	71.9	---	---	
			-	-

Location	Low	Med	High	Diesel	Propane
Fort Providence-hwy	70.5	75.5	---	67.9	45.0
Fort Providence	69.6	---	72.8	64.2	-
Fort Providence	68.4	---	---	-	-
Rae	71.7	---	---	-	-
Yellowknife	71.9	75.9	76.9	63.9	-
Yellowknife	---	---	78.6	62.9	39.0
Enterprise	69.7	---	---	57.9	-
Hay River	66.9	---	71.9	54.9	37.6
Hay River	66.2	---	71.2	-	-
Fort Resolution	79.9	---	---	-	-
Fort Smith	69.9	---	76.5	70.9	63.9
Fort Smith	69.9	74.9	79.9	-	-

Location	Low Cents/litre	Med ¢/L	High ¢/L	Diesel ¢/L	Propane ¢/L
Alberta					
Indian Cabins (close to NWT/AB border)	57.9	---	---	-	-
Meander River	59.9	---	---	-	-
High Level	57.9	---	65.9	57.9	34.9
High Level	58.4	62.4	67.4	59.4	-
Manning	55.9	---	59.9	53.9	-
Peace River	52.9	---	62.9	51.9	31.9

Totem poles at Kitwancool, BC

Description of Colour Pictures

Page **A**:
Class A motorhome and a very dirty towed vehicle Chicken,AK
Awesome Atlin, British Columbia, accessible only from Yukon
Fireweed on Campbell (and Dempster) Highway, Yukon

Page **B**:
Northern Lights Japanese Garden (non-public) in Terrace, BC
Lady Evelyn Falls, Kakisa, Highway #1, Northwest Territories
Solstice sunset/sunrise from atop the Dome at Dawson, Yukon

Page **C**:
Good Hope Lake, Stewart-Cassiar (#37) Highway, BC
Historic church at Hay River Dene Reservation, NWT
Local tourist during GNAF in July, at Inuvik, NWT
Author fishing at Liard River Rapids, BC near Alaska Hwy

Page **D**:
"Old Town" as seen from "The Rock", Yellowknife, NWT
Mountain sheep (goat?) on Alaska Highway, BC or Yukon
Bear Berries (red) and Cariboo Moss (white) in late summer

Page **E**:
The second Little Buffalo River Falls near Highway #5, NWT
Close-up of fireweed (we never did see the rare white variety)
Extreme close-up of Round Leaf Sundew
Tourist-made imitation of an Inukshuk, on Dempster Highway
Relaxing Liard Hot Springs on paved Alaska Highway, in BC

Page **F**:
Smoke from huge forest fire near Stewart Crossing, Yukon
Seed Yellow Avens near Campbell Highway, Yukon
Tombstone Mountain near beginning of Dempster Highway

Page **G**:
Lovely Liz trying her luck at the end of a rainbow, Smith Falls
En route to Keno Summit via Yukon's Silver Trail
Warm sand dunes in Carcross Desert, via Golden Circle Route

Page **H**:
'Class A' near Mount Elias Range, below Sheep Mountain, YT
Indian drummers + singers at Han Cultural Centre, Dawson, YT
Two canoeists returning from Hidden Lake, Ingraham Trail, NT

342

Appendix D: Three More Articles about Travelling "North of 60" in 1997-98

Author's note 1: I have tried to leave these diaries as they were written, modifying them very slightly only for clarity and consistency of spelling. Metric measurements and typographic errors are mine. Please remember these are diaries, which I think adds to the pleasure of reading them.

Author's note 2: If you or your friends have a diary, in any language, that you might like to have included in subsequent printings of this travelogue, please send them — as computer files or printed or hand written pages — to John Plaxton, 1362 Maple Road, Kelowna, BC Canada V1X 4Y4 or via e-mail to RVing@ogopogo.com. Copies of photographs or slides will be scanned at high resolution (450 dpi & 1200 dpi) then returned. There will be no financial compensation.

This article was received by e-mail and published with the permission of the authors, whom we met four times during our travels to and from Inuvik. Originally they provided us with several slides and a short narrative, then they E-mailed an almost complete diary of their entire trip by truck and trailer. The Sachs Harbour portion starts on July 20/1998.

This first article was written by photographers Steve and Laura Gasaway

'X-files' photo of shy photographers!

of Sandy, Oregon, USA who flew to Sachs Harbour while we stayed on the ground at the July 1998 Great Northern Art Festival. The authors also were there as volunteers, at the beginning and end of this annual event. They love wildflower hunting (Laura is a manager at a local plant nursery) and photographing and relaxing in [almost] unspoiled nature. They are in their mid-forties and have been married for 23 years; they have no children. They have camped in a tent, a tent trailer and now a trailer (with a bathroom, yea!), travelled north of 60^0N four times, visited the Canadian Rockies more times than they can count, and finally have succumbed to "Arctic Fever". They'll be spending the 1999-2000 Christmas and holiday season in Yellowknife, NWT (no RV this time) when there are very long nights. They expect to see the Northern Lights.

Flying to Sachs Harbour, and much more

Date: July 9/98
Starting Point: Home
Ending Point: Lac La Hache, BC, Canada
Morning (AM) Sky: Mainly Sunny
Mileage: 87567   Evening (PM): 88144 Total: 577 miles

It was a beautiful sunrise this morning. Left home at 6:05 am. I-84 west, to I-205 north. Freeway traffic not bad heading north but south very heavy. 57F degrees in Longview. Near Fort Lewis traffic picked up, heavy all the way through Seattle. Took I-405 "around" Seattle, 3 miles farther than I-5 direct shot. Back onto I-5 at 10:20. 70F degrees in Seattle, WA, USA. Very smoggy out. Stopped at rest area above Everett. 10:43 to 10:49. Trailer parking separate from trucks. Doe with spotted fawn next to freeway. Bellingham 11:35. Off I-5 and onto Hwy 542. More traffic in this area than in years past, lots of new homes around here. Stopped for fuel at Exxon (sorry) at Junction of 542 and 9. Corn 3 feet high here, ours at home is only 3" (very wet spring).
Sumac 12:34. Canadian Customs. Questions asked: Where are you from, Where are you going, Alcohol, tobacco, firearms? Did not ask anything about fruit or vegetables this year. Think

that was the easiest passing we have had. On to Hwy 1 East. Stopped at rest area before Hope, BC for a quick lunch, very nice out and nice rest area. Left 2:02 pm. Stayed on TransCanada Highway #1 through Hope, what a big town now. Fraser River is not as full as 2 years ago. Out of town, over the river and into the Fraser Canyon. Yale: 2:30 and passed a police lady with photo radar standing out next to her car with it. Not much traffic. Through the tunnels. Lots of people at the tourist trap, Hells Gate. Boston Bar at 3:06, stopped for pop at the drive-in (they had oyster burgers, ugh!). Diesel 47.9¢/L. It is very warm out.

Through the beautiful gorge near Skihist Provincial Park (PP) 3:55. We decided to go on even if it is a great campground, maybe on the way back. The river is beautiful. A few Blazing Stars are in bloom but not much else in bloom. Stopped for cherries at Spences Bridge. Yumm!!! Warm out and a little muggy. The fruit stand had lots of little tiny apricots, didn't look very good. Left 4:19. Wow!!! 4 big horn sheep on the hill on the west side of the road just outside Spences Bridge. This is the first time we have seen any in this area. (Cherries lacking in flavour this year) Cache Creek at 4:55.

A loon in a small lake along the road. More clouds but still warm out. Clinton, BC. Fire danger is extreme. Some nice Indian Paintbrush in bloom. There is still some green in the hills along the highway. 100 Mile House at 6:12. This town is growing, there is now a Super 8 Motel, big time! Visitor Centre still open, did not stop. Time to find a campsite.

To Lac La Hache Provincial Park (PP). It is about ¼ full, arrived about 7 pm, long day. Warm and muggy out. Campground had nice sites, we are in #23. A quick dinner and then a walk around campground. Decided to take the nature trail, big mistake without the bug juice. We were eaten alive, so we walked the trail very quickly. Nice trail, pretty level and through the woods, nice flowers in bloom. Back to camp to scratch and do the days paperwork. 67 degrees out.

Date: July 10/98 Friday
Starting Point: Lac La Hache PP, BC
Ending Point: Moberly Lake PP, Chetwynd BC

Morning (AM) temp: 46 (6 am)   Sky: Mainly clear
Mileage AM: 88144   Evening (PM): 88532 Driven: 388 miles

Left campground at 7:35. This is such a scenic area, green pastures with shallow lakes with yellow pond lilies in them. Really like this area. Mainly local traffic, very few RVs. Williams Lake 8:05. Yellow Bladderpod in bloom on pond. Stopped at Caribou Wood Shop to look around, nice store and the owner was very friendly. Left at 9:04, very nice out. Quesnel 9:50. Beautiful purple, pink & white petunias along road, sure makes the city look nice. Stopped at the top of the hill at Petro Canada for fuel. The attendant said there was a terrible thunderstorm here last night (none where we were). Onward 10:07. The road steadily climbs out of Quesnel.

More RV traffic now. Prince George 11:22. Stopped at Costco for fruit and vegetables. Had my birthday lunch there, hot dog & fries, nothing but the best for me! Hot outside. Left 12:47. Back onto Hwy 97, construction at junction. A buck near a stream in the hills out of Prince George. Bear Lake 1:50. Sky is now mainly cloudy. Stopped at MacKenzie Junction for a walk about. General Store is rather junky. Dark ugly clouds ahead. Diesel 55.9. Wow a lightning strike! This is where the road starts the windy climb to the summit. The fireweed looks good, the cow parsnip is almost through blooming.

Lots of frost heaves in the road, so very bumpy. Stopped by road construction, only 15 minutes, time to get rig dirty. Construction finished by Bijoux Falls (didn't stop this year, have good photos already). They are widening the road. Steeper climb after the falls to summit and then headed down. Alpine Fireweed in bloom, regular fireweed looked nicer at lower elevation. A bowless rainbow, real cool looking but no place to pull off to photo. Chetwynd 4:58. Dark, dark, dark clouds ahead, can see that we just missed a big shower. Stopped for fuel, the guys said that they really had a cloud burst about 15 minutes ago, they were soaked. Onward at 5:14 on Hwy 28.

A steep climb to junction for Moberly Lake, 2 miles to campground. Large campground on lake, the campground rather confusing. Lots of kids, just lots of people, don't think we will stay here again. Arrived about 5:30. The rain shower went through here so everything is wet, the poor people across from us have a flooded tent. Pit toilets. 61F degrees out. The park attendant didn't come around until 9:15 to collect campground fee. Another long day, too many miles for us.

Date: July 11/98 Saturday
Starting Point: Moberly Lake, Chetwynd BC
Ending Point: Summit Lake, BC
AM Temp:50   Sky: Clear
Mileage AM: 88532   PM 88925   Total: 393 mi

Left at 7:26 am. Dumped the trailer before we left, couldn't fill with water since there was no knob on it. [Author's note. Some are stolen. Other places remove the tap handles because they've had problems with children (and adults) turning on the taps and leaving them running for hours. Others such as Smithers and Inuvik use spring-loaded auto-turnoff taps, which can be a nuisance.] Strange campground. Back onto Hwy 28 north. Moberly is a long lake. Soon we started climbing again and that took us away from the lake. Another nice small lake, think there is a free campground here. No traffic on the road. Two does.

Over Peace River, next to the dam. Hudson Hope 8:14. Diesel 51. They have a new big school, lots of other building going on. Started climbing right out of town 79 km to Alaska Hwy. It was a short climb and then onto a plateau, then down a 6% grade. This is such a scenic road but may not be the best for fuel efficiency. We travel along the beautiful Peace River and then head back up into the hills. Two deer, another one and then a little fawn all by itself. These are mule deer. Pulled off at rest area at top of the hill to enjoy the view. 8:52. 10% downgrade and then head back up. 2 more deer.

Junction with the Alaska Highway 9:26. Charlie Lake campground is across the road from the junction, we need to check it out some time, when we have more time. We head west towards the Yukon and the Dempster. Wonowon 10:24. Diesel 62.9¢/L. Not many flowers but a few nice patches of fireweed. Had to stop for road construction, they are doing some paving work. Luckily not a long wait, really feel like we have to hurry.

Stopped at Pink Mountain (Mtn) for a walk about. A big RV caravan there, talked to one of the leaders, he thought we were nuts for heading to the Dempster. (We are, so what's new) Think he is nuts for being with a mega group of motorhomes. Onward and past Bucking Horse PP. 12:00. Stopped at pull out for lunch, very mild out. Made it to Fort Nelson at 2:15, still can't get over the welcome sign being so far from the real town. It sure has grown a lot since our first trip in 1989. A huge new motel. Fuel. 78 degrees. Onward. Past Liard Trail (Highway) junction, hope we can head that way again soon.

Went through a heavy rain shower. Through a huge land clearing, doesn't look like logging, really ugly. Arrived at Summit Lake Campground at 4:30. No trees here, so no privacy but great scenery. The campsites aren't terribly close together and there are pit toilets. Just got backed in when the thunderstorm came. What a downpour! Sure am glad to have the trailer. The storm lasted about 45 minutes, long enough for dinner.

Headed out to look around and then hiked up the ridge trail, great views from the top. The trail leads along the ridge in trees and moss- and lichen-covered ground. Good flower watching and also lots of berries (kinnickinnik, ligonberry and crowberry). It was so nice to get out and enjoy nature instead of driving, have been feeling more like we are in a caravan than our usual vacation travel. Why couldn't I have gotten more time off? Back down to camp. Campground noisy, lots of young adults in several of the campsites. Campground a little over ½ full. Bugs not bad out and the table had dried so sat out and enjoyed the scenery. During the thunderstorm the temperature dropped 10 degrees. 9 pm 54F degrees. Life is good.

Date: July 12/98 Sunday
Starting Point: Summit Lake BC
Ending Point: Watson Lake PP, Watson Lake YT
AM temp: 45   Sky: Mainly clear
Mileage AM: 88925   PM: 89168 Total: 243

Woke up at 4 am with the sun but didn't get up until 6. Walked around and took a few photos. A squirrel came out to greet us. Not many people up yet. Left at 7:16. Yucky looking to the north. Stopped at the next small lake to look for moss gentian, which we found after watching the ducks and photographing them. One mom had 8 babies with her, of course she headed away from us for protection on the far shore. Onward.

Got skunked! Not a single sheep or caribou. Road goes down by river and than backup. Everything is very green but not many flowers. Over the MacDonald River.

The avens were all in seed and they covered the gravel bar next to the river. Back over the river. This is such a scenic area, sure wish we had more time to explore. This is the second time up here but feel like it is all new and that we need time to get to know it. Muncho Lake Provincial Park 8:45. Fire danger is high here. Stopped along river for a look about. There was a small herd of stone sheep, of course people had to stop and try to get closer to these poor wild animals. People are so stupid sometimes. We headed off in the gravel to look for the Yukon Campanula, very few in bloom, too late. Not a single yellow avens in bloom in all the thousands of plants. Onward. Along the Trout River, the river has beautiful glacier water.

Over the Liard River and into the Liard River PP. The place is so crowded, no place to park, so the heck with it! Since we have already visited two years ago we will go up the road and walk around. Black bear just outside the park. Left 11:18. Stopped along the Liard River for lunch, what a scenic spot! 12 to 12:50. Partly cloudy but warm enough for wearing tee shirts. Cross over the Coal River and can see where it meets the Liard River. Just outside of the community of Fireside there was a fire camp with 4 helicopters.

The official Yukon entrance sign 2:43 which is right before Watson Lake. Got fuel at the Shell station then made a quick stop at visitor centre to check on forest fires. Didn't take time to look at signpost forest, once is enough for that. Left 3:22. Fire danger here is extreme. Out to Watson Lake PP which is off the main road and the side road was in very bad condition. Very dry, sure wouldn't take a chance with a campfire. Only one other camper in here, should be quiet. Water is "boil only" and pit toilets. Sure wish there were some good views of the lake, but it's only a quick walk to the lake.

Tried our new organic bug juice before our walk around campground, BIG mistake! Think that stuff attracted them instead of repelling them, into the garbage with that stuff. Needless to say a rather quick trip around the campground. Dinner. Spent a quiet evening catching up on paperwork and reading.

Date: July 13/98 Monday
Starting Point: Watson Lake PP, Watson Lake YT
Ending Point: Twin Lakes PP, before Carmacks YT
AM Temp: 45   Sky: Cloudy
Mileage AM: 89168   PM: 89532   Total: 364

Left at 6:55 am. 49F degrees when we left. Our loop in the campground about a third full. Back to the Alaska Hwy. Snowshoe hare along road, cute. Over the Liard River which is now a deep green in colour. Passed many road cuts with rock messages on them. Some very creative, others not. Some people coloured their rocks, some not. Moveable graffiti. Into a new section of road, looks like it was finished last year. Road construction, 3 km of very rough road.

Started to rain. Stopped at rest area for quick breakfast, crisp out. We got to the Continental Divide at 9:02. Just before Divide was an immature bald eagle in a tree next to the road. A nice display of fireweed along road, it is in prime condition. Swift River, an ugly junky place.

Into British Columbia, golden eagle. Nicer fireweed with a few white fireweed intermixed. Stopped at rest area for a walk about, there were a few nice flowers to look at. Out of BC. There is a birdhouse on a tree out here in the middle of nowhere. Teslin 10:32. Over Nisutlia River, huge! Nice community. This is a huge lake. Black spruce forest. Johnson Crossing 11:09 and the end of the lake. Over Teslin River. Can get to Canol Road from here (must do that some time). 59.9 for diesel. A rather dreary day out but at least it isn't raining now. Jake's Corner 11:52.

Foxtail grass: blonde, but it acquires a purple hue in the fall.

Spots of yellow fall colour on some of the trees. Tagish Lake, another big one.

Whitehorse 12:46. New visitor centre with RV parking, very nice centre. Left trailer there and walked through town looking for a record store, of course had to stop at a few of the shops too. It was nice to get out and move. Had to go to two record stores to get the CD we wanted, yeah-good music now! Not a lot of tourists compared to two years ago. Went and got fuel and dumped at the Shell on 2 Mile Hill (free to dump with fill up). Also had water there. Left 3:02. Lots of gas stations at top of the hill.

Fire danger moderate here. Heading onto a new piece of road for us. The guy at the gas station said that it had gotten up to 45°C (113°F) last week. Road goes through mainly pine forest. Vegetation looks very dry even in the rain. View of Lake Laberge. Campground is 3 km off the main road. Didn't go check it out. No flowers along the road except for the pest Sweet Clover, this plant has spread everywhere! There is just a quick view of the lake here and there. Road narrow and windy but not in bad shape, easy driving.

Fox Lake, think it would be pretty but clouds very low. Can smell the smoke from the forest fire. Fox Lake is pretty big. Drove through the burned area, which was several miles, looked like the fire was a very hot one by the damage. Today was first day that they let traffic through without a pilot car. Two helicopters were putting out hot spots with their dump buckets, one was dumping right next to the road. There was a crew of men on the ground directing the bucket. Nice to be back into green trees and not burned up ones.

Onward to Twin Lakes Campground at approximately 5 pm. Nice campground with great views of lake, large sites and pit toilets. There are more sites down at the lakeshore but like the view here and campsites down there have no privacy. Have to boil the water. Just one other camper on the top loop and several down below. It is breezy out so bugs not bad. The Mew Gulls kept us company while sitting out enjoying the view, also magpies here. Had dinner and then read for awhile.

Went for walk around campground and then crossed road to check out little lake. There was a beaver working, of course the cameras were back at the campsite. So we watched and enjoyed. Also several ducks with babies, one had 13.

Date: July 14/98 Tuesday
Starting Point: Twin Lakes Klondike Hwy YT
Ending Point: Tombstone PP, Dempster YT
AM Temp: 45   Sky: Partly Cloudy
Mileage AM: 89523   PM: 89794 Total: 271
When we left it was 55 out. Twin Lakes in the Nordenskiold River. Had heavy rain showers in the night. Left 7:12. A few more campers showed up in the night. Here the road is straight and level. Aspen looks sick. Lots of "moose marshes" but no moose, just ducks. A few arctic ground squirrels along the road. Naked looking mountains to the right. Aspen begin to look better near Carmacks. Carmacks 7:47.

Fire danger is 'extreme' here, it is very apparent. Carmacks just a stop in the road, nothing much. Over the beautiful Yukon River, there were a few canoes out on the river. Fire danger on this side of the river is only 'high', explain that one.

Road starts to climb past junction with road to Faro and back on road that we have travelled before. Stopped at Five Fingers Rapids for a quick look at viewpoint. Some idiot tenter put his tent right next to viewing platform, why couldn't he go into the woods a little bit. Left 8:32.

Through the 3-year-old fire, the very large aspen is starting to come back. Pelly Crossing at 9:30. Over the Pelly River to Stewart Crossing at 10:30. Over the Stewart River. There is minor leaf damage on aspen here, the trees all have white leaves. Everything is terribly dry here, even the willow leaves are brown.

Aspen leaf, with Leaf Minor

Stopped for lunch at first pull off in a very long time. Turnoff next to lake with out-of-bloom pong lilies, very nice here. There is a big bull moose across the lake, he left before we could set up the cameras, oh well. Left after lunch at 12:22. Tintina Trench, didn't stop this year, think once is enough on that stop. Along the Klondike River, which is very low, things are so dry looking. Dempster Corner. 12:50, stopped and got fuel. Left 1:20.

Over the Klondike River and onto THE DEMPSTER HIGHWAY! Of course stopped for road construction first thing, stopped for about 15 minutes. It must be over 70F out and mainly cloudy. Onward. Dust here we come. Road is in good shape, at least here. This is not the prettiest section of the highway but it is still great. Some type of medium size animal in road. (Looked like wolverine but video showed marmot).

Into Tombstone Campground about 3. Some flood damage in the campground from earlier July flooding. There are downed trees and part of the road looked like it had been washed out. Good our favourite spot, #20 is available. This spot is out in the open so great views and a breeze to keep the bugs down. Took the trail down to the North Klondike River and the ice flows, or what was left of them. Two years ago the ice flow was huge, this year very little ice left along the far bank. Would have had to cross the river to get up close, decided not to get wet. Explored the river and looked for flowers (not a lot but what was there was pretty). Lots of alpine fireweed and yellow potentilla.

Then sat down and enjoyed the beauty of this area, what a great place! This has to be one of the most scenic places in the world, better than the Colorado Rockies, Jasper or Banff , Alberta or anywhere else we have been. We were the only ones out here so were able to enjoy the peaceful scenery and daydream. It was hard to get up and head back but our stomachs said it was dinnertime. Got back to camp about 6 and then fixed dinner. Sat out at the picnic table and enjoyed the view with dinner. Campground is pretty full but most are down in the trees.

After dinner walked across the Dempster to photograph some pure white fireweed. Lots of moose tracks around the fireweed. A little windy but hope we got some good pictures.

Took showers (in the trailer), yeah! Settled in with a drink to do paperwork and enjoy the scenery. 61 degrees at 10 pm.

Date: July 15/98 Wednesday
Starting Point: Tombstone PP, Dempster Highway
Ending Point: Ogilvie View Point, Dempster Hwy
AM Temp: 37   Sky: Mainly sunny
Mileage AM: 89794   PM: 90088 Total: 294

Nice morning, 55F at 8:30 am. Left camp at 8:39 and headed up the Dempster. Stopped almost immediately at the viewpoint for Tombstone Mtn, what a great view! Had good lighting so took time to do some photography, hopefully got some good shots.

Ah well. It washes off. It really does wash off.

Next stop just down the road at the creek that had the huge ice flow two years ago, nothing here this year. Took time to explore and look for flowers before heading on. Left 10:24, wow approximately 5 miles in 2 hours (now this is our kind of travelling). We are feeling rushed because we need to be in Inuvik in two days, which is way too fast to do the Dempster.

Views of the southern Ogilvies, awesome. Spruce grouse with babies along the road, several batches of them. Passed Two Moose Lake, no moose but a great scenic spot (we should try to camp there sometime). Out of the rugged mountains into the northern Ogilvies. Stopped at gravel area to photograph the ice.

There was another family of spruce grouse just off the road, not terribly afraid of us so were able to get some good photographs. Warm out and bugs not bad. This area is so beautiful I couldn't explain it if I wanted to. Drive slowly, get out whenever you can and enjoy all! Through a washed out area, road fixed now. Did I mention that there is awesome scenery here? Several more wash out areas, road bumpy here.

Stopped at Engineer Creek Campground for a late lunch. 3:25. River is now next to campsites due to the last flooding. Sapper Mountain is across the river, makes nice photo spot. The campground has had some nice improvements from last time we stayed here. Still, potable water is out of river only, boil first. Clean pit toilets.

Left 3:45. Over the Ogilvie River. A beaver crossed the road, too fast to photo. Headed up to the Ogilvie View Point/ Rest Area. 5:30. Will camp here and enjoy the view. Crisp out and windy but still not bad for exploring. Took care of the pesky paperwork and then a late dinner. Went for a long walk and photographing. Very little traffic on the Dempster, no one else to share our lovely view. So peaceful it was hard to come in to bed. It is smoky to the southwest.

Lovely evening. Life is good.

Date: July 16/98 Thursday
Starting Point: Ogilvie/Peel View Point Dempster Hwy
Ending Point: Nitainlaii Campground, Ft McPherson NT
AM Temp: 59   Sky: Partly cloudy
Mileage AM: 89912   PM: 90088 Total: 176

62 degrees out when we left. The smoke rolled in sometime in the night; can't even see the mountains, darn! Sunset was about 1 am, never really got dark, there was an orange sky for short while. Then around 4 am the sky got orange again. Don't know why I couldn't sleep, maybe too quiet. The smell of smoke is bad.

Guess the good thing about the smoke is that we won't be stopping to photograph since we can't see much of the scenery. We are lucky, this is our second trip, too bad for first timers, but of course most of them drive so fast that they can't really see the scenery anyway. Destination is more important to most than the joy of getting there.

A lady in the visitor centre in Dawson told us on our first trip up here, that the Dempster Highway to her was a spiritual trip. I don't understand much about the natives' beliefs, nor am

I very religious but think I understand what she was saying. You get out and walk on the land and study and enjoy it and you come away with a wonderful feeling. Just can't explain it, it has to be experienced.

White Lousewort, beside Dempster Highway.

Now we are driving along a ridge. A porcupine! Can you believe it? Clear up here! Sorry, I think of porcupine in the tall forest not in trees that are less than 8 feet tall. He let us photograph him and then he took off like a bat out of hell. The mosquitoes were very bad here, they even bothered him. Wow! Approximately Km 268. Onward. Rock Ptarmigan. A lemming? More ptarmigan. A red fox, in the black phase (had the give-away white tip on the tail), moved too fast to even try to photograph. Lots of wildlife this morning.

Stopped along road for breakfast. Onward. Stopped a ways up to photograph the fireweed lining the road, looks like an English Garden, too bad that the fireweed is almost done blooming. Eagle Plains at 10:50. Got fuel and then looked around the small gift shop at the motel. Not many people around today. It is probably around 70 degrees out. The gas attendant said the smoke was from a fire at Mayo. Oops! A flat tire! Had it just 6 miles out of Eagle Plains on bridge over the Eagle River. There was a rock in the tire.

A German couple in a new Jeep Cherokee stopped and asked if we needed help. Arctic Circle 12:07. (90,003.3 miles on pickup's odometer). No views, smoky and windy out. The sky is clear above the smoke and sun keeps trying to peek through. Had lunch in trailer, too smoky to sit outside.

Stopped to help that same young German couple with a flat tire. It was really fun (to us). This guy was hysterical, and he was jumping up and down in the road waving his hands thinking we might pass him by. In his broken English he tried to tell us that their travelling partners, another couple in another new Cherokee were up ahead with only flat tires left and now they were down to no spares. After trying to calm him down Steve changed his tire (he didn't have a clue) we told him to drive slowly back to Eagle Plains and have them all fixed (bet that cost an arm & leg).

He told us they had been driving slowly but when they came up on us at Eagle River they were travelling fast. This guy kept saying "Why do they build roads out of this awful rock?", they should have never been on the Dempster. We went on up the road about a mile and came across the other couple and tried to explain to them that their friends were on their way back to Eagle Plains, they spoke no English.

Went past two other rigs with flats, both had things under control. Northwest Territories border 2:51, time change to 3:51.

Very windy here, think it must be like that most of the time (it was that way both ways last time). Tired and want to get to camp so did not stop. Smoke is starting to clear but still not good for photos. Leaving the Richardson Mtns. Past Midway Lake. Peel River crossing on the ferry, ferry waiting for us so had a quick crossing. (Ferry is free). To campground at 5:48. 85F degrees out. The camp host said very slow for tourists. We are the only ones here. There is a big music festival in Dawson. He said we would run into smoke tomorrow from the Summer Lake fire.

Had the pick of the campground, it is okay to have fires in the campground but we sure wouldn't, way too dry. Had a wonderful shower in the trailer and then dinner. Long day.

Date: July 17/98 Friday
Starting Point: Nitainlaii Campground, Ft McPherson
Ending Point: Happy Valley Campground, Inuvik NT

AM Temp: 59   Sky: Partly cloudy & smoky
Mileage AM: 90088   PM: 90296 Total: 208
Heard loons this morning, what a nice sound to wake up to. About 6 campers came in last night. Left 7:38, 62 degrees out when we left. Think we saw 2 sandhill cranes. Fire danger is

Calla Lily, on side of awesome Dempster Highway

moderate here. Calla Lilies at Km 106, not in bloom. Were able to drive right on to ferry, over at 8:45. Ferry stopped at Arctic Red River to pick up a vehicle. Short-eared owl (we think) sitting on edge of road, of course when we stopped it flew off. Another owl in a tree not far from the road. A bunny.

Blacktop at the airport (10 km out of town). Fire danger high here. Inuvik 12:13.

Through town to Happy Valley for a campsite. Almost drove through a red light. Oops. The staff haven't gone through the campground yet to see who had left but gave us the last site in the electric hook-up area. We got the two-week rate, it is the same for no hook-up or with electricity. The only problem with the hook-up area is that it is a parking lot with no privacy. Oh well, won't be around trailer much anyway. Walked down to the showers for a leisurely shower. Ah life is good.

Walked into town to mail a few postcards and then over to Boreal Books to say "hi" to Bob. It was good to talk to him in person instead of over the phone. Picked up a few books to have him send to Mom to keep her busy until we get home.

Could spend days in there looking at all the arctic books. He has a large area of collectable books that he has on commission, will look later.

Went over to the school to check in at the Great Northern Arts Festival. They didn't need help today but will need help first thing in the morning. Fine with us. Back to camp after a quick tour of the tourist shops in town. Made a quick dinner, really too warm for much.

Back over for the opening celebration for the festival. There was a blanket toss outside to watch, great fun to watch but not something I would have guts to try. Then everyone went indoors for the opening prayer. Matthew did drum dancing, and he is so fantastic, so smooth in his moves, could watch him forever. Then the local East Three Jiggers danced, these poor teenagers must have been dying in the heat in the building. It was hot just watching them, let alone trying to dance. They did a great job.

After the entertainment roamed the festival to look at the artwork, wow! Found Dawn Oman and made a date with her for dinner after we get back from Banks Island. Her artwork has changed some but still is great.

Back to camp around 11 pm. Kids still are playing in the street behind the trailer. Still hot out. Learned an important lesson, do NOT carry camera or video in the open so that the drunks can see them. It means tourist so they want to talk, none were mean or nasty but just over friendly. Sure more evidence of alcohol problems this year, maybe the warm weather.

Date: July18/98 Saturday
Starting & Ending Point: Happy Valley Campground, Inuvik
Low temp: 59   Sky: Clear
Miles: 0

Was a hot night and light all night, hard to sleep. The street behind us was noisy all night with kids playing. Up at 7 and down for showers. Noisy night is worth the wonderful shower.

Walked over to the school for the Great Northern Arts Festival to check in as volunteers. Started out with the good job of

360

emptying garbage (oh well, someone has to do it). With the maze of above ground pipes (utiladores) we got our exercise going up and over the pipes at least 3 times to get to the garbage bin. I put out names of the artists that were working around the table inside and for the outside sculpturers. Steve ran errands for the office, picking up things in town.

Went over to the college for lunch with Dawn Oman and a few of the other artists. It was *very* hot in the lunchroom. We were late so not much left but salad was enough for us. All of the staff is extremely nice and so are the artists, this is great fun.

Left GNAF about 2 for a break, it is also very hot in there. Over to talk to Bob at Boreal Books for awhile and then back to camp for quick nap. Back to GNAF at 5. Vacuemed, helped clear out the table and chairs for the night's entertainment.

Listened to fiddling and then outside to watch drum dancing. It was great but wish they would explain what the dances meant. It cooled off nicely so was a nice evening to sit outside. Stopped for ice cream on way back to camp. Got back about 10:30 pm, 71 out. 89F (31.7C) was the high today. Talked for awhile to a couple that we had met on the way up.

Date: July 19/98 Sunday
Starting & ending Point: Happy Valley Campground, Inuvik
Low temp: 65   High: 90   Sky: Clear
Mileage: 0

Quick breakfast and then over to GNAF. Picked up garbage again and then did misc. stuff until 1 pm. Time went fast. Talked to several of the artists. In one of the cultures - Inuit or Dene - feathers have different meanings i.e. ravens-change, unknown, eagles –wisdom. Feathers from different parts of the bird also have different meanings. It was very interesting, wish we could have talked longer.

Also talked to an artist that lived in Pine Point until it closed down, was one of the last out. Says nothing left, would like to go back there sometime. Back to camp, I tried to do laundry, there were 7 of us trying to do it with 2 machines but at least we had fun talking while waiting. All thought we were nuts for making the second trip up here. Steve cleaned out the back of the pickup while I was doing the laundry.

Drove out to airport to check on airplane tickets, okay, said to pay tomorrow before we leave. Stopped at visitor centre to get our Arctic Circle certificate. Back to GNAF to volunteer and watch entertainment. Back to camp late, got ready for trip tomorrow. Can't wait.

<u>July 20, 1998</u> We left on Aklak Air for Sachs Harbour on Banks Island. Aklak flies to the island three times a week in the summer. The flight takes you over the Mackenzie Delta and then over the Beaufort Sea. This is our second trip to the island, the first was two years ago in the middle of July. Then it was *very* cold and there were tons of icebergs in the bay.

A glacier that sheds huge blocks of ice is said to be "calving."

Today it is tee shirt weather and not an iceberg to be found.

Our hosts Roger and Jackie Kuptana, who run the Kuptana Guest House, picked us up at the small airport. There are no hotels or restaurants in Sachs Harbour. Before dinner (meals and island tour came with our package), we went down to the waterfront to look for wildflowers. The best wildflower hunting is in mid to late June but we still found plenty to photograph. With 24 hours of sunlight we explored late into the night.

<u>July 21, 1998</u> After breakfast Roger took us out to look for muskoxen and anything else we could find. The barren lands are anything but, flowers, birds, bees (yes, bees), spiders, lemmings, grasses, bright pink rocks and more. We watched 6 arctic fox kits play around the family den. Roger spotted a herd of 20+ muskoxen and took us in for a closer look. Muskoxen are very aggressive, so we viewed them from a safe distance. What a sight! Off to explore along the Kellet River where the alpine fireweed was in full bloom. We saw lots of bird species, sand hill cranes, snow geese and many more. Saw another herd of muskoxen and then several lone bulls. Back in time for dinner and a late evening stroll along the beach

<u>July 22, 1998</u> Since this was our second trip to the island Roger sent us out on the ATV to explore and photograph at our own speed. He did start us out first with a look at a lone bull muskox not far from town and then showed us where to go. He checked on us often and kept us heading in the right direction to a beautiful lake and a sand desert (no rattlesnakes) behind it. With no trees or large hills you could see for miles, what a view! Steve caught three arctic char from the lake but released them. Coming back to our ATV from the lake we were surprised by 2 bull muskoxen, got some great pictures! It felt good to get back to the guesthouse for a shower and then a wonderful dinner. The guesthouse has a cozy family room but it was too beautiful to stay indoors.

<u>July 23, 1998</u> Sachs Harbour is a hamlet of about 120 people but most were out on the land when we were there. There is a co-op store where you can buy food and a small assortment of souvenirs. Sachs Harbour is the only community on Banks Island. Peter, the mayor of the hamlet came over in the morning to tell us stories of years past and hunting for polar bears.

It was time to say goodbye to our hosts and climb quickly on the plane to take off before the wind got any stronger.

Date: July 24/98 Friday
Starting & Ending Point: Happy Valley
Low temp:? Cool   Sky: Cloudy & Windy   Mileage: 0
Fall has come to Inuvik (even some of the locals said that). Brrr. Over for showers. Breakfast. To the post office to pick up stamps and then to Boreal to do our book buying (ouch). Talked to Bob for awhile and then over to GNAF to do a little impromptu volunteer work. We were just going to roam but they asked for help, so why not.

Then did a little tourist shopping in town. Picked up a few more of the "Berry Bears" from Husky Insurance. Who would have thought that is where they would be? Have been looking for them to match our Cranberry that we got in Yellowknife in 1990. Two years ago we looked over Inuvik for them with no luck. Guess we just didn't look in the right place.

Had oil changed in the pickup and the tire fixed that went flat when we got here. Had more people stop to tell us that we had a flat on the trailer. I did a little laundry. To GNAF for the outdoor concert, it was chilly. Since our warm clothes are still in Sachs Harbour in our luggage, it will be a cold night. George Tuccaro was MC and also played guitar. He has a great sense of humour. It was a good concert with music and drum dancing. Was over about midnight. Bed after one.

Date: July 25/98 Saturday
Starting & Ending Point: Happy Valley
Low temp: ? Cold   Sky: cloudy & very windy   Mileage: 0

Over for showers and then to GNAF to volunteer. Mainly "security", which really is goofing off and visiting with visitors and the artists. Had lunch out, muskoxen & caribou hamburgers. Yum.

Went to the airport at 3:30, not a soul there, called the airlines from there and they said the plane left late, should be back here 5:30 to 6. Back to town to tourist shop. They asked for volunteers to help sand on the commemorative sculpture so we did. Luckily didn't make any booboos, could just see the headlines "Tourist from the States ruin Sculpture." Back to airport,

364

again no one there, finally found out the plane could not land and came back with the same passengers it left with and not our luggage.

Back to GNAF for free hamburgers & pop put on by the travel agency in town. The dinner concert wasn't very good. Inside at 7-ish for drum dancing, too cold outside for drums to work properly. Very good except for the Teslin, BC drummers. They went on forever and then asked for money, which we thought was not proper.

Jerry Alfred started outside about 11, it was cold! Very few people in the stands. He only played for about ½ hour. Inconnu played a little longer. Great music but brrr. Did I mention that it was cold! Sure wish we had our warm coats. Over at 12:30. Back to trailer and warmed up with hot cocoa. Bed around 2.

Two local girls trashed the women's washroom Friday night with soap powder and toilet paper. There are lots of drunks around this year. A few drunks hanging out below campground, cops were always in checking on them. One couple had their window broken in their trailer, not good PR for this town. It is too bad.

Date: July 26/98 Sunday
Starting & ending Point: Happy Valley
Low temp: Cold   Sky: Cloudy & windy
Mileage: 0

Up and to the last day of GNAF. Volunteered until 2. Cleaned up from last night's concert and "security." Visited with artists. Back to camp for pickup and out to airport, this time it was packed, big plane getting ready to leave. Sachs Harbour plane in at 4:10. They had our luggage!!!!! Yeah, life is good.

Back to GNAF, they were taking group photos when we got there, fun to watch. Closing started at 6-ish instead of the scheduled 5:30. All the thank you's and drum dancing and prayer. We were given a moose tufting that was very nice, still think we should have paid them for all the fun we had.

Wish we could do this every year but the drive is a little far. Said good-byes and then back to camp. Did some last minute laundry, had to wait for my turn. Fixed an easy, late dinner. Put laundry away, cleaned up trailer. Bed after 1.

Date: July 27/98 Monday
Starting Point: Happy Valley, Inuvik NT
Ending Point: Nitainlaii, Ft McPherson NT
AM Temp: 49   Sky: cloudy, drizzle
Mileage AM: 90296   PM: 90418   Total: 122

Didn't get up until nine since it was so late when we went to bed. The wind stopped in the night. Walked down for showers. Then we walked into town (the nice part about Happy Valley is it's in town so we don't have to drive like if we were out at the other campground) to play tourist and photograph the town.

Walked up to the DEW Line dome that now houses the cable TV & Internet office. They were kind enough to let us in to look and ask questions, it is really cool. They brought it down from Tuk on 3 flatbeds tied together on the ice road in March 1997. The dome weighs 20 tons and is 55' in diameter. The dome is on a base (not sure if it is wood or concrete) and this is the main office. They have made 2 more floors in the dome itself and they have started painting the insulation to look like the aurora. The dome and foundation is 65' tall. Can you imagine driving down the ice road with a little to drink and see this huge dome coming your way, ha!

Next to town hall to pick up an Inuvik pin and then back to camp to drop off camera gear. Then back into town to the Inuvialuit Building which is the 3 story building on the main street not far from camp. On the third floor (we had to ask, no signs for it) is a small gift shop, actually a room filled with fantastic art & craft work, most just piled here & there. What fantastic "stuff", Holman prints, carvings, stuffed muskoxen, etc. All good quality and had low prices. Found a hunter doll from Holman made out of caribou skins for only $150! Couldn't leave without it!

Stopped at "ToGo" for muskox and caribou burgers, yum!

Back to camp and got ready to leave, dumped and got water. Left 1:25. Bye pavement! South down the Dempster. 3 arctic loons in a small pond next to the road. Of course we stopped to photograph, there was also a duck of some kind with 3 babies. Sounded like bullfrogs, not sure if that is what they were. The sky has cleared up, so much nicer out. Made a few more stops to photo. This area is the least attractive part of the Dempster.

To ferry on the MacKenzie River, had to wait about 15 minutes for it, not bad. Road is dusty. To campground about 8 pm. The girls in the office gave us Eskimo donuts to eat, they had just made them, very good. Again only ones in the campground.

Grass of Parnassus

70 degrees out. Dinner and then paperwork. Saw 1 yellow pond lily in bloom, grass of parnassus and fireweed that was almost out of bloom. Road kill: 1 rabbit and 1 red fox.

Date: July 28/98 Tuesday
Starting Point: Nitainlaii, Ft McPherson, NT
Ending Point: Arctic Circle, YT
AM Temp: 51   Sky: mainly clear
Mileage AM: 90418   PM: 90503   Total: 85

Slow start. Breakfast and left 10:10. 2 more campers came in during the night. 72F out. Down to ferry, no wait. River is really down from when we came up. Starting to get cloudy. Stopped at Tetlit Gwinjik Wayside, which is a lovely spot, get out the bug juice! There was one Strawberry Blight plant, ligon & blueberries ripe. The cloudberries were in fall colour, great leaf colour. Rock Ptarmigan. Neat clouds, it feels like you can touch them.

Six cars that were very close together tore past us heading north. Scenery, what scenery?

A ptarmigan with 8 babies and then just down the road a grouse with 2 babies. Then another ptarmigan with just one baby, at least that is all we saw. Had to stop and photograph the interesting clouds, cooler out now. Stopped to try to photo a snowy owl which was off the road a ways but couldn't get close enough, he took off.

Wandered back towards pickup, stopped to watch a batch of ptarmigans and when we did we spooked up another snowy owl. It was right next to Steve, scared him to death! Ruined the snowy owl's dinner but we did get a few good shots (we hope) after we put our hearts back where they belonged. Really cool to watch.

Through the canyon which is always a fun place to poke around and we did. There was some alpine fireweed in bloom. Rain showers around us. Border 1:57 watches back to 12:57. Lunch. Started raining hard so took a three-hour nap, not that we were tired or anything. Boy it felt good! By the time we got up the rain had stopped so we went out and explored for awhile. All the rigs going by are all dirty but we are nice and clean, see, it was worth the nap.

On down the road to the gravel pit to examine the cannonballs, rock concretions that are very close to being perfectly round. They are huge, at least 400 lbs, we tried to move one but couldn't. Found a broken one so we got to see what the inside looked like. Neat rocks. Some arctic ground squirrels kept us company while we snooped around. Much warmer here than at the border which is about 5 miles back. Onward.

Wow, a beautiful rainbow! Just missed the rain shower that is to the east. Another rainbow! Had to stop to photo several times, really beautiful! Could see its double and the colours were so clear. Lots of ptarmigans and ground squirrels along the road.

Made it to the Arctic Circle about 8. Had a light dinner since we weren't that hungry. Breczy and cool out but it kept the bugs down so can't complain. Explored and photographed. Mainly clear out but there are thunderheads around the mountains. Sunset around 11:30, pastel orange/pink colours, not bad.

Really weird, the moon set not far from the sun, never saw that before. One other camper pulled in here for the night but they missed the sunset.

Date: July 29/98 Wednesday
Starting Point: Arctic Circle, Dempster YT
Ending Point: Ogilvie/Peel Lookout, Dempster YT
Low temp: 49   Sky: Clear
Mileage AM: 90503   PM: 90595   Total: 92

Beautiful morning, enjoyed breakfast outside. Left 9:37. The ground squirrels are very friendly and enjoyed having their pictures taken. On to Eagle Plains, population 22. Stopped for fuel at 10:56. Fireweed is done blooming or at the very top of spike only. It is clouding up as the day goes on. At Km 280 out of the "forest". Stopped to photo the picturesque little trees.

Found cloud berries ripe, actually slightly over ripe, kind of strange flavoured but not bad. Lots of ligon berries ripe, also crow berries, blue berries and kinnickinnik. The lichens and mosses were beautiful and offset the berries beautifully. Found a caribou horn among the berries. Have seen lots of bones along the highway for caribou but this is the first horn that we have seen.

This is a great place to explore, easy walking and very scenic. Km 278. Onward to Ogilvie/Peel Lookout 3:30. Rain showers around us. Took a shower in the trailer. Read and explored.

A small thunderstorm came through. Dinner. Only ones here. No good sunset here. Got skunked on animals today, didn't see any.

Date: July 30/98 Thursday
Starting Point: Ogilvie/Peel Lookout, Dempster YT
Ending Point: Tombstone Campground, Dempster YT
Low temp: 49   Sky: Cloudy
Mileage AM: 90595   PM: 90711   Total: 116

Fixed breakfast and then fixed a flat tire that happened on the trailer in the night. 53F out when we left. No one else stayed here last night. There was a small flat rainbow to the west near the mountains. Saw the elephant rock off in the distance, the rest area was washed out. This is such a pretty area, driving

A young Red Fox in the rocks.

along the river. A red squirrel with a cone in its mouth ran across the road. A duck with ducklings is in the river. Stopped to photo the yellow poppies, grass of parnassus and alpine fireweed.

Stopped along a black hill to snoop around. Saw a pika, ground squirrels, 4 angle white heather, yellow saxifrage and campanula. Started to rain. A dandelion! Took a lunch break. Some ice left on river but not much. 3 horses. Heard someone say in Inuvik that they saw wild horses, these are not wild just domestic horses on an open range. (Wonder why the gentleman didn't notice the bells around the horses' necks?)

One grouse, then another, this one with 9 babies! Damn driver tried to run over the mother, what a jerk! 13 horses along the road, 3 more grouse, 10 more horses. Found a beautiful patch of light pink fireweed, the biggest patch of light pink that we have seen. More scenic stops.

To Tombstone about 4:30. Our site (#20) available, of course we pulled in. Not many campers in yet. It is about 65F out so very nice and the bugs not bad. Fixed dinner. Walked down to river, the white gentian was in prime. Took our time enjoying the scenery. Back to camp.

Date: July 31/98 Friday
Starting Point: Tombstone, Dempster YT
Ending Point: Five-Mile Lake, Mayo YT
Low Temp: 34   Sky: Clear
Mileage AM: 90711   PM: 91010   Total: 299

Got up and left. Cold out last night. At 8:25 it was 42. Marmot along the road, think same one as when we came in. Goodbye scenery! Some of the poplars have some yellow fall colour. Dempster Corner 10:05. Bye, bye Dempster!

Towards Dawson. A red fox in the black phase. Into Dawson for the first-day issue of the Dempster Highway stamp. Stopped at visitor centre to see where the post office was, forgot from 2 years ago, hell to be old. Very warm out, so nice to walk around town for a little while. Lots of people in town, this is not one of our favourite places, wouldn't have come in except we wanted the stamps. This is the 100th anniversary of the Klondike Gold Rush. Stopped at the centennial office and got a few gifts.

Left 12:05. It is amazing the piles of tailings along the road, looks awful. Stopped at Dempster Corner for fuel. Left 1 pm. Headed south, some clouds coming in. Stopped at Tintina Trench to fix lunch. Can see the Dempster Hwy from here, didn't realize that when we stopped before. Saw a vehicle out in the middle of the bush, guess it must be the Dempster.

Stopped at Silver Trail Visitor Centre to check on the forest fire situation. No roads are closed. Left 3:24. Headed for

Mayo. Dropped the trailer at Five-Mile Lake Campground at 4:30. Just past the turn off for Mayo.

Headed up to Keno for a look see. Saw a squirrel, grouse and a moose & calf. The two moose ran along the road in front of us for a mile at least, the banks on both sides of the road were very steep. We stayed back not to scare them too much. They

Alpine Harebell, photographed near Dempster Highway

finally ran down a very steep embankment, I wouldn't run down it, heck I wouldn't even crawl down it.

On into Keno and up Keno Mtn to Signpost Summit or whatever it is called. Road not in great shape, very bumpy. Someone has done excavation right next to the sign post, some one living in a trailer up there, didn't come up and bother us and we didn't bother them. Very dry up here, very few flowers left. Someday we will catch this area in bloom; it is supposed to be great. Saw several marmots and pika. Nice evening out. Roamed around and looked at the cool rocks and the dried up flowers (oh well).

Headed back to camp, didn't stop in town since we did up the town two years ago. Not many people here in the campground, it is quiet. Can see the lake through the trees, an easy walk to the lake (and short). The sites here are very private. Pit toilets. Got back about 8:00 pm. Fixed dinner and enjoyed it outside. Took showers in trailer, yeah! Our hot water tank started to leak so Steve had to do a quick fix on it before we lost our water.

August 1/98 Saturday
Starting Point: Five-Mile Campground, Mayo YT
Ending Point: Spirit of 98, Whitehorse YT
Low Temp: 43   Sky: Clear
Mileage AM: 91010   PM: 91268   Total 258

Up late. 55F out when we left at 9:42 am. Oh well, we are on vacation.

This really is a nice campground. Lots of squirrels on the road. Back to the Klondike Highway 5 at 10:30. The aspen trees are full of leaf minor again this year. There already is some yellow of fall colour. Carmacks at 12:35 To the Toge Cho Hudan Int. Center and Craft shop. Not much in the way of crafts but a nice museum, even a short hiking path past interesting exhibits. The only problem was there were no signs on what the exhibits are. But it is still new, so maybe that will come later. Ate lunch in the trailer and then left at 1:30.

Sign says fire danger is "low", hard to believe. Cloudy out. Lots of magpies in the trees along the road. Past the Fox Lake fire, it is still smoldering in the hills. It really was a huge fire.

Into Whitehorse at approximately 4. Got fuel, water and dumped (free). To 'Spirit of 98' behind gas station to get site, hate private campgrounds but it is close to town. Walked into town but didn't make it to the grocery store before it closed at 6 (guess we are too American and expect grocery stores to be open to at least 9 or later). Roamed town for awhile. Then back to camp. Waited in line for over a half-hour to call the Moms. Our site is right next to main road so is very noisy, we are packed in like sardines. Saw yellow clematis on the walk into town. No place to sit outside so stayed inside and read.

Date: 8/2/98 Sunday
Starting Point: Trail of 98 Whitehorse YT

373

Ending Point: Snafu Lake Campground, Atlin Hwy
Low Temp: 41   Sky: Clear
Mileage AM: 91268   PM: 91493   Total: 125 miles

What a night! The road was noisy all night and made it impossible to sleep! Might as well have slept in the middle of I-5. Up early and went over and took showers but there was very little water in the restrooms. Grrrr.

Left 8:01. Fire danger high here. Headed towards Carcross. Stopped at Cinnamon Cache bakery for cinnamon buns (found this place two years ago) for breakfast and a loaf of flaxseed bread for the road. They make the best bread, yum!! Talked to the owners for awhile and then left 9:25. They had a photo of a white raven, never guessed there would be such a beast. Now we have something new to look for.

Onto Hwy 8 just outside of Carcross and towards Tagish & Atlin. Windy road with no shoulders in a narrow valley and then the valley opens up. Tagish 9:52. Tagish is off the main road, didn't have time to explore so went over lake, here road turns to gravel.

Onto Hwy 7 to Atlin just 2 miles before rejoining Alaska Hwy. Gravel. Little Atlin Lake very scenic and very large, road follows lake. Then road heads up a steep hill. A rabbit. Drove into Snafu Campground not made for our 20' trailer, more for campers and tenters. Very sandy soil. No fee, pit toilets and a view of the lake. Back to main road. 11:29. Tarfu Lake next campground, not far from Snafu.

Into BC and south of latitude 60. Drove along a very blue lake with snow on mountains. Vegetation also dry here. Atlin 12:30. Had to ask where visitors centre was, not well marked. It was behind a house that was built like a pyramid. Lots of old buildings and all of different styles, interesting. Town is on the lake with picturesque mountains around. Didn't take much time to explore town.

Went up Warm Road. The attractions on the road were not well marked. Missed the Glacier Overlook on way up. Warm Bay was too crowded to find a place to park, lot of campers parked wherever, all looked over used. Warm Springs, more campers around tiny little pond. Didn't explore, didn't look exciting.

On up to Grotto Parking Rec. Site, after almost driving past it, again not well marked. Found the grotto by walking up the road a short distance, it was small but pretty. Cow Parsnip, Yellow Coneflower and Corn Salad in bloom. Lots of ferns & foliage. Had lunch there. Pit toilet not useable; filthy is a kind word for it.

Back to Warm Bay and was able to find a place to pull off and park. Very scenic with clear beautiful blue water and snow capped mountains. The water was amazingly clear. Stopped at what we decided was the glacier viewpoint and then drove on down the road to pull off next to new house, guess this is the real thing. Nice view of Llewllyn Glacier and awesome water colour in the small lakes below us.

On down the road and stopped at pull off with short trail to the beach. A group of people partying here, lots of booze so left, a little too wild for us. Then down Surprise Lake Road to Pine Creek Falls, it had 3 or 4 tiers that dropped into a canyon. Nice.

Back to town for fuel and a few groceries. Headed back to camp. Think we were very lucky to have such a clear day to see the scenery but don't think we will come back (maybe that we are just grumpy about no sleep last night).

Decided to check out Tarfu Campground, it was 2.5 miles off road on a *very* bumpy one-lane road. Lake is not scenic, not a good place to camp. Back to trailer about 6. Not a planned campground but we ended up with a nice view of the lake. No drinking water here. It is a perfect evening and so quiet. Fixed dinner and enjoyed the quiet. Just a couple other campers here. Great sunset!

Date: August 3/98 Monday
Starting Point: Snafu Lake, Atlin Hwy
Ending Point: Rest area out of Iskut, Cassiar Hwy
Low temp: 36   Sky: Clear
Mileage AM: 91493   PM: 91925 Driven: 431

Up and tore down camp. Left 8:20. 2 hares. Onto Alaska Hwy at 9. Took us 244 miles to go 64 km via the Alaska Hwy. Oh well, it was fun to do once. Cool out but perfectly clear. Teslin Lake, very smoky, can't see much scenery. Funny, fire danger low here. Stopped at Rancheria Falls, walked the 1/3 mile trail to the falls. Saw some bunchberry in bloom. A fisherman down at bottom of the main falls, no luck but said he was having fun. Finally decided to try crowberry, not too bad tasting. It is still smoky and is muggy. Falls okay but not great, trail very easy walking and it was nice to be out of the truck. Left 12:30.

Stopped for fuel at Junction 37, massive line up for fuel. Left 2:17. Road starts out paved. Into BC and south of 60 and will stay south now, sure don't want to go home.

Dall Sheep, 6 females plus a baby. One has a crooked horn. They all looked very healthy and sleek. Too smoky for scenery pictures. 1 lone Dall Sheep. Stopped at Jade City, not much in their gift shop this year, two years ago an excellent selection. Jade is $5 per pound which didn't sound like much until we started weighing a few pieces, left them behind. Left 4:30.

Pavement ended 40 km before Dease Lake. Back onto pavement about 10 km out. Dease Lake at 6 pm. Lots of clouds in the sky now. A few red indian paintbrush along road and one orange iceland poppy. Back to gravel about 25 miles out of Dease Lake. Horribly smoky out, really yucky. On & off pavement. Iskut 7:10. Finally out of smoke a little. Decided to camp at a rest area that had an 8-hour limit. 7:30. Fixed dinner and ate inside. Parked next to lake but too smoky to be scenic. Trucker pulled in next to us for night. Very little traffic.

Date: August 4/98 Tuesday
Starting Point: RA out of Iskut
Ending Point: Meziadin Campground, Cassiar Hwy
Low temp: 41   Sky: Unknown, too smoky
Mileage AM: 91924   PM: 92075   Total: 151

Northern Monks' Hood

When we left at 7:30 it was 50F (10C) out. Can't even see the mountains across the lake due to smoke. Paved road here. This is a big lake. A grouse of some kind. On and off pavement. Out of smoke finally, high clouds. Tall orange Indian paintbrush. Nice scenery, some glaciers on the mountains.

Stopped at the brake check area to photo. Great place to camp just east of the brake-check pull off. Tall scenic mountains.

Back onto pavement at Km 330. Black bear on the run. Stopped for more photographs just past Bob Quinn Maintenance Station. Back to 'on again off again' pavement. A few raindrops. Yellow pond lilies in bloom. 3 grouse. Stopped at Bell II for a walk about. Diesel 65 cents per litre. Left 10:40. Black bear eating along the road.

To campground about 12:30. It is wonderful out. Got a nice spot right on the lake. Cleaned up the pickup and trailer. Hung out and enjoyed the scenery and the beautiful weather. What a nice afternoon. Fixed dinner and had our first campfire of the trip. It was great. They have added an upper level of campsites since our last visit. Campground didn't fill up until late. Roamed the campground and up to highway. Then sat around some more and enjoyed the great evening.

Date: August 5/98 Wednesday
Starting & Ending Point: Meziadin Campground, Hwy 37
Low temp: 53   Sky: Cloudy
Mileage AM: 92075   PM: 92182   Total: 107

Headed up with just the pickup at 7:51, 56 out. It rained in the night. Headed towards Stewart. Some fall colour in the trees.

Picture of three bears from previous trip.

One black bear couldn't be photographed because logging truck scared him.

Lots of log trucks and traffic. The log trucks let you know they mean business and get the heck out of their way.

Into Stewart, into Hyder to Fish Creek. Stopped at post office in Hyder to mail film first, opens at 8 Alaska Time (the only business that is on Alaska Time and that uses US funds). We heard that this is the largest salmon run in 20 years, last year there were very few salmon here (and very hungry bears, a grizzly killed another).

Too many people, very few bears (can't blame the bears with all the human noise). There was a mom brown bear and cub when we arrived but couldn't see it for the herd of people. After the crowd moved off we set up our cameras in different areas to wait and watch. A lone black bear came out a short time later but very shy so didn't stay in river long. Then there was four plus hours of watching the salmon and the people.

About 1:30 we went and took a bathroom and lunch break in town. Not a good idea to eat out at the creek but have seen idiots do it. Back about 3.

Were its eyes bigger than its stomach? Just about.

Not long after we got back and set up (together this time) the mom and cub came back into the creek upstream from the herd of people. The cub had the best time, he even caught a fish (didn't have a clue what to do with it). The cub must be a male since he really didn't obey Mom too well, rather independent. They were in and out of the creek for awhile. After that a mid-age brown bear came in to fish, he was awfully skinny but caught a lot of fish. He was in and out of creek at least 8 times.

Rained most of the morning, then cleared up and then started to rain about 5. It was pouring by 7. It was too dark to photo so left shortly after 7.

From what we heard that this is the last year for this un-controlled mad house. Guess that next year there will be a 4' boardwalk, no tripods allowed. A 12-car parking lot and then one up the road a ways for 15 cars, no RVs. Don't think that is fair for the people in the small motor homes that don't tow cars. But the tons of tourists have ruined it for themselves; the bear have to eat. Guess Fish Creek was put onto a German website so that has brought in even more tourists, the well kept secret is out and ruined. There were tons of people here today even in all the rain, most only stayed a few minutes.

I spent most of the day talking to a young couple from Grande Prairie, Alberta and a retired man from New Mexico, USA. Both first timers here and having a great time. Steve talked to a "photographer" that had been coming here every year since 1977. He and his wife carried walkie-talkies to keep in touch or look important.

Quick trip back to camp, no wildlife on the way. Got fuel at Meziadin Junction and back to camp about 8. Fixed dinner and then did paperwork. Partly cloudy but only 58 so didn't have a campfire.

There is now a custom office for Canada at Hyder. We were told it was put in to cut back on illegal amounts of tobacco, and poached bear parts.

———————

Thus ends the 1998 diary of Laura and Steve, except for, quote, "the really boring drive home with lots of miles and no stopping."

A totem pole seemingly abandoned at Kitwancool, BC

Salmon Glacier, Hyder, AK

Voyage to Canada's Northwest Territories:
June 12 - July 21, 1998

This article was extracted from a webpage (http://www.RVtimes.com) and published with the permission of the editor, Sheila De Groen and author Rejeanne M. Dion.

This article was written by Rejeanne M. Dion but typed on their new and first computer by her husband of almost 46 years, Jean. They are now retired in 100 Mile House, BC – many hobbies, too numerous to put on paper – and wondering "How did we ever have time to work and raise four children?" They often thought of writing about their travels but never seemed to find the time. This was their first article, thanks to the gentle persuasion of Sheila. In her letter giving permission and providing two photographs, Rejeanne also wrote "If I can help in some ways to promote our Great North, I'll oblige. Jean and I truly enjoyed that trip in the Northwest Territories."

We had been discussing it for a couple of years, debating to go with a camper or a motorhome. We decided on the latter. Of course, I should mention that Jean and I are outdoorsy people.

We left 100 Mile House, BC on June 12, 1998, but not before having heard all kinds of comments from friends regarding road conditions, as in, we should not take a motorhome there!

We travelled the "Deh Cho Connection" – Dawson Creek, Grimshaw, Manning, High Level, Hay River, Fort Liard, Fort Nelson and Fort St. John – and more. We did the whole territory, except Inuvik.

First of all, I should mention that the area is highly native influenced. They have eight official languages, a unique government, and their meetings are done in native tongues; you are invited to go to them if you wish.

Arriving at the 60th parallel, we visited the Twin Falls. We were taken by the beauty of it. By the way, the mosquitoes were not bad. The falls are on the Hay River; the formation of rocks and colours are breathtaking.

From there, on to Hay River; the hub of the territory. On the way we passed Enterprise, not much there. In Hay River we replenished our supply and headed south to Fort Resolution. To me, it is north east. A village of 500 people, 99% Native; very friendly and helpful people. It is on the south shore of Great Slave Lake. What an immense expanse of water, almost like a sea. There is wood, lumber and they have a sawmill.

By that time, Jean said he was ready to go fishing, and I was keen too. So we asked for some information on it; "Oh yes," they said, "there's a campground at 24 km south on the Little Buffalo River. It has just opened up to fishing." We spent three days at the river fishing for pikes and pickerels. We released the pikes and had a feast of pickerels (excellent fish). By the way, we had our licenses from the 60th parallel.

From there, we went south to Fort Smith on the Slave River. It is a very clean little town. We visited the Northern Lights Museum & Exhibition Centre, a great display with lots of history about the Slave River. On to Wood Buffalo National Park and the Salt Plains, "a sight to see". A world wonder. We went

24 pounds (11.5 Kilograms) of delicious fish.

back twice, and stayed overnight. It is a day use and picnic area. We were ready to leave if they wanted us to. It is an aftermath of the ice age: 370 square kilometres of salt mud flats. The plains provided salt for indigenous people for hundreds of years; and in the early days the Hudson's Bay Company and the Roman Catholic Mission harvested up to four tons of salt a year. Very very interesting. One of the highlights of our trip.

On the way back to Hay River, we stopped at Polar Lake; we were told that it was good fishing. We spent a day there and it was not good fishing, so we proceeded to Hay River, more supplies and laundry. It is a busy port on the Great Slave Lake.

On to Kakisa Lake, always thinking of fishing. But we could not get on the water because our boat was too small. So we proceeded to Lady Evelyn Falls, again just beautiful scenery.

Next we went on the northwest side of the Great Slave Lake. We had to cross the MacKenzie River and on to Fort Providence. The river itself is phenomenal. We were going north at all times and the terrain was changing, very rocky. We travelled through the MacKenzie Bison Sanctuary. We saw many bison and took lots of pictures. On to Edzo and Rae, two small villages and no services. We finally reached Yellowknife, and spent the night at Fred Henne Territorial Park — a nice park, the people were very helpful and they are in attendance 24 hours.

The next day, we left for the Ingraham Trail, another high-light of the territory. A recreational area: eight lakes, canoe trails, hiking and fishing. We stayed at Reid Lake for five days. Territorial Parks are just great and well kept. I had never seen so many people tenting. The Lake had sandy beaches, family facilities and good fishing. You should see Cameron Falls if you go.

Another one. Is this yours?

Back to Yellowknife and to Fred Henne Park. Spent two days in the city. We visited the Prince of Wales Northern Heritage Centre. We were overwhelmed with the place. It is more than a museum, it is the whole story of the North. Highly educational. The Information Centre is a great place also.

On June 30th, we celebrated our 45th wedding anniversary by having dinner at the Explorer Hotel; sampling the fares of the North. I had Arctic Char Mousse, and Muskox filet, well presented. Jean had Bison pate and the Satay plate, which consisted of Bison, woodland Caribou and lake trout; excellent dinner. While dining, we chatted with the waitress, who had come south, so we asked "Where were you before?" She said "Frobisher Bay."

On Canada Day, we decided to do something special. We took a fly-in-fishing trip to Blachford Lake. What an experience. Going in we flew in a Beaver aircraft, 20 minutes south of Yellowknife. We stayed in a log cabin with wood stove, and were fed at the cookhouse. We experienced the fishing of our lives! Just fantastic. We stayed there five days then flew back in a Twin Otter aircraft to Yellowknife.

We decided to take the Historical Walking Tour of Yellowknife. We had lunch at the Wildcat Café which had been built in 1930, walked up to the Rock, saw the Pilot Monument and enjoyed the fantastic panoramic view. All those places are in what is called Old Town (Sheila's favourite place in Yellowknife) and this is overlooking the Great Slave Lake, and the houseboats. There is so much more, I will skip them but, well, don't miss the Northwest Trading Post with its supply of native crafts — incredible is the word I use to describe it!

We were very impressed with the North; we were not expecting what we saw.

Now heading southwest to Fort Providence, across the Mackenzie River, and to Jean Marie River, a town of 75 people, all natives. Very friendly and welcoming. We spent 2 days there to fish (very good fishing).

From there on to Checkpoint. This is where the Liard Trail meets with the MacKenzie Highway, going north towards Fort Simpson. There again we cross the Liard River. It is located at the confluence of the two rivers. We visited the Papal Ground, and its monument to the four corners of the world.

Farther north again to Wrigley; a small settlement on the Mackenzie River, 200 people. They moved three times to escape the rising of the river. They moved all their houses, even the very old church. To go there, we had to board another ferry at Ndulee Crossing (Camsell Bend). Now just read this one: we had to back up on to the ferry with the motorhome and the trailer behind!

From there, we came back to Checkpoint and took the Liard Trail to Fort Liard. On the way we stopped at Blackstone Park. There we saw the high tech of the north in RV Parks. It is on the Liard River facing Nahanni Butte, breathtaking scenery. We had never experienced an RV park of this nature. All log buildings, gazebo, covered lunchroom and the list goes on. The shower room and restrooms were all stainless steel with flush toilets and state-of-the-art faucets — totally amazing.

We reached Fort Liard in the early afternoon, visited their Information Centre, bought a few souvenirs, and decided to proceed to Fort Nelson. Well, this stretch of road I would not recommend to anyone: 122 km which I believe took us four hours! But we made it home in one piece, regardless.

We have travelled miles and miles of gravel road. Over all we had a beautiful trip. Oh, I must not forget to mention the lovely hot and sunny weather and the Midnight Sun.

We arrived home on the 21st of July, just in time for our exceptionally hot summer here in 100 Mile House.

Is the NWT ready for RVers?

This article was extracted from an Internet webpage (http://www.RVtimes.com) and published with the permission of the editor, Sheila De Groen and author A. B. Robinson.

This article was written about a 1997 adventure to Yellowknife, NWT. The author is A. B. (Tony) Robinson, accompanied by D. A. (Dot) Richardson, of Kamloops, British Columbia.

They are now in their early 70's, and have owned RVs of one kind or another for most of the last 26 years, principally motorhomes.

Their first trip to Yukon and Alaska was via the Alaska State ferry system, disembarking at Haines. Since then they have travelled across Canada a couple of times and visited many of the United States of America. More recently they were to Inuvik in 1995 – few bug problems and unbelievably good weather – and Yellowknife in 1997. Their future plans include another trip across Canada.

Are you filled with the pioneering spirit?

Do you want to see wide-open spaces, cross mighty rivers, experience native culture, and come to grips with an important

Their still-clean motorhome on the Cassiar Highway, BC

part of Canada's history? Then think about adventuring to Great Slave Lake and the valley of the MacKenzie River in Canada's Northwest Territories.

Forewarned is forearmed, someone once said. Having been there, we would like to pass on to you the benefit of our wisdom.

So what, in general terms, is this part of the Northwest Territories like?

It is relatively flat, mostly below 200 metres in elevation, and covered with a mixed forest of poplars and evergreens. The summer weather is usually warm and dry, and wild fires are common. The north-eastern part is in the Canadian Shield, a glacier-scoured, rugged region of scrubby trees, bald outcrops of pink granite rock, and innumerable small lakes and ponds.

Communities are small and scattered. Only four have populations in excess of 1,000. The inhabitants are mostly Dene Indians, and many of the villages they live in are now named after posts established by the fur traders in the early 19th century. Fort Liard, Fort Simpson, Fort Providence, Fort Smith and Fort Resolution are examples. Yellowknife has a population of 16,000 and, besides being the Territorial capital and the centre of government, its economy depends on mining, transportation and tourism.

If you have already decided to organize a big rally, we must tell you that the Territories are hardly prepared for a massive influx of recreational vehicles. Private campgrounds are almost non-existent. The public ones are almost all small and primitive, and none have hookups. Showers and indoor plumbing are the exception rather than the rule. Few even have sanitary dumps or an RV-friendly water supply. So pack a shovel, pail, and funnel in case you can't find these essential services when you need them.

[Author's note: The situation was changed in 1998. Although there might not be as many private campgrounds as you would like, the new territorial campgrounds are excellent. Rather than repairing and fixing up the old ones, the NWT government decided to build many new parking sites from scratch. Some will even have full hookups - 110V electricity, drinking water, and sewer.]

The 'John Beren's' ferry between Wrigley and Fort Simpson. Note how the ramps are kept in good shape and how it always reaches the water no matter how low or high the river is.

On the positive side, the fee for most campgrounds in 1997 was only $12.00, and some of them were free. Many were located near some interesting natural feature. Several had excellent interpretive centres, with knowledgeable people on staff to answer your questions about the displays of arts and crafts.

What is the highway system like?

Some of the roads in the Territories are paved, but most are not. The gravel surfaces are usually well maintained and sprayed with a solution of calcium chloride to keep the dust down. But if you happen to get behind a tanker truck spreading the mixture of water and salt, or if it rains, you won't believe how dirty your rig will get. The bigger towns have truck washes where you can get cleaned up, and in a pinch, you can scrape the mud off your windows, after it dries, with a stiff brush. It is wise to carry two spares and a tire repair kit, because garages are few and far between. For the same reason, always travel on the top half of your tank, and it's prudent to carry extra fuel in a jerry can. You can get gas in most communities, even Wrigley which is just three degrees south of the Arctic Circle, and about as far as you can go on summer roads. But you first have to find the native lady who has the keys to the pumps for the storage tanks.

You will be crossing some of the rivers on free ferries that can carry, at most, only 10 cars or four big trucks. The landings are simply made of the sandy silt on the banks, and maintained by front-end loaders run by the deck hands. It is difficult to pack this kind of material hard enough to bear the weight of a heavy vehicle without rutting. As a result, boarding and disembarking can sometimes be stressful events. Just pretend you are a truck driver, and don't hesitate once you get your rig moving.

In the what-else-do-you-need-to-know department, expect flies in the summertime, lots of flies, swarms of flies, mosquitoes, black flies and horse flies. Dragon flies are all right; they eat the others. At one point on our trip, we swear, the mosquitoes were so thick that 25 got in our rig every time we opened a door. Bring along lots of repellent, for what that is worth. If these pests are a problem for you, you can purchase a hat with netting attached that covers your face and neck. It's hot and stuffy but effective.

You have probably already guessed that almost everything you buy will cost more than at home. Gasoline, for example, was over 70 cents a litre in 1997 at most stations in the Territories. If you are into photography, buy your films before you leave home and have them processed when you get back.

Buy the outstanding native arts and crafts – from Inuit soapstone carvings to coloured pictures made by the Dene from tufted moose hair – in the smaller communities rather than the bigger. You will get a better price and no less in quality.

If you are like us, you may want to book into a motel now and then to get cleaned up. We can tell you that the more remote the community, the more expensive the rooms are, and the poorer the housekeeping is. Reservations are recommended.

Whatever the hardships of travelling in the Territories, the rewards far outweigh them.

Just to see Great Slave Lake, larger than Lake Ontario or Lake Erie, and the big MacKenzie River which is the third largest in the world and over a kilometre wide in spots are reasons enough to go. There are also impressive waterfalls, some of them easily accessible from the highway system.

If they don't satisfy you, you can charter an aircraft that will fly you to 91-metre-high Virginia Falls in Nahanni National Park, perhaps the wildest and most spectacular sight to be seen in the Territories. More elaborate tours to the park are also available, including canoe and hiking expeditions. You can take charters to remote villages and fishing lodges, and others just to get a bird's-eye view of the north, if that is your interest. There is a wide variation in price for these flights, so check around.

If your budget is limited, the wild flowers along the highways are free, varied and beautiful, and you can purchase a book along the way to help identify them.

You should see some unusual wildlife, and we certainly did in Wood Buffalo National Park, one of the best areas for game viewing. Some 34 kilometres before we got to Fort Smith, we detoured off the highway onto a narrow track that took us to the Salt Plains overlook. It was perched on the edge of a steep escarpment, and below, the plains stretched off to the Slave River in the distance. The panel displays there informed us that salt oozes out of the ground at the bottom of the escarpment in such quantities that at one time it was commercially exploited by the Hudson's Bay Company. We hiked down the steep trail to the plains, 100 metres below the overlook and at the bottom we were rewarded with the sight and sound of two whooping cranes. They were about 100 metres away. They were strutting through the long grass with heads down, foraging, looking more like small deer than birds. Occasionally one would raise its head and long neck and bugle, a brittle, exciting territorial call that can be heard three kilometres away.

The next day, we drove south into Alberta, through Wood Buffalo National Park to Peace Point. It was sunny and hot and the flies were ferocious, and they swarmed around the lone wood buffalo we saw. It rolled in the dust on the side of the road for a few minutes to discourage the flies, then rose to its feet and sauntered down the road, looking very much like the largest North American land mammal it is supposed to be. We also saw a family of sandhill cranes in a swamp – the chick already half the size of its parents – and an Arctic loon having an afternoon nap in a beaver pond.

If you are a golfer you are sure to enjoy the novelty of playing courses with sand or artificial greens. And then there is the golf course at Yellowknife, an extraordinary nine-hole layout that we played for about $25.00 each, including a power cart. The sign at the entrance and the scorecards featured the image of a raven with a golf ball in its beak, and a local rule provided that no penalty is incurred if one of these birds steals your ball. There was no grass on the fairways, other than a narrow collar around the greens, and the tee-heads and greens were covered with artificial turf. How to play such a course? From the pro shop, we rented a piece of artificial turf, on which we placed and played any ball that landed on the fairways (no closer the hole, of course). It was necessary to sneak up on the greens because any ordinary pitch shot would simply carom off them, and downhill putts were lightning fast.

Yellowknife, because it has several tall buildings, looks like a much larger city than it is. It has most services you might want, even a Tim Horton's doughnut shop.

While there, we took a dinner cruise on Great Slave Lake (tickets available at the first-class visitor centre). It had been cloudy all day, but as often happens in Yellowknife, we were told, it cleared up in the late afternoon. We made our way down to the docks over a paved road made so uneven by frost heaving that it just about threw us into orbit. Our ship, the 30-metre long MV Norweta, was berthed next to a busy marina crowded with sailboats and power craft, and we got the last available parking space.

We climbed the gangway to the upper deck then enjoyed the view of the city as the skipper took us slowly out to the islands at the head of Yellowknife Bay. From there, strain our eyes though we did, we could not see the far shore of the lake. As for the dinner, 30 of us sat down in the saloon on the upper deck, not quite knowing what to expect. We were not disappointed. The galley crew first plied us with drinks (not included in the price of the dinner), then served both cold and hot buffets followed by dessert and coffee. The food was excellent, the crew were fun (we thought maybe they'd been matching us, drink for drink), and the service was excellent.

We took a guided tour of the legislative buildings in Yellowknife, built in the round and cleverly furnished to reflect the various cultures of the northern people. There we saw large Inuit carvings, wall hangings, paintings and photographs, and a rug made of a polar bear skin gracing the floor of the legislative chamber. The wall behind the speaker's chair was made of zinc, the principal metal mined in the Territories, and the chairs were covered in seal skin.

We also visited the Prince of Wales Northern Cultural Centre, large enough to contain sections devoted to wildlife, transportation, native arts and crafts. A. Y. Jackson, one of Canada's Group of Seven, painted extensively in the Territories, and many examples of his work were hung on the walls.

We should not end this article without telling you that there are two ways to get there.

The Liard Trail branches off the Alaska Highway 30 kilometres north-west of Fort Nelson, BC, while the MacKenzie Highway begins at Grimshaw, Alberta. (By the way. You can't get to Inuvik this way, except on ice roads in the wintertime. But that is another story.) We made a circle trip of our vacation, taking the first alternative on the way north and returning via the second. We drove about 3,500 kilometres in the Territories over a period of four weeks, about the right pace, we suggest, considering the state of the roads and all there is to see and do.

We should also tell you that the government and the people of the Northwest Territories are getting ready for more visitors. Every year, highways are being improved and the pavement is being extended. As for campgrounds, we were approached by an enterprising native in Fort Simpson who questioned us closely about the camping needs of RVers. He had a piece of property near town and the resources, he said, to put in a first-class RV park, including full hookups. Perhaps it will be ready for you.

To help with your advance planning, write away for information packages to the Department of Tourism, Box 1320, Yellowknife, NWT, X1A 2L9 (or phone toll free 1-800-661-0788), and to the headquarters for Wood Buffalo National Park, Box 750, Fort Smith, NWT, X0E 0P0.

And always take along a copy of The Milepost, the bible of travel in the north. [Author's note: In addition to this one, of course.]

When these two travellers heard about our complaints about not seeing many moose, they decided to send us a picture of one, a cow, in snow. And NO, it was not taken in July or August, but many months before.

Appendix E: 1995 Letter & 1992 Diary: Travelling in Canada "North of 60"

These two articles are extracted from a letter and a diary of two couples who travelled into many places, including Alaska, USA and in Canada's Northwest Territories, Yukon and northern British Columbia in 1995 and 1992. They have graciously consented to have it included in this book as a means of providing even more balance to our recorded activities. They had some good days and weather when we had bad, went to several different places than we did and vice versa, and we and they are couples with different desires and attitudes. Because they visited Canada's north several years before we did, their descriptions of road conditions, campgrounds, etc. might be considerably different than ours.

Author's note 1: I have tried to leave these missives as they were written, modifying them slightly only for clarity and eliminating irrelevant parts. Metric measurements and spelling/typo errors are mine. Please remember these are diaries, which I think adds to the pleasure of reading them.

Letter concerning a 1994 trip to Yukon and Alaska

Eric and Betty O'Dell have been married for more than four decades, but have been RVing for only seven, first in a motorhome and now in a truck and fifth wheel. They have lived in Caribou Country and the west coast of British Columbia and, when not wintering in southern USA, they hail from South Surrey, BC. Once again they have plans to travel across Canada (perhaps to visit Newfoundland which had been impractical due to bad weather and heavy Atlantic storms) and to return to north of 60 early in the next century. Eric telephoned from down south to give us permission to reprint his typewritten letter; to refresh his memory a copy was e-mailed to him.

October 10, 1995

Dear John & Liz Plaxton,

Just received your September 21st letter today that was kindly forwarded by Sheila of the RV Times. Interestingly enough, your letter came just days after reading your latest contribution in the current issue of RV Times. We are happy to pass along some comments on our experiences going to the Yukon and Alaska last year. Since we hope to do some travelling in Mexico ourselves, we will be most interested in hints and suggestions that you might have.

When taking a long RV touring trip, as we did across Canada in 1992 in a Class C motorhome and to Alaska in 1994 with a truck and fifthwheel, we like to think in terms of travelling an average of no more than 100-150 miles (160 - 250 km) per day. This seems to allow time to take short side excursions, visit points of interest or just enjoy a pause at a pleasant location.

For family reasons, we were not able to leave until July 26,1994. We missed the bug season but would recommend a bit earlier departure. After the Labour Day weekend (in Canada, usually the first weekend of September) we found that like many other parts of Canada and the northern United States, a number of campgrounds, attractions, and services had closed for the season.

Our route took us up BC's Fraser Canyon and on to Prince George and Dawson Creek to the start of the Alaska Highway. We followed the Alaska Hwy to Whitehorse, then branched north to Dawson City, then back over the Top of the World Hwy to Tok. On our return we left the Alaska Hwy at Watson Lake, taking the Cassiar Hwy to Stewart and Kitwanga, then via Hwy 16(Yellowhead) to Prince George. At Cache Creek we diverted over to Lillooet and the Duffy Lake Road, then on through Whistler area and home. Our trip totalled just under 6,000 miles, or 9,500 kilometres.

The Moberly Lake Provincial Park out of Chetwynd makes a nice stopping point with opportunities for swimming and walking.

The Dawson Creek Museum, the Kluane Museum of Natural History at Burwash Landing, and the Museum at the University at Fairbanks all have excellent animal displays. We thought the Burwash Landing museum to be the best.

Fresh vegetables in season are good quality at farms at the south end of the Taylor Bridge between Dawson Creek and Fort St. John.

In general, the main roads are all blacktop and in pretty good shape. Where re-construction is underway, and this is an ongoing challenge because of weather and terrain, there are rough and muddy sections. The longest we encountered was major re-construction from the Alaska/Yukon border to Burwash Landing. Chances are that most of this is now paved. The Yukon portion of the Top of the World Hwy was well graded, but the Alaska portion from Chicken to Tok was worse than we remember of the Caribou Hwy in the 1950's.

On the 450-mile (730 km) Cassiar Hwy, there are three separate 50-mile gravel sections: the rest is paved. The northerly two were fine, but the lower section leading to Meziadin Junction was muddy and rough. However, like you found in Central America, if you drive for the conditions of the road and tires, suspension, and running gear are in good shape, few problems occur.

The Provincial Park at Liard Hot Springs is adjacent to the hot springs and like most provincial parks, well spaced. We really enjoyed the pools as the day had been one of heavy rain.

Most people our age enjoy the Canteen Show put on each evening near the interpretive centre at Watson Lake.

You picked up on our story of Mukluk Annie's on Teslin Lake. We were pleasantly surprised by the swimming temperature in this Yukon lake. The George Johnston Museum at Teslin is worth a visit.

We had the misfortune to have our second gas tank close down on us at Fort St. John on our way north. So we made the rest of the trip using one 18-gallon tank, in a vehicle that did 8-9 miles per gallon, without having to rely on the two 5-gallon jerry cans we had along. (We had picked up a bad lot of gas at an Arco station in Las Vegas, AZ, USA on our way home earlier that year. Eventually after tune-ups and whatever, we ended up removing and cleaning both tanks, for a hefty cost.)

Virtually all the Interpretive Centres in the Yukon and Alaska were excellent. The one at Whitehorse was one we enjoyed. There are a number of things to do around Whitehorse to easily spend a few days.

We did not take the 486 mile (792 km, each way) trip from Dawson City, Yukon to Inuvik, NWT. It is a long drive over gravel roads that has to be retraced. Also, we had a short travelling range between gas stations; see note above. Another time we would probably leave the trailer at Dawson, taking only the truck to Inuvik. There are several flights available from Dawson as well.

Dawson City is exciting history. What more is there to say? With the help of Federal funding it is being turned into a 'living' museum for the summer months. The recitations at Robert Service's cabin are well done. The huge dredges and scars of gold mining tell quite a story. The view from Midnight Dome is a must, and easily reached by RV. Dawson was well worth a few days' stay. We took the day-cruise down the Yukon River to Eagle, Alaska and return. Recommended for a different look at the country side and the present way of life.

The Top of the World Hwy is aptly named and a neat experience. We found free camping at the West Fork Recreational Site 200km out of Dawson for our first night in Alaska.

There are two campsites a short ways into Denali National Park and Preserve accessible by private vehicle, at Savage River and Teklanika, but waiting time for a space and a permit may be a week. There is a large campsite at Riley Creek near the park entrance, there may be a day or two wait for this as well. We boondocked for one night a couple of miles north on a large gravel area between the highway and the Nenana River, in company with twenty or more other rigs. The tour bus trip into Wonder Lake is spectacular, especially if Mt. McKinley shows itself. This is a 170 mile (275 km) round trip on a school bus-type vehicle.

For those interested in old vehicles, tractors and trains, the Alaska Transportation Museum at Wasila is worth a few hours.

The Kenai Peninsula is one of the beauty spots of south-central Alaska. We camped at Land's End Campsite at the end of Homer Spit looking over Cook Inlet. From Seward we took a day boat tour to the Kenai Fjords National Park. For much less money there is a good closeup look at a glacier from a much shorter cruise from the Begich Boggs Visitor Center at Portage Lake. The Williway Forest Campsite there is a good stop before boarding the train to Whittier to catch a ferry to Valdez.

We stopped at the Eagle Trail Campground between Glennallen and Tok on August 31st to a beautiful display of fall colours. Some of the Alaska highway is subject to undulations from frost heaves. The worst we encountered was from Glennallen to Tok.

We attempted to take a side trip to Atlin, BC on the way home, but turned around halfway because of the muddy, slippery and very rough condition of the road. We came to the conclusion that the Alaska and British Columbia road maintainers could take a lesson from their Yukon counterparts. The gravelled roads we encountered in the Yukon were well maintained.

The weather was not favourable as we drove down the Cassiar Hwy so we missed out on much of the vistas. A very nice campground at the Kinaskin Lake Provincial Park. The side trip into Stewart was interesting to me as I was into there frequently in the late 60's when the only access was plane or boat.

The totems at Kitwancool remain a point of interest before getting onto Hwy 16 for the run into Prince George.

The alternate route from Cache Creek through Lillooet and the Duffy Lake Road to Pemberton and the 'Sea to Sky' highway adds another dimension to those of us used to the Fraser Canyon, Coquihalla or Hope-Princeton routes. Caution. The last run down the Duffy Lake Road is a long, very steep grade that deserves respect in an RV. We lost use of our overheated brakes about 1000 yards/metres from the bottom in spite of the truck being in low gear. This points out the unfortunate fact that many RV's are overbuilt (overweight) for the chassis that they are mounted on. Once cooled, the brakes were alright again.

The forgoing gives one couple's perspective of a wonderful trip. Hope there are some useful hints for you. If you have questions yet unanswered, please feel free to ask. ...

Eric and Betty O'Dell

Five Fingers Rapids, YT. Only one channel is safe for canoeists.

German motorcyclist tenting at base of Rock Glacier, YT

1992 Diary of Irene and Chris

As I sit watching a Black-capped Chickadee inspect my makeshift bird feeder I cannot help but recall the many places this feeder has hung, and the many places I should have hung it. This year we have seen many Provinces and Territories of Canada, many states of the United States of America, and a small part of Mexico. By the time we arrive back home in Winnipeg, Manitoba, Canada we will have travelled about 50,000 kilometres and twelve months will have passed. This portion of our diary concerns our northern travels, which included Canada's Arctic. ....

It was late spring of 1992 when we started to drive our way north from Winnipeg to Flin Flon, Manitoba and across the Hanson Lake Road to Lac La Ronge, Saskatchewan. The prairie provinces are not flat lands this far north. The Canadian Shield reaches west of Flin Flon and rolling hills, blue lakes and tall pines fill in the scenery.

Fishing became the order of the day, but because we did not have a boat, our fishing was done from shore or dock. We enjoyed many meals of pike and trout.

Driving beyond Prince Albert, Saskatchewan and Waskesiu Lake in Prince Albert National Park we entered the mixed farming area of the province. Farmers were starting to work the fields and plant spring seeds.

On to Edmonton and Grande Prairie, Alberta and Dawson Creek, British Columbia which now is the beginning of the Alaska Highway. (It is 80% in British Columbia and Yukon, Canada and only 20% in Alaska, USA.) We were now well on our way to the Yukon, Northwest Territories and Alaska where we would spend the summer months seeing the sights on the main roads and exploring as many side roads that we'd have time to investigate. Seeing birds and animals along the way would become an exciting part of our daily life.

Before we start telling about our journey along the Alaska Highway and later Canada's Top of the World Highway and Dempster Highway, I will fill you in on some of our preparations and the type of unit we chose for our travels, and a little background on who we are and how we planned to travel.

We, my husband and myself, are newly retired and are under 60 years of age. We both enjoy the outdoors whether it is biking, playing tennis, fishing, hiking or just simply walking and wandering and seeing what we can see. It also could be just sitting reading and watching the happenings around us. But the important thing is that we were outside enjoying nature and fresh air.

The outdoors became our livingroom without any boundaries or walls to keep us in. We will be living from our savings for a while so our funds are limited and we will have to live within a tight budget if we are going to travel the many months and the many trips that we hope will be in our future.

We bought a 19' (6 m) converted van that required some renovations and additions to the interior. It was an older Ford 3/4 ton truck chassis with a newer motor, both in very good shape. The extended roof made room for standing and lots of cupboard space. We equipped it with a propane stove, thermostatically controlled heater, a twelve volt system and a port-a-potti (portable toilet) for our boondocking (no electricity, water or sewage facilities) days.

Then the fun began of loading it without taking a lot of things that were only usable for one purpose. Because we had some experience canoe tripping and camping we basically knew what items were essential. The rule of thumb for clothing was that it all must mix and match and be the layered look for the cool or cold days. We also equipped ourselves with our sports equipment - tennis racquets, tennis shoes and balls, hiking backpacks and waist packs with water containers,hiking boots, fishing rods and hip waders. Since we hung our two mountain bikes on the back of the van we also needed our helmets along. All of these items are bulky but we found room and still had some room to spare for things we would accumulate on the way.

For our mental preparation we started reading books on the Klondike and in particular Pierre Berton's many books. This helped to acquaint ourselves with the history of the land that we would be visiting and the struggle for the gold and survival in a harsh land. We would be travelling on the famous Alaska Highway that had been started fifty years before and is still being improved upon. We found it impossible to remember all this information, but we wanted to have a very basic understanding and feeling for the country. After our trip when we reread these books we will see the land, hills and rivers in our minds and visualize life back then.

We also purchased "The Milepost" which is a must for anyone driving these northern roads. [Author's note. Our travelogue didn't exist then.]This book gives the traveller mile by mile notes of what to see, what to do, and the conditions of the road. It was well worn by the time we headed south down the Cassiar Highway in northwestern British Columbia.

I'm sure you may be asking what else we took along to make life easy. We were going to be prepared that if we found a place to stop and fish then we would not have to leave to find a store. We wanted the flexibility to do what we wanted to do when the opportunity arose. We stocked up on provisions, including canned meats as we did not have a freezer but only a small fridge. We packed along powdered milk for our breakfast, lots of pastas, rice, dried vegetables for soups, dried onion flakes, mushrooms, tomatoes (these have a fantastic flavour for a spaghetti sauce) and dried salami. When we were in a town that had a good grocery store we would stock up on fresh fruit, potatoes, salad makings and such. So life on the road was very easy as we had everything with us at all times.

Now that we have done some reading, have loaded the van, arranged for friends to check on our home and someone else to forward our mail, we are ready to leave. This just sounded very easy and very fast but the details and many lists to stroke off before the van was ready to leave took time.

Our drivers' licenses and insurance were due to expire before we were to arrive back home. To save some on auto insurance we removed the plates from our car and took out storage insurance. We took along all insurance papers and other documents that we thought we would need then took other important papers (including wills) to the safety deposit box.

We arranged our finances to have funds transferred to our current account on a quarterly basis. We made arrangements with the bank that we could have a fax of our account sent whenever we requested it. This had to be done in person as they required us to sign a form giving them permission to give information of the account. Since we would be travelling out of the country we would not have access to one of our bank branches and it was very helpful to have this arrangement so we would not be stranded without funds.

We travelled with major credit cards and always kept a separate set hidden away just in case we either lost our wallets or had them stolen. None of this actually happened I'm glad to say but we had a couple of close calls when Chris misplaced his wallet.

It is time to start travelling!

June 5 - Friday: Dawson Creek, British Columbia

After having pictures taken at Mile "0" we went for a beer and later a celebration dinner at the Alaska Café. It is a very old colourful building. The area has many Sudeten Germans - they left Germany in 1938 and settled here. We met 2 fellows from Holland and 1 from Brazil. We wrote cards, watched TV and watched the "Main Streeting" while parked on main street in front of Mile "0" and soon moved to a side street for the night. We picked a side street that was used as a race track so we moved again. All was nice and quiet until I heard 2 horses and riders go down the street and someone tried to open the door, but immediately left when he heard someone inside.

June 6 - Saturday: Dawson Creek to Pink Mountain, BC

Beautiful fresh sunny morning. Drove to the tennis court near the hospital and had 3 sets. We were the only ones playing. Many people were out walking including a lady with a German Shepherd in a wheel apparatus. He was paralysed in the back quarters - a genetic disease with the Shepherds. We mailed postcards, bought newspapers, washed our van, filled up with gas and headed down the Alaska Highway. Did a side trip to the Kiskatinaw Wooden Bridge - a very unusual curved bridge on the original highway. Saw a recently-hit dead deer on the road. The road is very good with shoulders and I'm sure this will change. There are many gas and oil wells along the way and at one point the smell of gas.

For lunch we stopped at Taylor Landing just before crossing the Peace River before Ft. St. John. This was a very nice place to stop. The river flows very fast. Saw one extra-long motor boat going upstream - at full throttle it was hardly moving. A single canoeist was also leaving to go downstream and float with the current (he wasn't wearing a life-jacket). On to Pink Mountain and parked for the night in the gas station lot. In front we could see the valley and mountains in the background. The fellow at the gas station had an ATV (all terrain vehicle, small, usually four wheels) which he was roaring around on and making lots of noise. We went for a long walk down the highway.

<u>June 7 - Sunday</u>: Pink Mountain to Summit Lake, BC

Soft drizzle this morning when we woke up. On down highway - saw coyote and then a cow moose with a calf. Very healthy looking animals. Terrific highway as far as Ft. Nelson and then it changed to 5 km of wide gravel road and immediately changed to a very narrow no shoulders and winding road. Stopped for lunch at a narrow turn-off. Raining all day, foggy and visibility not great.

We are slowly going up into the mountains. Reached Summit Lake at 1295 m. We arrived at 3:30 and decided to spend the night. The fog started lifting and we could see the partly snow-covered and bare peaks. The tree line is only about another 30 m (100 feet) up. The peak behind Summit Lake is Mt. St. George - 2260 m. We hope tomorrow will be clear so we can see this spectacular setting. We had a good pasta dinner with wine and a great view of Summit Lake and the mountains from our dining room window. After dinner the rain stopped and the lake was like a mirror with the mountains reflected in it like a double image. We went for a hike up the summit ridge. Spectacular!

We met a young couple from Tucson, AZ, USA who were going to help run a café in Alaska. We also met Cliff Wright from Wrangell, Alaska - a real character. His old and rusty VW camper died on a hill so he rolled it back down and went to work on it in a parking lot and he managed to get it running again.

We did not stay overnight in the campsite down by the lake, but chose to stay just off the road where the scenery is much more magnificent.

<u>June 8 - Monday</u>: Summit Lake to Liard River Whirlpool, Yukon

Today after much excitement we are sitting on washed up logs beside a whirlpool on the Liard River. It is 9 pm and we just finished having a black bear in one of the campsites. We are parked in a do-it-yourself campsite by the Liard Whirlpool. A young lady was in her tent and the bear appeared right outside. He finally sauntered off after tearing at a rug.

Just before that, a grandmother arrived with two 16 year-old boys. We had been out walking and she caught up with us and she was very worried as the boys had been gone too long. We all went walking where we thought they might be. They were only seconds away from drowning as they were standing on a downed tree that had become wedged against a rock and were trying to loosen it back into the churning and raging river. The tree was freed just as they stepped to the bank. The grandmother was quite shaken and was contemplating taking the youngsters back to her daughter - she was actually taking them to California for the summer.

We had problems with our video camera this morning as Chris had an accident with it and it is jammed. We saw 8 caribou today - a first. We had beautiful scenery along Muncho Lake. Raining and drizzle in the morning. At noon we arrived at Liard Hot Springs. We went to the far and more natural pool to get away from the masses. Cliff, whom we met yesterday, caught up with us on the walk. Met and visited with a couple from Australia.

The road turned rougher and stonier, in fact we got a rock chip in the windshield. The Liard River is magnificent, wild and huge. The roar at the whirlpool is quite something. After the day's excitement we all visited down by the river, a Swiss couple, a South Carolina, USA couple and us. We loaned the tenting couple our Bear Scare for the night because they were a little uneasy about the bear making a second visit.

Quite the day and quite the scenery!

June 9 - Tuesday: Liard River Whirlpool to Rancheria River, BC

We finally woke Clay and Betsy so we could get our Bear Scare back before leaving - they didn't need it during the night. The morning was brilliant again. We had lots of broken road today - it was harder driving. Stopped at a viewpoint of the Laird River where the "Robber Barons" attacked fur traders (possibly legend) and also went through British Columbia's 2nd largest fire - 400,000 acres burnt in '82. To Watson Lake.

We stopped for gas and Chris asked if they knew where we could store our bikes. We had not used them as there were no trails for riding and they were just bumping along on the back. He said he did and quickly took us to the Resources and Human Development Building.

We went back to the Husky station and had an oil change, shower and bought some groceries. Went on a reading tour of the sign posts at Watson Lake. We didn't have a sign to put up but found them interesting to read.

We may have a change of plans and leave the Dempster Highway until last, as the ice just went out and the rivers are still too high for the ferries to operate.

Tonight we are camped above the Rancheria River. Two campers are on the opposite bank and we are here by ourselves. We sat outside and read until it became too cool. It is interesting to watch all the traffic coming and going over the bridge. It is now 10:30 pm and the sun is above the horizon and I write without a light.

June 10 - Wednesday: Rancheria River, BC to Teslin, Yukon

Today we drove through some breathtaking scenery. Stopped at the falls at the Rancheria River just before the Continental Divide. We had clear sunny skies while driving along the river and a great view of the Cassiar Mountain Range. There were huge snow-covered high peaks with a new vista around very turn. It was really something!

We were stopped by road construction and talked to a truck driver's wife. They were heading to Inuvik with a load, but might be delayed because of the ferries not running as yet.

Had a super highway on to Teslin. We met a fellow from Vienna at the Falls and we followed them to Teslin. They imported and drove in a Mercedes motorhome.

We stopped at Mukluk Annie's to enquire about a fishing licence and ended up camping for free, having a barbecued salmon dinner for under $30, which included a 1 hour boat ride on Lake Teslin. Unbelievable! We got a camping spot by the lake.

The ground here is a very fine dusty clay so it gets into everything. We used shoes instead of our usual Birkenstocks. A few mosquitoes out tonight - have not been bothered much but trying out our Watkins product.

June 11 - Thursday: Teslin, Yukon to near Atlin, BC

Left Teslin Lake and on to Jake's Corner and tried to make some phone calls here. Stopped at Johnson Crossing for cinnamon rolls and to mail some letters.

The scenery going down to Atlin was fantastic! Mt. Minto dominated the vista. We had such a clear day we could see the coastal mountains. We stopped and watched about 10 mountain goats right down by the road - hopefully we have some good pictures.

We stopped at Lubbock Creek (drove in 3 miles on a one way road), we didn't see any Arctic Grayling - so drove into Snafu Lake. Chris caught a nice jack - so we will have a fresh fish for dinner. We met a school group enjoying themselves at Tarfu Creek. [Snafu: Situation normal, all fouled up; Tarfu: Things are really fouled up.]

Atlin is a pretty town by the Atlin Lake with snow-capped mountains all around. We continued to drive about 10 km south of town and decided to turn around as the road was becoming very rough with construction.

We stayed at a government campsite about 40 km north of Atlin. It was nice but the mosquitoes were the worst we have had. On this road we saw winter "survival shelters" for the first time. They are basic with stove, wood, matches and a bench. There was not a breath of wind on the lake - very warm when we went to bed, but the heater came on during the night.

We can read in the van even with tinted windows and no lights on until 11 pm. Quite something!

<u>June 12 - Friday</u>: Near Atlin, BC to Carcross, Yukon

It is 9:30 at night - I'm sitting on a walk bridge over the end of Lake Bennett. Chris and another fellow are fishing for Arctic Grayling. We can see the fish jump, but they are not biting. It was quite interesting to be fishing from the historic White Pass Railway bridge and the Lake Bennett Walkway.

We have had another remarkable day. We drove into Whitehorse today, fixed the video camera, made reservations for the Skagway/Haines (Alaska, USA) ferry on Sunday evening, had lunch in the parking lot of the Yukon College and watched people come and go for a presentation - Pierre Burton and NDP Leader Audrey McLaughlin and other dignitaries.

We drove back and arrived in Carcross in late afternoon. We stopped at Emerald Lake for pictures (it really is emerald colour). Carcross is a small and neat hamlet. We went for a drink at the historic hotel across from the railway. The liquor laws here are such that you can take a drink from the hotel and walk around. We enjoyed a glass of wine on the bridge while Chris was fishing. We visited for a time with James Krawchuk a local and part native. We stayed overnight in the parking lot of the railway station right across from the hotel.

<u>June 13 - Saturday</u>: Carcross, Yukon, Canada to Skagway, Alaska, USA

Left Carcross early as we want to take our time driving to Skagway. The scenery was indescribable - it went from moonscapes to snow covered peaks and valleys with ice-covered lakes and waterfalls. Chris stopped and talked to a couple who were going skiing and leaving from the road side. At the summit the lake was still ice covered and a huge high waterfall indicated the beginning of the melt.

As we descended into Skagway the White Pass Train was making its way around White Pass City and Dead Horse Gulch.

We drove into the area where the town of Dyea used to be and found the trailhead of the Chilkoot Trail. We walked it for about 2 km and it seemed to be mostly uphill. Then on to the abandoned town of Dyea and the cemetery where the victims of the April 3, 1898 avalanche are buried. The road to Dyea was very narrow and clung to the side of the mountain overlooking the Taiya River and the Taiya Inlet.

Then on into Skagway. It is quite touristy, but then that is their main industry. The Royal Odyssey Cruise Ship was in. We toured the town and then we went for a beer at the Red Onion, then parked for the night in a gravel parking lot. After supper we went for another walk around the town. We went back to the "Red Onion" to hear a good band playing Rhythm and Blues. We met the Australian couple whom we had met at Liard Hot Springs - small world!

June 14 - Sunday: Skagway to beach, Haines
This was a lazy day today after a busy one yesterday. This is a rainy, cloudy and cool day after beautiful sunny weather. Went for a walk before doing breakfast dishes and to a presentation at the Arctic Brotherhood Hall - it was well presented and quite entertaining.

Thought we would wash some clothes but at $4 to wash and dry a load, I thought it was highway robbery and will try to find a cheaper place later. Two cruise ships and one container ship are in the port today - Pacific Princess and The Discoverer.

It took about 1 hour to load vehicles onto the ferry for Haines. It was different from a regular ferry as the cars and motorhomes had to be driven on and then backed into position. It took much organization and some of the large rigs were not too happy with the set-up because they had difficulty backing into a tight area.

The one hour cruise to Haines was quite impressive with many waterfalls along the mountain sides. After driving off the ferry and going only a short distance we found a great place to stop for the night. A few other campers were already there including some we had met in Skagway. We were right on the ocean beach. We enjoyed a late glass of wine, candlelight and a view of the ocean out our front window. It couldn't be better!

<u>June 15 - Monday</u>: Haines to Desadeash Lodge (Mush Lake trailhead)

Slept in this morning and drove into Haines - a pretty setting, but town not as quaint as Skagway. Filled up with gas, water, some smoked salmon (not as good as the lox that Chris makes) and some cheaper gin. We drove out to Chilkoot Lake and Park to see the fishermen standing in the stream fishing for salmon. We didn't see anyone catch anything but there certainly was a lot of activity.

On to Haines Junction, YT, Canada. Very beautiful scenery but not as spectacular as driving from Carcross into Skagway. We stopped for gas and a treat of ice-cream at mile 33 Road House. It was very homey, clean and friendly - one of the nicest we have seen. Saw only a few bald eagles on the Preserve but maybe the main migration has not come in as yet.

We stopped at a trailhead into Klaune Park for the night. Another great view of Desadeash Lake and mountains from our dining room window.

<u>June 16 - Tuesday</u>: Desadeash to Jarvis Creek near Haines Junction, Yukon

Left our beautiful view and headed into Haines Junction. Did chores such as washing clothes and van, and made some telephone calls.

We drove only about 10 km and found a nice creek to camp beside. Chris tried his hand at fishing in the afternoon and evening - no luck even though we could even see them jumping. We had another camper join us and later walked to a viewpoint with him. We also walked across the road and visited with a nice Indian fellow who was helping the Ruby Mountain Trail guides. The horses were out in the fields somewhere. Later in the evening a chap from the University of Alberta stopped by to do some fishing. He knew the right place to go and caught a nice one.

He told us about some of the researchers at the station being treed by a grumpy grizzly so they now carry the pepper spray - Bear Scare.

At midnight 2 other motorhomes pulled in and were gone before 7 am. We started calling the "big rigs" LIFOs, as in Last In First Out. They seemed to drive too fast, stop real late, put on the generator, disturb the other campers and wake everyone else up when they leave at the crack of dawn.

One highlight while fishing - a brown mink came up to our feet and looked at us and scooted into the water.

June 17 - Wednesday: Jarvis Creek to north of Beaver Creek, Yukon

We were the last to leave the make-shift campsite. We enjoyed our leisurely breakfast, washed dishes and organized ourselves for the day. We didn't think that we would drive very far but nothing looked pleasing to stop at for the day and evening.

We ended up entering Alaska on the other side of Beaver Creek. The first gas station that we came to was closed and so filled up about 4 miles away. We were very close to empty.

The road was quite wavy with frost heaves and broken up in places. We passed miles of muskeg, bog and swamp land today with mountains in the background. We stopped at a wayside pull-off and the view from our dining room is the Tetlin National Wildlife Refuge and the Wrangell Mountains in the far distance. The sky is baby pink and blue with some darker blue clouds and the valley a dark green.

We watched the sun go down and it didn't disappear until 11:30. It was bright enough to read.

June 18 - Thursday: near Beaver Creek, Yukon to Bear Bridge near Tok, Alaska

When we left our night spot we saw a helicopter go over, and about 10 miles later we found the military being lifted out to fight a forest fire in Canada on the other side of the border. We stayed for some time watching the operation and talking to the local recruits and army personnel.

While we were at our lunch stop near Tetlin Junction we saw an old military convoy making their return trip up the Alaska Highway after the completion of the Highway in '42 and celebrating the 50th Anniversary. They had an RCMP escort and we later saw them in Tok.

We stopped for the night about 10 miles outside of Tok at Bear Creek. I tried to do some panning for gold. I got a few small flakes in black sand. I have to practice this but fun anyway.

June 19 - Friday: Tok to a mile above Tanana River, Alaska
Left Bear Creek and did not travel too far before we found a beautiful view overlooking the Tanana River and valley. We could see Mt. Hays and two others looming on the horizon. There was also one huge glacier.

When we stopped there were numerous planes overhead. Four groups flying in formation and one larger plane had 6 escorts and the other 4 large ones had 4 escorts. These were military planes commemorating the building of the Alaska Highway. They were flying over to Delta Junction. Delta Junction was the end of the military highway in '42.

Delta Junction was a tourist trap and had no information - only souvenirs at the Info Centre.

Another couple joined us for the night. They were in a rented camper and were from Munich. We sat and enjoyed a glass of wine with them in the evening.

June 20 - Saturday: Tanana River to Fairbanks
Summer Solstice!
Dull, dreary and a rainy day. Our Munich neighbours presented us with a small bottle of their brother's homemade schnapps which they brought along. This was very nice and appreciated.

It rained almost all the way into Fairbanks so there wasn't much sightseeing. We did see a cow moose and calf but in total we have not seen much wildlife.

The weather cleared in the afternoon so we did some walking around. We visited the Chamber of Commerce and Tourist Centre. They have a very good centre with lots of information and a very interesting park next door with a bronze statue recognizing the Inuit.

For dinner we had fresh salmon, new potatoes and a salad - delicious! The salmon was just beautiful - very light, delicate and especially fresh.

After dinner, which we had at the University Grounds parked at a viewpoint, we drove to a parking lot where a midnight race was to begin. Many were dressed in costumes for the run and were in great spirits. The army also took part in the fun. Then on to the finish of the race at Alaska Land. This is a park with artifacts about life in the north and the gold mining.

We met Jim Kowalchuk from McGregor, Manitoba and his wife and son. He was homesick for Manitoba.

At midnight the Square Dancers came out into the park and danced - it was all very colourful. A professional baseball game was being played without the aid of lights. We were able to walk in at the "bottom of the 9th" and get box seats from people who were leaving. The visitors from Los Angeles won 2 to 1 and it ended at 12:30 am. We stayed in the Safeway parking lot and it never really got dark, only a little dusky.

June 21 - Sunday: Fairbanks to Nenana River

On to Denali Park. We stopped at the touristy village of Nenana. As we came closer to the Park the scenery became quite wild, especially within 5 miles of the Park gates. We will spend the night on a pull-out above the rolling, white-capped Nenana River where rafters and kayakers are going down.

We drove to the park to reserve a bus seat for a ride into the park tomorrow. It is some view although a little windy as we can feel the van rock some.

<u>June 22 - Monday</u>: Nenana River

We left at 11:40 for the bus trip into Denali. It is a 66 mile (107 km), one-way trip. Part of the trip was pretty steep and narrow, but spectacular. We spotted many animals including 5 grizzlies - one mother with two one-year old pups, herds of caribou, 2 red foxes, moose with calf, golden eagles and lots of Dall sheep. We were unable to see Mt. McKinley due to cloud cover.

We arrived back to the van at 7:40 and we were quite tired. We had packed along food but still enjoyed dinner when we got settled back at our spot beside the Nenana River about 3 miles north of the park gate.

Just before going to sleep we spotted a bull moose floating down the river. At first we thought he was in trouble as he was going over some rough water, but then he nonchalantly headed for the shore and disappeared in the bush on the other side. This was a real climax to our animal watching and sightseeing.

<u>June 23 - Tuesday</u>: Nenana River to Talkeetna

We headed south from Anchorage. On our way we passed an annual and international wheel-chair race in progress from Fairbanks to Anchorage.

A clear day and a surprise - we had excellent views of Mt. McKinley. We stopped at two different spots to gaze and take pictures.

Chris bought his fishing license at Petrocash and the owner told us that fishing might be good at Petersville, which was only a 20 mile (32 km) gravel drive away. We rerouted and only went about 13 miles and the road was closed. One little bonus was a totally different view of the mountain, but it had disappeared as we retraced our route back to the highway.

Disgusted and disappointed we drove back then drove to Talkeetna - another side trip that sounded neat. Talkeetna is an old town and this is where the climbers stay and leave from for their ascent of Mt. McKinley. Rescue efforts are also organized from the airport here. Stopped for a beer at the Fairview Inn and met some unusual mountain characters. We also booked a salmon fishing trip for tomorrow evening.

We parked for the night outside the Inn and during the night a freight train groaned up the hill just beside us and everything vibrated.

June 24 - Wednesday: Talkeetna

A rainy day today, in fact it rained all night. We visited the museum of climbing expeditions which had a huge relief of the whole Mt. McKinley area. This year there have already been 12 deaths including 4 Canadians. We walked out to the cemetery where there is a memorial placed by Japan for the climbers who have died here.

We left at 5 pm for our fishing expedition. There were 3 paying clients, myself and 3 guides. We were taken by motor-boat — with our float boat piggybacked on the motorboat — as we were going to float back with the current. We had lots of excitement. Chris pulled in a 25 lb King Salmon and another fellow with us from New York, USA caught a 30 lb King. We saw a 2 ½ year old grizzly on the opposite bank looking for fish also. Some other people there shot off noise makers to scare the bears as they were staying the night and didn't like the company. The fish were cleaned by the guides and we arrived back home at 11:30 pm. We cut, filleted and marinated some fish, had a drink and went to bed about 2 am. Some day!

June 25 - Thursday: Talkeetna to Anchorage

Left Talkeetna in the morning - we sure had a good time there and we really liked the town. The people were quite a variety - some on welfare, some just making it, the climbing elite, the climbing guides, the fishing guides and the colourful characters.

We stopped for lunch at Eklutna beside an old Russian church. Here we saw our first red German bus called a Rotel. It seats and sleeps about 24 people.

We investigated Anchorage, we drove and we walked around the downtown area. Our mail had not arrived so will make another trip to the post-office in a couple of days before we go south to the Kenai Peninsula.

We spent the night at the Diamond Shopping Center with lots of other RV's. We checked out the shopping centre and they even have a security fellow keep an eye on the rigs that are parked there and everyone can stay 5 days.

June 26 - Friday: Anchorage

Woke up to rain; it had rained all night but just a nice drizzle. We bought sealers to can part of the salmon that Chris has caught as we could not eat it all. We canned 5 ½ pints of salmon and it looks real good. Decided to buy a pizza for supper after we did the canning in the parking lot.

In the afternoon we checked on our mail. It had been at the post-office all along, in fact they were going to send it back on Monday. It always pays to keep checking and ask the clerks to double check.

We also went to the museum. Excellent display on native art and life in the north. They have a very beautiful building also.

June 27 - Saturday: Anchorage

A real steady rain today. We went for an investigative drive around the residential area of Anchorage. We found large homes, large lots, and on a clear day a spectacular view of the harbor. Back to Diamond Center for the evening. It was a clear evening so we enjoyed a late walk.

Mt. Spurr erupted this morning and there was also a major earthquake in California not far from Desert Hot Springs.

June 28 - Sunday: Anchorage to north of Ninilchuk

As we drove south the scenery changed as soon as we left Anchorage. It became very mountainous and there was ocean frontage (the tide was out) along Turnagain Arm.

The traffic was unbelievable! The Alaskans are crazy drivers - they tailgate, pass on double solid lines and blind curves and seem to have no regard for speed limits. They seem to be on a suicide run.

We stopped at Portage Glacier. This was our first glacier up close. The floating ice is very blue.

From there we drove through majestic scenery and low marsh land. A sunny day to make the scenery even more contrasting. When we reached Kenai River and Russian River the fishermen were almost standing shoulder to shoulder.

On this trip we enjoyed the scenery but not the traffic and the service stations - this is a real tourist trap area. The Hamilton Service Station charged top gas prices, no water for windshields, pay for air, no towels and snarky people. Stopped at Clam Gulch campground - all lined up on parking lot stalls. It looked terrible so we left and stopped at a viewpoint 4 miles away. We had a view of Spurr (blew its top on Saturday), Redoubt and Iliamna.

Chris got his first haircut since we left home. There were no mosquitoes so we sat outside for the evening.

<u>June 29 - Monday</u>: Ninilchuk to Homer Spit

On the way to Homer we stopped at the historic town of Ninilchuk. We walked up to the Russian Church sitting on the hill and had a great view of Cooks Inlet. The Razor Clam diggers were all out in the mud - the tide was out and this was one of the best days to dig the clams. The tide was at its highest and lowest marks. We were shown how to dig them. Diggers are allowed 60 lbs (27.2 kg) per license.

We paid for our first camping fee of $3 to stop right on the beach on the Spit. The Spit extends about a mile into the ocean, and it is only wide enough for a road in some places and then it widens out for about 1/3 of a mile.

Chris tried his hand at fishing at the "Fishing Hole" but no luck. The salmon here do not bite so have to be snagged. Not too nice. A seal had come into the Hole and was bobbing up and down looking at the people. He of course was fishing.

After all this excitement we went to the "Salty Dog" for a drink. It is a very old lighthouse and still retains all the character of an old small historical building filled with lots of stories.

After a Fish and Chips dinner at a local restaurant on the beach, we watched the local guides weighing and filleting the halibut that was brought in. Some of the fish weighed up to 125 lbs.

June 30 - Tuesday: Homer

We spent the morning clamming for the first time. We bent the old Army shovel and bought a garden trowel - recommended by a young fellow in the hardware store. It also was the cheapest thing to buy. We only found one clam. We have decided to stay one more day and try our hand at it once more.

We went to the top of the hill above Homer to play tennis. The courts were quite good, but where else would you get such a view and location.

The chartered fishing boats didn't go out this morning as the sea was very rough so we have no halibut weighing to watch tonight.

July 1 - Wednesday: Homer to Soldatna

We were out clamming first thing in the morning. The tide was very low and we got a number of different types. Chris made a clam sauce for pasta and it was very good. I even cleaned the clams.

It was a perfect day - not windy and not cool. I think we have clamming out of our system. We went for another scenic drive above Homer and then started north.

July 2 - Thursday: Soldatna to scenic view, Hope

We leave town and the traffic is much heavier. As we near the Kenai River congestion a cyclist comes out from a side road, does not stop, sharply turns right and weaves into the traffic. He lost some balance due to a top heavy backpack he was wearing. Chris really swerved to miss him and just missed the on-coming traffic also. The driver behind had to do the same.

That was as close as we would ever want to come to hitting someone. We stopped again at the camp entrance and there wasn't any traffic behind us so he may have been hit.

We regrouped and drove on to Hope. It is a real old place, quiet and not many people. We filled up with gas and stopped for the night at a scenic view overlooking Turnagain Arm.

July 3 - Friday: scenic view, Hope
We went for a fairly long hike today near the campground area. It was great - first one for a while. We did some necessary laundry, some touring of the area and back to our scenic view for the night. Two other vans came in to stay also - one from Oregon and one from British Columbia.

The fellow from Oregon spotted the Tidal Bore coming in about 6:30. You could hear the roar as it approached and there was a least a foot of water coming in. This only occurs at the highest tides about once a month and is more pronounced in summer. It was quite a sight.

A beautiful day today, in fact, shorts weather. We stayed another night at our scenic view but were disturbed by some campers that came in late and walked over to the point.

July 4 - Saturday: scenic view, Hope
We decided to move to another scenic view as we didn't wish to drive to Anchorage until the holiday weekend was over. We can see the traffic across the Arm and it was bumper to bumper.

We could see and hear some boulders falling down the mountain behind us. Watched the Bore Tide again and it was quite dramatic with a strong wind blowing into it. We had a very nice quiet evening. Another motor home quietly stopped for the night too.

July 5 - Sunday: scenic view, Hope
It was "breakfast at Wimbledon" this morning. Steffi Graf won the Women's yesterday and Agassi won the Men's today. It was my turn to have a haircut. Chris read some stories to me while I was busy clipping. We did some more hiking in the afternoon and spent some time down by the ocean.

Our neighbour for the night was a fellow we had camped beside at Skagway and Haines. He drove a VW camper that had a broken windshield. Small world.

July 6 - Monday: Hope to Anchorage
On the way to Anchorage we stopped at Girdwood ski area. The weather was cloudy, cool and drizzly. The winter ski area looked a little desolate but quite alpine looking.

We took the van to Sears to have the front brakes checked and decided to have them redone. We had some more excitement as Chris mislaid his wallet at Sears. We searched high and low till we were resigned that it was lost when a clerk located it in the store. Were we ever relieved!

Back at the parking site we met a couple driving a Mercedes Unimog, a couple and a young boy in a VW camper and another couple in a truck camper. These were all German travellers. The Unimog couple will be on the road for 6 years travelling Africa, North and South America. The VW camper family is gone just for the summer, and he took part in the run down Marathon Mountain and skinned himself on both thighs when he fell. The truck camper couple have been on the road for 2 years and will be heading back to Germany soon.

July 7 - Tuesday: Anchorage to Glenn Highway, King River
We slept in this morning and enjoyed a morning paper with our coffee. We are on to Glennallen and Valdez. Just as we were leaving a delivery truck decided to pass a car on the shoulder of the road and broke an axle. We were pleased to safely leave Anchorage area without an accident.

We took the Palmer by-pass - not too scenic but better than the main road. We tried to drive down to 17 Mile Lake but couldn't find the lake or even see it. So back to the highway. The road was very rough.

We stopped by the King River for the night, and would you believe the Unimog stopped on the other side of the river? Chris tried his hand at fishing but never saw anything or caught anything - almost lost a hook but we got it out.

<u>July 8 - Wednesday</u>: King River to Willow Creek

A lovely clear morning and we could see the tops of the nearby peaks. Drove along the Matanuska River until we came to the glacier. It was spectacular from the campground and the highway. At the campground we met the couple with the Unimog. We thought we would drive around the base of the glacier as there was a road running parallel to the glacier but the entrance fee was $5 per person so we said "No Thanks. That is far too expensive" and left.

Ahead of us there was a four car pile-up so traffic was backed-up. No one was seriously injured.

At Glennallen we headed south to Valdez. We took the Copper Center Town Route and stopped at the visitors centre, and here again was the German couple with the Unimog. They were going to Kennecott and we to Valdez.

We stopped for the night at Willow Creek. There are diamond willows and hordes of mosquitoes in the area. Another couple also stopped so went looking for diamond willows together. Today we didn't stop until 6 pm, which is rather late for us. Surprisingly, we received a clear reception on the TV - better than in town.

<u>July 9 - Thursday</u>: Willow Creek to Valdez

We slowly got ready and drove towards Valdez. We made a number of stops including Worthington Glacier, Bridal Veil Falls and Horsetail Falls. We had foggy weather and it was really thick over the Thompson Summit. It was very poor driving conditions.

Valdez was rainy and cloudy and it is probably like that a lot. It has the highest record for snow fall in Alaska. We found a parking spot by the small boat harbor. We watched the tourist traffic and in the evening a number of locals gathered — between 3 and 14 people — and started to get quite drunk.

We also went to the museum in the afternoon. They have excellent displays about the earthquake in March/64 and the oil spill in March/89.

We decided to go for a walk about 10 pm and ended up at the ferry dock until midnight. We heard the boat whistles and the ferry from Seward to Valdez came in. The ferry was quite old and it unloaded cars, vans, motorhomes, bikes and motorcycles and trucks via a turntable which raised up to dock level and turned to drive the vehicle off. A very labour intensive operation. We were fascinated. Another ferry from Whittier was late due to a train derailment.

We walked back to the van, it was raining quite heavy by this time. We spent the night on the street by the small boat harbor.

July 10 - Friday: Valdez to Liberty Falls, Chitina

Even more rain and fog this morning. We drove into old Valdez and saw the remaining pier and streets after the 1964 earthquake. Drove to the floating dock and the area where the storage tanks are. The end of the Pipeline.

We saw hordes of fishermen fishing where stocked fish were. This area will be open for commercial fishermen on Saturday and then this is apparently chaos. Very dense fog until we were over the Thompson Pass again.

Our lunch stop was beside a creek and then we turned to take the road to McCarthy and Chitina and maybe on to Kennecott. We spied some nice diamond willow by a small lake. The Copper River Valley is immense and in the distance you could see the Wrangell Glacier.

At our campsite at Liberty Falls a fellow from New York climbed to the top and literally slid his way to the bottom after seeing a black bear at the top. Three women, 2 from Florida and 1 from Anchorage, shared our picnic table before going to McCarthy for the night. We had seen them arrive on the ferry the night before in Valdez. We were cleaning our diamond willow and another couple came to inquire what we were doing. This is a small clean and free campground - we hope it is quiet for the weekend.

July 11 - Saturday: Liberty Falls, Chitina

422

It started drizzling as we were finishing breakfast and preparing to leave. We had good pavement to Chitina. When we crossed the Copper River we saw fish wheels turning and people netting salmon. As the road climbed it started to deteriorate. It became very washboardy with many railroad ties surfacing. (This used to be the railroad bed to Kennecott).

At the Kalanuska River bridge people were gathering and preparing to bungee jump off the bridge. We stayed for 2 hours watching the proceedings. A little scary.

It was now raining quite heavily but we decided to try to go on. We only drove about 5 miles and decided to turn around as we had only gone about 1/3 of the way. It did not look like it would clear for some time because we could not see any mountains around and it was not pleasant driving.

We arrived back at Liberty Falls for the night. Some "Dip" fishermen almost sat on top of us for the night. They were inconsiderate of others, loud, and filthy as they left all their garbage for others to clean up. Campgrounds can do without this type of people.

July 12 - Sunday: Liberty Falls, Chitina to Tok

In the early morning another dip fisherman stopped to use our picnic table and he left a mess and noisily slammed doors at 7 am. It stopped raining when we left at 9 am.

We had an oil change at Glennallen and then on to Tok. We bought gas and parked in the service station lot at Tok for the night. We walked down to the Westmark Hotel, bought some T-shirts at their discount shop, and then went for a drink at the hotel. We visited with a local accountant and he bought us a drink - would you believe. The trip to Tok was very enjoyable and scenic. The road was very good also.

Just over the fence and in the woods behind our van, about 20 sled dogs were tied up and sitting on top of their houses. We didn't think much of it until it became dark and then the howling started. It was a very spine-chilling sound while they communicated with another group a few blocks away. They howled for about half an hour, but it was quite something to listen to.

<u>July 13 - Sunday</u>: Tok

We inquired at the local tourist bureau — a very lovely building and helpful staff — if they had tennis courts in town. We received directions to them and will check them out later. We enjoyed our dinner and walked to the recreation park. We were astounded with what we saw. Hoodlums had taken a truck and had driven it into the fences, ran over the tennis nets and stacks. Beer bottles lay broken all over the place. The locals had done a real good job on destroying this expensive facility. This is the taxpayer's money.

A cloud burst happened on our 2 km walk back to the van and we were soaked to the skin. It has been a long time since we got that wet but it was fun anyway.

<u>July 14 - Tuesday</u>: Tok

We went for a long walk this morning and met Paul and Shirley Klenke again - we first met them at Dyea and walked a distance with him on the Chilkoot trail. It is a real small world in the North. They are on their way to Dawson City also. Not much to do in this town so went for a number of walks and washed clothes.

<u>July 15 - Wednesday</u>: Tok to Chicken

Bright and sunny it isn't, just heavily overcast and raining. We took the Taylor Highway to go to Chicken. The road was very good with only some rough spots the first 15 miles and it narrowed before Chicken.

At Chicken we checked out the old and new town and settled for the old and stayed beside the old saloon, bakery and souvenir stand. We went to the old Saloon for a beer and met 2 fellows fromStorey, Wyoming, USA. One ended up buying round after round for the house. I refused a few but he spent lots of money as there were a few others in the lounge.

Dollar bills, pictures and hats and lots of other mementos were tacked to the walls, posts and ceiling. We had an excellent turkey sandwich for supper as we had finished the salmon for lunch. Chris talked to a few gold prospectors that came to the bar. One of them had some nuggets on him for sale. What an interesting place!

<u>July 16 - Thursday</u>: Chicken to Eagle

A great sunny morning. We took our time leaving and didn't pull out until 11 am. We watched tour buses come and go and had a fresh bun at the bakery. We watched a family of 4 children and 2 adults peel out of a VW camper and then go and spend lots of money at the bakery.

We had fantastic scenery on the way to Eagle. The road was pretty good, some spots a little rough and maybe narrow, but relatively smooth for a gravel road. Arrived at Eagle at 3:30. There hasn't been any rain here for a while so stopped and taped up the van as it is dusty.

We stopped at Fort Egbert and picked some strawberries. The berries were very small but loaded with flavour. We enjoyed a glass of wine in the van and then we went to the restaurant for a pizza as it was pizza night. They served one size - large. So we took some home, but still ate too much.

The library was showing a film on Eagle history and the 1992 ice-break-up on the Yukon River. This was extraordinary footage as it really ripped the shoreline and flooded the Indian Village just down the river from Eagle. The Yukon River is still very high and has a tremendous current. We spent the night at the local campground-it was free.

<u>July 17 - Friday</u>: Eagle to Alaska/Yukon (USA/Canada) Boundary

We joined a 10 am tour of the town which lasted until 1 pm. It was most informative and very well done. One part of the tour was given by the elderly wife of a prospector. She told of the hard times, of the isolation and the hard work involved with gold prospecting.

The drive back to Wade's Junction was not as spectacular as going into Eagle, and we also had to climb about 3000 ft. The rain really pelted down at the Junction and we stopped for gas at the border station. It was a real dump.

We drove another km and had a "top of the world view" so here we stayed for the night. The skies cleared and we walked to the top of the ridge and here we found the USA/Canada official boundary marker. We could see 2 mining camps in the distance which were not visible from the highway. This was one of the most scenic stops that we have had and there have been many. We watched 2 units drive through the border barriers and go on their way even though the border was closed for the evening. I wonder if they were caught.

July 18 - Saturday: USA/Canada Boundary to Dawson City, Yukon

The border was just up the hill. I forgot to mention the liquor and the repairs. I only mentioned the $25.70 for T-shirts and he waved me on and laughed and said I was a "big spender."

Away we went - we stopped at a viewpoint about 2 km down the road and lo and behold there stood the Unimog. We had not seen them since they were heading to Kennecott. We picked lots of "steinpilze" mushrooms on outcroppings and they lent us 3 eggs for an omelet.

He noticed the shield covering our water tank had come loose again so he and Chris took it off. It was a messy job, but glad to remove it if it was going to give us some more problems. We left it at the garbage dump near Dawson City.

This drive on the ridges of the rolling mountains on the Top of the World Highway is really something! A drive we would like to do again.

We stopped just before Dawson and had a view of the Yukon River valley. It was now downhill into the valley. We had about an hour wait for the ferry crossing into the City. The Yukon River was flowing so fast that the ferry was hardly moving at full throttle and then it was swept away. The captain was doing a good job but it just took time.

The Unimog was there ahead of us and also parked on Front Street. We picked up information on the Dempster Highway and such and went for a long walk before supper. We stopped at Minto Park to see the Folk Festival and met Ralph Benmurgei from CBC TV and Radio. We walked by Pierre Burton's , Robert Service's and Jack London's home; they were all within 1 block of each other. We walked by a beautiful home and complimented the local school teacher on her home.

We were thirsty and went for a beer at a typical Canadian bar - no character - all the others were filled or charged an entrance fee. We were parked by the dike so sat on the dike and watched the boat traffic for a while before going to bed. We stayed right on Front Street.

July 19 - Sunday: Dawson City to Km 116, Dempster Hwy, Yukon

It is dull this morning and it had rained very heavily during the night. The music festival closed down about 2 pm as there were quite a number of groups going through the street singing in the wee hours. They had to take the ferry across the river to the government campground on the other side.

We stocked up on groceries and stopped by to repay our debt (borrowed eggs) to our German Unimog friends. We said our goodbyes to them as we would now be on separate routes and would probably not meet again on this trip.

We left Dawson and followed the Klondike tailings of the gold field. We stopped at Bear Creek for a tour. This was certainly worth the stop and most educational about the gold rush and mining for gold.

Our next stop was at the Dempster Junction to fill up with gas and water and then down the road to Inuvik, NWT and the Arctic Ocean via the gravel road of the Dempster Highway.

The first part of the journey was the same type of terrain that we had been driving through. The road was very good and certainly better than the Top of the World Highway. Soon the valleys became wide and green and the clouds were playing tricks with the lighting. The mountains were some distance away but seemed relatively close. The landscape seemed to be plush and the mountains soft and spongy.

We stopped at the Blackstone River for the night. We went fishing before supper and Chris caught an Arctic Char, which we enjoyed for dinner. We enjoyed our late evening. Chris lost a hook and I snarled up the reel so we couldn't use it - or something was wrong with it. There were quite a few mosquitoes.

An elderly couple, in a new Roadtrek van, joined us for the night. They were university professors from Ontario, Canada. We would have liked to have visited with them longer, but they were leaving in the morning.

July 20 - Monday: Km 116 to Km 327 Eagle River Bridge, Yukon

It rained again during the night, sometimes quite light and other times quite heavy. Our neighbours quietly left at 6 am. We heard a cow bell ringing when we first woke-up and here were about 14 "wild" horses feeding along the road. I guess they were not too wild because of the bell but they were free to roam. The clouds were quite low but we had a good view of the mountain valleys and the cut rocks.

At noon we stopped at 140 km and tried fishing the Ogilvie River. We didn't have any luck but it was fun. Chris fixed my reel this morning so I am back in business. On we went to the first of three Continental Divides, which was an expanse of scenery. We then dropped down into a muskeg region and drove this for some miles. The flowers (fireweed) were brilliant along the roadside and framed the highway for some distance.

We did not need the extra gas we had taken along as we still had about 1/8 of a tank when we stopped at Eagle Plains for gas and water. The road so far has been very good with some rough spots and slippery on new construction due to the rain. We drove a couple of km down the highway and pulled into a new park area at the "Mad Trapper" Marker.

July 21 - Tuesday: Km 327 to Fort McPherson, Northwest Territories

It really rained during the night and then became quite steady. We were concerned about leaving this new parking lot as it looked quite soft now. It was soft and slippery but Chris made it just fine, although someone else had slid into the ditch. It continued to rain all day and we slowly continued on our way.

We stopped at the Yukon/Northwest Territories (NWT) boundary for lunch and it was really socked in, but lifted some when we left. Had some very interesting scenery for a distance through a river valley and then the road became very greasy and it was not easy driving, but most people drove sensibly except for a large motorhome driver and a passenger van full of passengers. We later saw the van in a ditch (about 10 passengers) but no one was injured.

We took the ferry over the Peel River and the banks were very rutted. Drove on to Fort McPherson, filled up with gas and parked for the night beside the old historical Anglican Church — where the NWMP Lost Patrol is buried — along the high banks of the Peel River.

July 22 - Wednesday: Fort McPherson to Inuvik, NWT

This morning we took the ferry across Arctic Red River and the MacKenzie River where they join together. Just after the crossing we spotted 2 birds walking on the road. They were either cranes or herons as they stood about 3 - 4 ft (1+ m) high. They were variegated rust, brown and white. We later inquired and we were told that they were immature Whooping Cranes.

It stopped raining but the roads ranged from exceedingly slippery to very good. The sun was shining when we arrived in Inuvik and the sky looked quite clear and it was very warm.

We came to Inuvik during the right week as the 1992 Circumpolar Conference and the Inuit Artists were meeting. At the Circumpolar Conference there were Inuit from Russia and from the east as far away as Greenland.

After a quick tour of the town we immediately went to the grounds of the MacKenzie school where all the activity was taking place. The blanket toss was in progress. We tried Caribou stew and fish, then visited with Irene from Nome, Alaska. She offered us cooked Beluga, but said she understood if we didn't have any.

Later in the afternoon we went into the local hotel for a drink and I met the owner, Walter Willkomm. As it turns out Chris and he had a mutual friend in Cassiar, BC many years before.

In the evening the Canadian (Air) Force's renowned aerobatic team, the Snowbirds, performed down over the MacKenzie River, and after that we went back to the grounds to listen to an Inuit group from Montreal, Kashtin. They were excellent and have produced a record or more. A very interesting day to say the least!

We ended the night by staying in front of the CBC building on Main street. The daylight was so bright at 1 am that we had to devise a cardboard insert for the skylight so we could sleep in the dark.

July 23 - Thursday: Inuvik

Drove over to the banks of the MacKenzie to have breakfast and afterwards we had to do our clean-up chores. We filled up with water and washed the van, but first we had to scrape the mud off the running board with a shovel. The mud was like glue so it took some work to get it to come off. We were a dirty mess so we cleaned up and headed to the airport for a flight to Tuktoyaktuk (or Tuk) on the Arctic Ocean. They have a lovely new airport at Inuvik and it is spacious and bright. Most impressive.

We were going in a 5-seater plane and another couple joined us, Susanne and Wolfgang Buder, a German couple who are now living in India. They left their 4 children in the campground in the care of the 16 year old.

The flight over the MacKenzie Delta was fascinating. We could see the trails of the Caribou, the many arms of the delta, and the vast flat land with pingos breaking the flat monotony of the tundra. The pingos are frozen "pimples" on the tundra, actually an underground lake that is frozen and rising to the surface about 2.5 cm (1") per year. One pingo is 500 years old and more are growing.

Tuk was a town that showed the harshness of the cold winters. The walls of the homes were very thick and quite drab. The only natural wood here is the drift wood that comes from the south via the river. The ice cap was out at this time of year so the water in the ocean was fresh water, and it is called the Beaufort Sea.

We had a native tour guide who drove us around and explained their life to us. The oil companies have storage tanks, equipment and personnel living there year around. Our tour guide, Boogie, took part in the Centennial Canoe trip across Canada with the Voyageurs, so he has travelled the country. Our short visit was over and we had briefly touched the most northerly part of our country.

We again searched the land as we flew back to Inuvik at an altitude of about 160m (500)'. It was fascinating.

Upon our arrival back in town we briefly met Mr. Willkomm again and then off to the school grounds again. The evening entertainment was by the Greenland Inuit and what a show they put on. It was the best I have ever been involved in. The whole audience became part of the entertainment. Before the evening really got underway there was a Bannock-making contest and the contestants had to make a fire and make the bannock. Chris was one of the judges and he enjoyed the tasting - this was right up his alley. The show and the singing weren't over until 12:30 and, of course, the sun was still up. The local dance was to start then. It had been a very warm and sunny day and a very busy day. We stayed the night on main street in front of the hardware store.

July 24 - Friday: Inuvik to Km 447, Cornwall River, Yukon

Again had breakfast by the MacKenzie River then we left Inuvik about 9:30 am. A beautiful sunny day, and the road is now dry and has been graded in some areas but rutted and rough in others. Magnificent scenery and we stopped many times to take pictures. The vastness of the land is not adequately portrayed in pictures as the distances are so far and deceiving.

We stopped for lunch at Fort McPherson and stopped where we had stayed the night by a river. The area was all rocks so there won't be any problem if it rains. It was just a lovely evening

- a little breeze, and not many mosquitoes. A red fox came right up to the van to check out some chips that we had dropped on the ground. We picked up all other crumbs as we didn't want any other unexpected visitors - meaning bears.

July 25 - Saturday: Km 448 to approx Km 250 viewpoint, Yukon

Had a terrific sleep and it was so quiet, but had hordes of mosquitoes in the morning so did not spend any time outside. We stopped at the Arctic Circle to take pictures and met some Eskimos from Alaska, who were travelling home after the Conference in Canada's Inuvik. We took many pictures as we had perfectly clear skies, hot sun and lots of dust.

Stopped at Eagle Plains for gas, water and a shower. A lady that I had met at the fair grounds informed us that a sow bear had been wounded near Eagle Plains and she had two cubs - so be careful!

We continued on to a large viewpoint overlooking an expansive valley with the Richardson Mountains in the background. Two other units also stopped and were going to spend the night. We went for a long walk and picked some cloudberries . Again the view here is indescribable - I would like to come back and just sit and look at this expanse of scenery and tundra, a river in the valley and mountains that look like they are soft and spongy like marshmallow, but must be mounds of gravel - ancient rocks.

The sky looks threatening, but we haven't had any rain so far. A forest fire was burning to the west but has burnt itself out tonight.

July 26 - Sunday: Km 250 to Km 116 Blackstone River, Yukon

We decided to have a slow start and ended up much later than expected. Chris came in after breakfast and said "We have a problem." Our right rear tire was low. He tried pumping it but it then went flat very fast. We had great problems taking off the safety nuts. (We will have them removed when we get to a service station.) After a couple of attempts at getting the van jacked up and actually stopping and asking a fellow to help him, they finally got the tire changed. The fellow had a good wrench that would pry off the nuts.

A passenger bus stopped behind us while we were having this trouble. The passengers were watching us but when they got on the bus the driver found out he had lost a bearing from the clutch. So now they had to swat mosquitoes and wait till he could fix it enough to drive the bus in one gear.

We also had a couple of units stop - one was only a couple feet from us. This was in a huge parking spot with a couple of empty acres. They ran their motors all the time they were eating or just plain sitting. We had to go and ask them to turn off their motors as they were stinking us out and we could not move. One couple got quite indignant that we would ask them to shut off the motor. It takes all kinds and some you could do without.

We finally got everything back in its place and headed down the road with no spare. The Yukon Highway Maintenance Shop was not too far down the road so we stopped to see if they could fix our tire. The fellow said he sure could. He was most pleasant and had the valve stem fixed in no time. He wouldn't take any pay as he said he was on salary and was being paid anyway, so we gave him $20 to buy some beer for the fellows. Now we felt more at ease to stay a few days at the Blackstone River.

We took our previous camp spot above the river. We went and tried our hand at fishing but didn't catch anything. A Hungarian fellow and his 2 grandkids stopped and tried also but they didn't get anything either. It was a beautiful evening and we walked to the top of the ridge. From the top we could see dozens of horses grazing in the valley. We are the only people here.

July 27 - Monday: Km 116 - Blackstone River

We took our time getting mobile. It cooled off and the sun went down further during the night. Itwas most peaceful and we slept like babies. Before we had finished breakfast, Jack and Joan Rodeen from Campbell River, British Columbia pulled in. We had met them in Inuvik.

We all went fishing, Jack caught his limit of 5 grayling and then Chris and myself had a circus. I caught my limit and then

Chris caught 2. They were a pretty good size for Arctic Grayling. We caught our mess of fish where the two rivers meet. We cleaned and scaled them and had a late lunch and early dinner. They were delicious! When we finished a Conservation Officer came by to take record of the catch. He never asked for our license although we both had ours or we wouldn't be fishing.

There was a lot of activity here in the afternoon with people stopping and fishing. We sat outside in the late afternoon and watched a ground squirrel and spotted a different bird and while we were fishing we saw the horses being herded down the road. The outfitter was collecting his horses for the fall hunting.

In late evening a red VW camper pulled in beside us and a French Canadian came over to say "You have new neighbours, and that they would be starting to cook their supper over the campfire." We said that in building a campfire here we would get all the smoke with the direction that the breeze was blowing and we suggested that they would have more privacy if they took one of the other areas. After some reluctance they moved.

But an Austrian fellow (tall, blond and good-looking and worked at the Sporting goods Store in Munich) and his girlfriend from Toronto, Ontario (PhD in Research Science) came over and we enjoyed a glass of wine together. We gave them 2 of our fish. They were still cooking supper when we went to bed and things were not harmonious between the French Canadian, the Austrian couple and a Swiss fellow. We were glad we had a quiet, smoke-free evening.

July 28 - Tuesday: Km 116 Dempster Highway - Blackstone River, Yukon

It cooled off enough in the evening for the furnace to come on a few times. Before the VW left in the morning the young couple came over to thank us again for the fish as it had been delicious. They had cooked it in tin-foil over their fire.

We went fishing at noon and new neighbours had pulled in. Eva (from Lucurne and Alaska) came with us and she caught a small one but I lost a good-sized one. Came home to have a fish lunch. Two more fellows stopped - one from Tiplitz and one from Tirol. Chris sold some flies and floats to them.

434

An ignorant fellow from BC wearing a Canadian hat almost parked on top of us. He had a 5th-wheel attachment on the back of his truck. Well anyway, he drove through and tore up a bunch of shrubs with no respect for anything - it is a shame how people act.

We tried our hand at fishing again in the late afternoon and this time we followed the creek in the other direction and then walked across the tundra home. Walking on the tundra is difficult and slow going. Well anyway we didn't catch anything.

Eva and Lorne asked us over for a drink while Walter and Mary were having supper and would come over later. It started to pour buckets and would you believe Walter noticed our boots were standing outside and he went and turned them upside down. How thoughtful.

Eva and Lorne were near 80-years old and had met in Libya but now live in Alaska. They come this far up the Dempster 3 times a year to fish and enjoy the scenery. She is the best fly fisherman we have seen, and they tie their own flies. She went out by herself at 11:30 pm and caught a few fish very quickly, but said it was rather eerie and came home.

July 29 - Wednesday: Km 116 Dempster Hwy to Km 18, Mayo on Yukon's Silver Trail

 Before we left the Blackstone River we walked up the hill to see the view and here we foundalmost a dozen wagon beds (minus the wheels) strewn around, 7 were in a circle around a fire pit. The timbers were 9x9 and 12x12 (30 cm x 30 cm). Solid stuff. There were a number of old tin cans and such.

Eva and Lorne gave us some homemade flies for fishing. Hope they work!

We had unbelievable scenery on the Dempster and the lighting was unreal. Stopped at Tombstone Interpretive Centre and found out about the 2 whooping cranes at Inuvik.

We picked up our first and only hitchhiker at this campground. He was a German fellow who had been waiting 5 hours for a ride. He was very nice and after we got gas and water and some food at the junction he came with us again as far as Stewart Crossing.

Oh yes, on the Dempster Highway we saw 3 groups of people with flat tires. One was on a trailer, another on an old jalopy and one on a new rental car. The Klondike Loop toward Whitehorse wasn't too exciting - a few pot holes and such.

The hitchhiker had more luggage than we had together on our trip to Europe. His pack weighed at least 60 lbs, a small duffel bag for food and a big guitar which he had bought in Whitehorse when he started out. He attended music festivals in Inuvik, Dawson City and was going to one in Edmonton, Alberta in 2 weeks. He had hiked the Chilkoot Trail with another fellow we had met in Alaska. Again it is a small world.

July 30 - Thursday: Km 18 Mayo to Elsa

Raining this morning and most of the night. Drove into Mayo and bought some fresh fruit. We did try to see if there was fishing from the Mayo bridge but the river was too high and swift so we decided to drive to Mayo Lake and see how it was there. We drove the old "Silver Trail" where they had originally hauled ore out to Mayo. It was a one way road, but not too bad, narrow and maintained. It was dry so there wasn't any problem.

Fishing here was also disappointing as the water was too high. We spotted lots more mushrooms and had them for lunch. Just delicious!

On to Keno and visited the information/museum log house and drove up the hill to the famous Sign-Post. On the top of the hill we watched a marmot, picked and threw some rocks and scared up a ptarmigan.

We came back to Keno but we were not too enthused about staying there for the night so on up the road to Elsa, the newest ghost town (the mine closed in 1989). We stopped for the night across from the school in the teacher's parking lot with a view over the river valley. You almost could hear the children in the school grounds as it had a real feeling of their presence. We walked around the town a little. All the buildings were in good condition, but empty and the only noise we heard was the watchman's dog barking. It looked like everyone had just left and the buildings looked ready for people to move in.

The sun has been shining today and the scenery has been great. This has been a most interesting and educational experience.

<u>July 31 - Friday</u>: Elsa to Wrong Lake

We took one last look at the town of Elsa — the stores still had signs up and everything was in good repair — before leaving and going to Mayo. Bought more groceries as they had a good store there.

We retraced our route to Stewart Crossing and stopped at Crooked Creek for fishing. I caught one small one which I threw back, but caught nothing else. Chris picked up some nice rocks with "Fools' Gold" in them.

Decided not to stay here as there was a fair amount of traffic, so we went a little further and stopped at Wrong Lake. I was driving and I went to turn in when Chris yells "No. No, this isn't right because the sign says Wrong Lake." We settled in and fished and fished and fished, but caught nothing although we could see some good-sized ones there, but they were not biting - not even nibbling. A very peaceful place off the highway and we even took our awning out as the sun was beating down.

We noticed that the trees are already starting to get their fall colours. It just isn't a long season here.

<u>August 1 - Saturday</u>: Wrong Lake to Km 30 from Junction

On to Pelly Crossing - lots and lots of garbage strewn along the highway. It is an Indian Settlement and at Minto Landing we drove down to see the Yukon River. Indians were busy fishing and had nets in the river and were camped there. They were very busy smoking fish and putting away supplies for the winter. They had a real nice, efficient camp set up.

Five Fingers Rapids we stopped and picked up some ash from a volcano 700 years ago. The white layer of ash is exposed in this area and is about a metre down. We had lunch at Five Fingers Rapids. This was a dangerous area for gold miners to cross, with fast water, rapids and huge boulders to navigate around. All tourists stop here for the view and the viewing area is nicely fixed up.

Stopped at another historical place - Carmacks. It is a very nice town with lots of new homes, good store and hotel.

Thought we would stop at Twin Lakes Yukon Campground for a rest. Two other units came in and one started a huge generator which was mounted on a special bracket on the rear of the van, and then came out with lunch on a paper plate. Further down the road we noticed lots of dead trees piled up - they didn't look burnt- but don't know why they died.

We found a small gravel pit with a great view of Lake LaBerge (Robert Service wrote about Sam McGee and this lake). It is a most unusual landscape and is very windy. This lake is known to blow up storms very quickly and quite unpredictably. We went for a walk down towards the lake and found a new development - some buildings going up, a large crane and satellite dish, etc. Interesting. Our overnight was very quiet and we couldn't get enough of the view as the clouds were playing with the light. Fantastic.

August 2 - Sunday: Lake LaBerge to Whitehorse, Yukon

We left before 9 am and drove to Takhini Hot Springs - what a disappointment. It was a commercial venture, the road was terrible and they wanted $3.50 for a swim. We decided to move on to Whitehorse. We finally stopped near the Cinema and made a great steak dinner. Because Whitehorse will not allow any motorhomes on their streets during the night, we parked for the night at a service station where we will have an oil change etc. done first thing in the morning.

The bars and cocktail lounges are all open on Sunday and The Cantina on Main street really had character.

August 3 - Monday: Whitehorse to Marsh Lake (Km 1421 Alaska Hwy), Yukon

Whitehorse is a good supply place, especially for groceries and doing laundry. We replenished the cupboards and moved on in the afternoon. Chris had an interview with the local reporter about the negative aspect of Whitehorse in not allowing visitors to park on the street as they want to push you into expensive campgrounds. The scenic stops near Whitehorse also do not allow you to stop for the night. Needless to say we only stayed as long as was required to pick up mail and do chores.

On our way out of town we stopped to look at the huge dam project and contemplated fishing but decided it didn't look inviting enough. The boat ramp area at Marsh Lake was our overnight home. It was a lovely place and very private. The lake was quite rough and some locals came to test their boat in the water and soon left. The mosquitoes were quite bad. We were staying at historic Mile 883 which was an old army highway construction camp for the building of the wartime Alaska Highway.

August 4 - Tuesday: Marsh Lake to Morley River Bridge Km 1251

Stopped at Johnson Crossing for some of their famous cinnamon buns and cake. We arrived at Morley River and immediately went fishing. I caught two nice graylings and then we lost two more as we didn't realize the net had a hole in it and they slipped out to freedom. We had a good fish dinner and two was all we could eat.

Went for a walk to the day-use area and found a package of cookies left by someone. We started feeding the squirrels and they were carrying whole cookies off to many hiding places. Interesting little creatures. As we were sitting by the river two very colourful kayakers came passing by. They were two Austrian fellows and they had the most up-to-date clothing and equipment. It was quite a sight coming down the river at 9:30 in the evening.

At 10:30 pm a Pace Arrow monster stopped almost on top of us and he pulled out at 5 am. What a ridiculous way to fly through the country when you go so far. At least he didn't put his generator on.

<u>August 5 - Wednesday</u>: Morley River Bridge, Yukon

Had full intentions of moving on today but went fishing first thing in the morning and caught lots of little ones which we let go. We drove up to the day use area for a change and started fishing in the afternoon and then it was too late to leave. We caught four nice trout whereas before they were grayling. After all this my reel needs some work as a piece came loose. Had a delicious dinner fit for a King and Queen - fresh trout (fried whole with onions), boiled potatoes, green salad with feta, white wine and vanilla pudding with sherry sauce.

Spent the evening watching our tape of Denali and south. It really was spectacular scenery and we have been quite fortunate with the weather.

We had a terrific day today and Chris said "I defy anyone in a big rig having anymore fun than we are having."

<u>August 6 - Thursday</u>: Morley River to Cormier Creek, Cassiar Hwy, BC

Dull and dreary day and sprinkling some. We made a stop in Watson Lake to pick up mail, make phone calls and fill the tanks. We picked up our bikes and they were kept just fine. Drove through construction area along the Swift River and the Rancheria River. The big rigs are really moving now. Or at least that is the way it seems to us as we just pull over and let them disappear down the road.

We drove along about 20 km down the Cassiar (BC Highway 37) and found a place for the night. A lot of people had been stopping at this make-shift campground and it was pretty dirty. Some blackwater holding tanks had just been dumped on the ground. It is hard to imagine that people act like this.

<u>August 7 - Friday</u>: Cormier Creek to Tanzilla River, BC

Raining and more rain. It was a good day to visit the town of Cassiar, although it is quite depressing to do so this week. The town will officially close in a few days and most of the people have moved out. Everything is being sold including the mobile park model homes. The mine has closed down so Elsa,

Yukon is no longer the youngest ghost town as Cassiar is replacing that distinction. The mine office was full of workers coming and going and the atmosphere was jovial with sarcasm. Many of the workers will not have jobs and may need retraining somewhere else.

It was a beautiful side drive up to Cassiar as you are right in the mountains and the town was located in a nice wooded area. We could see the mine and the road from the town where many miners had died working and mining asbestos.

On to Dease Lake. We picked up a gas cap at the Good Hope station and traded it for another at Dease Lake as we had left ours in Watson Lake. We stopped for the night at a rest stop by the Tanzilla River. This was not your ordinary type of rest stop as it was a free campground with dry toilets and camp spots. We had a great spot which backed onto the creek. We didn't have any luck fishing but our neighbour had too many and gave us two and he even baked them over his fire. Delicious! We had planned spaghetti, but only had to make potatoes and zucchini.

August 8 - Saturday: Tanzilla River to Beaver Pond Creek
Km 280

We left at 10:30 but most others vacated the camp at 7:30. It was a lovely campsite. We had a lovely drive and the road was much better than expected as there was new pavement after Iskut. We saw the coastal mountains and some glaciers.

Drove past the avalanche area where a Swiss couple had just caught a 24" (60 cm) fish, a Dolly Varden. We stopped and tried fishing, had supper, and tried fishing again. Oh well maybe another day. We needed lights for reading at 9 pm and it was pitch dark at 10 pm. The mountains got in way of the sun.

August 9 - Sunday: Beaver Pond Creek to Bear Glacier, BC

We had 40 km of rough gravel and then the rest of the road was good. We took a side trip to Stewart, BC and Hyder, Alaska. A very impressive drive and excellent highway. Drove along the Salmon River out of Hyder to watch the salmon spawning and the bears catching salmon. We saw two black bears and one was only 40 ft (12 m) away. We met a German couple, Werner and Hilde Brockmann, who were most impressed with Canada. We bought some post cards, visited the bar (lots of $1 bills posted to the walls), washed the van and drove out to the Bear Glacier rest stop. A majestic panorama viewpoint just across from the glacier and 3 waterfalls to the back of us. What a view from our dining room window!

August 10 - Monday: Bear Glacier, BC to 30 km east of Terrace, BC

Clear skies for our view of the glacier. I cut Chris' and my hair before we left in the morning. We witnessed a near accident between two Alpenlite 5th wheelers and a logging truck - a real smell of rubber.

Stopped at Kitwancool and Kitwanga to see the totem poles.

We travelled BC's Yellowhead Highway along the Skeena River. Thought we would fish for salmon but didn't buy our permit from the Indians. We stopped beside a creek and will stay the night. Chris noticed a leak from the radiator and thought the overflow was dripping, we caught the drips and found the bottom hose had sprung a leak. We had a quick supper and decided to change the hose ourselves as we had a spare hose. Well we did it and refilled the rad. We will have all the hoses checked in Terrace tomorrow. Ford in Winnipeg was supposed to have done this. We had a beautiful clear stream for washing water and extra water to put in the rad. The water was very soft.

August 11 - Tuesday: 30 km east of Terrace to near the Skeena River, BC

Left first thing to go to the Ford dealership in Terrace, and we got an appointment to come back later. Did some shopping and had a new windshield installed. It took a lot of time as he had some problems with it being glued on. Then to Ford to have 2 more belts replaced — alternator and fan belt — and change the radiator fluid. We left at 6 pm tired from all the waiting.

We splurged and went to the Pizza Hut for supper - it was very tasty. We walked around and decided to stay in town. We found a very nice place beside a creek, and very quiet and a distance from the highway. Decided to go for a walk and went about 2 km to some log jams from where we parked and will retrace our steps when we go fishing tomorrow.

August 12 - Wednesday: Skeena River

Walked to the Skeena (about 2 km) across an old river bed, down a good road to a gravel pit, then on a 4X4 trail to the log jam, over the logs to the river and beach area. In the 2-3 hours we were fishing there Chris caught 6 red Sockeye. The first one we landed had the hook come out when I got him in the net. Chris lost 4 salmon and the last one was a riot.

The fish was so strong that it took the line so Chris kept backing up and backing up until he fell backwards over a large timber (which he had just sat on to have lunch) and hit his bottom and head. He said he was almost knocked out. A teacher and his son were just walking by and grabbed his rod. In the meantime the fish was mixed up in my line and wrapping around my legs. I got him nicely in the net and then realized what was happening on shore. Two tired people walked back.

It was almost 30^0C - a sunny glorious day in the mountains. The van was in the sun when we returned so we got some cool water from the creek to put the fish in.

We moved to a lovely site backing on the Skeena River. Our neighbour was Rudi Rabhan (German/American and ex-Sergeant Major) and he ended up loaning Chris his portable smoker so we smoked our fish over mesquite chips on our stove. He thought we had not cooked it long enough so did it some more and it was excellent. Later we sat out by the river watching the full moon come up over the mountains and the reflections on the river.

Some day!

August 13 - Thursday: Skeena River

We were bothered by a few mosquitoes in the early morning. We enjoyed morning coffee at Maria and Rudi's and he showed us all the fishing equipment, pictures etc. We spent a very lazy day. I read some and Chris had a nap and tinkered around. It was a nice lay-about day. We needed it after our exciting time the day before.

Rudi and Maria drove to Terrace for bread and water and 2 "yahoos" stopped in their place and we were somewhat concerned that something might be damaged. More mosquitoes at night but we are parked right among the bush and it is nice and shady for the day. We saw 2 seals bobbing in the water in the evening.

<u>August 14 - Friday</u>: Skeena River

Off to Prince Rupert. The day was clear so we took the gondola to the top of the mountain to see the city from the Chalet. A very pretty city except for the horrible smell from the pulp mills as we neared town. We toured the museum and we took time to look around the town and left about 6 pm. We found another spot along the Skeena River. It was nice and bright and we had a lovely evening with the river at our feet.

<u>August 15 - Saturday</u>: Skeena River to the Kitimat River Bridge, BC

While having breakfast we saw seals float out with the tide.

On to Terrace and the scenery was again beautiful and we continued directly on to Kitimat. This was an excellent highway. Stopped at one of the best tourist brochure places we have seen and picked up a number of maps of Vancouver, BC. Drove to the Alcan plant — which is a huge set-up— and had lunch at the old hospital and town site called Hospital Beach. Then we drove to the 500 year-old Sitka Spruce — huge tree — and found tennis courts and could not resist 2 games of tennis. We had not played since Homer so it was quite enjoyable. We went to the townsite and found it very clean and all the industrial plants are in another area so there was hardly any smell in town. Our heads felt funny when we were near the pulp mill.

We found a site by a bridge about 28 km out of town. A group of about 14 young people came for the weekend and made lots of noise so we moved across the river. We were glad to be over there with all the rock throwing, yelling etc. that was going on.

August 16 - Sunday: Kitimat River Bridge

The groups were quiet and left before 11 am. We tried our hand at fishing. Chris talked to 3 German fellows who were very well equipped. In fact one caught a pink salmon and gave it to him. We tried smoking it but it was mushy so we had to throw it out. It is in between a run so we are seeing a lot of dead chum (dog) salmon coming down the stream. A mother bear (black) and her small cub were spotted down on our side.

Two campers from California, USA pulled in with an old GMC truck and at least a 35' (11 m) 5th wheeler - it also must be one of the first produced. They are headed to Alaska to live for a year. She hung out flower pots, umbrella, table and rungs. Unbelievable. The husband does not say much but she doesn't mind ice and snow and she "boogies the unit up the mountain" regardless of the conditions.

It is really dark at 9:30 pm now - it is a real change from Inuvik in July. Spotted a blue stellar jay in afternoon.

August 17 - Monday: Kitimat River Bridge

The lumber trucks and logging trucks all started moving about 3 am and we decided to move back across the river. We found a very nice spot with the river right out front. We threw our rods in a few times and I can now handle the spinning rod. We read books and set-up the screen door for the first time. It was just a beautiful day!

August 18 - Tuesday: Kitimat River Bridge

We fished, read and sat and watched the scenery go by. We went for a long walk along the river and met a fellow from Smithers, BC and he did up a lure for us. It was made from a colourful pompom. It was sunny and hot but the evenings are cool.

August 19 - Wednesday: Kitimat River Bridge

Another busy day with a lot of fishing, reading and walking. We still did not catch anything but another German fellow caught a nice pink salmon just in front of our place. Our neighbours Emery and Sonny Goddard moved to another spot where it is quieter. We were invited over to visit in the evening. We had lots of laughs. The northern lights and stars were very bright when we went home. Almost need the furnace at night now. There is a campfire ban due to the hot dry weather.

August 20 -Thursday: Kitimat River Bridge
More R & R, visiting, fishing and before we knew it the day was gone.

August 21 - Friday: Kitimat River Bridge
Another sunny day!
The river has really dropped so the Coho will not come up the river until there is a real good rain. The river has a couple of low spots that the salmon cannot get through unless it is high - so they are sitting in the channel waiting. We fished this morning and I caught a rainbow trout. We had it for lunch and it was excellent. We have been visiting quite a lot and it is rather nice since we have not done this for a few months. The parents of the boys who made all the noise gave Chris some lures and brought some beer. They felt bad and apologized and were disappointed as they had trusted their children.

August 22 - Saturday: Kitimat River Bridge to 10 km before Moricetown, BC
We had a real send off by Emery and Sonny and the fellow from Edmonton. It was very nice. Stopped at the campground to dump and met a Bavarian couple that we had seen around.
We did our shopping in Terrace and left quite soon as we had enough of the city. We stopped at a provincial park for lunch but there was so much smoke that we both had a headache for the rest of the day. We had a beautiful day of travelling. Drove through Hazelton and stopped to see the ancient village of 'Ksan. We stopped at an old gravel yard for the night and 2 other groups came in. One couple was Mervin and Eveline Hermann from Minnesota. We visited with them until quite late, watched the northern lights and off to bed.

August 23 - Sunday: Moricetown to another gravel pit

Drove to Moricetown Canyon to watch the Indians fishing at the falls. Lots of beer cans around and an extra chubby Indian boy kicked the cans into the canyon instead of picking them up. He was also selling fish which is illegal. The country around Smithers was very pastoral. We played tennis in Burns Lake and then carried on.

Stopped at another gravel pit for the night and another huge rig came in and Chris asked him not to run his generator near us. He moved quite some distance away and we could still hear it. He also could not remember where he had stayed the night before as he has been travelling about 12 to 14 hours a day.

August 24 - Monday: gravel pit to 30 km before Quesnel, BC
Drove on to Prince George, nice country with rolling hills although extremely dry. The plywood plant was on strike so we could not take a tour. Stopped at a way-side for the night.

August 25 - Tuesday: 30 km before Quesnel to Maple Shopping Centre, Quesnel
Drove into Quesnel and then on to Barkerville. We really enjoyed our day in the historical town - it is very well done. It was authentic and the guides did a great job of telling about the life of Barkerville. On return trip to town we stopped at the Cottonwood Roadhouse - it had been in use until the 1950's and was in excellent condition. The shopping centre advertises free parking for RV's for the night and Quesnel was a well marked and easy town to drive through.

August 26 - 28: Quesnel to 100 Mile House to Lillooet to Meadowlands Ranch, Pemberton, BC
We settled into my sister-in-law's cottage for a few days before heading into Vancouver, BC.

This is the end of our 1992 Alaska, Northwest Territories, Yukon and northern British Columbia trip in a converted camper van. It was fantastic with many, many highlights.

Appendix F - Complementary Publications & Miscellaneous Trivia

RVing into Canada's Arctic – by ourselves, John and Liz Plaxton, is an excellent travelogue. It's a collection of interesting and sometimes humourous articles and diary entries that tell more than "Just the facts, ma'am". Of course many useful facts are there as well. [ADVERTISEMENT]

There are several books and publications that do provide facts, facts and many more facts than our book, and the following might be useful to you. We have used them all, although some issues were more than a year old.

First and foremost, **Tourist/Visitor Information Centres** should be visited wherever you happen to be. Use all those free government publications.

These locations are usually well marked on highway signs in all cities and towns. (You can easily find them on the maps that you can get at each centre once you've found them and are inside the building.) Usually there is adequate temporary parking for almost any size of vehicle, but not camping facilities.

These centres contain a wealth of information such as provincial, territorial and state and local community maps, campground descriptions, scenic routes, etc. Many of the information centres, especially those in northern BC and Alberta, also will have publications about Yukon, Alaska, and Northwest Territories. Many commercially distributed pamphlets and brochures and newsprint will be available. After being used all are good for starting fires in fire pits. Better yet, recycle them by passing them onto people you meet who are going to where you have been.

Ask many questions of the staff in tourist or visitors information centres. The staff are usually very knowledgeable on local areas of interest and about currents events worth going to. They also possess general knowledge about several other locations.

Being familiar with southern BC, Liz and I used only the "Accommodations Guide" and the "North by Northwest Guide" in the Super Natural British Columbia series.

In addition, write to or telephone the Yukon Territory and Northwest Territories (NWT) tourist agencies for printed material. If your travel dates are known, let them know. Order early because Canadian mail service is not the fastest in the word, nor the slowest.

"Canada's Yukon Vacation Guide" and more can be ordered by contacting **Tourism Yukon**, PO Box 2703, Whitehorse, Yukon, Canada Y1A 2C6 and by telephone: (867) 667-5340 or fax: (867) 667-3546 or on the Web: http://www.touryukon.com and via Email: yktour@yknet.yk.ca .

"The Explorers' Guide" and more can be ordered by contacting **NWT Arctic Tourism**, PO Box 610, Yellowknife, NT Canada X1A 2N5 and by telephone: (867) 873-5007 or fax: (867) 873-4059 or toll free from Canada and USA: 1-800-661-0788 or on the Internet: nwtat@nwttravel.nt.ca .

If you know place names, such as 'Atlin British Columbia', 'Fort Simpson Northwest Territories' or 'Faro Yukon', you can also use an **Internet** search engine to find the hundreds of community-sponsored Web pages. I'm still amazed at some of the URLs I discover. Search engines are a blessing for users (and advertisers).

The **Canadian Automobile Association**, an affiliate of the American Automobile Association, produces several excellent books and publications, although I found that many smaller non-member facilities were not included. "CampBook, Western Canada and Alaska" includes brief information on recreational vehicle (RV) and tenting sites, and the "Western Canada and Alaska TourBook" provides information on many hotels and motels, cities and towns, as well as things to do and see. These books are updated yearly. And they are free if you belong to either the CAA or AAA, or if you can find a copy in a laundromat or campground book exchange.

"**Alaska Yukon and British Columbia Travel Guide**", of the Bell's Mile-by-Mile series, provides many details about things to see and do as you travel. In discussion with various people, it seems that Tim Bell visits each location himself, every one or two years. If true, this book is as up to date as you are going to find. Of particular importance for travellers with lots of time to take side trips or stop at viewpoints is the recording of sights and sites against kilometrage and mileage travelled. For example, 'at 1163.5 km (723 mi) from Dawson Creek along the Alaska Highway is the Continental Divide sign where two of the world's largest river systems split: the Swift river flows into the Yukon river system and into the Bering Sea; and the Rancheria River flows into the MacKenzie River and into the Beaufort Sea.' Also important to travellers is the location of propane, water and sani-dump stations, gasoline and diesel stations, and fishing information such as '... Grayling and Dolly Varden. Use small black flies or spinners. Fishing is best in August (1106 km, 687.3 mi).'

We had so many books that Liz, my wonderful navigator and en route narrator, could not use them all. This was the first one she put aside.

Published in 1997, "**Yukon**" by Dieter Reinmuth is an excellent book for back packers and cyclists, and a useful book for those travelling by motorhome or trailer. It also covers several canoe routes. Its historical comments are informative and its kilometrage records are very detailed, as appropriate for those travelling at a truly leisurely pace. This book probably has the most detailed information on radio stations, community activities and who and how to contact locally – police, hospitals, airports – than any other book. And there is no commercial advertising.

"**The Milepost**" is another excellent travel guide, if you don't mind wading through hundreds of advertisements, both as ads and descriptions. If you think a particular description of a facility sounds very good, check for the word [ADVERTISEMENT] at the end of the description. I'm surprised the publishers charge for this book because I think the advertisers would have adequately covered all publishing costs, but I suppose the distributors and retailers have to make a profit as well.

"**The Milepost**" provides comprehensive coverage of the Northwest Territories, Yukon, Alaska, and direct routes through British Columbia and Alberta. In addition to mileage comments and city current and historical information, it does include many highway and city maps. It also discusses the marine access routes, i.e., travelling by ferry up and down the west coasts of British Columbia and Alaska. It too provides information against mileage (kilometrage) travelled. For example, 'DC 710 (1180.9 km) Historic Milepost 733, Swift River Lodge with food, gas, lodging, car repair, pay phone and highway maintenance camp. Open year around.'

If you can afford to buy only one other book besides our "**RVing into Canada's Arctic**", "**The Milepost**" is probably the one you should get. However, we did find several entries that were outdated. Also a small percentage of entries were in the wrong order which resulted in missed turnoffs or backtracking. Turning a motorhome around in the middle of a two-lane highway is not my favourite sport.

Phonetics - Phooey

Phonetic adj. 1. Representing vocal sounds 2. (Of spelling etc.) corresponding to pronunciation. **Phonetically** adv.

Phonetics n.pl. (Usually treated as *sing.*) 1. vocal sounds 2. The study of these.

One of the discoveries Liz and I made when travelling in Latin America was that the Spanish language (español) is much more phonetic than English, which is made up of words from many different languages and cultural backgrounds. That is, if a word contains certain characters in a certain arrangement, that group of characters will [almost] always have the same sound. It is easier to learn to understand oral Spanish or to write Spanish than it is to do so in English.

Liz and I play a lot of word games when we choose to relax around our dinette, games such as 3-D Scrabble (our own invention) and Boggle. Having been alerted to the phonetic inconsistencies in English, we have compiled a short list of words which have made it to our "fonetix fooi" list.

As you travel along Canada's northern highways, you might try to think of a few of your own.

The following words have the same *spelling*, but completely different sounds.

grave (hole) - *grave* (accent)
polish (wax) - *polish* (nationality)
tear (rip) - *tear* (eye water)
lead (verb) - *lead* (metal)
dove (verb) - *dove* (bird)
use (noun) - *use* (verb)

The following words have the same *sound*, but different spelling.

sane - seine	*plane - plain*	*weight - wait*
ate - eight	*draft - draught*	*lone - loan*
aught - ought	*lief - leaf*	*rale - rail*
mourning - morning	*chaste - chased*	*been - bean*
roomer - rumour	*moose - mousse*	*led - lead*
ceiling - sealing	*to - too - two*	*off - cough*
cease - peace	*four - fore - for*	*slew - slough*
t*ow* - d*oe* - d*ough*		

The following words have the same groups of *letters*, but they are pronounced differently.

h*ave* - gr*ave*	d*one* - g*one* - b*one*
f*our* - fl*our*	st*and* - w*and*
h*ere* - wh*ere*	h*oot* - f*oot*
d*oll* - dr*oll*	*sch*olar - *sch*nitzel
off - c*ough*	m*outh* - y*outh*
ab*ove* - m*ove* - st*ove*	

The following letters have the same *sounds* but are spelled differently

sn*uff* - en*ough*
burr*ow* - thor*ough*
*gn*at - *kn*it
feign - *fain*t
p*eas* - s*eize*

Trivial Tips

One can use an Invertor or an uninterruptible power supply (UPS), which produces 110 VAC from 12 VDC, to charge a rechargeable razor.

One can even use an Invertor or UPS to power hair clippers or a small portable mixer for use by a cook/chef, provided that UPS's electronic circuitry has adequate amperage output, which most would have. I use a 400VoltAmp or 250 Watt UPS.

When disconnecting a car or RV battery, I prefer to disconnect the Ground, which is usually the Negative post, first. If I then touch metal with a wrench while undoing the Positive connection, I am not greeted with a blue arc or sparks. Been there, done that until I smartened up.

After your 'clicker' or piezoelectric fire starter has run out of fuel, it can still be used to light propane or butane stoves and, with care, propane barbeques. A spark is all that is necessary to ignite those flammable gases. I would strongly encourage your getting the longest clicker possible so your hand is far away from the flames. Of course, if the back of your hands are extremely hairy, you might want a short clicker so you can singe off some of that hair.

Remember to open the lid of your barbeque before you light it. I've been told of stories where the top was blown open violently enough to break its hinges.

When finished your shower, keep the door to the bathroom closed until the next person has his or hers. This will be much appreciated when in the high mountains, or in early spring or fall, when the outside temperature is hovering around 10 ^{0}C (50 ^{0}F).

Toothpaste tubes can be kept shortened with an elastic band. Roll-up or fold the end of the tube until the paste is squeezed tight, then wrap an elastic band around the folded-up end.

Occasionally, after driving for a couple hundred of kilometres, you might want to stop and feel your tires and even the centre of your vehicle's wheel hubs. If the tires are very hot, they might be under-inflated or your brakes might be very hot. Hot brakes, especially drum brakes (which are usually on the rear wheels) can mean that there is no braking ability. If the centre of your wheels are hot, too hot to keep in contact with your hand, then the wheel bearings might be failing or the nuts holding them in place might have loosened. This condition should be checked by a mechanic as soon as practical to do so.

Interesting enough, my motorhome has dual rear wheels. If each tire in each pair of 'duallies' is not inflated to the same or nearly same pressure as the other, the centres of my wheels get hotter than usual. Consequently, I bought a small hammer that I use to pound on my tires before I drive off each morning. I can tell from the sound if the tires are inflated equally.

I brought along a portable electric screwdriver, which I use primarily as a drill. With a small grinding wheel, I've sharpened then re-sharpened a brand new axe which I foolishly lent to man who obviously had never used such a tool before.

Dried mud from northern BC is almost mortar once it dries and seems like excellent material for adobe. It refuses to fall off door side panels or sides of our motorhome. Perhaps I'm going to have to drive into a lake or river and soak it off. Or maybe I'll drive into a placer mine and use their hydraulic nozzle to blast if off. (With so much pressure, flakes of the brass-gold paint will probably be found in the mud, which could result in some interesting reactions.) However, neiether action was necessary. I just used many, many buckets of water and a sponge or rag.

Always try to take mud off while it is still wet, even if it means dipping your squeegie in a puddle of dirty water during a rainstorm. You'll be glad you did. It could even be worthwhile to drive through several puddles in an attempt to wash mud out of wheelwells and off heavily loaded frames, tanks, etc.

Our sewer cap was glued in place by mud and sand, and I had to use an oil filter wrench to turn the cap and break this seal.

Dust was a problem in two rear cupboards. But no more, I used a half a roll of the RVers' essential material — duct tape — to fill any and all cracks and holes I could find. I also discovered that bad engineering design left a huge hole between the open-to-the-highway holding tanks and one hidden compartment that was next to the under-the-sink cupboard. I filled that hole with a piece of cloth cut from the blanket that I use to lie on when working under my RV (for example, replacing a lost tail pile clamp with a U-bolt). I duct-taped one side of the porous material to create an impervious shield to dust.

Our motorhome has a rubber or neoprene connector at the water inlet. Often this flexible connector does not mate tightly with the brass threads of our water hose, which results in a small but wasteful drip of water. I've stopped the drip every time by wrapping a small amount of Teflon tape (plumber's tape) or black eletrical tape around the threads before attaching the hose. When we disconnect, I make sure the tiny piece of non-biodegradable tape goes into our garbage container.

I use a computer mouse holder to keep my rechargeable razor out of the way but next to an electrical outlet. The holder is mounted on the outside of our bathroom cabinet where every thing is readily accessible for touch-up jobs, and it frees up scarce space inside. Also these inexpensive holders have a slot for mice tails, which is great for slipping the razor's charging cord in and out whenever I use my electric shaver.

Once a year I use vinegar and a non-abrasive nylon scrubbie to wash down the sides of our fibre glass shower. Biodegradable vinegar is a lot cheaper than other products, and also can be used for cooking or as a condiment for fish and chips. Then I polish it with hard-coat car wax.

If you have any interesting tips or techniques, please write and let me know. Thank you.

John (& Liz) Plaxton
RVing@ogopogo.com

456

Index

E

Eagle 82, 83, 86, 87, 88, 240, 241, 242, 280, 425
Eagle Plains 107, 277, 369, 428, 432
Eagle River 358
Edith Creek 78
Edzo 188, 304
Ekali Lake 173, 174, 176, 301
Eklutna 415
Elsa 287
Emerald Lake 62, 231, 408
Endako 207
Engineer Creek 111, 356
Enterprise 323

F

Fairbanks 413
Faro 148, 290
Fish Creek 379
Five Fingers Rapids 147, 288, 353, 437
Folded Mountain 294
Fort Fitzgerald 318
Fort Liard 296, 310, 385
Fort McPherson 123, 140, 151, 259, 265, 429
Fort Nelson 1, 159, 160, 162, 164, 295, 296, 348, 386
Fort Providence 177, 303, 304, 311, 383
Fort Resolution 314, 315, 316, 382
Fort Selkirk 146, 147, 287, 288
Fort Simpson 2, 164, 165, 166, 168, 169, 297, 298,
          299, 300, 301, 385
Fort Smith 189, 302, 316, 318, 321, 382, 390
Fort St. James 207
Forty-Mile 143
Francis Lake 291
Frog Creek 115, 119, 259
Frog creek 113

J

Jade City 376
Jake's Corner 56
Jake's Corner 407
Jean Marie River 385
Johnson Crossing 223, 439
Junction 37 376

K

Kakisa River 311
Kamloops 201
Karstland Trail 191, 320
Kathleen Lake 236
Kelly Lake 213
Kelowna 1, 4, 6
Kenai Peninsula 398
Keno 151, 285, 286, 372, 436
Kinaskin Lake 216, 217, 398
King River 421
Kitimat 24, 51, 210, 211, 444
Kitimat River 445
Kitwancool 21, 22, 380, 398, 442
Kitwanga 21, 54, 395, 442
Klondike Highway 62, 64, 145, 255, 287
Klondike River 248, 260, 353
Kluane Lake 236
Klukshu 235
'Ksan (Gitksan) Village 209

L

Lac La Hache 6, 202, 203, 344, 345
Lady Evelyn Falls 311, 383
Lake Bennett 408
Lake LaBerge 438
Lake Teslin 407
Liard Hot Springs 157, 294, 396
Liard River 157, 291, 297, 349, 405
Liard river 165

R

S

V

Valdez 421
Vale Island 313, 314
Vanderhoof 206
Virginia Falls 390

W

Wade's Junction 82, 83
Wade's Junction 425
Warm Bay 375
Watson Lake 47, 49, 50, 221, 222, 228, 291, 349,
        396, 406, 440
White Pass Summit 232
White River 237
Whitehorse 1, 49, 53, 62, 66, 90, 150, 199, 222, 223,
        227, 228, 229, 230, 280, 283, 306, 351,
        373, 397, 408, 438
Whittaker Falls 302
Williams Lake 8, 9, 203
Willowlake River 299
Wood Buffalo National Park 193
Wrigley 2, 168, 169, 171, 173, 298, 299, 385, 389
Wrong Lake 437

X

Y

Yellowknife 119, 164, 178, 179, 181, 182, 198, 271,
        299, 303, 305, 306, 307, 308, 309, 383,
        385, 387, 391, 392
Yukon 229, 276, 277
Yukon River 47, 86, 89, 103, 104, 143, 146, 151, 230,
        240, 242, 243, 248, 254, 255, 287, 288, 289, 425

Z

Notes / Comments / Corrections

Notes / Comments

Notes / Comments

Notes / Comments